From Girl to Goddess

From Girl to Goddess

The Heroine's Journey through Myth and Legend

VALERIE ESTELLE FRANKEL

McFarland & Company, Inc., Publishers
Jefferson, North Carolina, and London

LIBRARY OF CONGRESS CATALOGUING-IN-PUBLICATION DATA

Frankel, Valerie.
    From girl to goddess : the heroine's journey through myth and
legend / Valerie Estelle Frankel.
        p.   cm.
    Includes bibliographical references and index.

    ISBN 978-0-7864-4831-9
    softcover : 50# alkaline paper ∞

    1. Women — Folklore.   2. Heroines — Folklore.   3. Women
heroes.   4. Women in popular culture.   I. Title.
GR470.F68   2010
202'.13 — dc22   2010033639

British Library cataloguing data are available

Front cover: *from top right* statue detail of Medusa, Loggia della
Signoria, Florence (© 2010 Shutterstock); *The Birth of Venus* by
Cabanel, Alexandre, 1863 (Pictures Now); sculpture of Athene
(© 2010 Shutterstock)

Manufactured in the United States of America

McFarland & Company, Inc., Publishers
  Box 611, Jefferson, North Carolina 28640
    www.mcfarlandpub.com

To my mom,
who sews clothes, crochets baby blankets,
grows corn and persimmons, makes soap, cures olives,
cans jam, teaches dance, leads international tours,
writes gossip columns, records our family lore,
collects songs of the old country, tells stories, sings lullabies,
listens to the spirit world.
And to all the other wonderful women who do likewise.

Acknowledgments

Books aren't created in a vacuum, and this one owes its thoroughness to the advice and support of many special friends. I'd particularly like to acknowledge Benjamin Leitner, Cliff Winnig, Christl Denecke, Donna Frankel, Eve Noonan, Faith Henderson, John Scimone, Kevin Frankel, Linda Cohn, Margarita Kudlov, Marti Sterin, Mary Lowd, Miriam Plotkin, Phillip Chatoff, Shirley Ginzburg, Steven Frankel, Steven Ginzburg, and all my long-suffering roommates, who listened to an entire summer of mythology lectures.

Table of Contents

Introduction

Many readers know Joseph Campbell's theory of the hero's journey: how every man from Moses to Hercules travels the road from childhood to adulthood, seeking acceptance. But that very statement — every man — leaves out a great deal.

In the hero's journey, the boy grows up in the ordinary world — the countryside for King Arthur and Bilbo Baggins, the mundane world of Muggles for Harry Potter. Then a mysterious herald appears summoning him to an adventure. You see, he has ... a destiny. The hero often rejects this call — it is too strange, too mysterious, but, at last, he accepts. He goes on adventures along the way, aided by his friends and companions, with sometimes a token female. Unfortunately, that's all Campbell saw.

Even before reading Campbell, I knew the hero's quest intimately. I was one of those bookworm kids, reading since age two the way my mom tells it, tottering out of the library under an ever-growing stack. These tales of my multicultural childhood told of Japanese Izanami and Izanagi, Russian Vasilisa the Beautiful, Ojibwa Little Burnt Face. I also read books of my parents' childhoods: Robin Hood and King Arthur, the Bible, Arabian Nights.

But I was more than a silent reader — I was a storyteller. Each day on the elementary school playground, I'd retell the tales I'd been reading — not prosaic Cinderella, but exciting tales from far-off lands like "The Lion's Whisker" from Sudan or "The Brocaded Slipper" from Vietnam. Thank goodness the school library had a big enough stock even after I had finished the colored fairy books.

By sixth grade I knew *all* the Greek myths — not just major characters, but all the obscure ones out of my beloved and battered dictionary. I knew Norse myth too, and Native American, and Australian, and all the others that come in big round-the-world collections. Now I did my storytelling while babysitting, or channeled the performance energy into theater camp. I was devouring a book a day at least, all fiction, with lots of folktales and their longer adaptations. In high school I wrote my first novel, a children's fantasy in a *Wizard of Oz* style, which was far too awful to ever see the light of day. I'm embarrassed to admit that the bad guy apologized at the end and promised not to try to destroy the world again. It's buried ten feet deep in my files. The world it took place in had elves and dwarves, but also kappas, thunderbirds, hamadryads, and kelpies. In a world with limited use for a teenage storyteller, my tales were still finding outlets.

I remember my first real mythology class, day one of college. There in Comparative Literature 6, I studied the Indian *Ramayana* and *Mahabharata*, the Irish *Tain*, the African *Mwindo Epic*, and many more. It was an exciting realm beyond Beowulf and the Odyssey, one offering the best stories ever written the world over. I remember inspiration snatching my pen from me as I scribbled an adaptation of Gilgamesh among my class notes. In fact, that short story went on to be reprinted a dozen times and win awards — although the researcher for a Gilgamesh television special seemed disappointed it wasn't autobiographical.

Flash forward to me studying in England, touring every castle I could find, churning out (and occasionally publishing) a hard drive full of stories. The first *Harry Potter* and the *Star Wars* prequel were hitting the big screen, *Lord of the Rings* was coming to theaters soon: Everyone was excited about the big surge in fantasy. And still I was having rough luck getting my big children's novel out there, the story of a girl who fights goblins to rescue the elves from annihilation, with a magic gem glowing on her brow (I did write my more saleable Harry Potter parody that year, but that's another story).

While I mapped my fantasy world of Calithwain and devoured thousands more myths and epics in a new country of libraries, similarities in the "chosen one" story leapt out at me. I started cataloguing these patterns, for I wanted to decipher this most popular plot: the quest, the descent into darkness, the desperate rescue. I charted Siegfried and King Arthur through their battles, Psyche and Persephone through their underworld quests. *The Mists of Avalon* fit too, as did *Romeo and Juliet,* along with so many other popular novels and fantasies and romances and movies and fairytales.

I finally stumbled upon Joseph Campbell's groundbreaking *The Hero with a Thousand Faces*, and I instantly understood. Here were my theories, clearly delineated, divided into the hero's setting forth, seizing the magic sword, battling the dark lord, and returning with new wisdom to lead his tribe. As Campbell relates: "The hero feels something's lacking in his life. He then goes off to recover it or to discover a life-giving elixir. There's a cycle of going and returning."[1] At the climax of this quest, the hero confronts the ultimate enemy — a figure that represents his dark side, his evil and submerged half. This conflict also represents a war with the father figure and a struggle for dominance. This struggle is most apparent in works such as *Star Wars* ("Luke, I am your father") and King Arthur, where the son and opposite covets the father's place. These were the secret yearning primitive tellers and modern novelists alike employed to frame their universal struggles. This was the destruction of evil, the quest for adulthood, the triumph over the deepest fears of the subconscious. Here was everything in my favorite tales. But where was Snow White?

The hero's mentor bestows on him Excalibur, Campbell explained. But none of the fairytale heroines carried swords. He faces the dark lord, his shadow and other-self, all the things he is not. Well, there the wicked stepmother fit. He descends into death, Campbell added, offering the story of Inanna's descent. So the "hero" could be female. But I was seeing patterns that weren't the sword–young warrior–dark lord–kingship struggle.

I read other respected commentaries: Clarissa Pinkola Estés' *Women Who Run with the Wolves*, Maureen Murdock's *The Heroine's Journey*, Joan Gould's *Spinning Straw into Gold*, Maria Warner's *From the Beast to the Blonde*. These were nearer, and I see my book fitting closely among them. But nowhere did I see described the true heroine's journey in myth, step by step, from magic slipper to triumphant motherhood.

Campbell had called the feminine the "goal" of the quest — the princess needing rescue. While the hero represented the logical, powerful side of the personality, the feminine offered him creativity, nurturing, and intuition: "The mystical marriage with the queen goddess of the world represents the hero's total mastery of life; for the woman is life, the hero its master and knower."[2] But the queen goddess, like Arthur's Lady of the Lake or Perseus' Andromeda, is static and shallow. This hero quest of all-powerful Luke Skywalker and sidekick Princess Leia (in her gold bikini no less), or valiant Harry Potter with bookish Hermione, provides an unbalanced and unfair view of the world. In today's society, women oppressed by hero myths see only two choices: Be the helpless princess sobbing for rescue, or be the knight, helmeted and closed off in a cubicle of steel, armored against the natural world, featureless behind a helmet. Only men or those who act like them, with business suits and power lunches and strategy charts, will succeed.

However, the heroine's true role is to be neither hero nor his prize. What about the dynamic, valiant, thoroughly feminine girls in *The Chronicles of Narnia*, *Coraline*, *Twilight*, *The Princess Diaries*, *Inkheart*, *The Wizard of Oz*, *Ella Enchanted*, *The Golden Compass*, *A Wrinkle in Time*, *The Lioness Quartet*, *Beauty*, *Caddie Woodlawn*, *Little Women*, *Anne of Green Gables*, *Pippi Longstocking*, *Alice in Wonderland*? And that's just in children's books. All these clever, creative heroines are not simply modern products of a growing female awareness — they have always existed, as far back as the ancient Great Goddesses who battled the darkness.

The archetypal goddess, or Great Mother, dominated all mankind. She was the earth, the sea, the font of all life. Along with her feminine qualities of beauty, imagination, and compassion, she also offered death and savagery. Across the world, this primal mother goddess reigned uncontested: "Ishtar, Astarte, Cybele were cruel, capricious, lustful; they were powerful. As much the source of death as of life, in giving birth to men they made men their slaves," writes Simone de Beauvoir in her celebrated *The Second Sex*.[3] The Mother was worshipped as the ultimate creator, the vessel of emerging power and source of all life. Girls emulate that path on their journeys by forming a family circle they can rule as supreme nurturer and protector. Here emerges a different story veiled beneath the hero's, but just as ancient, just as valid, just as universal and empowering. Here is the heroine's journey.

The true goal of the heroine is to become this archetypal, all-powerful mother. Thus, many heroines set out on rescue missions in order to restore their shattered families: a shy princess knits coats of nettles to save her six brothers from a lifetime as swans, Psyche quests for her vanished lover. Demeter forces herself into the realm of the dead to reclaim her daughter, while Isis scours the world for her husband's broken body. Little Gerda in Hans Christian Andersen's tale quests all the way to Finland to rescue her playmate from the unfeeling Snow Queen. This goal does not indicate by any means that the girls are trying to "stay at home" or "play house." Though they redeem beloved family members or potential husbands, these heroines work as hard as any fairytale hero. And they do it without swords.

Epics and Folktales

As Joseph Campbell commented in one of his later books:

In *The Odyssey*, you'll see three journeys. One is that of Telemachus, the son, going in quest of his father. The second is that of the father, Odysseus, becoming reconciled and related to the female principle in the sense of male-female relationship, rather than the male mastery of the female that was at the center of *The Iliad*. And the third is of Penelope herself, whose journey is ... endurance. Out in Nantucket, you see all those cottages with the widow's walk up on the roof: *when my husband comes back from the sea.* Two journeys through space and one through time.[4]

The problem is that Odysseus and Telemachus cross oceans and (in the case of Odysseus) encounter fearsome monsters. Penelope outwits suitors with her weaving for 20 years, all the while maintaining her faith and chastity while protecting her son and island. However, this journey involves no battles or flashing swords. It is a quiet task of patience and fortitude.

Here we discover the one-sided nature of epics. Most are of warfare: *The Song of Roland, Shaka Zulu,* the *Cid,* the *Mahabharata.* The heroes become

COMPARISON OF MODELS
THE STEPS OF THE JOURNEY

Campbell's Hero's Journey	The Heroine's Journey	Stages
The Ordinary World	The Ordinary World	Innocence and Discovery
The Call to Adventure	The Call to Adventure	Innocence and Discovery
Refusal of the Call	Refusal of the Call	Innocence and Discovery
Supernatural Aid	The Ruthless Mentor and the Bladeless Talisman	Innocence and Discovery
The Crossing of the First Threshold	The Crossing of the First Threshold	Journey through the Unconscious
The Belly of the Whale	Opening One's Senses	
The Road of Trials	Sidekicks, Trials, Adversaries	Journey through the Unconscious
The Meeting with the Goddess	Wedding the Animus	Meeting the Other
Woman as the Temptress	Facing Bluebeard	
	Finding the Sensitive Man	
	Confronting the Powerless Father	
Atonement with the Father	Descent into Darkness	Meeting the Self
Apotheosis	Atonement with the Mother	
	Integration and Apotheosis	
The Ultimate Boon	Reward: Winning the Family	Meeting the Self
Refusal of the Return	Torn Desires	Meeting the Self
The Magic Flight	The Magic Flight	
Rescue from Without	Reinstating the Family	
The Crossing of the Return Threshold	Return	
Master of the Two Worlds	Power over Life and Death	Goddesshood and Wholeness
Freedom to Live	Ascension of the New Mother	Goddesshood and Wholeness

legendary for their actions *in battle*: Beowulf slays monsters, the kings of Persia defend their thrones. Women are rare on the battlefield, though not unheard of, thanks to warrior goddesses like the Morrigan, Athena, and Anat.

Of course, within these battles, Helen of Troy beguiles thousands in the *Iliad*, Blood Moon quests for adulthood in the *Popol Vuh*, and Durga destroys an army of monsters as the Indian pantheon cowers. For this reason, many memorable heroines hail from these hero epics. Who can forget Brünnhild's vicious revenge that destroys two kingdoms or Tiamat gnashing her dragon jaws? For this and other reasons, Joseph Campbell overgeneralizes when he says, "All of the great mythologies and much of the mythic story-telling of the world are from the male point of view."[5] Ancient pantheons, too, are more balanced. Most countries offer creatrix mother goddesses like Isis, benevolent protectresses like Kwan Yin or devourers like Kali. Gods and goddesses equally share the events of the Norse *Poetic* and *Prose Eddas* or Japanese *Kojiki*.

Women's heroic epics, though rarely of battle, do appear, such as *The Burden of Isis, Hymn to Demeter, The Legend of Miao-shan, Cupid and Psyche*, and *The Descent of Ishtar*. Many heroines are subjects of ballads like the Scottish *Tam Lin* or Chinese *Mu Lan*. Antigone and Medea are title characters for their classical plays, as are the Trojan women, Electra, Iphigenia, Alcestis, Andromache, Helen, and others. And many devotional hymns are still sung today in Native American, Neo-Pagan, and Hindu cultures to the Great Goddess. Non-Europeans have worshipped her for millennia, spinning such epics as *Pele and Hi'iaka* from Hawaii and *Devi-māhātmyam* (Glorification of the Great Goddess) from India. Side by side with these are the "newer" epics — African and Native American oral epics only recently transcribed as the storytellers are fading from our modern world. While the African ones I found were mostly phallocentric, I discovered new and valuable Native American works of the Great Goddesses: *Diné bahané: The Navaho Creation Story, The Fourth World of the Hopis,* and *Daughters of Copper Woman*.

Though these epics once proliferated, they, like so many books discarded and altered through the centuries, can be difficult to unearth. Often male chroniclers, particularly Spanish missionaries in the New World, focused on male practice and gods, leading to a set of one-sided narratives recorded firsthand from now-extinct civilizations. Chroniclers were excluded from women's ceremonies such as the Eleusinian Mysteries, thus shrouding them in secrecy for all time. With the exception of some famed writers such as Sappho and Enheduana, male authors far outnumbered females, leaving the ancient world with far more Virgils and Homers.

But it is likewise true that sourcing these epics written by literate men are the myriad of folktales spun by women around their hearthfires. These were learning tales, psychological tales, tales that influenced children of both genders immeasurably. They were passed along by wisewomen, teaching girls how to change their beast into a prince, or transcend the abuse still far too common today. These were teaching tales about girls who rescued themselves, tales that originated in now-vanished *"rites de passage* and initiation rituals ... most of them celebrate the metaphoric death of the old inadequate self as it is about to be reborn on a higher plane of existence."[6] All cultures in the world have great stores of tales, usually passed through the women, emphasizing cleverness and patience and smaller magics along with the great creation magic, descent into death, and resurrection that mark the passage to adulthood for heroes of both genders. The men might have written, but the women told.

The Brothers Grimm tales, for example, derive from interviews with female tellers.[7] Thus, many of their heroines take center stage: Cinderella, Sleeping Beauty, Snow White, Goldilocks, Little Red Riding Hood, Clever Gretel, Tattercoats, Rapunzel. Before the Victorians' program of censorship and diminutizing heroines (and Walt Disney's even more extreme version of the same), fairytale heroines were brave, resourceful, and clever, accustomed to saving themselves and their princes. Gretel rescues her brother, Molly Whuppie outwits giants, the girl in "East o' the Sun, West o' the Moon" walks the entire world to free her lover.

These were teaching tales about women's fears: child abuse (Tattercoats, Hansel and Gretel), marriage to a monster (Beauty and the Beast, Bluebeard), and facing death (Snow White, Sleeping Beauty). These most archetypal tales that shape our childhoods are the tales of women's growth and understanding.[8] As one critic explains:

> Women's oral history ... is a feminist encounter, even if the interviewer is not herself a feminist. It is the creation of a new type of material on women; it is the validation of women's experiences; it is the communication among women of different generations; it is the discovery of our own roots and the development of a continuity which has been denied us in traditional historical accounts.[9]

Folktales, more ancient and widespread than the great epics, are integral to humanity, the imaginings and hopings that separate us from the animal. Fairytales are the bedtime stories of the collective consciousness. Their dreamers employ them as wish fulfillment, conflict resolution, and self-discovery. "Fairytales and mythos are our initiators; they are the wise ones who teach those who have come after."[10]

While these listed are all Grimms' tales, the stories themselves echo across cultures. With a little reading, one can stumble upon the Tahitian Rapunzel, the Arabic Bearskin, the Indian Bluebeard. They're all the same tale, after all. The most ubiquitous is Cinderella, the story of the persecuted drudge who becomes the greatest of all. This is the story that resonates across boundaries, as a fantasy of a better life. As Jack Zipes notes in his *The Brothers Grimm: From Enchanted Forests to the Modern World*:

Perhaps the most striking feature of the tales is that, at their beginning, the majority of the protagonists, whether male or female, are either poor, deprived, or wronged in some way. They come largely from the mercantile, artisan, or peasant class. By the end of many tales, these protagonists, whether male or female, experience a rise in fortune which enables them to win a wife or husband, amass a fortune and power, and constitute a new home.[11]

Generally with a girl in the title role, this is the tale of bravery and constancy in the face of persecution, the woman's struggle for autonomy in the world of myth.

Sources

As I started my research into the world's great tales, I originally planned to use the oldest, most authentic versions — with Sumerian Inanna preferable to Babylonian Ishtar. However, Greek legends that predate Homer are startlingly different from the "classic" versions, and many Brünnhilds forego slumbering in their legendary rings of fire. In these and other cases, I found myself drawn to the popularized versions, the ones people best remember. So I used *The King James Bible*, Wagner's *Ring of the Nibelung*, Homer's *Iliad* and *Odyssey* with translations by Evelyn-White or Butler. For the many, many other works I read in translation, I once again selected well-known editions that were often classics in themselves. The Internet Sacred Text Archive and interlibrary loan system were invaluable. Continuing to winnow, I selected Euripides' famous *Medea* and *The Bacchae*, though he also wrote epic plays on Alcestis, Andromache, Hecuba, Helen, and Iphigenia. A small amount of Shakespeare slipped in as he, like Italo Calvino, Angela Carter, Jane Yolen, and others, used a great deal of folklore as a base for his tales.

Like most Americans, I was most comfortable with the Bible stories and European fairytales, the Greek myths and Arthurian knights. Some areas of the world, like Central America or the South Seas, were a mystery. Luckily for me, I found incredible assistance in the politically-correct scholarship of the last few decades. I live in the multilingual, multicultural Silicon Valley, with three major universities and extensive public library systems. These bulged with multicultural folktale collections, strong women around the world collections, religious texts, Wiccan compilations, international Cinderella projects. *Ancient Mirrors of Womanhood* by Merlin Stone and *The Book of Goddesses and Heroines* by Patricia Monaghan proved the most useful of many outstanding anthologies, as they scoured elusive corners of the globe for warrior women, strong-hearted girls, and mighty goddesses. I remember coloring in a world map to make certain I'd reached just about everywhere (not every country but most geographical areas, as well as cultures known for major epics and folktale tropes). There was a big blank over Antarctica, but otherwise, the earth seemed well-covered.

To find all these, I looked up the storybooks from my childhood or discovered new collections, combining two or three tales into a retelling if there were multiple sources. Often, my search led me straight back to the classics: The best known stories of Aphrodite and Demeter derive from the Homeric Hymns, while many of my remembered tales came straight from the *Kojiki, The Book of the Dead,* or the *Poetic Edda.* As I researched, I discovered new ones, and my childhood tales of Lilith and Sheh Hsien stepped aside to make room for Copper Woman and Ix Chel. I delved into the maiden-mother-crone triad, which has become our modern goddess myth. Still, I'm glad I ended up with one tale each by Andersen, the Brothers Grimm, and Lang, the fairytales that shaped the baseline of my childhood, along with their more multicultural cousins.

Mindful of my weaker areas, I checked out West African tales, Peruvian tales, Zuni, Australian. While I was at it, I scooped up the rest of the library shelf on my way out and read more legends, more commentaries, more psychology, history, and sociology. I think over the past six months, I've read about four of those books per day — an obsessive load even for me. Every book offered a deeper perspective on the tales, and hundreds of those often-clashing viewpoints inform my work. From all these sources came bibliographies and websites that led to more books, more references, more articles, and especially more tales.

Though I read stacks of anthropology, historical and current, I determined to keep my research centered on myth, supporting the great sagas, rather than overwhelming them. At the same time, these theories of the hero's journey are based on humankind's universal drives: love, fear, the challenges of adolescence, the dark side of the psyche. As such, exploring myth means exploring the psychology of Jung and Freud, along with Jungian mythographers like Maria Tatar or Toni Wolff. However, I consider this book fairytale analysis, rather than psychoanalysis. There are no case studies, no "real life" tales, save those of historical heroines such as Joan of Arc and Cleopatra who have transcended history into legend. As I researched, it became clear how I could easily write this book entirely about historical personages, children's books, classic novels, television, or nearly any other medium, for this is the universal journey of women, one that has existed as long as our gender.

The Great Goddess as Devi, Gaia, and Danu was once revered above all. From this, the roles cycled until the great goddess epics dwindled into gossipy tales about Baba Yaga, witch of the forest, or Saint Bridget and her gentle favors. The ancient tales of multiracial, multiaged heroic women have faded, though modern writers try to recreate them forcibly with tales of "Iron Joan" and "Miss Ali Baba." While this type of tale is a kindly-meant gesture, it suggests that powerful women are a creation of modern times, rather than an archetype that has always existed, from Inanna to Deborah, Scheherazade, Ying-Ying, the Wife of Bath, Lady Macbeth, Jane Eyre, Queen Lili'uokalani of Hawaii, *Their Eyes Were Watching God, The Woman Warrior*, and *Like Water for Chocolate*.

The heroine's journey is a path of cleverness and intuition, buoyed by water and earth. It is a path of circular logic, of kindness, of creativity so forceful that the world shapes itself to a wish. It is a path of birth and patience, or guardianship, but never of passivity. Women's work, nowadays devalued as folk craft and biological urges and time wasting, is the work that has conquered and preserved nations. It is as White Buffalo Calf Woman told the Lakota women: The work of their hands and the fruit of their bodies keep the people alive. "You are from the Mother Earth," she said. "What you are doing is as great as warriors do."[12] This is the path of the great mother goddess, destroying mountains and creating civilizations. And each woman journeying toward insight, toward adventure, toward motherhood, toward wisdom is following this path, just as great Astarte, valiant Judith, passionate Isolde, and even sweet Cinderella once did. "It is important to realize we are not women channeling the goddess or pretending to be her — we *are* the goddess pretending for a single lifetime to be a mortal woman."[13]

Ibid 135

❖ Section I ❖

STEPS OF THE JOURNEY

Growing Up:
The Ordinary World

CHAPTER 1

Whispers in the Darkness:
The Call to Adventure

The Wild Swans (Denmark)

Far away in the land to which the swallows fly when it is winter, dwelt a king who had eleven sons, and one daughter, named Eliza. The eleven brothers were princes, and each went to school with a star on his breast, and a sword by his side. They wrote with diamond pencils on gold slates, and learnt their lessons so quickly and read so easily that every one might know they were princes. Their sister Eliza sat on a little stool of plate-glass, and had a book full of pictures, which had cost as much as half a kingdom. Oh, these children were indeed happy, but it was not to remain so always. Their father, who was king of the country, married a very wicked queen, who did not love the poor children at all.

She transformed the boys into swans, who flew off into the horizon. Next, she sent Eliza to a peasant cottage and, when her father sent for her, the stepmother browned her skin with walnut juice until she was quite unrecognizable.

When her father saw her, he was much shocked, and declared she was not his daughter. No one but the watch-dog and the swallows knew her; and they were only poor animals, and could say nothing. Then poor Eliza wept, and thought of her eleven brothers, who were all away. Sorrowfully, she stole away from the palace, and walked, the whole day, over fields and moors, till she came to the great forest. She knew not in what direction to go; but she was so unhappy, and longed so for her brothers, who had been, like herself, driven out into the world, that she was determined to seek them.

She plunged into the forest, finding it a place of secret beauty and healing. There, a little old woman gave her berries and advice, and Eliza watched the skies. At last, she found her swan-brothers, who, as she discovered, could wear human form only at night, and could visit their home only 11 days a year. Together, they wove a blanket of rushes so Eliza could travel with them far across the sea, to a land of safety. When they arrived in that new land, she prayed with all her heart that she might dream of a way to save her brothers.

> And this thought took such hold upon her mind that she prayed earnestly to God for help, and even in her sleep she continued to pray. Then it appeared to her as if she were flying high in the air, towards the cloudy palace of the "Fata Morgana," and a fairy came out to meet her, radiant and beautiful in appearance, and yet very much like the old woman who had given her berries in the wood, and who had told her of the swans with golden crowns on their heads. "Your brothers can be released," said she, "if you have only courage and perseverance. True, water is softer than your own delicate hands, and yet it polishes stones into shapes; it feels no pain as your fingers would feel, it has no soul, and cannot suffer such agony and torment as you will have to endure. Do you see the stinging nettle which I hold in my hand? Quantities of the same sort grow round the cave in which you sleep, but none will be of any use to you unless they grow upon the graves in a church-yard. These you must gather even while they burn blisters on your hands. Break them to pieces with your hands and feet, and they will become flax, from which you must spin and weave eleven coats with long sleeves; if these are then thrown over the eleven swans, the spell will be broken. But remember, that from the moment you commence your task until it is finished, even should it occupy years of your life, you must not speak. The first word you utter will pierce through the hearts of your brothers like a deadly dagger. Their lives hang upon your tongue. Remember all I have told you." And as she finished speaking, she touched her hand lightly with the nettle, and a pain, as of burning fire, awoke Eliza.

She fell on her knees and silently thanked God, and then gathered the nettles to begin her spinning. The ugly nettles burnt great blisters on her hands and arms, but she bore it all for her brothers' sake.

One day, a king discovered her in her mossy cave. Though she didn't say a word, he was charmed by her and took her to his castle. When Eliza saw how carefully he preserved her single finished nettle coat and her hard-won thread, her heart softened. He asked her to be his queen, and she accepted.

They were happy together and she loved him, though she could not tell her tale. Each night she crept from the king's side to keep weaving her nettle coats of mail. However, the archbishop accused her of witchcraft for her beauty that had captivated the king, for her refusal to speak, for her prowling in grave-yards to collect her precious nettles. She persevered in spinning through accusations, through imprisonment, through condemnation to be burned at the stake. All that while, not a single word fled her lips.

> Even on the way to death, she would not give up her task. The ten coats of mail lay at her feet, she was working hard at the eleventh, while the mob jeered her

*and said, "See the witch, how she mutters! She has no hymn-book in her hand.
She sits there with her ugly sorcery. Let us tear it in a thousand pieces."*

*And then they pressed towards her, and would have destroyed the coats of mail,
but at the same moment eleven wild swans flew over her, and alighted on the cart.
Then they flapped their large wings, and the crowd drew on one side in alarm.*

*"It is a sign from heaven that she is innocent," whispered many of them; but
they ventured not to say it aloud.*

*As the executioner seized her by the hand, to lift her out of the cart, she hastily
threw the eleven coats of mail over the swans, and they immediately became
eleven handsome princes; but the youngest had a swan's wing, instead of an arm;
for she had not been able to finish the last sleeve of the coat.*

"Now I may speak," she exclaimed. "I am innocent."

*Then the people, who saw what happened, bowed to her, as before a saint; but
she sank lifeless in her brothers' arms, overcome with suspense, anguish, and pain.*

*"Yes, she is innocent," said the eldest brother; and then he related all that had
taken place; and while he spoke there rose in the air a fragrance as from millions
of roses. Every piece of faggot in the pile had taken root, and threw out branches,
and appeared a thick hedge, large and high, covered with roses; while above all
bloomed a white and shining flower that glittered like a star. This flower the
king plucked, and placed in Eliza's bosom, when she awoke from her swoon, with
peace and happiness in her heart. And all the church bells rang of themselves,
and the birds came in great troops. And a marriage procession returned to the
castle, such as no king had ever before seen*

[Selections from "The Wild Swans" by Hans Christian Andersen (1838)].[1]

Here is the heroine's quest: battling through pain and intolerance, through
the thorns of adversity, through death and beyond to rescue loved ones. As
A.B. Chinen explains in *Waking the World: Classic Tales of Women and the Heroic
Feminine,* "When goddesses embark upon heroic journeys, it is to restore what
has been broken or injured. Isis searched for the pieces of Osiris's body to resurrect him; the Shekhina gathers up Jewish souls in exile; and Nu Kwa, a Chinese goddess, went through the world after a holocaust, repairing the cosmos."[2]
In the tradition of these goddesses, Eliza quests for her family. She achieves
marriage and queenship, but the story can't end until her brothers regain their
humanity.

In the Aarne-Thompson Index, the standard classification guide for folktales, "The Six Swans," with its many variants, is known as AT 451: The Brothers Who Were Turned into Birds. Arabic, Russian, Greek, Armenian, and other
nationalities offer stories of remarkable similarity, varying only with which
type of birds her numerous brothers become. The Grimms appeared fond of
AT 451 tales, since they kept three in their collection: "The Six Swans," "The
Seven Ravens," and "The Twelve Brothers." Famed folklorist Jack Zipes theo-

rizes that they valued the tale for its message of family fidelity through adversity and separation.[3]

Swans represent devotion, thanks to the popular belief that they mate for life. The brothers return whenever their enchantment permits, and their steadfastness echoes Eliza's own faith as she struggles to free them, swordless, speechless, and vulnerable. This is the true heroine's journey: Achieving adulthood through love and intuition, understanding that the craft of weaving and the passivity of silence can be mightier and more stalwart than the hero's sword.

Needs

Most fairytale children grow up with evil stepfamilies or foster-parents bewildered by their adolescent desires. This will soften the wrench of leaving home. In his signature studies, Freud notes that this is a common children's fantasy: After the parents somehow disappoint or dissatisfy the child, he dreams that he is adopted, the child of distant royalty.[4] As fairytale analyst Maria Tatar adds, "The child-hero stands as a victim of parental malice; he has been neglected, chastised or abandoned by one of his parents. Like every 'persecuted' child, he dreams of running away."[5] From here come our fairytale champions with magical destinies.

New desires are blossoming, like swans flying just out of reach, so the adolescent ventures into the forest to connect with herself. As Joseph Campbell describes it in his lectures on the hero's journey:

> What's running the show is what's coming from way down below. The period when one begins to realize that one isn't running the show is called adolescence, when a whole new system of requirements begins announcing itself from the body. The adolescent hasn't the slightest idea how to handle all this, and cannot but wonder what it is that's pushing him — or even more mysteriously, pushing her.[6]

Adolescents enter the forest because a part of themselves is missing — in Eliza's case, her swan brothers and their magic. On the surface, she longs to reunite her beloved family, but beneath, she seeks to reintegrate.

"I will go and seek my brothers," she says. "I'm leaving the parents who are no longer my protective source. I'm going out to develop into a whole person who can stand independently. But I need to evoke that masculine strength hidden inside me. I'm going to quest until I find it." As swans, her brothers have the freedom of flight, the magic of transformation, and the masculine power of will, all characteristics Eliza seeks by seeking them.

"The Call to Adventure," as it is most often named, implies hearing. In this way, "Inana's Descent" begins with the great goddess opening "her ear to the Great Below," as she desires to make the dreaded journey "from which no traveler returns."[7] Thus, she abandons her temples, as Eliza departs the palace.

Not all adventures are so profound; one can attempt something new, like sky-diving or running for office. Or one can quest to reclaim one's lost childself, the most innocent and playful part of the personality. One may seek true love, or quest to destroy the evil demons of one's soul. This is a questioning, a setting forth, an opening of one's attention to the forces of the universe and the faint whisper of the unconscious from deep within. Humans can shut their eyes, but the ears always remain open; even in the passive world of sleep they await danger or alerts. To detect the call to adventure, however, the questor must be in a receptive state.

Heroines begin their adventures in a myriad of ways. Some boldly stride into the forest, some make rash promises, some flee their families. Others declare, "I won't marry the man you've picked for me," or "I want to do something different with my life." As Campbell adds, "With the refusal of suitors, or the passing over a boundary, the adventure begins. You get into a field that's unprecedented, novel. You can't have creativity unless you leave behind the bounded, the fixed, all the rules."[8]

> Tétiyette was pronounced ready for marriage when her mother noticed how she seemed to glow with a quivering radiance. Her budding prettiness had blossomed into beauty, a beauty as fascinating to the eye as the dew is to dragonflies in the cool of the morning. And to her suitors, she was lovely, more lovely than the rumor of rain conjured up by thirsty foliage during a drought, and more lovely than the pearly intimacy within the convolutions of a shell, and (to be precise) as lovely as the salty glitter of the sea when the sun beats down with impossible heat, hammering it smooth.
>
> More than one suitor moaned, and myself loudest among them, "O light of her beauty, O!" Unfortunately, the beauty herself finally realized this and began putting on airs, sashaying her backbone like a wiggling snake, so stuck up her long eyelashes dripped with disdain: no one was good enough for her!"[9]

Fascinated by the Otherness of the forbidden, the call of magic lands far distant, Creole Tétiyette insists on a livelier destiny than her village offers.

While marriage may not seem a very independent goal, one analyst describes it as a far-reaching political decision. "In choosing husbands for themselves, these women are choosing as well, the family and the tribe within which they will live their future lives; in this setting, they will not only rear children, they will exercise their skills in horticulture, weaving, food-gathering, and much else."[10] Some heroines achieve marriage in their quest (as some modern women still do), but others rescue family or slay monsters, showing interest in a wider circle. The recurring theme is a completed family, a goal which heroines risk life and health to achieve.

The man's task is often to conquer and rule, as with Jason, Perseus, and Theseus from Greek mythology. This, of course, reflects the archetypal quest to find a career, win battles, and assume the father's throne. Women have only recently started looking toward career goals rather than simply marriage goals.

Hundreds of years ago, a perfect marriage was the popularized goal because a career was not even in their sphere of reference. Women in our modern culture are no longer confined to the home. However, they have rebelled — perhaps too far. "Feminine wiles," "simple handicrafts," and status as "just a housewife" are discarded as weaknesses rather than the mighty energies that once toppled empires.

Many women today, determined to compete in the workplace, "have been content to be men in petticoats and so have lost touch with the feminine principle within themselves."[11] If women have lost touch with the feminine principle, they have lost the power to lead the family and household in their ancient roles of strength. Girls learn that to compete with boys they must never show fear or emotion, never risk being called "hysterical" or "shrewish." Getting "tied down" will end their careers, and so they must choose strength or femininity, never both.

Inside, this ball of frustration churns: Act against one's own nature or seem weak. The girl tries to sort through her complex emotions but nothing in this world of discarded rules and absent standards offers guidance. The feminine principle, buried and pressed into the darkness of her unexplored soul, whispers within her.

> All night I could not sleep
> because of the moonlight on my bed.
> I kept on hearing a voice calling:
> Out of Nowhere, Nothing answered "yes."[12]

The *Zi Ye*, a collection of sixth to third century B.C.E. Chinese folk songs, are traditionally ascribed to a single female poet of that name. This one shows a woman's frustrated disassociation. Here the moonlight, a feminine goddess symbol, is calling to her, awakening her. This longing from her buried feminine self is crying, and something deep within, this "nothing," is answering. Here is a summons of the inner feminine.

While the hero journeys for external fame, fortune, and power, the heroine tries to regain her lost creative spirit, this image of moonlight or swansong calling her forth from her empty bedchamber. Once she hears the cries of this lost part of herself needing rescue, her journey truly begins.

Silenced

To redeem her brothers, Eliza must exceed anything she's done before. She must transform into a creatrix and, upon finding her brothers, "birth" them, recreating them as human. As she shapes each shirt, she builds them human arms, shoulders, chests, remaking them in her own image. This is the primal energy of creation, something every woman grasps on her path to adulthood.

As she weaves, Eliza is more prosaically learning to make cloth, the creative task of an adult woman. "She must learn to work in a skillful way with a plant that is a strict taskmistress. Loss of concentration, or careless hurry, would be immediately 'stung' back into mindfulness."[13] Eliza's fairy asks a hard task, but not a masochistic sacrifice. The nettles' thorns can be avoided if Eliza stays deliberate and focused.

The harder task is Eliza's silence, which condemns her to isolation, even while she is surrounded by people. She cannot seek aid or even proclaim her innocence. She is vulnerable to the king, to accusations, to loneliness, to death itself.

Silenced women in myth echo silenced women in today's world, illiterate and confined to cleaning and childbearing. Throughout history, stories were the exception to the drudgery of life, a way for women to express themselves and their culture. Some wove or built or sculpted. Though illiterate, the women spoke out through their intricate crafts. Those confined to their homes, deprived of voice like Eliza, or Philomela in the following Greek myth, found weaving to be their only means of speech.

King Tereus married the lovely Procne, and then conceived a passion for her sister. While bringing young Philomela to his home for a visit, Tereus dragged her into an old forest where he locked her in an abandoned house and raped her. She screamed, and he was frightened someone would hear, so he sliced off her tongue. As Ovid describes it:

> Mutilated, she could not communicate with anyone to tell her injuries and tragic woe. But even in despair and utmost grief, there is an ingenuity which gives inventive genius to protect from harm: and now, the grief-distracted Philomela wove in a warp with purple marks and white, a story of the crime; and when 'twas done she gave it to her one attendant there and begged her by appropriate signs to take it secretly to Procne.[14]

Upon receiving the tapestry with its secret message, Procne rescued her sister, and killed her son in vengeance, serving him to her husband at a banquet. As the maddened husband chased them, sword drawn, the compassionate gods changed all three into birds.

Philomela sends the tapestry to her sister — one who will read her hidden message, bound as they are in the secret sisterhood of women. "Ironically, Philomela, the innocent woman who spins, becomes the avenging woman who breaks her enforced silence by simply speaking in another mode — through a craft presumed to be harmlessly domestic."[15]

Vocalizing is a source for power, and is sometimes even a means for casting spells, which Cinderella does in her tale, crying, "Shake, shake, hazel-tree, Gold and silver shower on me!"[16] This power, predominantly employed by the

Grimms' females, is "an imperative addressed to natural powers," emphasizing women's constant connection with nature.[17] The Greek sirens or German Lorelei have beautiful voices which lure sailors to doom. Mermaids are known for song, as are Germanic fish-tailed nixies and the seductive slavic Veelas, whose charm makes men forget food or sleep. Even as Eliza weaves and sews, she is cut off from the greater feminine magic, that of nature and the supernatural, until her voice is restored.

Fairytales show silent, virtuous maids like Cinderella and the little mermaid, who never complain of their vicious treatment, and even more silent, virtuous but dead mothers. Contrasted with this are the vocal witches and stepmothers giving orders. While silence teaches discipline and patience, the heroine must absorb her adversary's voice in order to ascend. She becomes queen, the one who gives orders and decides fates. She becomes the sorceress Circe who enchants men into pigs or Snow White's stepmother with her magic mirror. But the magic awaiting mastery is volatile, primeval. Thus, the heroine must journey through the forest of the self, the underworld and beyond, in order to claim it.

Seeking the Self

Jungian psychology teaches that man has a feminine side and woman a masculine side, anima and animus respectively. For the man, his anima is his intuition, wisdom, empathy, compassion. As he travels into the forest and meets the Great Goddess, she taps into these qualities in him. This is the growth of the unconscious: the needs and longings and understanding which only exist below conscious thought. On his spiritual quest, the Goddess represents his inner anima, his submerged gentler side, as he quests to integrate all of his fragmented parts into a powerful whole.

By contrast, the heroine quests for her source of strength. When the woman meets her lover, he acts as animus and evokes masculine traits within her: logic, rationality, intellect. Her conscious side, aware of the world around her, grows, and she can rule and comprehend the exterior world.

As with Beauty and the Beast and other tales of meeting the male power, "The Wild Swans" shows Eliza growing through her relationships with the masculine, as her six brothers and husband support and teach her. At the most superficial level, the animus represents brute force and power, like the unsympathetic kingly father who rejects Eliza. She learns

STAGES OF ANIMUS GROWTH
IN THE QUESTING HEROINE

1. Brutishness and Physical Force
2. Initiative and Planning
3. Law, Rule, and Order
4. Wisdom and Spiritual Fulfillment

from this injustice and then encounters men who teach her the next higher animus stage. This is initiative and thought-out action: The swans plan with their sister to take her to safety. The third, more developed, stage is law, rule, and order. Eliza weds these qualities in her kindly royal husband, and incorporates them as she becomes a proper queen. The final stage is wisdom. The animus in its highest stage "gives the woman spiritual firmness, an invisible inner support that compensates for her outer softness."[18] In the end, Eliza restores her brothers and they gather around her. She returns to life as they do, all through their mutual devotion.

For both the questing hero and heroine, the opposite sex brings forth their untapped powers, evoking the man's gentleness and woman's strength. Further, the highly developed animus connects the woman with her spiritual side, making her even more receptive to her own creativity. Thus, the heroine, as well as the hero, obtains the mystical feminine energy that offers endless emotion, sympathy, nature, magic, insight, and perception. For both, this integration leads to maturity and wholeness on the journey to adulthood.

CHAPTER 2

Sleeping Beauty's Chrysalis: The Refusal of the Call

Brünnhild and the Ring of the Nibelung (Germany)

Bold and wise, Brünnhild was daughter to Father-god Wotan and the Earth-mother Erda. Leading her sister Valkyries, she would fly over battlefields on her magic horse, Grane, byrnie drenched in blood, and bright rays shining from her spear. She had the power of fate and prophecy, wielding Wotan's magic runes and determining how each mortal man might die.

One day, Wotan sent her to warn the hero Siegmund that the gods had decreed his death. Brünnhild promised him a glorious afterlife in Valhalla, where heroes ate and drank beneath a thatching of golden shields. However, Siegmund rejected her. He had fallen in love with Sieglinde, his own twin sister. Though they'd been parted many years before, upon first meeting, they were irresistibly drawn to each other. As Sieglinde lay sleeping in the forest, curled up around the unborn child they'd conceived together, Siegmund pleaded for Brünnhild's help, refusing to abandon his true love, even for paradise.

Brünnhild, much moved, vowed to protect them both. Though Siegmund died battling Sieglinde's vengeful husband, Brünnhild rescued Sieglinde, whisking her away on Grane and prophesying that she would give birth to "the noblest hero of them all."

Wotan punished Brünnhild for her disobedience by banishing her to earth. Stripped of her divinity, she would lie asleep on a rock, awaiting whoever could awaken her. Brünnhild protested, and demanded that only the greatest hero, one "freer than a god" and immune from fear, come to her. Wotan agreed. With the prick of a magic thorn, he plunged her into a profound sleep and then surrounded the sleeping Valkyrie with a ring of magic fire.

Meanwhile, Siegfried, son of Sieglinde, grew up in the forest and reforged the shattered sword of his father. Eager to learn about the fear he had never felt, he killed the dragon Fafnir and won its vast treasure. He tasted its blood, and in so doing, gained the speech of animals and the power of deep insight. He also claimed the dragon's helm of invisibility and a magic ring. However the ring, forged from the Rhine maidens' stolen gold, carried a dreadful curse that whoever did not possess it would desire it, and whoever possessed it would suffer unhappiness and death.

Wotan hoped that since Siegfried still did not know fear, the curse would not affect him. As he told Erda, the Earth Mother:

> Void of all envy,
> On him shall fall harmless
> Alberich's curse,
> For no fear does he know.
> Soon thy child and mine,
> Brünnhild,
> Shall be waked by him;
> And when waked
> Our child shall achieve
> A deed to redeem the world.[1]

Guided by the chattering birds, Siegfried climbed the mountain and discovered the ring of fire. Fearless, he plunged into the flames, which willingly parted before him. There he saw a mysterious figure, armed and armored, lying beneath a vast shield. He stripped the armor from Brünnhild, slicing away the shining mail to reveal the girl within, and was struck by her beauty. However, with this awe came fear at the glorious power of the anima, the woman born to complete him.

> Magical rapture
> Pierces my heart;
> Fixed is my gaze,
> Burning with terror;
> I reel, my heart faints and fails![2]

He called upon his mother for help, even as he trembled, fear overtaking him at last. Thus the curse took hold.

He bent and kissed the golden maid, and at his touch, Brünnhild awoke. Upon seeing Siegfried, and knowing him for the greatest hero of the world, she fell instantly in love. Recognizing Brünnhild as his protector and goddess, Siegfried pledged himself as an extension of her, her will personified.

> Then every deed that I dare
> Will be achieved through thy virtue;
> All my battles thou wilt choose,
> And my victories will be thine.
> Upon thy good horse riding,
> And sheltered by thy shield,

> No longer Siegfried am I,
> But only Brünnhild's arm.[3]

Brünnhild offered him her love, laughing as he seduced her. At last, she willingly relinquished her virginity and divine status, ready for human love as she cried:

> Farewell Walhall's
> Radiant world,
> Its stately halls
> In the dust laid low![4]

Siegfried gave Brünnhild the ring as his love-pledge, and she gave him her magic horse. They swore eternal devotion, unaware of the ring's unleashed curse.

> Those oaths remember
> That unite us;
> The faith and truth
> That are between us,
> And evermore
> The love we live for;
> Brünnhild in thy breast
> Will deeply burn then for aye![5]

They parted, and Siegfried arrived at the castle of Gunther and his sister Gutrune. But the treacherous dwarf Hagen had already convinced them to steal Siegfried's vast treasure of the dragon's hoard, and win Brünnhild for Gunther. Gutrune offered Siegfried an enchanted drink, and when he swallowed it, he fell desperately in love with her. Thus, when Gunther asked Siegfried's help in winning Brünnhild for himself, Siegfried readily assented. Using the Tarnhelm, the shapechanging helmet he'd taken from Fafnir's hoard, he disguised himself as Gunther.

Siegfried and Gunther swore blood-brotherhood upon the bargain:

> To-day from the bond
> Blood-brotherhood spring!
> But if broken the bond,
> Or if faithless the friend,
> What in drops to-day
> We drink kindly
> In torrents wildly shall flow,
> Paying treachery's wage.
> So — sealed be the bond!
> So — pledged be my faith![6]

Siegfried, disguised as Gunther, passed through the flames and found Brünnhild waiting. Upon discovering a strange man in her sacred circle, however, Brünnhild was horrified, crying, "Who art thou, frightful one?"[7] She had saved herself for the best hero, the one who had won her heart, and this intruder could not be her Prince Charming.

Brünnhild panicked and called for Siegfried's ring, the love-pledge between them, to save her. However, Siegfried yanked the ring from her finger and commanded that she submit to the marriage.

When Brünnhild came to Gunther's castle to wed him, she found Siegfried there, wearing her ring. At once, she knew how she had been betrayed. Thus came Brünnhild to wreak her revenge upon the houses of Siegfried and Gutrune.

After wedding Gunther, she urged her new husband to murder Siegfried, and avenge his betrayal. Gunther was afraid, as he and Siegfried had sworn oaths of brotherhood, but the scheming Hagen offered his help. Brünnhild told Gunther and Hagen of Siegfried's weakness: Though she had used her magic to ward him from harm, she had left his back unguarded, knowing that he would never flee from a foe. Gunther and Hagen resolved to lure Siegfried on a hunting trip and murder him.

As Siegfried wandered through the forest, the Rhinemaidens urged him to return the ring and avoid its curse, but he ignored their tidings of doom. They swam away, predicting that Siegfried would die and that his heir, a lady, would treat them more fairly. Hagen restored Siegfried's memory of Brünnhild and then treacherously stabbed him in the back. Mourning his betrayal of his one true love, Siegfried the great hero died.

Sorrowfully, Brünnhild ordered an immense funeral pyre and claimed the ring, instructing the Rhinemaidens to pluck it from her ashes, once fire had cleansed it of its curse. The pyre lit, Brünnhild mounted Grane and rode into the flames, uniting herself with her lover forever in death.

Brünnhild the warrior woman echoes through our hearts as the epitome of strength, grace and magic, the collector of souls and weaver of spells. Her and Siegfried's tale dates back to tenth century C.E. carvings in Sweden, and from there the tale developed to the 13th century Icelandic *Volsung Saga* and *Poetic Edda* to the German courtly romance of *The Nibelungenlied*, to popular novels and movies today. In Wagner's opera, *The Ring of the Nibelung*, Brünnhild has been expelled from the tomboyish paradise of the Valkyries, condemned like a medieval maiden to marry a human stranger. Her sin is in loving Siegfried, but this is a childish love, a love from the safety of home, with fathers and sisters to guard her. As she puts it:

> O Siegfried! Siegfried
> ...
> Prisoned I lay,
> Because thought it was not,
> But felt alone!

> For what the thought was —
> Say, canst thou guess it? —
> Was love of thee, nothing but that![8]

While she gushes in childlike infatuation up in heaven, she hesitates at leaving home for the mortal world, marriage and adulthood. As always in these tales, outside forces (Wotan in this case) force her out. But this expulsion is too momentous, too shocking, for her to transition smoothly.

Confronted with family pressure to marry or the terrors of the unknown forest, the heroine balks. Leaving safety to ride off on an unknown prince's horse or go seeking the water of life is an overwhelming task. How will she be treated? What will she find? Daughters often lamented leaving home for the unknown household, illustrated by a touching lament in the Finnish *Kalevala*.

> At home a maid has it made!
> In her father's house she is
> like a king in his castle
> with only a sword missing.
> But a poor daughter-in-law!
> In her husband's house she is
> like a Russian prisoner
> with only a guard missing![9]

Thus, the heroine desires nothing more than to hide, to finish growing up before she leaves, to conceal herself from all eyes.

In so many fairytales, the adolescent heroine isn't certain she's ready for Prince Charming, but having the prince choose someone else would be intolerable. How to cope? Sleep allows her to withdraw, to come to terms with her changing self and then to reappear when she's ready to try adulthood and the sexuality it entails. This sleep is a defensive maneuver, allowing the self to deal with the insurmountable stress of change. Thus, heroines appear surrounded by shrouding thorns or rings of fire, forcing away all interlopers. In the earliest version of this tale, from the *Poetic Edda*,

> Sigurth rode up on Hindarfjoll and turned southward toward the land of the Franks. On the mountain he saw a great light, as if fire were burning, and the glow reached up to heaven. And when he came thither, there stood a tower of shields, and above it was a banner. Sigurth went into the shield-tower, and saw that a man lay there sleeping with all his war-weapons. First he took the helm from his head, and then he saw that it was a woman. The mail-coat was as fast as if it had grown to the flesh.[10]

Likewise, in Wagner's Ring Cycle, Brünnhild lies "in full shining armor, her helmet on her head, and her long shield covering her, in deep sleep."[11] Rather than a seductive image, this is one of wariness, of Athena-like virginity guarded by sword and shield.

Often, women in career-oriented lives detect something missing around midlife. A period of seclusion and reflection can help them connect with their submerged feminine side. "Women and artists know instinctively that there are times in life where we must be unreachable, times when we must insist that those around us, especially those nearest and dearest, remain at a distance if anything significant is to develop inside us," explains Joan Gould, author of the fairytale analysis *Spinning Straw into Gold*.[12]

Sleep becomes a place of safety for the frightened heroine, and this cocoonlike state is a necessary step in reaching adulthood. "During puberty, sleep is the refuge in which an adolescent girl can absorb the new sense of herself that she gains from the prick of the spindle, and changes from girl to woman: a transformation more radical than from boy to man,"[13] explains Gould. Young women have developed new powers — they can produce new lives inside of them. Their bodies change and develop sooner than expected. More horrifying still are the catalysts that propel them into adulthood — Snow White's apple or Sleeping Beauty's spindle, suggestive of original sin and sex, respectively. This moment is too frightening, and will take time to absorb. Thus, the heroine flees deep inside herself, refusing to take the final step into adulthood.

Sleeping Beauty, Rapunzel, and Maid Maleen, to name a few, are kept from the eyes of the world at the behest of a witch or foster mother. While this classic Terrible Mother seems cruel, she, like the prince and other characters, is enacting the young princess's sublimated desires, walling her up in a tower or hiding her behind a hedge of brambles. "You mustn't leave yet, you mustn't grow up," the crone cackles. "Stay and be my daughter longer — aren't we happy?" And they are. The child grows up under the mother's influence; she is the source of all love, nourishment, comfort. This overwhelming authority is difficult to escape. In fact, the mother often reinforces this, sometimes unconsciously. "I'm going to have to keep taking care of you. You'll always need me," she says. However, this protector is too demanding, too all encompassing; if she wishes to survive and grow independently, the princess must break away from the inner voice that tempts her to remain a child. In *The Uses of Enchantment*, Bruno Bettelheim observes the destructive safety of stagnation in Snow White's or Sleeping Beauty's sleep state:

> Whether it is Snow White in her glass coffin or Sleeping Beauty on her bed, the adolescent dream of everlasting youth and perfection is just that: a dream. The alteration of the original curse, which threatened death, to one of prolonged sleep suggests the two are not all that different. If we do not want to change and develop, then we might as well remain in a deathlike sleep. During their sleep the heroines' beauty is a frigid one; theirs is the isolation of narcissism. In such self-involvement which excludes the rest of the world there is no suffering, but also no knowledge to be gained, no feelings to be experienced.[14]

When she awakens, the heroine must give birth to herself. She cannot remain asleep, cannot remain confined to her mother's tower, under her control.

"The child, whether seven or seventy, can only break that unconscious bond with the mother world when it realizes it has a soul of its own, which has been born onto this earth through the body of the mother but does not belong to her (or to anyone else)."[15] The new task for the questing boy or girl is to differentiate the self from the mother — to learn where one ends and the other begins. The woman's task then is to reconnect in a new, healthier way.

Clarissa Pinkola Estés, author of *Women Who Run with the Wolves*, adds, "While the metaphor of sleep can denote unconsciousness, here it symbolizes creation and renewal. Sleep is the symbol of rebirth"[16] Snow White lies unconscious, perfectly preserved in glass, but at the same time, the coffin is like a crucible, transforming her from frightened child into powerful queen. This sleep, of course, symbolizes the heroine's descent into death, where she must confront her mortality and gain wisdom from the experience. When she wakes, she has become stronger. "Snow White's period of 'death' involves a reiteration of the overall cycle of transformation. She is bathed ceremoniously, purifying baptismal waters being necessary for the final spiritual and physical union of marriage." The glass coffin is likewise significant as a symbol of the vessel of transformation.[17] Glass is magical, as invisible as air and yet hard and protective. Thus glass isolates, preserving what it holds. Within its sheltering case, Snow White grows strong and pure as its surface, distilled down to her essence.

When the princess has absorbed the trials of puberty and the labor of her initiation, she is ready to awaken. "Okay," she says. "I've thought this all through. I've decided I'm ready for marriage and children." As soon as she does so, a prince appears, ready to marry her and complete her needs. The thorn hedges part to receive him on the very day she's stirring again. "Is it you, my prince?" she asks. He, like all fairytale characters, is an aspect of herself, the male persona or animus who represents her completion. "This is every girl's dream," Gould writes. "To fall asleep at the beginning of adolescence.... When she's ready, she'll wake as a woman, her problems resolved, and the perfect man leaning over the bed."[18] The maiden has reconciled these new parts of her personality and thus welcomes a new stage of development. Within a fairytale paragraph, they fall in love, wed, and have children, just as she's planned. All that remains is the happily ever after.

Creating the Animus

Brünnhild's path is more complicated, but she too, awakens for romance and the next stage of growth just as the heroic Siegfried arrives. Valuing herself highly, she tests the heroes, lying in a ring of flame that only the greatest can penetrate. Who can seduce and charm his way past all her barriers?

Siegfried is guided to Brünnhild by a bird, a creature he understands because of his animal insight. Likewise, he wields the feminine talismans of helm and ring along with his father's sword. He is not only the dragon-slayer, mightiest of heroes, but he also possesses the sensitive power of perception. For the unschooled kitchen maid, the animus is a powerful prince, but for the warrior woman, the ideal mate is gentle and intuitive. Thus he is a fitting consort for Brünnhild.

Wotan himself guards the way with his spear. He thunders:

> Fear thou the rock's defender!
> My might it is
> Holds the maiden fettered by sleep.
> He who would wake her,
> He who would win her,
> Impotent makes me for ever.[19]

As Brünnhild's father, he is another barrier the hero must prove worthy to pass. Siegfried shatters the spear; enlightened by his feminine gifts, he surpasses the all-father's purely masculine energy.

After withstanding the ring of fire, he removes her helmet and slices off her armor, coaxing away her self-imposed barriers one by one. Though Brünnhild, sleeping and now armorless, is ostensibly vulnerable, she holds the relationship's power. It is Siegfried who is weakened by this moment, as he sings:

> What if her gaze strike me blind!
> How shall I dare
> To look on their light?
> All rocks and sways
> And swirls and revolves;
> Uttermost longing
> Burns and consumes me;
> My hand on my heart,
> It trembles and shakes![20]

He realizes he is a supplicant, brought here at his goddess's desire to lead her into adulthood. He is fettered, bound in her power, there to fulfill her will. The sleeping maiden's story is her own and not the hero's.

On waking, Brünnhild, who protected him before birth, greets him as a goddess to her creation, the beloved son who would soon become her lover.

> O Siegfried! Siegfried!
> Hero most blest!
> Of life the awaker,
> Conquering light!
> O joy of the world, couldst know
> How thou wert always loved!
> Thou wert my gladness,
> My care wert thou!
> Thy life I sheltered

Before it was thine;
My shield was thy shelter
Ere thou wert born:
So long loved wert thou, Siegfried![21]

Even after dreaming up her perfect animus and meeting him, Brünnhild hesitates. She toys with the ring, wondering if this love is worth forsaking her heavenly home and growing up. Her ring, Siegfried's love pledge, is cursed, just as her love with Siegfried is cursed. When her Valkyrie sister urges her, "The ring upon thy hand — Tis that: ah, be implored! For Wotan fling it away!,"[22] she is echoing Brünnhild's own doubts. Should she keep waiting? Will Siegfried truly return for her? Is love worth trusting?

The ring symbolizes the marriage contract which Siegfried soon breaks, winning her for Gunther rather than himself. While Brünnhild remains isolated, the ring that she hoards has thrust the earth into chaos. In this way, the land projects her own feelings — while she is in torment and separate from her animus, it writhes. As this is her tale, all the characters echo her thoughts and desires: Wotan as protector of her childish virginity, Siegfried as handsome prince and charming animus, the ring as the blessed and cursed torment of her pledge to him. Eventually, every character in the saga is thrown into conflict over the ring (i.e. Siegfried's broken marriage-pledge).

Brünnhild, who has reserved herself for the best, is furious when she discovers Siegfried's betrayal. She doesn't set out to reclaim him; instead, she demands her honor be restored, and murders most of the main characters while seeking it. Her oath and determination to wed the best hero lie in ruins. Thus she declares war on the world. Only when Siegfried and Brünnhild unite at the tale's end is the curse lifted and order restored in the world.

Despite her apparently passive sleeping state, Brünnhild is one of the most vibrant and memorable heroines in myth. Once she abandons her sky sisters to adventure on earth, she truly comes into her own, a formidable warrior-maiden equally determined in love or revenge.

CHAPTER 3

All the Better to Guide You With, My Dear: The Mentor

Tam and Cam (Vietnam)

Long ago in Vietnam, there lived a girl named Tam. She was skilled at pottery and cooking, and was generous to all she met. Her parents had died, and so she lived with her father's co-wife and her daughter, Cam. Every day, she cooked three meals and brought them to her lazy stepmother and spoiled stepsister. Every day, she swept the cave where her father the chief had ruled. Tam drew water from the deepest wells, cut wood in dangerous places, and undertook all the hardest chores.

One day, their stepmother told the girls, "Go catch crabs and shrimp in a basket for me. I'll give a new red dress to the one who brings home the most." Tam worked for hours, scooping up the small creatures in her basket. Meanwhile, Cam wandered along the riverbank, picking flowers and enjoying the sunshine.

When it was time to go back, Cam said, "Sister, your hair is full of mud. Better wash it out or mother will scold you."

When Tam stepped into the river to wash, Cam snatched her basket and poured all the fish into her own and ran off. When Tam saw her sister had stolen all the fish, her heart sank and she began to cry bitterly.

The blue-robed Goddess of Mercy materialized before her, carrying a lovely green willow branch. "What is the matter, dear child?"

Tam gave an account of her misfortune and added, "Most Noble Lady, what shall I do? My stepmother will say I've been lazy and will beat me hard."

"Perhaps things aren't so bad. Look in your basket to see whether there is anything left."

Tam looked and saw a lovely little fish with red fins and golden eyes.

"Now, take him home and care for him."

Tam smuggled the fish home, and slipped him into a pond behind the cave. After that, Tam visited him after each meal, with a few grains saved from her bowl of rice.

The fish grew large, and would slide up onto the bank whenever he saw Tam. Despite her stepmother's beatings and harsh words, Tam delighted in her friend.

"Where's Tam taking that extra rice?," the stepmother asked. She followed Tam, and watched how she fed her pet. After Tam left, the stepmother peered into the pool. However, the intelligent creature hid itself away.

After days of trying to catch the giant fish, the stepmother concocted a plan. "Tam, your coat's filthy," she said. "Leave it here, and I'll wash it while you go out." She sent Tam off to the fields to care for their water buffalo and she slithered into the girl's discarded coat. Upon seeing her, the fish obligingly slid up onto the bank. The stepmother smiled. "Such a waste of rice, all on a pet. Still, he's big enough for my daughter and me to feast tonight!" She clubbed the fish over the head, cooked him up and ate him.

When Tam returned, she called and called, but the fish didn't appear. She spied blood on the water and cried, "Great Goddess, where is my little fish?"

The Goddess of Mercy appeared. "Your family has eaten your fish. But don't cry. Gather the bones in four jars. Put one under each of the legs of your bed and see what may happen."

And Tam did.

The time came for a great festival. Of course, Tam's stepmother and sister busied themselves in donning their finest clothes, leaving Tam sitting on the dusty floor. Tam slipped into her bedroom and sat before her bed. "Can you help me go too?" she whispered.

She peeped into the closest jars and found a cloak of azure kingfisher feathers and delicate golden slippers embroidered with phoenixes, dainty as air. The other two jars held a scarf and a fine gown of silk. She quickly hid them all back under her bed.

"May I go too?" she asked her stepmother.

The stepmother mixed a basketful of unhusked rice with the basket of clean rice Tam had prepared the previous evening. "You may go to the festival when you have separated this grain. If there isn't any rice to cook when we return home, you'll be beaten." And she and Cam hurried off.

"Goddess, can you help me once more?" Tam asked.

"What is it, child?" the goddess asked, appearing before her.

"I must sort out all this rice before I can go to the festival."

"Bring your baskets to the yard," said the goddess. "Perhaps the birds will help you." The birds came and pecked and fluttered until, in no time at all, they had divided the rice into two baskets. So Tam put on her pretty new clothes and hurried to the festival.

Surrounded by music and good things to eat, Tam danced and laughed and had a wonderful time. Then she spied her relatives nearby. "That girl looks like our Tam," she heard her stepsister say. At once, Tam rushed home so fast she lost a slipper. She hid her fine clothes back in their four jars and sat again on the dusty floor.

One of the festivalgoers found the shoe and sold it to the king; upon seeing it, he was struck by its delicate beauty. He ordered every girl in his kingdom to try it on, but none could wear it. Mesmerized by the thought of finding its owner, the king traveled farther and farther on his quest for the maiden with the delicate feet. At last, his travels carried him to Tam's cave.

"It's mine!" shouted Cam, plunging her bony foot as far as it would go, until the stitches creaked. Tam stood behind her, dressed in rags, eyes modestly downcast. Yet the warlord could see the recognition in her face as she watched the slipper. Under her rags, Tam's extraordinary beauty shone through, as did her whisper-tiny feet.

When she tried the shoe on, it fit perfectly. The king smiled. "You are modest and gentle," he said. "You wear the slippers of a princess, but that is nothing compared to the beauty of your face and the grace of your soul." He put Tam in a beautiful palanquin and they rode off to his palace, where they were wed.

They lived happily for a time, but when Tam visited home to offer food on the anniversary of her father's death, her stepmother concocted a horrid plan. "You must make an offering of betel to your father," she said. "Climb that tree and pick some nuts for him."

Tam climbed the tree and when she was at the top her stepmother took an axe and began to chop it down. The tree trembled and Tam shrieked, "What's happening?"

"Don't worry, I'm just chasing off the ants," her stepmother said. She continued to chop until the tree and Tam fell with a great crash and Tam was killed. The stepmother took Cam to the palace, dressed in her sister's lovely clothes. She explained sorrowfully that Tam had died by accident, and asked him to take Cam as his substitute queen. This the king sadly did.

As Cam was enjoying life in the palace, sewing decorations on the king's robe, she heard a nightingale singing outside her window. Then the nightingale said, "Be careful with my husband's robe and don't tear it."

Cam raced outside, but the king had already seen the pretty bird, and was enjoying its sweet song. "Dear bird, if you are my wife, please come to my sleeve," he said, and the bird did. He placed it in a golden cage and listened to its melancholy tunes day and night.

On her mother's advice, Cam killed the nightingale, cooked it and threw the feathers into the Imperial Garden.

"Where is my nightingale?" the King demanded.

"She must have flown away," said Cam.

The King was very sad but there was nothing he could do.

The feathers of the nightingale grew into a calamander tree with a single fruit. The scents that emitted from it flooded the garden, and gladdened the heart of a little old gardener. "Please, lovely fruit, drop into my bag," the old woman called. And the calamander dropped straight down to her. She took it home and put it on a shelf, where its sweet smell filled her entire hut.

When she returned the next day, she found the hut had been swept and a hot meal was awaiting her on the table. Day after day, this went on.

One day, the old woman pretended to leave, but instead hid just outside the door. She saw the calamander open and a beautiful girl come out and tend the house. She rushed inside and embraced her. "Beautiful child," she said. "How kind you are! Stay and be my daughter." And Tam agreed.

One day the king was passing, watching the skies and looking for his lost nightingale; the old woman saw him and offered him water. She served betel nuts with it, and when the king tasted them, he thought he had never tasted anything so good or so familiar. "Who prepared these?" he asked.

When he heard it was the woman's daughter, he insisted on seeing her. And out came Tam, fresh and sweet as she had been before.

When Cam saw that Tam had returned, she feared for her life, and hurried to ingratiate herself to her sister. "You look lovelier than ever, dear one. Tell me how you got so beautiful."

"It is very easy," answered the queen. "You need only jump into a basin of boiling water." Cam believed her and did so, but she died instantly. Once her mother heard, she dropped dead like a stone. And Queen Tam lived happily with her husband forever after.

To guide them toward their goals, epic heroes have mentors like Merlin or the centaur Chiron who raised Hercules and Jason. The kindly advisor is mostly tutor, brimming with all the wisdom of the world, incredibly powerful, yet gentle and kindly. He is the elderly king the young hero hopes to become after he defeats the evil overlord and establishes a more beneficent reign.

This tutor's female equivalent is the fairy godmother who has replaced the Goddess of Mercy throughout the centuries. "Ask the birds for help, look beneath your bed," the goddess says, prompting Tam to peer beneath the surface, pay attention to voices outside her conscious thoughts. The old gardener, too, cares for Tam, protecting her from her murderous stepsister and helpless husband until Tam is ready to reenter her palace.

More loving and real, however, is Tam's beautiful fish, which loves her and offers companionship. The Chinese Cinderella, Sheh Hsien, has the golden

fish but no kindly goddess to advise her. Likewise, Russian Vasilisa the Beautiful has the wooden doll her dying mother leaves her, which can speak and
perform tasks. In a manner similar to Tam, Vasilisa feeds her mother's doll with
her own scanty meals, going without when needed. "The doll's help comes
with a cost. Vasilisa must nourish the doll, the spirit of her mother as well as
an alter-ego, and must sacrifice in order to empower it."[1] This magical pet is
the heroine's support, offering sage advice and magical gifts when the psyche
can no longer cope.

Children in real life cry and vomit, make messes and panic parents. Thus,
Tam feeds and protects her beloved fish as preparation for motherhood. Even
Disney's submissive Cinderella sews coats for her tiny animal helpers. From
caring for animals, loving, and being loved, Cinderella learns she has value.
She discovers herself, while the stepsisters only polish their exteriors. From
there, it's only a matter of changing clothes.

As the hero's mentor bestows the magic sword, the heroine's mentor offers
beautiful garments that reveal her pupil's inner beauty, golden spindles and
rings to woo a beloved, or careful instructions on how to win him back. As
wisewoman or elder of the tribe, this mentor teaches spinning, singing, or magic
to prepare her pupil for her ordeal.

In Apache tradition, an adolescent undergoing her Changing Woman ceremony required such a mentor. Parents would offer a prospective godmother
an eagle feather and turquoise prayer stone, along with many gifts. The godmother, chosen for her good moral standing and character, acted as attendant
during the girl's ceremony, and watched over her all her life. Her attributes of
strength and wisdom, a friendly manner and healthy children were passed along
to her protégé.[2] The godmother advised the girl through the ceremony and
massaged her, giving her "a vigorous and erect body to meet the demands of
womanhood."[3]

In this way, the mentor's qualities transmit to her goddaughter in an act
more magical and divine than a mother's qualities transferring genetically.
Nowadays, our culture offers fewer mentors as teachers are overburdened with
pupils and personal contact fades into emails and statistics. The mentor offers
different wisdom than the parents, but wisdom that is no less valuable. However, to learn the most difficult lessons, the heroine must face a far crueler
teacher.

Watch the Witch

If Cinderella's stepmother were kinder, the girl wouldn't have a clue how
to run a household. She learns how to cook and clean and sew, while her step-

sisters have only mastered preening in front of suitors. Cinderella's kitchen chores weed her down to her very essence. Her stepsisters have never made breakfast or mended their own clothes; their mother has babied and spoiled them. Their hands, like their bodies, are soft and pudgy. By confiscating Cinderella's life of safety and privilege, they force her to care for herself and others. A heroine with no one to do her laundry learns to wash it herself. And a heroine with only a single companion, that prized doll or fish, learns to mother it in a way her stepsisters can't understand, as they discard hundreds of dolls and buy newer ones.

As teacher of independence, the evil stepmother is essential to the story. She's not only the antagonist; she also balances the far-too-generous fairy godmother or angelic absent mother. Cinderella's helper, whether doll, fish, goat, mother's grave, or wide variety of other characters, gives liberally with no price, save the spell's inevitable limitations (return by midnight, or else...). In Perrault or Disney's version, the godmother appears because Cinderella is good, worthy, and mistreated — so good, in fact, that she has summoned a divine helper. Certainly, this is a great fantasy: that good things happen to good people if they're patient.

Instead of awaiting handouts, most Cinderellas eagerly escape their gawky, soot-covered states. The Grimms' Cinderella (Aschenputtel) doesn't cry by the fire when her stepfamily goes to the ball. She deserves to dance and feels ready to enter the world of romance, so she requests help from her mother: "Shake, shake, hazel-tree, Gold and silver shower on me!"[4] She proudly scrubs off the soot of gangly adolescence and dons her prom dress. "At the moment of transformation, Cinderella falls in love with herself ... her fairy godmother has filled her with pride, which shines through her body and looks from the outside like a gold and silver gown,"[5] notes Joan Gould in her book of fairytale analysis. The godmother can clothe inner beauty in a visible gown, but Cinderella has to learn the lesson for herself: she has worth.

Since Cinderella has gained a spectrum of adult skills, as her stepsisters have not, she is the hotter catch, outshining them with more than her gown and magic slippers. Across the ballroom, the prince notices the one woman who glows with inner light, who isn't fawning or oozing the need to get married. There he spies a self-possessed, confident woman shining with innocent wonder at her first ball. He's captivated.

Rather than swooning helplessly as her stepsisters do, Cinderella challenges the prince to find her as she flees the ball each night. Unlike her marriage-obsessed sisters, so desperate they maim their feet, Cinderella wants a prince worthy of her, one who will pursue her each night, and recognize her in any guise. Only if he can see through her rags and place the slipper on her foot will she take him.

Stepsister

This story falls under the Aarne-Thompson index as AT 510: Cinderella, but also AT 403: The Black and White Bride. Tam weds the king, but the story hasn't yet ended. Here, "the more disturbing story begins," Gould says, describing these false bride stories. This theme of the neglected stepsister or witch taking the young queen's place appears in several Brothers Grimm tales: "Sleeping Beauty," "The Black and White Bride," and "The Goose Girl," among others. "Just when a woman thinks that she is about to enter into a permanent union with a man, when there seems to be nothing to do but live happily conjoined ever after, this fairytale tells us that she splits in two," Gould adds.[6]

The sweet, polite, gentle half (Tam) has been raised to adore marriage, willingly give up her old identity to be queen, put her husband's needs first, be two instead of one. But part of her balks.

She doesn't know how to grow suddenly from housemaid to queen, with no warning or training. "But it will all work out," she tells herself. "I've found my Prince Charming. I'll never be unhappy or angry or regretful. This is the best time of my life." Upon hearing this, the Black Bride destroys the White Bride, chopping down her wobbling perch of affirmations and killing her. "This intruding Black Bride is aggressive, dynamic, mercenary (often for necessary reasons), on fire with jealousy, self centered, and self-reliant ... she is the subversive force that has been repressed in maidenhood until it explodes on the way to the wedding."[7] Thus the Black Bride arrives at the palace, demanding control, and is often uglier, crueler and needier than the new husband had fantasized when he proposed to his sweet princess. More often, he doesn't even notice — this is the story of her transformation, not his.

Like Brünnhild's sleep, Tam's death is a withdrawal from the world, a rethinking of priorities, a hiatus. And like Brünnhild, Tam isn't sure she's ready to return. "Cam killed me and my husband did nothing," she thinks. "Will this happen again? Is this world of violence and treachery really what I want?" She perches outside the king's window and watches. Only then can she decide what she truly desires.

Bird-women (or even bird-men) are popular mates in folklore. Aside from their beauty and elusiveness, most cultures link them with the spiritual, as birds transport the dead or fly souls to heaven. Ancient Egyptians carved a hawk symbol on coffins to represent the spirit taking flight. The Toltecs believed hummingbirds were warriors killed in battle, while Mediterraneans saw seagulls as lost sailors.[8]

As nightingale, Tam flies away and sings sadly. "I'm too little for marriage. Cam will be better at it," she muses. Then she discovers Cam can't manage the household. "You're doing it wrong," the hidden polite one calls to the raging, destructive powerful one; order calls to chaos. "The king's sad, and you're making a mess of things. Maybe I should rein in my destructive side. Maybe I should stop hiding behind these dark rages and rule after all."

"No," screams the dark bride and tears her to pieces. "I'll never give way." Cam destroys her sister a second time. Yet Tam finds herself blooming in her withdrawn state, safe in the garden. Away from the demands of stepmother, of husband, of queenship, her undeveloped maidenly side grows into something nourishing and wonderful, a calamander fruit that brings gladness to everyone.

While the Black Bride is trapped inside the palace, flirting with the king and subsisting on surface appearance, the White Bride extends her roots deep into the ground. Relying on only herself, she grows independently in the wilderness and gains strength each day, becoming the one who will stand by the king for a lifetime and mother his children and bloom past angry adolescence into adulthood.

"You've grown enough," says the gardener, an old grandmother who's watched her own children grow and marry, who's tended plants all her life. "You're perfect now." She takes the fruit home and coaxes Tam out of her shell. Still, Tam doesn't disclose her identity or return to the palace. She stays in the gardener's house doing chores. The house is like the one she grew up in, where she feels herself: White Bride awaiting the king once more. "Am I the one the king wants?" she wonders. "Or does he prefer Cam? Maybe I'll wait and see if he comes looking." She hides, like the European Cinderella in her peasant house, waiting for the king to seek her out and tell her she's the best, the one he truly desires. She wants to be appreciated for her inner beauty beneath the ragged apron, for the strength and independence she's gained. Only by penetrating her hiding place can the king prove he recognizes the woman within. And only then will Tam feel ready to face down her dark sister and the darker figure waiting behind her, the stepmother.

Wicked Mothers

Merlin would never ask King Arthur to gather nettles, nor kill and eat his beloved pet. Why then are the cruel stepmothers so often the girls' mentors? "The gaps from housewife to career woman; from wife to widow; from widow to lover; from lover to single woman again: all involve pain and ungainliness and a change of consciousness," notes Gould.[9] These girls will someday need the strength to give birth, to lose a child, to face an emergency. And that's not even addressing adolescence.

In the original "The Little Mermaid," the ambivalent sea witch sends the little mermaid to find her prince. In a twisted mirror of Cinderella, she warns that her potion will cause

> ...great pain, as if a sword were passing through you. But all who see you will say that you are the prettiest little human being they ever saw. You will still have the same floating gracefulness of movement, and no dancer will ever tread so lightly; but at every step you take it will feel as if you were treading upon sharp knives, and that the blood must flow. If you will bear all this, I will help you.[10]

The sea witch is harsh (though she's not malicious like her Disney alter ego). She doesn't hurt her charge through desire to torture; this pain is, significantly, the price for humanity. "If you want to be a human woman, there's pain and bleeding ahead," she says. "There's no way around it." Even the mermaid's grand-mother is callous towards her suffering.

> "Well, now, you are grown up," said the old dowager, her grandmother; "so you must let me adorn you like your other sisters"; and she placed a wreath of white lilies in her hair, and every flower leaf was half a pearl. Then the old lady ordered eight great oysters to attach themselves to the tail of the princess to show her high rank.
> "But they hurt me so," said the little mermaid.
> "Pride must suffer pain," replied the old lady.[11]

With these unfeeling older women guiding her to adulthood, is there any won-der the little mermaid endures endless sorrows before she dies, sacrificing her life for the prince who doesn't love her? The mermaid's story is pathetic, not only for her tragedy, but also for the cruel lessons that fill her journey.

Notably, these vicious stepmothers only show up to bully the passive princesses; Snow White, Sleeping Beauty, Rapunzel, and the Little Mermaid lack sympathetic female role models, just as most Cinderellas do. The step-mother supports her own daughters. They're extensions of herself, after all. But this upstart stepdaughter, this ugly duckling in her nest, can't be allowed to inherit — not her father's love, and not the prince's kingdom. The young beauty has her whole life waiting, with a myriad of choices and suitors. When she mar-ries and becomes queen, the dowager stepmother will have nowhere left but the crone's tower. Thus the queen becomes "the devouring mother who through her jealousy and envy of her daughter's talents and potential freedom tries to imprison her."[12] While the heroine understands the natural world, singing to her animal friends and picking flowers, the evil queen dominates the adult world: castle, servants, and politics. She clings to her position fiercely by keep-ing the princess a child or pawn. These stepmother-witches often represent the heroine's internalized denigration of the feminine — these marriage-hungry, power-thieving sexpots are dark parodies of women, devouring what they don't control. This antagonist must be faced, even accepted, for the heroine to grow into a balanced adult.

Though cast as the princess's deadliest foe, the witch-queen offers priceless knowledge of sensuality and lust that the virginal heroine must embrace. Disney's evil witches are voluptuous, uninhibited, and brutal. They daringly wear black and violet, disdaining Snow White's childish puffed sleeves and hair ribbons. But they are the real queens, masters of magic. The princess needs these skills to marry and rule.

In the Roman "Cupid and Psyche," the most startling aspect is Venus's debut as one of the first recorded evil stepmothers. The divine goddess of love and beauty turns into a spiteful, competitive shrew when confronted with another beautiful woman. Worse yet, her son Cupid has chosen mortal Psyche as his bride. The crone's tower beckons.

Enraged, Venus forces Cupid to hide himself and Psyche in their sheltered womb of a magic castle, turning himself into Psyche's invisible lover. "Cupid's mother's antagonism inspires his furtive behavior: her envy of Psyche, his fore-knowledge of her furious disapproval of his relationship with her, require the clandestine, unseen lovemaking: his mother turns him into a mystery pres-ence,"[13] Marina Warner comments in her famed analysis, *From the Beast to the Blonde*. When Psyche lights a candle and beholds him in the darkness, she is thrust from paradise and Cupid must return to his mother. Venus then thwarts Psyche in her goal of finding Cupid, imposing cruel tasks on the pregnant woman.

This goddess who best knows the nature of love sneers at pathetic, preg-nant Psyche cowering on the floor of her temple. "Can't you do anything? Know anything? Be anything?" Venus demands. "Who are you as a person? What have you accomplished? How are you prepared to be Cupid's wife and take my place?" Sheltered Psyche, the innocent White Bride, has no answer. Venus gazes haughtily at the useless usurper of Cupid's love. "The marriage is not between equals ... and cannot be held to be legitimate."[14]

Venus's initiation of Psyche is demanding in the extreme. Psyche suffers torments and afflictions; she despairs of accomplishing her tasks and becomes suicidal. But these strenuous labors develop her consciousness and her capac-ity to love.[15] The Terrible Mother is the heroine's catalyst. She represents the dark, unexplored side of the heroine, a side Psyche still must face. As Silvia Brinton Perera comments in *Descent to the Goddess*, "Until the demonic pow-ers of the dark Goddess are claimed, there is not strength in the woman to grow from daughter to an adult who can stand against the force of patriarchy."[16] Psyche quests to become Cupid's equal: wife and goddess rather than mortal mistress. She has spent her life deficient in vital Black Bride qualities: strength, domination, sexuality, wrath. Venus embodies all these; thus, Psyche must learn at her feet to become whole.

Like Tam's stepmother, Venus imposes tasks, but these are teaching quests, which offer Psyche the skills she will need as adult and mother. Each time Psy-che completes a task, she gains a new intellectual capability. For her character, who reacts far too instinctively and emotionally, these abilities make her more balanced and assertive. Sorting seeds represents assessing priorities and making difficult choices. In fact, it is a balancing act — if one can sort grain, then one can watch the baby, the stove, the door, and the toddler, all at once.[17] Thus the young woman learns to supervise a household, to prioritize, to manage the household's food. Gathering precious golden fleece while not getting trampled by the fire breathing rams shows her ability to gather worldly power (represented by the costly fleece) and yet remain uninjured and uncowed. The eagle who advises Psyche on entering the underworld offers an overhead view — an unusual perspective and necessary distance. Finally, Psyche must ignore pleading ghosts, underworld food, and finally a box of forbidden beauty and return untempted if she wishes to emerge stronger from her ordeal.[18]

In the great Mayan epic, *Popol Vuh,* the heroine Blood Moon has been impregnated by an invisible lover in a tree, who spits on her right hand to make her conceive. When her family threatens to sacrifice her for not revealing the father, she craftily sends them a nodule of sap in place of her heart, and quests to find her mother-in-law, who by tradition must adopt her into her new family. This mother-in-law, like Venus, sets impossible food-gathering tasks for the pregnant heroine. Blood Moon enters the garden, only to discover a single corn plant, unlikely to produce all the food required. She only succeeds by invoking all the goddesses of the harvest to regenerate the plant, so that it will fill her gathering net. Thus her mother-in-law accepts her, and she gives birth to the divine twins Hunahpu and Xbalanque.[19]

Snow White's stepmother laces her so tightly she can't breathe, and Venus beats Psyche and makes her labor to the edge of her sanity. Despite their cruelty, these evil stepmothers teach valuable lessons. Cannibalistic witches teach Gretel to clean house and Vasilisa the Beautiful to cook. These monstrous women teach and threaten as one, until the gift of an apple or the order to cook supper turns deadly. The Fairy Godmother, like doll or fish, offers comfort and love. Thus the heroine trains with both fairy godmother and villainess, growing from all these lessons into an adult, a woman unafraid to offer both discipline and mercy.

CHAPTER 4

Dude, Where's My Sword? The Talisman

The Cauldron of Cerridwen (Wales)

The Goddess Cerridwen (whose name means Cauldron of Wisdom) lived on the isle of the Sidhe, known as The Land Beneath the Waves. On this island, she bore a son and named him Morfran because he resembled a raven. She worried because he was so ugly, so she decided to gift the son with her magical powers to make his life easier. She began to prepare the Cauldron of the Deep, the cauldron known as Aven. Only three drops from it would provide foresight and magical power for a lifetime.

She poured into it the waters of inspiration and prophecy. Carefully observing the orbits of the sun, moon, and every single star, she added each herb and the foam of the ocean, all at the proper times of the sky's cycle. The waters simmered with the scents of vervain, wort, and cress. Nine druids of the Isle of Sein breathed on the cauldron with their holy breath. Cerridwen found a blind old man to stoke the fire, and a lad named Gwion to stir the cauldron's precious elixir. It seethed for a year and a day.

As the potion neared its potency, Cerridwen sank into exhausted sleep. Beside her, Gwion kept stirring. Three precious droplets of the boiling brew splashed on his hand, and, instinctively, he licked them off. The poisonous remains of the water split the sides of the cauldron asunder and poured out upon the ground.

The thundering crack of the cauldron woke Cerridwen from her sleep. Using his new powers, Gwion transformed into a hare and fled. Cerridwen took the form of a greyhound and gave chase. She had almost caught up with him when they came to a river and he dove in, as a fish. She became an otter and still pursued him. He took flight as a sparrow, but she chased him as a hawk.

At last, he became a grain in a vast pile of wheat. Cerridwen transformed into a black-crested hen. And peck, peck, peck, she swallowed him.

Cerridwen thought she had ended matters, but the tiny grain of Gwion took root in her womb and began to grow. When she discovered she was pregnant, she swore she'd destroy the child as soon as it was born. However, on the day of his birth, she relented, hesitating to harm the newborn child. At last, she placed him in a leather sack and threw him into the river.

Floating toward Aberystwyth, the infant drifted to the weir of Gwyddno Garanhir, whose son Elffin discovered him on Calan Mai (May Day). "Dyma dâl iesin!" (what a beautiful forehead), the boy exclaimed. So the child was named Taliesin. He became a great poet, and eventually, according to many tales, became Merlin of King Arthur's court.[1]

Like Athena with her owl, or Isis with her throne, Cerridwen always appears with her regenerative cauldron, symbolic of the holy, life-giving womb. Here is the source of Taliesin's poetry, his endless creativity, the shape-shifting powers of Merlin. He usurps the goddess's feminine generative powers, tricking her into providing his shape-shifting magic, to birthing him, to setting him on the waves of the unconscious for his first journey.

> He is the son of the goddess and dwells in the divine land, but he is also a culture-hero stealing from the divine land. Perhaps the myths reflect the encroachment of the cult of a god on that of a goddess, his worshippers regarding him as her son, her worshippers reflecting their hostility to the new god in a myth of her enmity to him.[2]

The powers he steals from her are feminine in nature: voice, craft, water, wisdom. Thus Cerridwen has double cause for rage as Gwion appropriates these skills, like Zeus giving birth to Athena, or Coyote stealing magic from his mother. "Her anger at Gwion may point to some form of the Celtic myth of the theft of the elements of culture from the gods' land. But the cauldron was first of all associated with a fertility cult, and Cerridwen must therefore once have been a goddess of fertility, who, like Brigit, was later worshipped by bards."[3]

According to feminist Adrienne Rich, women were the pottery-makers in prehistoric times, guarding their skills jealously from the men. She suggests the theory that

> the woman potter molded, not simply vessels, but images of herself, the vessel of life, the transformer of blood into life and milk — that in so doing she was experiencing, celebrating and giving concrete form to her experience as a creative being possessed of indispensable powers. Without her biological endowment the child — the future and sustainer of the tribe — could not be born; without her invention and skill the pot or vessel — the most sacred of handmade objects — would not exist.[4]

Far from passive, the pot is transformative, representing the generative power of the enclosing, encircling woman. Like her womb, the goddess uses the cauldron to bring new life to the tribe and sustain it, linking crafts with the deepest biological mysteries.

Cerridwen was not only mother of birth, but also of death and transformation. In another legend, she offers Bran the Blessed her magical cauldron, which can resurrect the dead warriors placed inside it. This Cauldron of Regeneration, womb of the death mother, was one of the most famous treasures of Celtic myth.

Bran later was transmogrified into the Fisher King of Grail legend, with the Cauldron of Cerridwen recast as the Holy Grail. The cup, as a universal symbol of the mother-element, water, reflects the womb-vessel, and later, the chalice of resurrection, "the female-symbolic bowl of life-giving blood."[5] As for its feminine characteristics, the Grail dispenses both material food and spiritual solace. It preserves youth and maintains life. It heals knights wounded in battle. It radiates light and a sweet fragrance; it rejoices the troubled heart. In all these ways it is a source of solace and spirituality, elevating man above the animal and toward the divine. It is the guiding symbol, the anima, for which man quests.[6]

Chalice, Not Blade

Men may quest for the grail, but each woman already bears the feminine deep within, and only needs evoke it. Her talisman helps her do so, but this token of her inner femininity cannot be a sword. In one Scottish tale, a woman weaves a cloak from duck down and carves a harp from seal bones, trimming both with her long, golden hair. She trades her treasures for a path into Fairyland and the return of her child. In "East o' the Sun, West o' the Moon," the heroine carries a golden spindle, comb, and apple. "Heroines of folktales are often the recipients of domestic items made out of gold," Maria Tatar points out, "tokens of the way in which the ordinary can take on the quality of the extraordinary."[7]

Bluebeard's heroine has an egg, rose, or key she must keep pristine. Radha, lover of the handsome god Krishna, has a necklace of gunja berries he once wore. Girls in "Bearskin," "The Seven Ravens," "The Armless Maiden" and "Tattercoats" are identified by their rings. Red Riding Hood's cape. Andersen's red shoes. A golden ball. Seven league boots. Flowers.

Clothing and jewelry are common, as are tools of the home, all woman's everyday objects imbued with an aura of the mystic. Eggs, apples, and other spheres represent the fertile life cycle which is a woman's power. In the same vein, womblike bags or purses often appear, as in the following legend from the Welsh *Mabinogion*.

Pwyll and Rhiannon were deeply in love, but she had another suitor, named Gwawl. When he arrived at the wedding feast and asked Pwyll for a boon, Pwyll foolishly offered anything he had.

"Give me Rhiannon," Gwawl said. Rhiannon managed to delay her marriage to him by arguing that the wedding feast was supplied by her father and was not Pwyll's to grant, but Gwawl would not give up his claim to the bride. Rhiannon came up with a plan. At her following wedding feast, this time to Gwawl, Pwyll came to the door disguised in beggar's clothes and requested a boon.

"Anything, if it is reasonable," Gwawl said, not planning to fall into his own trap. But Pwyll held out a small bag and only requested it be filled to the brim with food. Everyone agreed this was reasonable. But no matter how much they poured into the bag Rhiannon had enchanted, it remained empty. Pwyll explained that only a nobleman stomping down the bag's contents could fill it. Gwawl did so, and Pwyll quickly closed the bag up, only trading Gwawl's freedom for his eager bride.[8]

Keys are likewise significant, as the lady of the house kept them on her belt, dispensing goods and distributing largesse among her people. Keys allow guardians to open doors or bar them, controlling the wealth men receive. Mielikki, the forest mistress of the *Kalevala*, has a set of golden keys, which lock the shed where wild animals are kept from hunters. Keys were also attributed to Proserpina, Roman guardian of the underworld. As William Thomas and Kate Pavitt comment in *The Book of Talismans, Amulets and Zodiacal Gems,* "The key talisman was a very important one with both Greeks and Romans. It is the joint symbol of Janus (or Apollo) and Jana, his wife (Diana, or the Moon), and was worn for Prudence, and for Remembrance of things past, and foresight of things to come."[9] Janus was the two-faced god, suggesting balance and sober judgment. His ring of keys provided access from humankind's prayers to the gods. "Diana, or Jana, his wife, presided over doors and thresholds and was the special protectress of childbirth, and as keeper of the Gate of Heaven held the key of light and life."[10] The birth passage was a doorway that could be opened or shut like a locked gate; thus, European Jewish women in labor used to put the temple key in their birthing beds. This was an egalitarian custom; if the temple key were unavailable, the women would borrow the one from the church.

Weaving, too, had sacred powers. The Micmac women of New England and Eastern Canada had to sew their future husbands beautiful clothing to prove their skills, and the resulting designs were most prized as a source of magical protection. Likewise, Cheyenne women would create sacred designs from porcupine quills and beads. In this case, the act of making the object, rather than the object itself, was considered sacred.[11]

Spider Woman spun a web across the world, and fashioned people from the clay of the earth. She spread a covering of creative wisdom over them, fashioned from her own being. To each soul, she attached a strand. "Each person has a delicate thread of web connected to Spider Woman, connected to the doorway at the top of the head. Those who do not know this allow the door to close, but it is only when we keep the door open by chanting through it, that we may draw upon this link to the creative wisdom of Spider Woman," notes Merlin Stone, in her worldwide examination of goddesses, *Ancient Mirrors of Womanhood*.[12] Thus, weaving and spinning, women's magic, create humankind.

As creatrixes, goddesses have many enchanted objects, though rarely weapons like Zeus's thunderbolt, Poseidon's trident, or Thor's hammer. Saint Brigid of Ireland had a mantle which locals would leave out overnight before her festival, hoping she would touch it and bring prosperity. In her earlier incarnation as goddess, Brigid kept a sacred well that could cure all illness ... if the asker was worthy. The goddess Isis wore a jar-shaped amulet representing her fountain of living water. Norse goddesses Frigga and Freya wore flying cloaks of falcon feathers, which allowed them to shapeshift and visit the nine realms. The more militant Hel, Norse goddess of the underworld, frequently vanished under her helm of invisibility, the Helkappe. The bodhisattva Kuan Yin had a luminous pearl that allowed her to safeguard the entire world, and a peach of immortality. In Navaho tradition, Changing Woman often tossed a set of magic hoops in all colors of the earth. Pele, volcano goddess, had a magic spade called a *pa-oa,* Inanna, a veil of rainbow colors. A black pot was the symbol of the goddess Kali, and farmers hung it in their fields to avert the evil eye.

More famous is the girdle of Venus, which could bestow irresistibility on its wearer. In *The Iliad,* Juno borrows "the curiously embroidered girdle into which all her charms had been wrought — love, desire, and that sweet flattery which steals the judgment even of the most prudent."[13] Upon offering it, Venus says, "Take this girdle wherein all my charms reside and lay it in your bosom," promising that with it, Juno's task of seducing her husband from the battlefield will be fruitful.[14]

Venus's symbols were the fragrant rose and myrtle, gleaming pearls and shells, and the mirror (Venus gazing in her mirror is the modern symbol for woman). Rather than a sign of vanity, this mirror was a divine soul-catcher, or passage to the spirit world, as it was considered universally. Amaterasu's mirror is her *shōtai,* her god-body. When she bestows it on her grandson, earliest emperor of Japan, she says, "My child, when thou lookest upon this mirror, let it be as if thou wert looking on me. Let it be with thee on thy couch and in thy hall, and let it be to thee a holy mirror."[15] Today it is the most sacred image of her at her shrine at Ise.[16] Celtic women were buried with their mirrors, as a gateway to the afterlife, and Buddhist and Christian teachings describe a future in which we can see beyond the shallow reflection of our current existence. Snow White's stepmother seeks her mirror's advice as from an oracle, and some magicians trap their victims as "slaves of the mirror" forever. In Egypt, the word for life and mirror is the same (*ankh*). One reflects the other. In fact, the ankh symbol is an image of the goddess, round head over outstretched arms and upright body. It became known in Egypt as a symbol of sexual union, feminine circle and male cross united. Thus it came to represent immortality, worn by the gods to show their eternal life.[17]

Unlike delicate Venus, war goddesses travel armed, though rarely with swords. Artemis has her silver bow, and Hecate a whip, both distance weapons. Pele needs only the devastating power of her lava. Devastating oceans and storms are the province of many water goddesses. In the same mode, the Irish war goddesses do not participate in battle, but instead undermine or demoralize armies through trickery to accomplish their desires. Sometimes they even trap an army into turning on and killing one another. One of the most threatening tasks of the Morrigan is washing clothes. When she does this, whoever owns those garments will soon perish. Women, even the war goddesses, most commonly fight at a distance, using the magic of birth, growth, and destruction rather than swordplay:

> Then the *Badb*, and *Macha*, and *Morrigu* went to the hill of hostage-taking, the tulach which heavy hosts frequented, to Temhair (Tara), and they shed druidically formed showers, and fog-sustaining shower-clouds, and poured down from the air, about the heads of the warriors, enormous masses of fire, and streams of red blood; and they did not permit the Fir-Bolgs to scatter or separate for the space of three days and three nights.[18]

Sword, Spear and Lightning

"Swords belonged to men in pagan Europe when most other things — fields, houses, furniture, utensils — belonged to women."[19] Thus they were a symbol of their nomadic owners, greatly prized, and were buried with them. The magical sword, along with lance and spear, is a masculine hero symbol, divinely endowed as a sacred trust. "Often the breaking or loss of the sword signaled the loss of royal authority or of heroic mana, and the hero's consequent death."[20] Upon this, the magic sword generally returned to the sea, or underground, or fairyland where it had been forged. Most famous is Excalibur, though it has many companions: Lancelot's Arondight, Saint George's Ascalon, Roland's Durendal, Charlemagne's Flamberge, Paracelesus's Azoth, Siegfried's Gram, Muhammad's Zulfiqar, El Cid's Sword of Tizona, Beowulf's Naegling, and Laevateinn — the sword Surtr will use to bring down the dome of heaven at Ragnarök.

In ancient Scythia, the war god was an iron sword anointed with human blood, while Japan's mythic creation stems from a jeweled spear thrust into the water. Other masculine symbols include the ladder, pillar, obelisk, plow, and scepter. Often these are phallic symbols, when the jeweled spear is dipped into the life-giving ocean, or the lance of Christ is displayed plunged inside the Holy Grail, like the Indian lingam-yoni. *From Ritual to Romance* explains that the lance and cup are "sex symbols of immemorial antiquity and world-wide diffusion, the Lance, or Spear, representing the Male, the Cup, or Vase, the Female, reproductive energy."[21] Likewise, the Celtic Spear of Lug "had such destructive force that its head has always to be immersed in a cauldron so that the town where it was being kept did not go up in flames."[22]

However, as symbolist Barbara Walker notes, more is happening below the surface.

> Apart from obvious phallic connotations, long motifs represent the patriarchal vision in various ways. The up and down, the ladder between heaven and hell, the ferocious dichotomy between the weapon's point and its hilt fitting the hand: These are the emblems of differentiation, one thing from another, We from They.[23]

In a world in which man was learning to walk upright, and reaching toward heaven as the source of divinity, towers and ladders were signs of strength, of civilization, of contact with god-force. Thus upright man is separated from animal, sky parted from earth.

By contrast, the circle was one of the primary female signs, representing a protective or consecrated space, a room where all were equal. "The universe begins with roundness; so say the myths," Walker says. "The great circle, the cosmic egg, the bubble, the spiral, the moon, the zero, the wheel of time, the infinite womb; such are the symbols that try to express a human sense of the wholeness of things."[24]

While the hero's sword clearly echoes a phallic symbol, the heroine's possessions are only slightly more subtle. Ovens, cauldrons, and shoes denote feminine sexuality, representing the genitals and womb. Hoops and rings offer equally suggestive openings. Sappho cried out to her patron goddess, "Queen, Cyprian/ fill our gold cups with love/ stirred into clear nectar."[25] From a Freudian interpretation, the metaphor is clear.

Cinderella's shoes are echoed in the shoes tied to honeymooners' cars, to the Old Woman in the Shoe who "had so many children she didn't know what to do"— most likely because her life was centered on reproduction! Among the Chinese, tiny feet were a source of beauty, prompting both Tam's tale and crippling foot binding. As Joan Gould observes in Cinderella:

> Hundreds of maidenly feet from all over the kingdom are poked out from under the owners' skirts toward the hand that holds the slipper, each maiden playing the male role by trying to thrust her foot into the slipper where it doesn't belong, unless she happens to be the rightful claimant. The sexes seem to be reversed here, but sex is a versatile and ambiguous game: A bride holds out her fourth finger, left hand,

like a penis, while the groom slips the ring over it, mimicking the sexual act in reverse, both partners consenting to both roles in this private theater of intimacy.[26]

Along with rings, Freud links women with images of the home, forests and flowers, jugs, and bowls.[27] Jung lists ploughed fields, gardens, magic circles, mandalas, caves, springs, wells, "various vessels such as the baptismal font, or vessel-shaped flowers like the rose or the lotus."[28] As he adds, "Many things arousing devotion or feelings of awe, as for instance the Church, university, city or country, heaven, earth, the woods, the sea or any still waters, matter even, the underworld and the moon, can be mother-symbols."[29]

Flowers are delicate fertility symbols, while forests and potions bear the dark mystery of the unconscious. Water evokes the deep feminine, interconnectivity and flexibility. It offers a chance to let go, to let intuition and nature buoy the woman forward. All these represent the domestic or magical world where woman rules, the magic of fertility, sex, and birth, the wisdom of the unconscious — power men can only gain in the feminine sphere.

Swordless Strength

Perhaps in the days of tales by the fireside, the girls looked on wistfully as their brothers rode off to war. "There's magic in our lives, too," their grandmothers would say. "We can disguise ourselves as men and pick up swords, be warrior queens like Maeve and Atalanta, or we can follow our own path." From there emerged stories of spinning (Rumpelstiltskin), gardening (Rapunzel), weaving (The Wild Swans), housework (Cinderella), washing clothes (East of the Sun, West of the Moon), holding a loved one (Tam Lin), caring for relatives (Red Riding Hood), child rearing (Electra), and marriage (nearly all of them).

As Campbell notes, generally the male is questing out in the world, while the woman quests in the home. Still, actions in the so-called "women's domain" save the men and allow the heroines to accomplish their goals: Electra achieves vengeance on her mother, Clytemnestra, for slaughtering her father only by raising her young brother and protecting him. Janet must clasp Tam Lin in her arms whatever shape he takes in order to steal him away from the fairy queen. More daring folkloric heroines use Shakespeare's "bed trick." Many, like Rumpelstiltskin's heroine, guess riddles. All of the heroines accomplish their quests without violence, valuing shrewdness and fortitude over Excalibur. "The point is not that women must stay in the kitchen. The point is that in the ordinary, in the familiar, we will find the tools we need and in the humble, we find transformation." A simple kitchen fire and pot are magical, turning eggs into omelets, and flour and sugar into gourmet cakes.[30] From here comes women's magic of the home.

The tale of how Oonagh cleverly protects her household and husband Finn from the giant Cucillin demonstrates the power of "hearth craft," even at defeating the most powerful of adversaries. Cucillin, whose footsteps shake mountains, comes seeking Finn, and Finn is terrified of losing the fight. Oonagh hides her husband, and when Cucillin arrives, she explains that Finn has already gone to meet him. Then, using a skilled combination of Irish bluff and blarney, she describes her husband as the most ferocious man ever to walk the earth. As Cucillin starts to regret his visit, Oonagh asks him to do a few chores in exchange for hospitality, chores she assures him her husband would do were he home. Cucillin cannot refuse.

She has him lift the house up and turn it to reduce the wind exposure, and clear the side of a mountain to provide the house with a spring. As a reward for his help, she generously bakes him "Finn's bread," but he cracks his teeth on the griddle she bakes into it. Then, as he groans in pain, she asks him to check on the baby, and Finn, hiding in the cradle, bites off the finger that gives Cucillin all his magical strength. Suitably chastened, Cucillin departs, never to return.

Oonagh outwits a giant while staying at home with her husband hiding behind her. She even does some vast remodeling, determined to use all the giant's abilities in practical ways, before stripping him of them. This is woman's valor — using wit and hidden domestic magic to cow her enemies.[31]

The taletellers never confused the woman's domain with passivity. Among the Aztecs, who ranked their afterlives by heroism, warriors who died in battle ascended to the same heaven as mothers who died in childbirth. These heroisms are comparable, as the mother gives over her own life for another's, for the good of the tribe.[32]

Heroes wield their gifts in a more straightforward world, where their powerful swords kill antagonists and defend the helpless. Heroines, however, live in a more treacherous, shifting world, where even their mentor can seek their death. Just as the outdoor world threatens the hero, the interior world of the home offers shocking treachery for the heroine, which she must defeat in order to rule. Only through valor and ingenuity, not swordplay, can the heroine survive this surrounding threat to one day preside over her own household.

Journey through the Unconscious

CHAPTER 5

Crossing Over: The First Threshold

Hina, the Fairy Voyager (Samoa)

The highborn maiden Hine-te-iwaiwa lived in seclusion, surrounded by palisades. Waited on by a stream of constant attendants, she served her family's ceremonial duties each day. Her parents were the wealthiest on the island Nukutere, boasting as they did of a rich breast ornament, beautiful white shell bracelets, and — more precious than all these — a gorgeous headdress of scarlet and black feathers, with a frontlet of crimson berries. One day, Hina tried on these treasures over her pure white shift and admired herself in the sunlight. How bright and glittering she looked! But the arch-thief Ngana saw her thus. He charged from a nearby thicket, hoping to snatch Hina's ornaments. The frightened girl darted away.

Ngana realized he would need to change his approach and knelt on the sand. "Forgive me for insulting you, lovely maiden. But you look so fine in those treasures. I wonder if I would look as fine. Please, may I try on those bracelets?"

Hina was reluctant, but after much begging, Ngana persuaded her to invite him into her house and let him try on all the ornaments. She locked them both in, though, as she didn't fully trust him not to steal. Garbed in the finery, Ngana danced joyfully about the house, eyes darting toward all the barred windows. When he discovered a tiny crack in the shutters, he slipped through it and away, still wearing the treasures. "Beware of listening to flattery, O Hina, the lovely and well-meaning!" he laughed.

When Hina's parents returned, they were furious at the theft, and thrashed her with coconut branches. As they beat her, a *manu*, or divine spirit, possessed Hina, and uttered in a strange voice —

> Most sacred is my person
> And has always been untouched;
> I will go to the Sacred Isle,
> So Tinirau alone may touch it.

Now Tinirau, chieftain of Sacred Isle, was a great magician, who commanded the fish of the ocean and used sharks for his messengers. He had two bodies he could switch between: one a man, the other a giant fish. Having uttered her prophecy, Hina sneaked down to the beach, but she had no idea how to reach Sacred Isle, far toward the setting sun.

There on the beach, her elder brother Tangikuku found her. Fearing lest he should inform her parents of her flight, Hina snatched his bamboo fishing rod and stomped on it. Taking a sharp fragment, she sliced off the tip of Tangikuku's tongue, so he couldn't speak. Then she kissed him goodbye. Looking desperately about, she noticed at her feet a small fish named the *avini*. Knowing that all fish were subjects to Tinirau, she cried:

> Ah, little fish! Art thou a shore loving *avini*?
> Ah, little fish! Art thou an ocean loving *avini*?
> Come bear me on thy back
> To my royal husband Tinirau,
> With him to live and die.[1]

She mounted the narrow back of the *avini,* but unaccustomed to the burden, it flipped over, and Hina tumbled into the shallow water. Angry at this wetting, she repeatedly struck the *avini,* hence the beautiful stripes on the sides of that fish to this day, called "Hina's tattooing." Next she tried a larger fish, the *paoro.* When it dropped her in the lagoon, she likewise struck it, leaving long blue streaks. Hina next tried the *api,* which was originally white, but when it upset Hina at the outer edge of the reef, her curses rendered it black. She now tried the sole, and it bore her all the way to the breakers, where Hina experienced a fourth mishap. Wild with rage, she stamped on the head of the unfortunate fish with such energy that she flattened it.

At last, a shark consented to bear her. She grew thirsty on the way, and the shark raised its dorsal fin so she could use it to pierce one of the coconuts she'd brought. But the fin wouldn't break it, so Hina thumped the shark's head with her coconut, and raised a lump that is still called "Hina's bump." At this, the shark too dumped her into the water, leaving her to swim. As the islanders still sing:

> Like a tall solitary tree is the fairy
> Who committed herself to the winds.
> [H]ina invoked the aid of many fish
> To bear her gaily on their backs;—
> The lordly shark to convey her safely
> To the royal Tinirau o'er the sea.
> Alas, the bruised head of the angry monster.

Who hitherto had obeyed the trembling maid,
Who opened a coconut
On her voyage to the Sacred Isle.[2]

In the water, Hina struggled and gasped, wondering if she would ever arrive, and fearing that she would find Tinirau in his monster-form. As a fish, would he swallow her? Hina shuddered and considered sinking herself to the bottom of the ocean. As she drifted there, her legs grew together until they became a fish's tail, and thus she swam to Sacred Isle.

There, she gazed about and saw numerous saltwater pools teaming with fish but no people. The only house was empty as well. In the middle sat a great wooden drum, and she beat it until its sweet notes filled the entire land, and even reached to No-land-at-all, where Tinirau was visiting that day. Intrigued, the king of all fish returned to his islet dwelling.

Hina hid behind the drum, because she wanted to see him first, but when she beheld his handsome human face, she came out straight away. They were married, and Hina gained the ability to pass between the spiritual world and the world of men, thanks to her adventures in the water. In time, Hina gave birth to a daughter named Ature and a hero-son named Koromauariki. And thus, Hina reached No-land-at-all, a sacred spot attained by few.[3]

When the heroine poises herself on the edge of the unconscious world, she hesitates. On the one hand is safety, familiarity, a high palisade with sturdy walls. Beyond this is the deep forest or the glittering sea: the magical realm of the unconscious. Fairyland. The Otherworld. The Realm of Death. Here fears manifest themselves as monsters, frogs speak, and fairy godmothers appear. Prophecies and wishes are always fulfilled. A tossed comb can be a bramble thicket; a mirror, an ocean. And here is where the heroine grows into her hidden powers and discovers the mermaid or enchantress she is waiting to become.

Hina, like her myriad of sisters worldwide, leaves home desiring adventure. She will no longer submit to her parents' abuses; she is a woman nearly grown and she wants a romance. Like Brünnhild, she offers herself to the best chieftain available, as a mark of how highly she prizes herself.

Hina's ornaments in red, black, and white are goddess colors, evocative of Snow White and other girls on the cusp of adulthood. She is a maiden (white) longing to become a grown woman (red). To accomplish this, she faces death and gains powers of the spirit (black). Likewise, her adventure begins by dressing the part, wearing the sacred garments of a priestess and so becoming one. Ngana's acts, from beguiling her with fair words to accepting an invitation to wear her sacred clothes and enter her house, can all be viewed as sexual, a first foray for the maiden.

As Hina tries on the crimson and black feathered headdress over her white shift, playing at becoming an adult, she asks the universe to fill her with divine spirituality. She waits for her life to change ... but nothing happens. In fact, she has outgrown her island, and the prospect of becoming its priestess no longer appeals. She needs a new adventure, a breaking with her island's ties. Perhaps the smooth-talking Ngana can provide this, if she shares the sacred gifts with him, and closes up the house to keep him bottled in, she thinks. But Hina herself is incomplete, still searching and growing. Like Cinderella, she must discover and fall in love with herself before marrying — a man cannot solve all her problems. Only when she's lost everything — her parents' trust, the sacred garments of her former aspirations, the flirtatious young man — can she commit the unthinkable in order to leave her stifling childhood.

Ariadne and Medea of Greek fame echo this pattern as they aid their lovers (Theseus and Jason respectively) in stealing their families' sacred treasures. To speed their escape to new islands and new adventures, they murder their brothers, betraying and sacrificing their old families to start new ones. As Patricia Reis explains in her analysis of Ariadne's tale, the woman at a transition to her life must dismember the hyper-masculine side of the psyche in order to let the feminine elements grow unhindered. If the brotherly masculine energy is misdirected (in Hina's case, toward keeping her a child on her island), she must tear it apart to properly direct it.[4] Thus, Hina parts forever from her childhood, silencing the masculine impulse of her brother who would speak out to confine her. The sacrifice of her childhood complete, Hina sets her eyes toward the Sacred Isle under the setting sun, more imagery of the near death Hina must face to reach her love.

In the ocean, near drowning, she discovers and claims her own sea power, transforming into a mermaid. These beautiful creatures of the unconscious are universally identified with sexuality and magic, signaling Hina's readiness to summon her perfect mate. This is Tinirau, whose name literally means "forty millions," suggesting the innumerable fish under his care.[5] He is godforce incarnate. As shapechanger and sea creature, he is a swirling manifestation of the unconscious world, dreamed up by Hina and made manifest by her *manu* and drumming, as this is her tale. Her journey from the provincial and demanding Ngana to ocean god Tinirau is, like Ariadne's journey, "not just a turning from one man to another; it is a move away from projecting one's power onto a solar heroic 'other,' toward finding an inner source of empowerment in the natural flow of life," as Reis explains.[6] Thus No-land-at-all offers Hina far more than a mate — it evokes her strongest self.

Entering the Unconscious

Once upon a time. These words beckon us to the otherworld, a place of magic, strangeness, vagueness: A fairyland where earthly rules may not apply.

This is the threshold to transcendence itself, the passage from reality to dream metaphor, time to eternity. It offers mystery and a taste of chaos to the hero — and far more to the heroine.

On her quest, the heroine will cross "the crack between worlds," the entrance to a new geography and a new psychological landscape. It is ambiguous in time and space, without familiar referents, a place where a different type of awareness comes to prominence, where deeper archetypal energies can emerge. "One cannot draw near the nucleus — be it self or soul or spindle core — and the meaning of life, without also being on the edge of falling into greed, darkness, and the field of encircling shadows."[7]

The forest, a feminine symbol, represents the dangerous side of the unconscious, its ability to destroy reason. As foliage blocks the masculine-centered sun's rays, it becomes a hidden place, a place of unknown perils and obscurity. This setting forth reflects the adolescent's inner turmoil, as the unconscious intrudes into the everyday world. Since innovative psychologists like Freud and Jung represented myths as part of the masculine cultural unconscious, femininity was constructed as the unconscious of the unconscious, the dark continent of the dark continent.[8]

To Jung, the unconscious is "everything of which I know, but of which I am not at the moment thinking; everything of which I was once conscious but have now forgotten; everything perceived by my senses, but not noted by my conscious mind."[9] It is the desires one doesn't even realize exist, but which whisper beneath the surface.

Upon approaching the Otherworld, a moment of transition presents: A shimmering barrier into fairyland, deep in the forest. A long, twisting tunnel into the realm of death. A mountain where one can don winged sandals and launch into the heavens ... or catastrophe. This forest, dark and mysterious, is a font of feminine power, the deep unconscious made manifest. As the heroine travels it, she explores the deepest recesses of her soul. Though shrouded in the trees' shade, the unconscious represents invaluable wisdom, if she can only learn to tap into it.

All these thresholds are dark, fluid environments, places where one cannot perceive the shapes below the surface. Fears and dreams become reality here, so that trees snatch at one's gown or a sea monster rises from the depths. These are places with dual natures: water meets land, trees protrude into sky, womblike tunnels descend to the underworld. This split echoes deeper dichotomies: masculine and feminine, the physical world and the spiritual, life and death. To Freud, hybridization, ambivalence, polarity, duplicity, and dualism suggest fear and confusion. But they also symbolize the sacred.

Mermaid and fairykind are born into this realm of magic and mystery, where one's deepest fears and greatest longings manifest themselves as demons and angels. Animals speak, wishes come true, and belief changes the world in an instant.

Most heroines, however, watch from their kitchen doors, dreaming of a world somewhere east of the sun and west of the moon. There they may find handsome princes, glittering festivals, gowns as silver as the stars and golden spinning wheels that fit in one's palm. There will also be shrieking banshees, witches with gnashing teeth, dragons that tear and bite and snatch. But even watching from the world of kitchen chores and walled up towers, the untried girl cannot resist the otherworld's call. For the adolescent, it is the road to adulthood, the journey up rugged cliffs and down through the valley of death into a kingdom indescribably magical, initiation into the secrets of life and love and growth.

The Liquid Element

Water is dual; it both saves and kills. Purification and regeneration. Tears, perpetuity, drowning, inundation. Amniotic fluid.

> It is in the dark that the passage from prebirth to birth takes place — in the maternal womb, the embryo, in the earth, the grain of wheat that Persephone represents.... The sea, the womb, Eleusis — all are places of birth and transformation, where the enigma of generation is concealed, containing all manner of snare and wonder, pleasure and mystery, the dangers of the sea became metaphors for the dangers of the feminine realm.[10]

Water is dark and secret, always changeable. It is the coolness of yin, rather than the hot wind of yang. From there are born the perpetually varying sea spirits, like Proteus (who gives us the word protean) or genies set adrift in their bottles.

Water is maternal, as all life springs from it. The sea, treacherous and changeable, infinitely potent, was often regarded as the domain of the goddess. Oya, goddess of the Niger River, was the goddess of change, transition, and the chaos that often creates it. Shifting endlessly between her forms as woman and water buffalo, she created the storms and waves.

Water offers prophecy and wisdom to those attuned to it. Heroes enter this realm, and depart, like Odysseus, with the experience to rule.

Water holds the power of healing, of renewal, of purification, as sacred waters have been used from time immemorial for all these purposes. Dipping in water is returning to the Goddess and being reborn. To the Greeks, the river Styx was imagined as a stream of goddess blood, emanating from the earth's womb.[11] An oath made on it would bind even Zeus to honor it or die a betrayer of the feminine mysteries. The goddess Thetis dipped her son Achilles in its divine fluid to make him immortal. This, like all baptisms, is a return to the life-source, a second birth.

Even those who commit crimes against maternity can find salvation in water's healing. Ino, a classic "wicked stepmother" and queen, bribed the women of her country to parch the grain, which consequently never sprouted. The oracle, whom Ino had also bribed, prophesized that the famine would cease when King Athamas sacrificed his children by his first wife, Nephele, to the goddess Demeter. The outcast Nephele begged Zeus for aid, and he sent a golden ram to fly the children to safety. When the enraged king learned of Ino's actions, he killed Melicertes, his son by Ino, and pursued Ino into the sea. There, she changed into the Siren Leucothea, she who saved Odysseus with her magic veil. Though Ino is a classic Terrible Mother, destroying her stepchildren, in water she reincarnates as a savior of the vulnerable.

The Little Mermaid, too, dissolves into sea-foam. Betrayed by the prince who will never love her, she sacrifices herself and dives into the sea.

> The knife trembled in the hand of the little mermaid: then she flung it far away from her into the waves; the water turned red where it fell, and the drops that spurted up looked like blood. She cast one more lingering, half-fainting glance at the prince, and then threw herself from the ship into the sea, and thought her body was dissolving into foam. The sun rose above the waves, and his warm rays fell on the cold foam of the little mermaid, who did not feel as if she were dying. She saw the bright sun, and all around her floated hundreds of transparent beautiful beings; she could see through them the white sails of the ship, and the red clouds in the sky.[12]

Here, blood, icy ocean, and hot sun blend, reincarnating the dying mermaid into an air spirit. While she begins as a creature of the borderlands — sand and sea, woman and fish — she is reborn into divinity, insubstantial and angelic. Like Leucothea, she becomes a protector of others, guarding the world's children.

While men enter the sea and then return, like Odysseus, Achilles, or Beowulf, many women embody the sea, like the mermaid. Thus, the most spiritually gifted heroines submit to the water's regenerative energy, integrating it so fully that they never leave its influence.

On a small island near Taiwan, a woman with many boys prayed to the goddess of mercy. Soon after, the woman conceived the girl she'd prayed for. As a baby, the daughter was very quiet, so she was called Lin Mo (silent). However, she quickly developed remarkable intelligence and an eidetic memory. At four years of age, Mo knelt in front of a statue of Kuan Yin and received the power of second sight. At age ten, she studied Buddhism, and at thirteen, ascended to Taoism. When she turned fifteen, a sea creature erupted from the water before her and offered her a bronze disk, which helped her predict when the waters would be calm enough for fishing.

Lin Mo was at home weaving a tapestry when she suddenly had a vision that her father and brother were in danger. Clutching the bronze disk, she transported herself instantly to their fishing boat. Pushing her brother to safety, she swam for shore with her father clenched between her teeth.

Meanwhile, Lin Mo's mother saw her daughter (as it appeared) slumped over the tapestry in a deep trance. She shook Mo awake, breaking the trance so that Mo's father drowned. Sorrowful, Mo could only return to the water to retrieve his body.

In her grief, Mo distanced herself from others, turning to spirituality and holy works. Her family pressured her to marry, and two great warriors professed their great desire for her. Untempted, Lin Mo challenged the pair to fight her, insisting that they serve her forever if she won. Armed with her priestly training in martial arts, she beat them both soundly.

Lin Mo's death at twenty-eight was as remarkable as her birth. She climbed a nearby mountain, all alone, until she was encircled by clouds of dense fog. To the accompaniment of enchanting celestial music, she floated into the heavens in a golden glow, with a rainbow trailing after her. To honor her great humility and enlightenment, Lin Mo was elevated to goddesshood as the sea deity Mazu. Tens of thousands make the eight-day pilgrimage to her oldest temple in Taiwan each year, and, to this day, sailors from China to San Francisco pray Mazu for a safe voyage and thank her upon their return.

CHAPTER 6

Where the Wild Things Are: Allies and Enemies

Ix Chel (Maya)

Ix Chel, first woman of the world, graciously gifted the people of the Yucatán with ease of childbirth and knowledge of healing. It was she who flooded the entire world, just as she floods women's wombs once each month. Crowned with eagle feathers, she made the birds her messengers, and, copying the spider, she taught weaving to the women of earth. She was the shining moon up in the heavens, the cleanser, goddess of tides. Standing by the beds of the ill, she held a reed cradle, signifying her power over life, even as she fed the sick with turkey broth and the sap of the rubber tree.

At the very beginning, she dwelt in the heavens beside the sun, and was just as bright as he. The sun, gazing at her from across the sky, swooned with love for her. But since her grandfather guarded Ix Chel jealously, the sun borrowed a hummingbird's shape and flew to her window.

Ix Chel welcomed him with the honey of tobacco flowers, but as they spoke, a clay pellet flew through the air and buried itself deep within the hummingbird's side. He tumbled to the ground. Ix Chel cried out, for she knew her grandfather had shot her first friend. She carried the bird to her room and nursed it tenderly until it recovered.

They resolved to run away together, and sun and moon paddled through the heavens in a cedar canoe. Infuriated, her grandfather hurled a lightning bolt that killed Ix Chel in an instant. As she lay there at the bottom of heaven's marshy stream, dragonflies gathered, mourning with their soft buzzing. They blanketed her with their vibrating bodies as they prepared for her 13 hollow logs. On the 13th night, the logs cracked open. From 12 crawled the awesome great snakes of heaven, and from the 13th, Ix Chel herself, well and whole.

63

The overjoyed sun proposed marriage, and they dwelt together happily up in heaven.

However, all was not perfect. The sun's handsome brother, Chc Noh Ek, was a constant visitor. Soon, the sun, overcome with jealousy, accused them both of adultery. Turning on Ix Chel, he flung her from heaven.

She landed with a thump near the lake of Atitlan, in the land of volcanoes. Brimming with anger at the false accusations, Ix Chel gazed at the sky, uncertain what course to take. "Poor child, you look like you need help," a voice squawked. Ix Chel turned, and there was the king of the vultures.

"I don't know where to go," she confessed. Her treacherous brother-in-law had stolen her husband away, perhaps forever.

"Come to my mountain and stay with me a while." Confused and vulnerable, Ix Chel agreed to stay with the vulture, and at last became his lover.

When the sun spied her there, his jealousy burned hotter than ever before. He covered himself in a deer hide and huddled on the ground. When a vulture arrived, he leapt on its back and was carried to Ix Chel. There he knelt before her and poured out apologies like rain on the ground.

Ix Chel gladly forgave him and returned to the sky. But once again, jealousy consumed the sun. Berating Ix Chel for her beauty, which shone indiscriminately on all the beings of the earth, he began to beat her. He rained down blows on her face, determined to scar her so badly no one would ever want her again. As her brilliance dimmed, her will grew stronger, until she flew off into the night.

There she dwelt, alone, traveling the heavens. Many offered her marriage, but she rejected them all, saying, "The sun is my husband," though she hurried off whenever she spied him approaching. She became a protector of women, encouraging them to journey as they pleased, especially to her shrine on Cozumel Island, the Isle of Women. From then on, Ix Chel came and went as she willed, sometimes disappearing for days, ever solitary, ever one-in-herself.[1]

Ix Chel was revered throughout Southern Mexico and Central America, from about 600 to 1500 CE. In her tale, she has a myriad of animal protectors: the dragonflies that restore her to life, the vulture that, as nonthreatening lover, protects her from the world. These are small, benevolent helpers like the bees and ants who aid the Grimms' heroes and heroines on their quests. Zipes describes them as "small creatures or outsiders — those creatures who are marginal and live on the border between wilderness and civilization, between village and woods, between the earthly world and the other, sacred world."[2]

In *The Snow White Syndrome*, Betsy Cohen focuses our attention on the dwarves as a force for altruism:

The dwarfs, Snow White's rescuers, are the helpers who seem to come into our lives magically, just at the moment we need them. In the "real world," these helpers may be therapists, friends, relatives, mates, ministers, or just a stranger on a bus. In the story of Snow White, the dwarfs are humble, nonthreatening, empathic, understanding, nurturing men with qualities that present a true contrast to those of the wicked queen. The dwarfs are miners. They dig deep into the earth, seeking precious gems and metals. They help Snow White mine for what is precious in herself. The dwarfs bring Snow White down to earth. They watch over Snow White and try to guard her from her envious mother. They warn her, they support her, and give her a role, a purpose in life.[3]

These creatures are a part of the heroine, the unconscious voices that creep forward to help, to comfort, when the task is too hard. Famed fairytale analyst Bruno Bettelheim theorizes that "both dangerous and helpful animals stand for our animal nature, our instinctual drives."[4] They are the tiny voices that operate on the intuitive level: "Don't go there! Stop and think first. Trust yourself." They provide encouragement and strength, acting as the heroine's hands and eyes to solve her puzzles.

Pets and familiars are common in tales, providing more than a friendly ear. Like the dwarves, they can be the animus to the heroine's anima, supplementing her female intuition with male intellect, or vice versa. Cinderella has her helpers, while Psyche has the sympathetic ants and birds that help her complete her tasks. From the Nunivak tribe of southwest Alaska comes a tale of a girl who hunted with a muskrat as her companion. Together they killed caribou and seals, game considered the province of male hunters. In this way, she earned enough food to care for them both, along with her grandmother, who stayed home and did the "women's work." For the Nunivak, the huntress and her pet represented a traditional male and female pair (the male as a magic totem animal) who together lived in perfect harmony.

These protectors give more than advice, guarding the heroine's back as she travels. For, just as she has small helpers, she has small enemies — guardians or monsters who block the path, forcing her to outwit or outmaneuver them.

Monsters

When the heroine enters the forest, or another realm of the unconscious, she has left the world of logic and entered that of the spirit, the anima. Therefore, this female-centric realm offers female monsters and symbols, creatures of the borderlands and crossroads of the unconscious which the hero of either gender must conquer.

These guardians are of split natures, emphasizing the bridge between two worlds. Spying the monster guarding the gate, the questor hesitates. Does he or she truly dare cross into the realm of the magical, the unknown? These creatures guard the border between land and sea, or life and death. Often dwelling in caves open to the air or deep in the forest, these creatures test the heroine: "Do not pass," they say. "Are your eyes or ears better than mine? Do you have a magic token or hidden talent? Only one who knows the secret of life, only one who is clever, or anointed in women's mysteries, may step into the shrine. For all others, death awaits."

In this world, the heroine is weak, still a student beside the ageless power of the god-imbued immortals. Both heroes and heroines need the advice of tiny creatures magical amulets of the goddess, song and mirror, sacred cloaks of invisibility, or other feminine powers to defeat these twisted voices of the unconscious. Thus the sphinx, half woman and half lion, defends her threshold, demanding a riddle of the nature of life itself. She is monster and woman, as chaotic and magical as the unconscious itself, a figure of nightmares. In facing her, the hero Oedipus faces the knowledge of mortality, the terrifying feminine, and the magical gateway.

> Myth images of half-human beasts like the mermaid and the minotaur express an old fundamental very slowly clarifying communal insight: that our species' nature is internally inconsistent, that our continuities with and our differences from, the earth's other animals are mysterious and profound, and in these continuities and these differences lie both a sense of strangeness on earth and the possible key to a way of feeling at home here.[5]

Egyptians prayed to gods half-human and half-animal, considering them interceders between the two worlds: Sekmet the lioness, Hathor the cow, Bast the cat, Thoth the ibis, and Horus the falcon. Houyi, of ancient Chinese legend, shot a number of these mixed guardians: Yagu the centaur, Zuochi the ogre, Quiying the monster that kills with water and fire, Dafeng the great bird that unleashes the wind Fengxi, and Xisushe the giant serpent.[6]

These creatures possess wisdom and insight beyond that of the questor, often symbolized by magical eyes. The snake heads of Medusa and the Hydra had many eyes, as did the three-headed Chimera. Argus the Many-eyed was the goddess Hera's servant, ever watchful. The gnarled old Graeae, who knew all the world's secrets, passed one magical eye among them. According to the Hindu *Lalita Sahasranamam*, the Great Goddess destroyed and created the universe just by opening or closing her eyes.[7] Eyes were such a feminine symbol of the ancient world that the patriarchies vilified them as the still-dreaded evil eye.

The three-headed canine Cerberus, whose heads can see in three dimensions, had unnatural perception. Though male, he too was a guardian of feminine mysteries, as dogs were sacred to the Celtic mother goddess and to Hecate, reigning crone of the underworld. Wolves, too, appear in myth as goddess-protectors or as the Great She Wolf of the Sabines, foster-mother to Romulus and Remus. As Clarissa Pinkola Estés explains about her book *Women Who Run with the Wolves*:

Healthy wolves and healthy women share certain psychic characteristics. Wolves and women are relational by nature, inquiring, possessed of great endurance and strength. They are deeply intuitive, intensely concerned with their young, their mate, and their pack.[8]

Both wolves and women have been denigrated and forced to the shadows, falsely blamed for aggression and deviousness. Still, they are a powerful symbol of women's wild natures.

In the epic *Beowulf*, the monster Grendel slithers from the wildness of forest and lake to menace the soldiers in their stronghold. Grendel's mother, too, is a borderlands creature, associated with water and the wilderness. She is called *brimwylf*, wolf of the lake, *grundwyrgen*, accursed monster of the deep, and *merewif mihtig*, mighty woman of the mere — all water associations. She is a hag or monster-woman (*aglec-wif*) of dark intent. At the same time, however, she is twice called *ides*, the term used for a lady of high standing.[9] In the adventure of Beowulf against Grendel's mother, "a sense pervades the scene rather of nature's terrible wonder than of moral evil and crime.[10] She is like a goddess of the wild, husbandless, defending her realm beyond the civilized castle and sending her monster son out to battle.

In over 30 years of field research, Marija Gimbutas discovered that an overwhelming number of Stone Age figures blend woman and water bird. Neolithic paintings through Cretan Bronze Age pottery depict women as the bird-woman hybrid, linked with running water.[11] The Irish battle goddess, the Morrigan, flew over battlefields in the form of a crow, helping the hero Cúchulainn with her powerful magics.[12] There are many other bird women of sea, land, and sky, like the shrieking harpies and furies, possessing wings of feathers or brass. Bird women offer passage to the afterlife as ravens, as feather-cloaked Valkyries, as angels. They are creatures of the unconscious, both terrible and tempting. Many are shape-shifters, or are cruel and kind by turns.

When faced with male monsters, men slay them. Theseus doesn't hesitate to kill the Minotaur, though he represents the mating of the cow-horned moon priestess and her sacrificed bull-king.[13] But a surprising number of monstrous guardians are outwardly female, embodiments of ancient wisdom. Heroes of both genders generally outwit them in order to pass beyond their barriers. Orpheus plays beautiful music, conquering the Sirens with his creative talents, and then sings Cerberus to sleep. Perseus shields his eyes from Medusa. Hermes tells Argus hundreds of tales, waiting patiently for him to drowse. Theseus, fighting a handful of guardians, learns to use their strength against them. Hercules slays the Hydra, but again this takes cunning, as do the Chimera and Medusa; all these monsters are too deadly to approach without a careful plan.

More terrible still are the deadly pair that Jason and Odysseus face, steering carefully through the dreaded straits: Scylla, like many feminine monsters of Greek myth, offended one of the gods; in this case, she was the lover of the sea-deity Glaucus, who in turn was loved by Circe. Circe poured a virulent poison into the nymph's bathing pool, which Scylla stepped into down to the waist, leaving her lovely nymph above, and six ravenous dogs below.

> She has twelve mis-shapen feet, and six necks of the most prodigious length; and at the end of each neck she has a frightful head with three rows of teeth in each, all set very close together, so that they would crunch any one to death in a moment, and she sits deep within her shady cell thrusting out her heads and peering all round the rock.... No ship ever yet got past her without losing some men, for she shoots out all her heads at once, and carries off a man in each mouth.[14]

On the opposite side of the channel "lies the sucking whirlpool of Charybdis. Three times in the day does she vomit forth her waters, and three times she sucks them down again; see that you be not there when she is sucking, for if you are, Neptune himself could not save you."[15] Reportedly, Charybdis was a greedy woman who devoured her neighbors' cattle, and thus was changed by the gods into this deadly devourer of ships. Odysseus later describes encountering her, saying:

> As she vomited it up, it was like the water in a cauldron when it is boiling over upon a great fire, and the spray reached the top of the rocks on either side. When she began to suck again, we could see the water all inside whirling round and round, and it made a deafening sound as it broke against the rocks. We could see the bottom of the whirlpool all black with sand and mud, and the men were at their wits ends for fear.[16]

"This was the most sickening sight that I saw throughout all my voyages," Odysseus says of this deadly pair, both in their own ways borderlands creatures.[17] Scylla is half charming woman, half zoomorphic monstrosity. But Charybdis is the deadlier threat, as a passage to an unknown world, a sucking hole in the ocean. Circe is wise when she cautions Odysseus to sacrifice six crewmembers to Scylla rather than the ship to Charybdis, but it goes deeper than that. An animalistic guardian of water and land, canine and human, is a precursor, a less deadly threat, to a gaping passage to the underworld.

Serpent Guardians

Snakes and their dragon counterparts were frequent guardians, like Ladon, coiled around the golden apple tree in the Garden of the Hesperides. Nāgas prowled ancient India, at times benign or terrible. Coatlicue of the Aztecs was part anthropomorphic, part zoomorphic. She was clearly female, and yet dual, with her masculine side represented by eagle parts, and the female by the snake.[18] The chthonic, or underworld deity, Lamia, slithered over the shores of Libya, while nearby sea serpents engulfed entire ships. Python guarded Gaia's sacred caves, just as Cerberus and the Chimera, both snake-tailed, warded other shadowy passages.

The vicious Furies, too, punishers of those who broke the gods' justice, were perpetually snarled with snakes as they lurked in the underworld. As Ovid's *Metamorphoses* describes their leader:

> The baleful Erinys stood ... stretching her arms entwined with tangled snakes, and shaking out her hair. The snakes, dislodged, gave hissing sounds; some crawled upon her shoulders; some, gliding round her bosom, vomited a slime of venom, flickering their tongues and hissing horribly. Then from her hair she tore out two with a doom-charged aim darted them. Down the breasts of Athamas and Ino [her sisters], winding, twisting, they exhaled their noisome breath.[19]

In Hebrew and Arabic, the word for magic comes from the word for serpent, while the Sioux word for serpent also meant wizard. From the Southwestern United States to Greece, certain snakebites were known for giving insight and prophecy. Throughout the world, these chthonic figures were, in fact, "infinitude indicating omniscience."[20]

> Snakes, or serpents, as they are often called in Greek myth, are also known for their transmutational power, which is exemplified in their ability to shed their skin. This life-death-rebirth cycle is the energy of wholeness and the ability to experience anything willingly and without resistance. It is the knowledge that those things which might be poisonous, hurtful or uncomfortable may be ingested, experienced, integrated and transmuted if one is in the proper state of mind ... thereby producing divine, cohesive energy.[21]

According to Cambodian legend, the nāga, or snake-people, dwelt in their empire in the Pacific Ocean. The nāga king's daughter married an Indian Brahmana named Kaundinya, and gave birth to the Cambodian people. The gigantic bird-man Garuda once offered the nāgas the elixir of life and immortality, placing it on the ground, but the god Indra hastily confiscated it. Unseen, a few drops remained on the grass. The nāgas licked up the drops, but cut their tongues on the grass, and since then they have been fonts of wisdom and immortality, but their tongues have been forked.

As Merlin Stone notes in her groundbreaking *When God Was a Woman*, "Despite the insistent, perhaps hopeful, assumption that the serpent must have been regarded as a phallic symbol, it appears to have been primarily revered as a female in the Near and Middle East and generally linked to wisdom and prophetic counsel."[22] Sumerians worshipped the great Mother Serpent of Heaven, and the snake was found coiled around many Great Goddesses such as Asherah, Ishtar, Athena, and Hathor. The Minoan snake goddess likewise dominated Crete, leaving behind figures of woman and snake entwined. The snake tempted Eve, offered prophecies, allowed Cleopatra's triumph. "The symbol of the Serpent was the one most widely used to represent or adorn the Goddess of the Ancient Near East or to depict, or mediate, the relationship between goddesses and human culture," explains Mary Condren in *The Serpent and the Goddess.*[23]

The snake reflected the Great Goddess, changing from young to old and then cycling back to young as the world renewed in the spring. It contained the insight only known to priestesses of the time, and it shed its skin, like a woman birthing a new organism from itself. Depicted coiled in several successive rings, the serpent mimics cyclical evolution and reincarnation. It coils sinuously as the seasons and the fluidity of female cycles, devoid of straight lines.

"The serpent represents immortal energy and consciousness engaged in the field of time, constantly throwing off death and being born again."[24] The snake that sheds its old skin, or eats its own tail, is a Goddess symbol of constant decomposition, constant renewal. Thus the Aegypto-Greek Ourobouros or Norse Jörmungandr (Midgard serpent) surrounds the cosmos, biting its own tail in a symbol of perpetuity and infinity, never ending, always regenerating.

Across the ocean in the Solomon Islands, Walutahanga was a female snake, daughter of a human woman. When her frightened family cut her into eight pieces, they grew together again and she revived. Again they cut her in eight pieces, this time eating her. Then Walutahanga summoned eight enormous waves, which drowned the village. She saved the only woman and child who hadn't eaten her body, and created yams, taro, and coconuts for them.[25] Death could not stop her reemergence, and she repaid both cruelty and kindness with godlike strength. This mother snake cycles effortlessly from death to life, guardian of the seas and of the earth's magic, nurturing and terrifying.

Meeting the Other

CHAPTER 7

Taming the Beast:
The Shapechanger as Lover

Tam Lin (Scotland)

While Janet was walking through the forest of Carterhaugh, a holding of the castle her father had gifted her, she wandered toward a deep wishing-well, her green skirt blowing softly in the breeze. There she spied a brilliant double rose blooming, like a dream of fairyland, aromatic and bright with potential. As she plucked it, a young man appeared, as if out of nowhere. "Who are you," he asked, "and why do you pluck my roses so boldly, in my forest without my leave?"

"Why, Carterhaugh is mine, a gift from my father," she retorted.

His gray eyes darkened. "This is fairy country, and it's not wise to wander here. Take some friendly advice and go."

She tossed her red hair. "I tell you this land is mine. And I'll go where I please in it."

He started to speak, but hesitated and then finally said, "I beg your pardon, then." He gazed about the woods, with their shadows and secrets. "It's been long since I've traveled here."

"Why is that?" she asked. And though he seemed disinclined to tell her, they chatted for hours of all manner of things. Despite his earlier gruffness, Janet reflected that she had never met a man so wise, with his knowledge of the hidden pathways through the forest, and the hiding places of hares and deer. She had never met one so handsome, either, with his wide grey eyes that watched her every gesture as if trying to read her. At last, they made love on a velvety patch of moss, the plucked double rose lying tumbled beside them.

"Come," she said after. "Come and stay a while."

Tam Lin, as he was called, shook his head sorrowfully. "You believe me a traveling bard or wanderer, but I'm not like you. You must return alone."

"Are you so faithless then? Or an elf-knight from another world?"

He took her hands. "Mortal as you, but the elf knight isn't far off. For I was an earl's son once, long ago. But I fell from my horse and who should rescue me but the Queen of Fairies, who bound me in service. I cannot stray far from her kingdom, or from this forest."

"Must you serve her forever then?

He closed his eyes. "I pray so."

"What!"

He snatched at her hands as she tried to tug them away. "I would gladly spend my days on earth with you, Janet. But I am the Fairy Queen's in life or death, as she would have me."

Janet felt her ruddy cheeks pale. "Death, you say?"

He nodded. "Each seven years, the fairies pay a teind to hell, a single life to protect them all. And if the queen tires of me, I may become that sacrifice."

"Can I save you?"

He shook his head. "The Queen has the prior claim, and would never accept yours. Farewell, dearest Janet." And he vanished between one breath and another.

As the months passed, Janet discovered that she was carrying Tam's child. She hid her condition as long as she could, but soon the maidens in her bower and the soldiers in the field had all begun to gossip of it. When her father discovered what had happened, he chided her for losing her maidenhood to an unknown stranger. "He's no stranger, but a fairy knight all in gray," Janet boasted, but her family would have none of it. They swore she had disgraced them with some good-for-nothing, and that they would be shamed forever in the eyes of the world for her wantonness. At last, in desperation, Janet walked to the shady forest well, for at its base grew clinging herbs that would help her lose the child.

No sooner had she begun plucking them, soft damp leaves, smelling sharp between her fingers, when she spied another glorious double rose. She rushed over and plucked it, and there was her lover.

"Who are you," he asked, eyes shining like clouds over the sun. "And why do you pluck my roses so boldly, in my forest without my leave?"

Janet smiled, relieved beyond words at his teasing. "You came. Now, when I best need you." She clasped her hands unconsciously over her belly.

"But *you* are here to rid yourself of my child," he said, and looked so sad that she reassured him that she would never do such a thing. He smiled, but his melancholy remained.

The thought fluttered in Janet's mind that he seemed fey and flighty, as he stood there in the shadows. "Are you well, Tam Lin?"

"Well enough," he said. "But this child is all that will remain of me — tonight is Hallow e'en, and the Queen is sending me as her tithe to hell."

"No!" Janet said, surprising them both with her ferocity. "She shan't have my lover. Tell me how to save you."

Tam hesitated. "This child between us gives you claim. But this will tax your courage to the limit."

"I'll do it, whatever needs must."

"At midnight, all the fairy folk will ride and I with them, all swathed in cloaks of gray."

"Then how will I know you?"

"Let the black steed and the brown one pass, fair Janet. I'll be riding the milk-white one. And I'll loosen my hair and ride with my left hand glove-less — by those tokens you'll know me. Then you must pull me down from my horse and hold me tight in your arms. And if you can hold me till dawn, why then, the time for tithing will have passed, and I'll be yours forever."

"Just hold you? There must be more."

"Aye. They'll transform me in your arms into a hissing snake, a famished bear, a lion, a living flame. But you must hold me close with courage, whatever form I take. I'm your babe's father, Janet, and your true love forever. You must trust in me, and in yourself. Only then can you reclaim me."

That night lay gloomy, with eerie curls of mist rising over the path. Janet waited, wearing her green wool mantle, stout leather shoes and thick-knitted socks against the chill. A soft jingle brushed her ears, rhythmic as a horse's trot: belled bridles, and many of them. Her breath stopped. All the fairies rode by in beautiful company, cloaks gray as the mist shrouding their finery. Janet let the black horse pass, and the brown. But she ran to the milk-white steed and yanked its rider off.

As they hit the ground and rolled, Janet smelled hot meaty breath as a wolf's jaws snapped at her, inches from her eyes. Janet shut them tight and clutched her lover with all her strength. He gnashed at her with lion's jaws, hissed with serpent's tongue, stank with a bear's greasy fur, and crackled with fiery heat. Still she clung, though she shook with terror, and longed to thrust away his hideous form.

At last, dawn sparked in the sky, and there lay her lover, naked and human in her arms. She wrapped him in her mantle and gazed up at the fairy queen on her palfrey who had been watching all the while. Still she clutched him close, though she doubted the lovely queen could take him now that dawn had come. "He's mine now, by the feat I've done this night, by the child in my belly, by our love for each other."

A terrible cloud passed over the Queen's countenance. "An ill death may you die — you've stolen the fairest knight in my company." Her gaze turned to the cloak-wrapped man. "And you, Tam Lin, I'd have plucked out your gray eyes if I'd known you were plotting this."

Janet's arms closed around him. "It's daylight now, and I've won. So you must return to Fairie now and leave him to me."

So the fairy queen rode away into the forest. And Tam Lin and Janet dwelt happily together for the rest of their lives.[1]

In the game of love, the hero and heroine each view their partner as a shapeshifter. This "other half" they must cleave to like themselves has frightening mood swings and unpredictable desires. Hence, many tales appear about enticing swan maidens from the sea or taming beastly monsters into Prince Charmings.

This type of story "places the male lover, the Beast, in the position of the mysterious, threatening, possibly fatal, unknown, and Beauty, the heroine, as the questor who discovers his true nature," comments Marina Warner in *From the Beast to the Blonde*.[2] In these tales, such as "The Tiger's Bride" or "The Frog Prince," the monsters are memorable, but the heroines are abstract and universal. Their names like Beauty and Psyche (soul) represent every woman questing for love and desire in the heart of someone so foreign, so unimaginable that they may be devoured.

For Tam Lin and Janet, the situation is identical — he takes on monstrous forms, gnashing at her with gleaming teeth. However, as with Beauty, Janet must show faith in Tam Lin under his frightening transformations. If she can hold him close and accept him as magical other, slavering beast, and masculine lover, she drains him of all power to intimidate.

This monster is the animus, the submerged male side of the heroine. For the man, the anima represents the hidden perceptive, spiritual side. For the woman, the animus offers a source of rules, logic, and order, an objectivity that strengthens her through her tasks. Often, she must quest for him, entering a growing awareness of her own explored masculine side. As noted by Jungian scholar Marie-Louise Von Franz:

> The conscious attention a woman has to give to her animus problem takes much time and involves a lot of suffering. But if she realizes who and what her animus is ... instead of allowing herself to be possessed, her animus can turn into an invaluable inner companion who endows her with the masculine qualities of initiative, courage, objectivity, and spiritual wisdom.[3]

By integrating the animus into herself, the heroine journeys toward wholeness, adding to her power before she need face the more terrible initiation through death. Sometimes this is fulfilled through animal helpers, dwarves, or other male companions, friends and confidants who teach her needed skills. More often marriage or love, often an achievement before the tale's end, induces her masculine nature as well as the feminine, completing her. With beast-lovers, the animus is the magical side beneath her perception, a creature of the ocean or the forest, one she must integrate into herself to absorb its powers.

A group of Samish maidens were gathering shellfish on the beaches of the Pacific Northwest. One girl kept dropping the clams and having to chase after them until she stood in water up to her waist. A hand grasped hers and she screamed. "Do not be afraid," a voice in the water said. "I only want to admire your beauty." From then on, each time she gathered shellfish, the voice would come to her and describe the beauties of the world under the sea.

One day a young man rose from the water and asked to marry her, but her father refused. Then the merman scowled, and the shellfish became scarce. Fish vanished. Streams and springs dried up. At last, the father allowed his daughter to go, if the merman promised she could visit home. The merman agreed. The maiden walked into the sea, long hair streaming behind her, and all of the food returned.

She visited as promised, but her people noticed changes in her. First barnacles sprang from her hands, then her arms, then her face. She seemed increasingly unhappy out of the water. So her people agreed that she didn't have to visit them. Though the young woman didn't return, she made sure her people had plenty to eat. And when they looked out into the water, they saw her long drifting hair and knew she was watching over them.[4]

Often, Beauty enters a magical world, with the Beast its most magical offering. She integrates the magic into herself and grows from it. This is a melding of personalities and traits, the perfect balance of male and female abilities, yin and yang. This is a marriage.

Cupid and Psyche

Psyche grows up completely naive until the god of love, Cupid, sends the west wind to whisk her away. He then offers her the traditional taboo bargain: She can be his wife but never see his face. Though Psyche has entered the Otherworld of magic and possibility, she cannot grow, ensnared within it as she is.

Psyche's life with Cupid, instead of the ostensible paradise, is a cotton cocoon. She receives servants, gowns, a glorious palace, everything she desires. She has no needs, no challenges, and certainly no growth. Cupid shelters her from death and suffering, but also from life. As a god, he holds all the power. Psyche might as well be doing housework and caring for the kids during her lonely days, but she doesn't even have that — just an endless parade of playing dress-up and embroidering. With no friends and no occupation, she's like a wife who can't balance the checkbook, doesn't know how to hire a repairman, and calls her mother daily to ask for help.

Psyche, in fact, is so innocent that Cupid has to inform her when she becomes pregnant. Using condescending and fatherly language, he calls her "a girl as open-hearted and simple as yourself," adding, "Though you are still only a child, you will soon have a child of your own."[5] As a "child," she is not

Cupid's equal. She is a kept lover, not the lady of the house and decision-maker. She is not, in fact, adult enough to become a mother, despite her pregnancy.

In the original Roman legend by Apuleius, Psyche lives mindlessly and contentedly, never questioning the paradise in which she lives. Psyche might never leave the womblike seclusion, except that her sisters make their way to her very door, pounding on it and calling for her. They are the catalyst needed to shove her toward growth. "You've never seen him?," they demand, looks of shock on their faces. "All right, our palaces are small, but at least we rule our households. You may be his mistress or his victim," they insist, "but not his wife. Meet his friends, join the country club, plan a dinner party. Whatever you do, get out into the world."

Cupid, concerned with any outside influences touching Psyche, forbids her to admit them.

> The unhappy girl spent the whole day crying and mourning, constantly repeating that now she was utterly destroyed: locked up in this rich prison and deprived of intercourse or speech with human beings, she could not bring comfort to her sisters in their sorrow or even set eyes on them. Unrevived by bath or food or any other refreshment and weeping abundantly, she retired to rest.[6]

At this emotional display, Cupid relents and allows them in.

Here, Cupid is not only the all-providing lover. He is also Psyche's adversary, defending her innocence at the cost of her soul-growth. "When the youthful spirit marries the predator, she is captured or restrained during a time in her life that was meant to be an unfoldment,"[7] warns Clarissa Pinkola Estés in her groundbreaking *Women Who Run with the Wolves*. Though Cupid offers well-meaning love, he plots, like Bluebeard, Rapunzel's witch, and Snow White's stepmother, to trap Psyche in total innocence. When her sisters insist Psyche light a candle and look upon her lover, suggesting Cupid may be a monster, their diagnosis is all too accurate. Psyche's smothering existence cannot continue.

Stifled thus, every heroine must open the cottage door, taste the apple, turn the shining key. For Psyche, lighting a candle is not "destructive feminine curiosity." She only seeks the equality denied her and takes her first step toward loss of childhood innocence. She cannot linger in the empty paradise of Eden when the tree of knowledge beckons.

How many spouses secretly follow their partners, read their mail and diaries, seeking evidence of infidelity? This is no different than Psyche's candle. Psyche breaks Cupid's trust, but Cupid himself has transgressed first, hiding so much of himself that he remains a whisper in darkness. Psyche tears down that divide, forcing Cupid's confidence, his true appearance. Only then can they abandon the flawless god and exquisite princess relationship and accept each other as flawed, imperfect lovers, as real people.

"To fall in love is to project that particularly golden part of one's shadow, the image of God — whether masculine or feminine — onto another person. Instantly, that person is the carrier of everything sublime and holy."[8] This in-loveness obliterates the humanity of the beloved — we love the projection we imagine, but not the flaws and reality of the other person. When we finally light the candle on what we find distasteful in the other person and accept it, we grow and can love truly and honestly.

In a tale from Uttar Pradesh in India, a barber tells his friend, a farmer, that his bride-to-be is homely and cannot cook. Believing these statements, the farmer blindfolds himself before the ceremony, determined to never look upon his wife or eat her cooking. The wife resolves to end this behavior. While her husband is gambling with the barber (without his blindfold), she joins them, pretending to be a stranger. Beguiling her husband, she wins all of his fortune in the form of rings, necklaces, and bracelets, over many visits. The wife then persuades her mother-in-law to conceal the jewelry in sweets called *laddus* and serve them. Confronted with his foolishness, the husband accepts his wife and abandons the prohibitions.[9] When the wife forces away the blindfold, the husband can stop idealizing/denigrating her, and begin to relate to her as a person. No longer shut out, the wife can become part of his life.

Within the heroine's journey, a moment occurs at which the heroine realizes her father (or his representative) is not the all-powerful god she envisions. He is insecure, fallible, mortal. When Psyche's family sacrifices her to a dark, mysterious monster, the bewildered girl finds herself married to a shadowy figure always cloaked by night. Indeed, relationships offer strangeness, uncertainty, changing rules. To many, this lover seems a shapechanger, with personality and desires too changeable to comprehend.

Psyche lights the forbidden lamp and gazes on her lover as he sleeps. There she sees not a monster, but the god of love, handsome and helpless. Psyche pricks a finger on his arrows and falls desperately in love. As the tale states:

> As soon as the light was presented and the secret of their bed became plain, what she saw was of all wild beasts the most soft and sweet of monsters, none other than Cupid, the fair god fairly lying asleep ... utterly lost as she was, as she gazed and gazed on the beauty of the god's face, her spirits returned.[10]

Though Cupid's divine beauty is mesmerizing, his real attraction lies in the fact that his mystery and menace have vanished. He is no longer an invisible monster stifling Psyche and waiting to devour her. His deception ended, Psyche can love him as an equal. Erich Neumann analyzes this change in his *Amor and Psyche: The Psychic Development of the Feminine*:

> In the light of her new consciousness she experiences a fateful transformation, in which she discovers that the separation between beast and husband is not valid. As the lightning bolt of love strikes her, she turns the knife against her own heart or (in other terms) wounds herself on Eros' arrow. With this she departs from the child-like, unconscious aspect as well. Only in a squalid, lightless existence can Psyche

mistake her lover for a beast, a violator, a dragon, and only as a childishly ignorant girl (but this too is a dark aspect) can she suppose that she is in love with a "higher husband" distinct from the lower dragon. In the light of irrupting love Psyche recognizes Eros as a god, who is the upper and the lower in one, and who connects the two.[11]

In her mind, Psyche has divided beast and god, fleeing the former and clinging to the latter. She is divided too, forfeiting her independent side and clinging to her persona of a weak insipid princess.

Archetypal fairy tale figures yearn for their total opposites. Thus, the vilest villains vie for the purest maidens, while temptresses lose their hearts to the gallant hero. "What is it about you?," the dainty princess asks the ruffian. "You're unlike anyone I've ever met." Within this compelling danger lies the attraction. Cupid represents the heart and Psyche the soul. These opposites crave each other, incomplete without their complement. Psyche is the most beautiful woman, while Cupid literally fades to invisibility. Cupid compels the most powerful gods, while Psyche is a helpless princess, married off by her father's choice. When she takes charge, she learns that her lover is both god and beast, and that she contains similar qualities in herself: passion, rage, guile, strength.

Changed by this encounter, the heroine realizes that her male "protector" is not an omnipotent god worthy of her blind devotion. He can be her equal, but he no longer commands her every thought or desire. Thus she understands she need not rely on her father, or men at all, to rescue and protect her.

After Psyche discards the curtain of innocence surrounding her, she begins her quest toward true adulthood. With one flare of candlelight, innocence flees; knowledge and understanding flood in to take their place. As in Eden, the price for immortality is leaving paradise. Psyche finds herself pregnant and alone in a grassy meadow, Cupid and his delightful palace vanished. Now she can cease to be a pampered shut-in.

From the Beast to the Blonde, by famed fairytale commentator Marina Warner, states, "'Cupid and Psyche' represents Eros biding his time, waiting for his bride to prove herself and earn him. This story is her journey. She has to expiate her error."[12] While Cupid is clearly waiting for Psyche to succeed and even earn him, I still dispute the "sin of feminine curiosity" plot device. Yes, Cupid is waiting for Psyche to prove herself, but only because it is her journey to complete. He cannot offer the pampered princess godhood; the Psyche who seeks him must become a goddess.

Beauty and the Beast

In the traditional tale, Beauty tames the husband and brings out his princely qualities through her love, something every medieval bride aspired to accomplish. At the same time, the Beast's monstrous appearance conceals a gentle, patient heart. He is willing to wait as long as Beauty needs to make her comfortable. In the classic version from the French court, he proposes to Beauty each night after an elegant dinner. When she refuses, he accepts it with courtly grace and deference.

As fairytale analyst Terri Windling notes, the original Beast from Madame Gabrielle-Suzanne de Villeneuve in 1740 is far less inhibited:

> The Beast is a truly fierce figure, not a gentle soul disguised by fur — a creature lost to the human world that had once been his by birthright. The emphasis of this tale is on the transformation of the Beast, who must find his way back to the human sphere. He is a genuine monster, eventually reclaimed by civilité, magic, and love — and it is only then that Beauty can truly love him. In this story, the final transformation does not occur until after Beauty weds her Beast, waking up in her marriage bed to find a human Prince beside her.[13]

Ancient beasts are equally frightening. Norway offers several tales of being carried off by a giant bear, deep into the swirling snow. Zeus swims away as an enormous bull, the frightened princess Europa clinging to his back. From Italy comes a Cupid and Psyche tale featuring a green snake. When he rescues the princess, she begs him to leave, screaming that she would rather die than face him. The Brothers Grimm girl who loses her golden ball must eat dinner with the frog to whom she made a promise, and then carry him upstairs and welcome his slimy body into bed with her. Even the Native American girl who cries to the heavens that she would do anything, even marry a buffalo, to feed her starving family, must face more than she intended. On first meeting, these lovers are bloodcurdling and grotesque, making the maiden fear for her life.

Animal Bridegroom stories embodied the real-life fears of women promised to total strangers in marriage, who did not know if they'd find a brute or a gentle lover in their marriage bed. From here derive Bluebeard tales of murdered wives and savage husbands. The husband is unknown, frightening, even monstrous. Often Beauty fears he will "gobble her up." In a Creole version of Bluebeard:

> "You disobeyed me," snapped the devil, and carrying her off to a stifling red room, where he undressed her on a canopy bed wider than it was long and, without even admiring her beauty (the obsession of my dreams), he took off his own clothes, exposing to the livid light his hairs and scales and even his beastly and infernal turgescences. What happened next was gruesome: licking his chops, he sprinkled her with salt, pepper, aromatic spices, and a bit of oil he produced from a drawer in the bedside table. Then he explained to her (but she'd probably already guessed): I'm going to eat you!" And Tétiyette screamed.[14]

This scene is horrific in its lurid detail. We expect rape but witness something even more grotesque as the devil prepares literally to devour Tétiyette. Her family finally rescues her, but only from the devil's belly.

The predator exists in everyone — the force that longs to devour the world, the insatiable greed that will take the entire psyche for itself. The demon lover, or killer animus, lures his victim out of life. He seduces her, shrouding her in lies, trying to convince her she's helpless. "And he will succeed unless she has the courage to bring him to consciousness.... Because the ego is afraid, it looks at the unconscious with fear and animosity, thus constellating the demon face that stares back."[15] Facing and overcoming this predator is a necessary lesson. By facing it, we can understand its weaknesses and so deprive it of its murderous energies.

The Bluebeard tale is a challenge for the psyche. Will the girl come to realize that her lover is a murderer before it is too late? If she does, she survives, and learns not to be fooled by charming manners masking a murderous heart. If her hidden instincts don't emerge in time, if she cannot use the one key of perception to open the door blocking her knowledge of who Bluebeard truly is, her body will end up dismembered in his trophy room.

Her bloody key (or egg or rose) signifies the knowledge of the murderer that stains her. She has not lost her "virginity" by entering the forbidden chamber; she has lost the innocence of her happy marriage in which she had faith in her husband. This shock of knowledge is permanent, leaving a stain the once-innocent bride can never wipe clean.

Though she can't return to her mindless, sheltered bliss, she can move on, find a better man, and marry again, after she escapes the wounding stiflement Bluebeard exudes. "Women find that as they vanquish the predator, taking from it what is useful and leaving the rest, they are filled with vitality, intensity, and drive."[16] In this way, Bluebeard's craftiness, absorbed by the heroine, becomes instinctual understanding of the universe. His rage becomes strength. And his murderous nature becomes the power of death-dealing Kali or Hecate, to kill off those aspects of the spirit that weaken her, when it is their time to die.

At the same time, modern readers crave the beast, savage and unprincipled — the pirate, the foreigner, the barbaric lover who carries the heroine off from her safe world. All versions, from "The Brown Bear of Norway," to "The Green Snake," to "Bluebeard" take place in the prince's castle, far from Beauty's home village. Often there is heavy snow or a set of enchanted barriers divorcing Beauty from her old life. The servants may be invisible, adding to the isolation. This is a tale of honeymooning, reveling in the savagery and the diversity. As Bettelheim notes:

> Beauty and the Beast foreshadows by centuries the Freudian view that sex must be experienced by the child as disgusting as long as his sexual longings are attached to his parent, because only through such a negative attitude toward sex can the incest taboo, and with it the stability of the human family, remain secure. But once detached from the parent and directed to a partner of more suitable age, in normal development, sexual longings no longer seem beastly — to the contrary, they are experienced as beautiful.[17]

This time apart from her family allows Beauty to explore his beastly side and accept it, evoking the beastly side of herself. Angela Carter tells several sensuous versions of Bluebeard and Beauty and the Beast, including "The Tiger's Bride," in which the heroine's fear and desire war until she finally approaches the Beast.

> He will gobble you up.
> Nursery fears made flesh and sinew; earliest and most archaic of fears, fear of devourment. The beast and his carnivorous bed of bone, and I, white, shaking, raw, approaching him as if offering, in myself, the key to a peaceable kingdom in which his appetite need not be my extinction.
> He went still as a stone. He was far more frightened of me than I was of him.
> ...
> He dragged himself closer and closer to me, until I felt the harsh velvet of his head against my hand, then a tongue, abrasive as sandpaper. "He will lick the skin off me!"
> And each stroke of his tongue ripped off skin after successive skin, all the skins of a life in the world, and left behind a nascent patina of shiny hairs. My earrings turned back to water and trickled down my shoulders; I shrugged the drops off my beautiful fur.[18]

Beauty becomes a Beast as she taps her raw, sensual side, removing all her barriers. Here sex is allowed to be primitive and even violent, rejecting the courtly manners of the outside world in favor of magic, emotion, and sensation. The hidden is revealed, crude desires made manifest. For the heroine, this sexual initiation fulfils every fantasy, every dark desire. Just as she is the well-brought-up innocent, he is the lover, all passion and danger. And she loves him for it.

Of course, the twist is that Beauty actually falls in love with the beast, not the prince. In many modern classics, from *The Phantom of the Opera* to humorous interpretations like *Shrek*, the gallant, well-mannered prince looks weak and foppish compared with the brutish, snarling beast lacking in social graces. This monster is actually a desirable figure, the "bad boy" from the wrong side of the tracks, the suitor the parents will disapprove of, the misfit. His courtship, in or out of the bedchamber, is all the more sensual for its illicit nature. Whether these include shy dates at a magnificent table with France's beast, or fiery nights in a magnificent bedchamber with the invisible god of love, the beast is a seducer into the realm of physical pleasure. He rages and storms, but loves his lady with such devotion that he will die without her and languish into nothing.

Still, this idyll of passion cannot last forever. The princess must eventually have children, and not beastly ones. She must have a proper society husband with a steady job, a good provider, one who can appear at the country club. In other words, when the honeymoon ends, she needs Prince Charming on her arm, and not the ferocious beast. Often her family intrudes at this point:

"Who is this man whom you've moved in with? Can we meet him? How much money does he make? Is he a good catch?" This moment spurs Beauty to realize that she needs more — she needs a proper husband by day as well as a fantasy lover at night.

She breaks the spell by lighting a candle, by accepting a proposal, by admitting her love — by taking the next step. "The emphasis shifts from the Beast's need for transformation to the need of the heroine to change — she must learn to see beyond appearance and recognize the good man in the Beast."[19] Unveiling her mystery lover or admitting her feelings pushes them into a relationship as equals, not one of seducer and naive seduceé, or mystery lover and kept mistress. Thus, her complete acceptance of him transforms him into the next stage — a proper husband and provider for the family. Now the heroine can marry him in a glorious ceremony and begin an orderly life with the proper prince, abandoning her affair with the beast, in search of permanence.

CHAPTER 8

Unholy Marriage: Confronting the Father

Tattercoats (Germany)

Once upon a time, there was a princess who was very beautiful, with long, golden hair and deep blue eyes. She had gotten these features from her mother, who resembled her very closely. The queen had been ill for a long time, and finally, she was close to death. She turned to the king beside her. "Dearest, will you promise me something?"

"Anything, my beloved."

"I know that after I am gone you will marry again, and give this country a new queen. But please, promise me that she will be as beautiful as I am, with long, golden hair."

"Beloved, I could never dream of marrying again. In spite of what my subjects will wish, you are the only one that I could ever love."

The queen again begged for this promise, which the king gave. Then the queen closed her eyes for the last time.

Years passed, and the king stopped grieving and wished to remarry. His servants searched through his kingdom, and through all of the neighboring ones. But nowhere could they find a woman who was as lovely as the queen had been, who also had long golden hair. Finally the king decided that he must wed his daughter himself.

The princess was horrified when she heard his command. Thinking quickly, she asked for a gift before the marriage took place.

"Anything you wish," the king promised, relieved at her silent acquiescence.

"Then I wish for three dresses. One must be as gold and glittering as the sun, one as pure and silver as the moon, and one as radiant and sparkling as the stars themselves. And these three dresses must all be packed into a walnut shell. And, along with these, I must have a cloak fashioned from a piece of skin from every beast in the kingdom." If the king couldn't fulfill her requests, she would have a concrete excuse to escape the marriage.

"Done," said the king. He summoned his most skillful seamstresses to spin the three gowns, which had to be the most dazzling ever made, and yet fine enough to fold into a nutshell. His best hunters were sent to take a piece of skin from each animal in the kingdom. Then he went off to plan the wedding.

At the end of a month, the princess entered her chamber to find a large walnut shell on her bed. Below it lay a fantastic cloak, of many different skins. Fearfully, she opened the shell and found the three magnificent gowns. It seemed the king was determined that the wedding would go forward.

That night, the princess dressed herself in the cloak, and smeared her hands and face with soot. She concealed her rich golden hair beneath the hood of the cloak, and took from her room a tiny golden thimble, a gold spool, and a gold ring. Then she took the nutshell with the three dresses and stole away from the palace. She wandered through the forests for days, eating roots and berries. One day, she heard a great sound of hoofbeats. She scrambled up a tree just before a large party of soldiers galloped into the glade. One of them pointed up at her. "Look, it's a bear."

"Not like any bear I've heard of," another soldier said. "It's some strange magical beast. We'd best stay away."

"I say we shoot it down," said a third.

"No, no!" cried the princess. "I am but a poor child, abandoned by father and mother. Please have mercy and take me with you." The soldiers agreed, so the princess climbed down from her tree. They brought her to the palace of the king they served, where she asked for any kind of a job. They finally agreed to let her help the cook.

One night, there was a ball, and the princess begged the cook to let her go watch the dancing.

"Very well, but mind you stay behind a curtain, Tattercoats (for so she was called because of her cloak). I'll not have the guests seeing your ragged form. And mind you're back bright and early tomorrow." Tattercoats rushed to her small, barren room, and opened up her walnut shell. She washed away the soot and put on the dress as golden as the sun. Then, looking like the beautiful princess that she was, she went to the ball.

When she entered the room, everyone gasped at her beauty. The king himself came forwards and asked her to dance. As they danced, everyone could see that the king was entranced by her clever and modest conversation. As dawn was just about to break, Tattercoats quickly pulled her hand from the king's, and raced away. When she was safely in her room, she pulled off the golden dress and folded it into her nutshell. Then she put on her fur cloak, smeared her hands and face with soot, and raced to the kitchen.

When she got there, the cook had crossed arms and a scowl on her face. "It's about time you got here," she grumbled. That evening, Tattercoats asked for permission to make the king's soup. The cook agreed, since Tattercoats was a skilled cook. After cooking the soup, Tattercoats dropped the thimble into the king's bowl, and then had the king's servant carry it to the table.

When the king finished his soup, he found the golden thimble at the bottom of his bowl. He sent for the cook. "Who made this soup?" he asked.

"I did, sire," the cook responded, knees knocking against one another.

"That is not true. This soup tastes different than yours usually does. I must see the person who made this."

So Tattercoats came before the king and curtsied meekly. "Who are you?" he asked.

"A poor creature abandoned by father and mother," was all she said.

So the king let her go back to the kitchen, where Tattercoats was scolded by the cook. "Likely you dropped one of your hairs in the bowl," she said. "See if I'll ever let you make the soup again."

A few days later, there was another ball, and again Tattercoats was allowed to watch if she stayed out of sight. She scampered upstairs and washed her hands and face, then put on her dress as silver as the moon. She gracefully made her way into the ballroom. When the king saw her, he immediately claimed her as his partner, and they danced the night away. This time, Tattercoats couldn't help noticing how handsome and well mannered the king seemed.

When dawn came, she ran from the ballroom and hurried back to her room, where she again disguised herself as Tattercoats. After being scolded by the cook, she finally got permission to make the king's soup once more. This time she dropped her golden spool into the broth. Again the king sent for her after sending for the cook, and again Tattercoats assured him that she was a poor orphan.

The third night, Tattercoats wore her gown that was as beautiful and glittering as the stars themselves. Her eyes met the king's across the ballroom, and they immediately moved towards each other and danced the night away. This time, Tattercoats was so overwhelmed with love for the king that she lost all sense of time. As dawn slowly appeared, rosy outside the ballroom windows, Tattercoats dashed from the king's arms, to the safety of her room. She didn't notice that this time the king had slipped a golden ring onto her finger. She had no time to change before she was expected in the kitchen, so she threw her fur cloak directly over her sparkling dress and pulled her hood up close, rather than covering herself with soot. She endured a well-deserved scolding from the cook, and dropped her own golden ring into the king's soup, still not noticing the one he had placed on her finger.

When the king summoned her, the first thing he noticed was the ring on her finger. He took her by the hand and refused to let go. Blushing hotly, she struggled to leave, and the hood fell back from her magnificent, gleaming hair. The king pulled back the cloak to reveal her gown of sparkling stars, and he knew that she was the princess that he sought. They soon were married, and lived very happily after.

The father is the king or sky god, unassailable head of the household. As such, he has total control, which often extends the power of life and death over his children. As with many motifs in fairytales, this control often takes a sexual turn.

This story is of Aarne-Thompson type 510B, a variant on the 510A story Cinderella. While this is the classic Brothers Grimm version, AT 510B stories appear across the world, emerging as "Delgadina" (New Mexico), "Hanchi" (India), Katie Woodencloak (Norway), The Princess in the Suit of Leather (Arabia), Wooden Maria (Italy) and Catskin (England).[1]

The oldest surviving account is found in *The Facetious Nights* of Giovanni Francesco Straparola, from 14th century Venice. Straparola's story contains the introductory episode that starts most tales of type 510B into motion — a widower's incestuous advances toward his daughter, ostensibly prompted by his wife's dying wish.[2]

The dying wife forces her husband to promise that his second wife will be as beautiful as she is. In some versions, the new wife must perfectly fit her ring, clothes, hair color, etc. Many tales shift the blame onto the dying wife and even onto the helpless daughter for fitting the conditions. As Tatar notes, "Even when a tale turns upon a father's incestuous urges, the mother becomes more than complicit; she has stirred up the trouble in the first place by setting the conditions for her husband's remarriage."[3]

Perrault shows the king "going mad" and later "recovering." The queen's forcing the king's promise likewise absolves him of blame, while the daughter's trying on of her mother's ring in some versions kindles the king's interest. Pilinovsky notes in her essay on Tattercoats how many of these tales show society blaming the daughter. However, "the denouement of the tales indicates a framing societal agreement that such attitudes are biased, unfair, wrong" — society gets its comeuppance in the end.[4]

It appears the wife is setting these impossible (so she thinks) conditions because she does not wish to be replaced. She plans, possessively and almost maliciously, to deny the continuing cycle of life: remarriage and more children for the husband, leaving him stuck as grieving widower. Of course, denying life's cycle can have brutal effects in fairytales, as the queen's commands provide the ideal excuse for the king's incest. When the daughter is the only one who fits the ring or description, she is forced into competition with the mother or, rather, the mother's memory. Can she take her dead mother's place and become a reigning queen?

In Jane Yolen's insightful and tragic "Allerleirauh," the dying queen has a different request:

> "Promise me that you will love the child," she said, for even in her dying she knew his mind, knew his heart, knew his dark soul.... "And promise me that you will not marry again, lest she be..." and her voice trembled, sighed, died.
>
> "Lest she be as beautiful as thee," he promised wildly.... "Lest she have thy heart, thy mind, thy breasts, thy eyes..." and his rota continued long past her life.[5]

Clearly, this queen wants a kindly stepmother for her daughter, but the king, obsessed with surfaces and his own well-being rather than his daughter's, misinterprets her request. Terri Windling's "Donkeyskin" shows the queen requesting a second wife "better than me," with king and queen having similar assumptions as in Yolen's story.

After her father proposes marriage, Tattercoats takes her first steps toward her mother's role by copying her. She sets a list of impossible demands that the king must meet (again, to stop any marriage from taking place). "In some variants, the princess asks directly for the source of her father's wealth, such as the skin of the donkey, which excretes gold in the French 'Donkeyskin,' or for items more extravagant than any possible article of clothing in the Russian tale 'The Gold Lantern.'"[6] Lavish gowns make sense for a princess, but the skins of forest creatures make an odd trousseau. In her father's home, she only wears the grimiest of her gifts, the coat of many furs or cloak of donkeyskin, regressing into a wild beast rather than a marriageable princess. The furs suggest the abusive carnality she faces — by disguising herself metaphorically as her oppressor, the heroine can inherit his power and escape with it. Her cloak is not merely warmth and disguise; it is "a resource that allows her to tap into a deeper part of nature and thus succeed in her future attempts at happiness through craft and cunning, where her past attempts had failed."[7]

Though Tattercoats is a Cinderella figure, she summons all her will to cleverly escape her father and triumph. Tatar notes:

> She begins with a strong assertion of will, resistant to the paternal desires that would claim her. Fleeing the household, she moves out into an alien world that requires her to be inventive, energetic, and enterprising if she is to reestablish herself to claim her royal rank. To be sure, her resourcefulness is confined largely to sartorial and culinary arts, but these were, after all, the two areas in which women traditionally distinguish themselves. Donkeyskin dazzles with her dress, and she successfully uses her cuisine to draw the prince into romance.[8]

While some view the daughter's incestuous marriage as an Oedipal fantasy (If Mother weren't around, I could have Daddy all to myself), the story is truly one of child abuse. The daughter's horror at the proposal and her androgynous or animalistic disguise all reflect her revulsion and determination to disassociate herself from it by running away.

Many references to father-daughter incest appear throughout mythology, beginning with Lot's fathering children on both of his daughters, or Greek Merope wooing her own father. Tane, the creator-god in Maori myth, tries to marry his mother, Papa, but she rejects him. Then he models a woman from soil and breathes into her mouth. Her name is Hine-ahu-one (Woman-heaped-up-from-earth). They have a daughter named Hine-ata-uira (Pattern-woman), and Tane, as a fertility figure, weds her as well. But when she realizes the incest, she cringes with shame and rushes down into the night below the earth. There, she becomes Hine-nui-te-po (Great-goddess-of-night), goddess of death.[9]

This descent into death, like Tattercoats' flight, is a panicked withdrawal from the scene of abuse. As Tatar adds, "A flight into nature offers numerous imperiled women an unlikely, but surprisingly common, refuge from sexual pursuit."[10] Some heroines wall themselves up in suits of wood, like Daphne hiding in her tree, praying that Apollo leave her be. Others disguise themselves as cats and donkeys, claiming the protective coloring of nature. When Tattercoats asks for work at the kitchen, the servants consider her disguised self a strange creature, rather than a maiden. She has rejected all aspects of gender, preferring to go around the house in a sweatsuit too big for her, covering the body at which her father leered, the body she wants no one ever to see. She hides in the kitchen, face dirty with soot and refuses to tell the king her name. And yet, she finds herself peeping out at the balls and the handsome prince who awaits her when she's ready. Over time, the beast's skin gives her strength, until she can stand to leave it behind and transform into a princess.

The prince must discover her femininity despite her disguise. In fact, he must identify her and accept her in her dirty fur. At the balls, she courts him, representing herself as the prince's whole world (sun, moon, and stars). She further teases him through trinkets in his soup, suggesting the water of life. The items she drops are gold to suggest her royalty and feminine symbols (thimble, spool, and ring) to offer herself as a suitable mate. Thus the prince is prepared for the final revelation. This is the erotic unveiling: "The nubile and sophisticated woman appearing from under the ashy face and furry pelt."[11] She is ready to become human once more and wed her prince.

Confrontation

Many versions of Tattercoats conclude without the heroine confronting her father, leaving him unpunished. However, her simple relief to have escaped robs her of a valuable stage of growth. In Robin McKinley's *Deerskin*, the heroine has a chilling encounter with her father, where she forbids him to marry a local princess after his treatment of her. The father is indeed cowed and humbled, while Deerskin ascends to near-goddess power. Finally, Deerskin confesses to her prince that she still feels flawed and cannot promise to love him forever, in a conclusion that echoes with realism. As Helen Pilinovsky comments in her insightful "Donkeyskin, Deerskin, Allerleirauh: The Reality of the Fairy Tale," "The sad reality is that this sensation of being harmed beyond healing or repair is part of the cycle of abuse, continuing on long after physical scars fade."[12]

To the young heroine, the father is a godlike force, powerful and indisputable. At the start of the journey, he has all the power; the girl, none. In the English ballad "Catskin," he banishes the girl from his presence, commencing her adventure. When she returns, a happily married and triumphant queen, it is to find him pitiful and dying. He has learned his lesson and begs her forgiveness; he has lost his power and she has gained it.

> Her father repented too late,
> And the loss of his youngest bemoan'd;
> In his old and childless state,
> He his pride and cruelty own'd.
>
> The old gentleman sat by the fire,
> And hardly looked up at my lord;
> He had no hope of comfort
> A stranger could afford.
>
> But my lord drew a chair close by,
> And said, in a feeling tone,
> "Have you not, sir, a daughter, I pray,
> You never would see or own?"
>
> The old man alarm'd, cried aloud,
> "A hardened sinner am I!
> I would give all my worldly goods,
> To see her before I die."
>
> Then my lord brought his wife and child
> To their home and parent's face,
> Who fell down and thanks returned
> To God, for his mercy and grace.[13]

In yet another variant of this tale, "Why Meat Loves Salt," the youngest daughter is cast out when she tells her father she loves him only as much as meat needs salt on it. She marries the prince in a story identical (from here on) to that of "Tattercoats." However, the important twist appears at the tale's end when her father arrives, unknowing, to celebrate the wedding. She orders no salt placed in his food and, when he declares his dinner inedible, she reconciles with him, revealing that she loves him the most of all.

Thus the male aggressor must pay for his transgression and earn forgiveness in order to be integrated as the heroine's animus. As folklorist Marion Woodman notes, "We see the frozen gods we can no longer worship. We thaw these frozen images with our tears, restore the stone gods to life by enacting them in our own flesh. We endow them with the blood of our own suffering."[14] If we can thus sympathize with the once-powerful father, integrating him into the self, his lessons can be ours, his intellect ours as well. Thus we know our inner strength. "We move from a place of total abandonment to a place where we can never be abandoned. In that moment of knowing, soul and Self are one."[15] We are no longer dependent on the stifling patriarchy, no longer weak or afraid. At last, we have found wholeness and can open ourselves to love.

In "The Frog Tsarevna" Vasilisa the Wise and Clever is born more intelligent than her father. Outraged, he transforms her into a frog. She performs many helpful tasks in this guise, but her husband, intimidated in this case by her magic, burns the frog skin. As penance, he must seek her in the underworld before she is restored to him. In this case, it is the prince who must develop his anima side to win back his wife, and so he trains with Baba Yaga the forest crone and quests for a magic needle. Only then will he have earned his bride.[16]

"The Queen and the Murderer" features a similarly threatened princess. After her father imprisons her in a tower, a murderer peeks in at her over and over, until she slices off his hand. Thanks to a clever disguise, the murderer wins her as bride, and Bluebeard-like, drags her off to his castle. She flees and he pursues, until she finally marries a foreign king, making him promise to keep her hidden away. When the king succumbs to his subjects' curiosity and shows her off, there waits the murderer in the crowd. He tries to kill her once more, but this time she slays him with his own pistol, ending his tyranny forever.[17]

The murderer forces her to rely on herself more and more, as father and new husband both remain oblivious to her cries for help. Like the antagonizing stepmother, he is an impetus for growth. At last overcoming her victim state, she faces and defeats her devourer.

Changed by her adventure, the heroine realizes that her father is not the omnipotent god in whom she had once completely believed. She has her own power now and her own success. In this moment, the heroine realizes that she need not depend on her father, or men at all, to rescue and protect her. She is the heroine, equally as valid as the hero.

Often, this encounter takes place in the middle of the epic quest, before descending into the final conflict with the witch. Though a resting place, it is also a revelation. By returning home, the heroine can see how far she has evolved. Beauty visits her family and chooses between magic and the mundane. Dorothy returns to the Wizard but discovers him a humbug. Cinderella returns from the magical world of the ball. Now she must cater to her stepsisters and pretend that she is the same person. Her night of glamour is over. Yet, she finds that the status quo no longer fits her, if indeed, it ever did. She is a different person more suited to the prince's world than her own.

At this stage, the heroine has outgrown her father's power and influence, but to become a Great Mother herself, she still needs her own mother's guidance to complete the final challenge. The father represents the parent or authority figure, but a reader must remember that each fairytale character represents a part of the self. The father, in fact, is the guardian, the intellect and system of rules meant to protect the self. Usually, in fairytales, the father fails to protect the daughter, or foolishly bargains her away (as in Beauty and the Beast). He rarely understands the connection between the conscious and unconscious world — that things are not always as they appear. This lack of guidance reveals the young woman's innocence at the beginning of her journey. At the end, she returns as a goddess or teacher, powerful beyond the dreams of the once-authoritative father. This leap in power represents the growth in soul and knowledge that the heroine has achieved.

CHAPTER 9

The Deepest Crime:
Abuse and Healing

The Armless Maiden (Xhosa, South Africa)

Once there was an elderly couple who had two children, a boy and a girl. When the father was dying, he summoned them both. "My son," he said. "Shall I leave you my property or my blessing?"

"Property," he responded quickly.

"And you, my daughter?"

"I would like your blessing."

So it was done. After time passed, their mother grew very ill. "Children," she said. "Will you have property from me or my blessing?"

"Property," the son said.

"A blessing," the daughter said.

After the mother died, the brother went into town and bought yams and rice and beans: enough food for an enormous feast. He brought it home and told his sister to cook it all.

"But why?" she asked. "Who could possibly eat it all?"

"It's to be our wedding feast," he replied.

"But I can't marry you; you're my brother!"

"And everything in this house is mine. If you want to stay here, you'll have to marry me."

"Then I'll leave," she said. She packed up her few clothes and turned to go.

Filled with rage, her brother snatched up his knife and followed her out into the forest. When he reached her, he sliced off both of her arms! "Now let's see you survive alone," he said. And he left her there.

A gentle rain fell, staunching the girl's bleeding. She raised her head and drank. As she wandered through the forest, she encountered a rough heap of boulders. She couldn't climb over them, or budge them without arms. At last, she found a small, rough hole that animals had dug. Wriggling and kicking, she managed to slither through. So famished that all her strength had vanished, she tumbled into the grove beyond. She was so hungry, but couldn't pick fruit off the trees to feed herself. Surrendering to her weariness she hid herself in the bushes and slept.

When morning came, the girl longed to eat. But even though she knelt under a fruit tree, she couldn't reach a single piece. Overcome with despair, she curled up behind a bush and started to weep.

A young prince was hunting in the forest that day and heard her. He followed the sobs until he stood just on the other side of the bush. "Who are you?" he asked.

"A poor girl without father or mother," she replied. "Don't come any closer. I don't want anyone to see me."

"All right," he said. "But you need help. Here, I know what to do." He called for the servants who carried his bow and arrows and ordered them to bring a palanquin. She stepped inside and he joined her, and then pulled the curtains shut around them both. Thus hidden, they proceeded to the palace.

In the palanquin, the prince fed the girl fruit with his own hands. Even though she had no arms, he was touched by her beauty and strength of character. By the time they reached the palace, he had fallen in love with her.

His parents were less than pleased when he presented as his future wife a girl with no arms, who could not even take care of herself. Still, the prince was so in love and so eager to marry her that they gave the young couple their blessing. The prince married her, and placed his ring on a chain around her neck. The servants fed her and dressed her in fine linen. Her new husband made her a pair of silver hands that made her look almost normal, even though they didn't move. As time passed, she managed to win her new parents over with her grace and kindness.

One day, the prince was summoned to war. He made his parents promise to care for his wife. Since she was going to have a child, he bade her an especially tender farewell before departing. Some months later, the girl gave birth to a baby boy who shone like the sun. Even though she had no arms to care for him, she doted on the baby and fussed over him. The king and queen wrote to the prince, exclaiming their joy over the birth.

By bad luck, the messenger stopped in the very village where the girl's brother lived. He was married now, and he and his wife offered to let the royal messenger stay the night. "You're bringing good news, I trust," the brother asked him that night.

"Oh, the best news," the messenger said. "The princess has just been safely delivered of a baby boy. She has no arms, but everyone in the palace is so happy to have such a beautiful prince."

The brother realized who the princess must be. That night, he stole the letter from the messenger's bag, and switched it with one of his own. When the messenger delivered the letter, shadows crossed the prince's face. The letter read, "The queen has given birth to a monster. Now she crawls about like an animal, eating kitchen garbage." The prince was stunned. At last, he wrote back, "Care for both my wife and child; I will see them when I return."

On the road back, the brother and his wife again welcomed the messenger and again switched the note. This time it read, "Kill them both. I never should have married a mutilated woman who cannot even care for herself."

The king and queen were heartbroken, but after all, the prince had the right to decide. They showed the maiden the letter and she nodded silently. "Dress me in a plain gown and strap my baby to my back and I will leave. Tell the prince I died in the forest."

"But you cannot care for the child without hands. Leave him here and we'll care for him."

The maiden shook her head. "If my husband has deserted me, this child is all I have, and I will keep him." She walked out into the forest, baby on her back. When she had left sight of the palace, she knelt down on the forest floor and wept and wept.

Her baby woke and began to fuss, but she had no way to feed or change him, no way to soothe him except with the sound of her voice. Neither of them had anything to eat that night, and the baby's cries sliced through her like a knife's blade. In the morning, she kept walking as the baby howled, since she couldn't think what else to do. At last, they arrived at a sparkling river. The maiden knelt, very carefully, to drink from it. At just that moment, the baby kicked! The jolt loosened his swaddlings and sent him tumbling into the river.

The maiden dived in after him. Without thought, she reached out underwater to find him, to save him. To her shock, a pair of strong, healthy arms stretched out before her. She easily snatched her child, and swam them both to safety. On the riverbank, she cuddled and nursed her child, marveling over the firm brown hands she had regained. Had the river spirit rewarded her for her bravery? Or had the forest embraced her and her suffering child? Whoever it had been, the maiden blessed her.

Child in her new arms, she walked for several days. Now she could pick fruit and nurse the baby. Even though she felt a sense of renewal coursing through her, she didn't feel ready to return to the palace. At last, she came across a little hut. An elderly couple lived there and welcomed both the maiden and her child. The maiden scrubbed the house inside and out, baked the bread, planted pumpkins, sewed up the holes in the old couple's clothes and helped them until they regarded her as part of the family.

Meanwhile, the prince returned from the war. "Where are my wife and child?" he asked.

"But you told us to kill her. In the end, we couldn't and we sent her away."

"I did nothing of the sort. Even though she gave birth to a monster."

"The baby was beautiful beyond words; someone deceived you."

And so the truth came out about the lost letters. The desolate king couldn't believe that his wife had died, even with no way to care for herself. He resolved to wander through the forests until he found her. After weeks of wandering, he heard a sweet laugh coming from a house. He looked through the window and spied a beautiful woman tossing a baby in the air and catching him in her two perfect arms. "She can't be my wife," the prince thought. "Though she looks and sounds so like her." Just then, the maiden turned and saw him through the window. "It's you," the prince exclaimed upon seeing her face.

"And you, my husband. Why did you send me away?"

The prince told her the entire story. "Come back to the palace with me," he begged.

She shook her head. "When you married me, you took pity on me, as one might a wounded animal. Now I am whole again and you must court me properly, as a woman you admire."

The next morning, the old couple called her to the window. The king's mother had arrived, leading a string of cattle. Each carried fine cloth, jewels, all manner of sweetmeats, and even a singing bird. The queen placed her own crown on the maiden's head and begged forgiveness for sending her away. The maiden gave lavish gifts to the old couple and then, son in her arms, she rode back to the palace. That night they held a proper wedding, and the prince placed her wedding ring on her finger. "Now you are truly my wife at last," he said.[1]

This tale, featuring mutilation and often incest at the hands of a close relative, appears all over the world as Aarne-Thompson type 706: The Maiden without Hands. It is "The Handless Woman" from Japan, "Rising Water, Talking Bird and Weeping Tree" from French Louisiana, "The Girl with the Maimed Hands" in *The Pentamerone*, "The Maiden without Hands" in Grimms, and "The Girl Swallowed Up by a Stone" in the Libyan version of the tale. In the last one, the maiden hides under an enormous stone, refusing to let her amorous father or rival mother enter. Only her innocent and childlike little brother can join her in her refuge.[2]

Why was this story told by the fireside around the world? It echoes the assaults which far too many young women endured in the male-dominated world. As Zipes notes, "In the main body of Grimms tales, there are 25 tales dealing with children being abused (not counting abandonment or kidnapping). This reveals the prevalence of child abuse at the time."[3] The Middle Ages especially offered stories of innocent virgins stalked by their own fathers, though the Grimm Brothers hastily censored these events.[4] Still, echoes remain in this tale, when the father or brother mutilates the suffering girl, as the unthinkable horror of having one's hands cut off captures the unspeakable trauma of rape and incest. Thus, the extremely grotesque violence and torment of these stories show the aftereffects of this devastation, still present in our modern society. While many might reject this story as fantasy, some cultures permit and even endorse women's mutilation today, as female circumcision remains a part of girls' initiation ceremonies in some African tribes. Throughout cultures, this story guides many types of victims through suffering to wholeness.

Some variants of this tale keep the mutilation and subsequent healing, yet censor the incest, rather like the tamer versions of the Tattercoats legend. In the Grimms' "The Girl without Hands," the devil tricks the father into offering the girl, and threatens the man's life if he doesn't mutilate her.

> The miller's daughter was a beautiful and pious girl who lived without sin, and when the devil came for her, she wept on her hands to cleanse them, and he could not touch her. Angered, he threatened the miller: "Chop off her hands, or you will be mine."
>
> Seeing her father's plight, the girl held out her hands, saying: "Father, dear, do with me what you will. I am your child." She stretched out her hands and the miller cut them off.
>
> Then he said to her: "Because of you I am wealthy. Now I want to take the best care of you, for as long as you live." But she answered: "I cannot stay here," and she set forth on foot.[5]

This story is made all the more pathetic for the father's quite literal excuse (the devil made me do it!) and the daughter's martyred compliance.

Without the water and fertility of her tears, with which she defends herself, she is destroyed, crippled. Water represents the life-giving feminine; thus, severed from inspiration and innate power, the girl stands helpless. In this way, the heroine's strength lies in receptivity, but here we see its dark side — unquestioning compliance. Thus she sacrifices her feminine power and her living hands, all to preserve the patriarchy. "It is easy to see how a child, abused by the principal authority figure in her household — the individual who should be her most powerful protector — could see herself as being without hands, the human extensions that most directly allow us to manipulate and control the world outside ourselves," writes folklore scholar D. L. Ashliman.[6] The father's attack is a type of castration, representing her confinement to the world of the home, and male society's strictures.

For young women, the father's approval and validation is the earliest lesson on how to relate to men. If he approves of her, she forms a foundation for healthy relationships later. "But when the father is predominantly critical of his daughter or largely unaware, uncaring, or demeaning of her femininity, he sells that blooming possibility to the Devil,"[7] comments Gertrud Mueller Nelson in *Here All Dwell Free: Stories to Heal the Wounded Feminine.* As an adolescent girl, she is forbidden to speak out — and with one brutal attack, authority cripples her forever.

Meanwhile, the father is not terribly concerned about the shocking destruction of his daughter. Frustrated and afraid as the devil threatens him, he offers up a weaker substitute in his place. Zipes comments:

> He finds a way to vent his frustration by attacking his child and then rationalizing it. He simply expects her to forgive because he cannot help himself, because he is afraid of the devil. His violation of her is not treated as a crime but rather as an emergency; she is made to feel guilty if she does not relent.[8]

As with many fairytales, the father's brutality is excused and softened by the retellers, spreading the blame from the abuser to other characters. His needs must supersede hers until she is truly helpless and handless, without means to defend herself.

For Chinese Miao Shan, defying her father and becoming a nun goes against every tenant of filial obedience. Her infuriated father ensures that the nuns treat her harshly, and when she won't relent, he decides to murder her and burn the monastery to the ground. Miao Shan miraculously escapes and descends into the realm of death, where her compassion transforms hell into a paradise. Disgusted, the ruler of the dead sends her back to earth with a magic peach that sustains her and eventually makes her immortal. Meanwhile, Miao Shan's father is critically ill as punishment for his actions. The only cure, say the doctors, are the arms and eyes of a pure person. Miao Shan sacrifices these to cure her father. Though she reconciles with her parents, she can no longer live on earth and thus ascends into heaven.[9]

The father, as the heroine's choking restraint, represents part of the self that must be overcome. He is a force for tyranny and domination, the opponent in gender warfare, society's demands that the armless maiden surrender all traces of independence and give herself up to be mutilated. He is the predator, maiming the woman's soul along with her body, and presenting an obstacle the heroine must conquer and absorb. Still, he is not the only criminal. The evil stepmother or sister-in-law often plays a role in this tale, inciting the father or brother to wickedness. In some versions, she even kills her own child merely to blame the death on the virtuous heroine. These two work in concert to destroy the heroine's spirit and viciously hack away all independence.

Afterwards, the Grimms' maiden refuses her father's generous settlement and leaves forever, severed arms strapped to her back. She cannot remain in a house where her father would maim her and her mother would watch silently.

As Midori Snyder comments in her essay on the armless maiden, "There can be no return to a childhood home corrupted by such cruel violence. The girl must move forward in her journey to a new destination where she will reconstruct not only her severed arms but her identity as an adult woman."[10] Only by acknowledging her own power (her arms) and needs (her child, the inner child crying out inside her) can she grow past her childhood victimization and be whole.

Outcast

Twin agonies war within, crippling her: The loss of her arms, though tragic, is a symptom of her betrayal by the closest family, and the shame of incest. "With hands severed from their arms, the heroine's body stands as an emblem of disempowerment, helplessness, and victimization."[11] This mutilation plunges the heroine into the world of the unconscious in a brutal call to adventure. The everyday hands that have aided the heroine through her quiet, sheltered life have been pruned away; she requires more powerful tools to accompany her future rebirth. Until she can fashion these new hands for herself, her psyche must compensate, biding her time until the whole woman can be reborn.

Thus, she wanders animal-like through the forest, helpless to care for herself. Still, this very rejection of humanity and society protects her as it does Tattercoats; she is a beast, not a princess-like sex object. As she pitifully nibbles at hanging pears, "we realize the extent to which her bodily state has forced her to become a foraging creature and reduced her to pathetic dependency on nature's bounty."[12] Nature offers healing and comfort, disguise and sustenance. Thus buried in the sheltering femininity of the dark forest, she regains a fragment of herself.

Among the Cherokee, the sun was a lovely young woman named Unelanuhi and the moon her brother. After Spider Woman wove a net and dragged her to earth so the people would have heat and warmth, Unelanuhi lived pleasantly. The grateful people visited her, and she had a lover as well, who visited in the dark each month and wouldn't tell his name. One night, she smeared his face with lamp soot. But when her brother joined her for breakfast, she saw the soot on him. In horror, she sliced off her breasts with her crescent-shaped knife and flung them at him, crying, "You desire to taste me — devour these as well." She lit a lamp, and, going outside, ran around and around in a circle until she spiraled up into the air. Her brother snatched a lamp and followed her, but his wick blew nearly out, which is why the moon gives light but no heat. She fled into the sky and he pursued her throughout time, hiding his face in shame as the month passed.

Likewise, in a poem from the sixth century B.C.E., Subhā of Jīvaka's Mango-grove, a Buddhist nun living in the wilderness, met a libertine who tempted her with the joys of the flesh. She explained with great detail how she had renounced sensuous pleasures in favor of quiet contemplation. Though she taught him her philosophy, he ignored it, continuing to praise her beauty:

> Eyes hast thou like the gazelle's, like an elf's in the heart of the mountains —
> 'Tis those eyes of thee, sight of which feedeth the depth of my passion.
> Shrined in thy dazzling, immaculate face as in calyx of lotus,
> 'Tis those eyes of thee, sight of which feedeth the strength of my passion.

Though thou be far from me, how could I ever forget thee, O maiden,
Thee of the long-drawn eyelashes, thee of the eyes so miraculous?
Dearer to me than those orbs is naught, O thou witching-eyed fairy![13]

Upon hearing how much he admired her eyes, she unhesitatingly ripped one from her head and offered it to him, retorting, "If you like it so much, you can have it!" Horrified, his lust vanished, the man begged her forgiveness. Subhā, thus vindicated, prayed before the Buddha, who restored her eye to its rightful place.[14]

When beauty becomes a tool for exploitation, the heroine wraps herself in her tattercoats and vanishes into her forest refuge. Maimed by herself or others, she is no longer a sex object to be brutalized and threatened. The forest is empty and dark and shields her with sharp thorns and twisting branches until she feels ready to reenter civilization.

Feminine Symbols

There in the forest of the unconscious, she finds comfort at the prince's palace, as he protects and succors her. Before wedding her, the prince of the unconscious kingdom restores her beauty, if not her independence, by giving her silver hands. Silver echoes the spirit power of the moon and the water (both feminine symbols). Still, they distance her as her maimed state does, since these hands don't conduct feeling. She is still hiding from her abusers and thus rejects connecting with the prince and with herself. "Because she does not know her feelings, she cannot feel the feelings of others, which is empathy and is the deepest requirement, essential to love and the creation of a better society."[15] While the artificial hands do not restore the girl (they're useless, in fact!), they faintly echo the arms she will earn back for herself once healing takes place.

Servants bathe her, dress her, and feed her, all services supplied by the prince. Snyder comments, "She is not whole, not the girl she was nor the woman she was meant to be.... Without her arms, she is unable to fulfill her role as an adult."[16] Thus, like Psyche, she regresses to childhood, welcoming the prince's protection as an all-powerful substitute father. The heroine, shivering and abused, is content to stay in this warm shelter, unmotivated to grow past her maiming into adulthood. She would remain there forever, if not for cruel nature pushing her into the world.

The prince's palace is not a proper ending for the maimed, unequal heroine. Though it provides safety, it is also a place of patriarchal restrictions, echoing with spiritual emptiness. Andersen's little mermaid ventures to the palace for romance, but discovers that giving up her tail, voice, and magic to live in the male-centric world cannot satisfy her.

As the days passed, she loved the prince more fondly, and he loved her as he would love a little child, but it never came into his head to make her his wife; yet, unless he married her, she could not receive an immortal soul; and, on the morning after his marriage with another, she would dissolve into the foam of the sea.[17]

"Sleeping outside the prince's door on a cushion implies that the little mermaid is something of a waif, an exotic pet for the prince," notes Maria Tatar.[18] She cannot find the loving relationship Beauty and the Beast achieve, but only shallow admiration. This is another tale of maiming, all the more tragic because the heroine inflicts it upon herself. As Zipes notes:

Andersen only allows the mermaid to rise out of the water and move in the air of royal circles after her tongue is removed and her tail is transformed into legs described as "sword-like" when she walks or dances. Voiceless and tortured, deprived physically and psychologically, the mermaid serves a prince who never fully appreciates her worth. Twice she saves his life. The second time is most significant: instead of killing him to regain her identity and rejoin her sisters and grandmother, the mermaid forfeits her own life and becomes an ethereal figure, blessed by God.[19]

The problem is the total one-sidedness of the relationship, and thus the self-sacrifice. As the story describes her dancing, "Every one was enchanted, especially the prince, who called her his little foundling; and she danced again quite readily, to please him, though each time her foot touched the floor it seemed as if she trod on sharp knives."[20] She dances, she smiles, she loves, she suffers, she dies, all to surrender her entire life to the prince who only looks on her as a favored pet. This self-sacrifice is no better than abuse. True, her "goodness" allows her to ascend into an air spirit. But this is counterpointed by her lack of achievement on earth. When heroines cut themselves off from their innate magic and unconscious, dismemberment, suffering, and death are inevitable.

Thus, the Armless Maiden cannot stay forever in the prince's castle, unequal, pampered and coddled, or she will wither away like the mermaid. Her expulsion from the castle forces growth. The maiden could abandon her child and venture forth without him. As a spiritually crippled wreck, she can't care for him, can't handle motherhood without her husband's all-encompassing protection. "Bent by the burden of the child bound to her back, and with two stumps for hands, she represents a supremely abject portrait of helplessness."[21] How easy it would be to desert all responsibility! Yet the heroine clings to her baby, the first step toward regaining self-worth and capability. Instead of surrendering to despair, she discovers the healing nature and refuge the forest, like the sea, can offer.

When her child tumbles from her back, the armless maiden thinks beyond herself. "To reach out, even inept hands, and begin to accept may be the young Queen's most heroic task — to embrace and accept her cross, her heroic deed," Nelson adds.[22] Clearly, the heroine has untapped strength of which she's only unconsciously aware — her hands wait within her. With no helpful fairy godmother in sight, she recovers her arms in an instant to rescue her inner child, the innocent bundle of desires and self she's repressed for so long. "By doing for her own child what she needed done for her in her own growing up, a woman often heals herself.... Her feeling hands restored, she makes order and value of all the feelings that now flow freely from her heart."[23] Surrounded by feminine water and intuition, she reclaims her suppressed self; she has chosen to heal and thus regrows her arms and becomes a healer of others. Thus, the threat of death creates life. Only when no one but her can save her child does she snatch her arms and use them, asserting her status as mother rather than victim.

In an Inuit tale, the beautiful Sedna makes the mistake of marrying a dishonest seagull, who starves her. After a long winter, her father rescues her, but, afraid of the squawking, pursuing seagull, he pitches her out of their kayak. As Sedna clings to the side, her father slices off her fingers and then her hands until she drops to the ocean floor. In the transformative water, her severed hands and fingers transform into whales and seals. There, Sedna builds herself a shimmering home under the water.[24] As an ocean goddess, she feeds the local people, but only when they help her by combing her tangled seaweed hair — since she can no longer do it herself. Even with her hands severed, she has grown from mutilated victim to divine life giver, a figure of triumph.

It's no wonder the armless maiden insists her husband court her. She was his sheltered, crippled shut-in, like Psyche before her apotheosis. Now she is a whole woman, balanced between the worlds of spiritual and physical. She waits in the woods while he ventures on his own initiatory journey, seeking his lost anima. At last the two reunite. For the first time, she can marry her prince as an equal as he affirms her as a self-sufficient person. Thus, the damaged woman is reborn and finds peace at last.

CHAPTER 10

"With This Ring...":
Sacred Marriage

Scheherazade and Dunyâzâd (Middle East)

King Shahriyar was anticipating with great joy the visit of his brother, Shah-Zeman. However, Shah-Zeman arrived late, pale and emaciated with distress.

"What has happened?"

Shah-Zeman related that just as he had set out, he had turned back, and discovered his wife asleep with one of his slaves in her embrace. Executing the pair, he continued to his brother's palace.

King Shahriyar did all he could to console his brother. Nothing would do it. However, one day, Shah-Zeman discovered his brother's wife kissing a slave in her gardens, surrounded by naked slaves of both genders. "My brother's lot is far worse than mine," he mused, and he cheered up immediately.

When he told his brother and King Shahriyar beheld his wife cavorting with the slaves, reason fled, and he executed them all. The brothers resolved to travel the world until they found someone who had been wronged more greatly than they.

As they were resting by the shore of the sea, a black pillar of smoke rose from its depths, and behold, it solidified into a genie bearing a large wooden chest. He opened it and drew from it a glass case, which he unlocked. From thence emerged a fair maiden. "Noble lady whom I carried off on her wedding night, I desire to sleep," the genie said. He laid his head into her lap and drifted off.

The damsel, however, slipped from under the genie's head and beckoned the two kings to approach. When they hesitated, she called to them again, threatening to wake the genie if they didn't make love to her.

When both had done everything she wished, she showed them a loop with 98 seal rings strung on it. "Now give me your rings," she said. "I will add them to my collection. The genie has walled me in two caskets at the bottom of the sea, but that cannot stop a woman who is truly determined."

The two kings decided the genie had a greater misfortune than either of themselves. They returned home, and King Shahriyar vowed to rid his country of treacherous women. Each night he wedded a virgin, and in the morning he beheaded her. No tears or pleas would stay him from his course. For three years this continued, until nearly all the young women were dead or had fled the country.

Scheherazade, who was the oldest daughter of the king's vizier, went to her father, and to his horror, volunteered to be the king's bride. Nothing the vizier said could dissuade her, and at last, she was offered up.

When she had been dressed well and was brought before the king, Scheherazade wept.

"What ails you?" King Shahriyar asked.

"Oh, king," she said. "More than anything I wish to take leave of my young sister."

So the king sent for Dunyâzâd and seated her at the foot of the bed. When the king had taken his pleasure with Scheherazade, and lay sleepily beside her, Dunyâzâd spoke up, as her sister had previously arranged. "Sister, relate to us a story to beguile our waking hours."

"Most willingly," she said. "If this virtuous king permit me."

King Shahriyar assented and Scheherazade began her first story.[1]

This tale, of a genie determined to take his unjust revenge on the world, continued so long that it was soon morning, and time for the king to commence his tasks. He spared Scheherazade for a single night to hear how the tale would end. But this first story was an intricately woven net of tales, with more budding inside one another until the tale was not finished for many more nights, and after that a new one had begun.

As she told her thousand-and-one nights of tales, Scheherazade bore the king three fine sons. When she had finished them all, she knelt at the king's feet, and, calling for her three sons to be brought in, she begged to be preserved, as she could care for them better than anyone. The king wept and embraced his children. "Oh, Scheherazade, I pardoned thee before the coming of these children because I saw thee to be chaste, pure, ingenious, pious." And so all the country rejoiced. Dunyâzâd wedded Shah-Zeman, and they and their people lived on in prosperity and joy.

This frame tale of *Arabian Nights* is a story of storytelling: how tales can deter the mighty from violence and teach them a better way to live. Scheherazade, the architect of these tales, means to bring order to protect the vulnerable;

to provide security in the realm by eradicating distrust and dangerously erratic behavior.[2] Thus, she tells of wise kings, good and virtuous princesses, and wicked deceivers who are punished commensurate with their crimes.

Shahriyar and Shah-Zeman live in entirely masculine worlds. The only females present are their adulteress wives, without a trace of a positive anima. Unsurprisingly, the men raised thus consider women the enemy. These men are savage and unmerciful, without the tempering emotions of mercy or sympathy. As Jung notes, "Permanent loss of the anima means a diminution of vitality, of flexibility and of human kindness. The result, as a rule, is premature rigidity, crustiness, stereotypy, fanatical one-sidedness, obstinacy, pedantry."[3] Shahriyar demonstrates a distrustful rage against women, untempered by mother, sister, or lover as a mitigator. He attempts to form a positive anima bond by wedding a new bride each night, but he destroys those women before they can wound him further.[4]

Scheherazade has chosen a particularly feminine manner of dealing with the king: Rather than assassinating him, she will cultivate the stunted anima within him, and with it, understanding. After wedding the king, she shares her stories with him each night, born from her creative presence. These tales provide positive role models, as wise young women rescue transformed heroes, and a maddened genie shows mercy in return for stories, just as Shahriyar is doing. Scheherazade can heal the king's madness based on her feminine knowledge of healing, sexual passion, and tale-telling.[5] While she tells her tales, she conceives and births the king's three sons, all the while remaining chaste and faithful, displaying a paradigm of women for her husband. Likewise, she draws out his rage and turns his course through stories of forgiveness and altruism. Finally, she passes on her tales of women's wisdom to Dunyâzâd, preparing her for her own womanhood and her own journey to civilize a king.

> Through listening to her sister's tales as the representative of other young Muslim virgins, she will be prepared to cope with men like Shahriyar and to turn a male social code to her advantage. In fact Scheherazade teaches Dunyâzâd how to plot and narrate her own destiny to achieve an autonomous voice, which receives due respect from Shahriyar at the conclusion of all the tales.[6]

This instruction shows Dunyâzâd how to succeed in Muslim society with wisdom and courage. Through all these heroic deeds in one, Scheherazade rescues all the young women of the kingdom.

"Given the patriarchal nature of the Arabic culture, it would seem strange that Scheherazade assumed the key role in the *Nights*. Yet, a woman exercised more power in Muslim culture during the Middle Ages in Baghdad and Cairo than is commonly known."[7] Though the media is festooned with images of women draped head to toe, Islam and the *Qur'an* were quite progressive towards women, granting them divorce and property rights many centuries before equivalent European laws. Female scholarship was also popular, with precedent for it set by Muhammad's wives. The wife shared in the disposition of her dowry and was absolute ruler of the home, children, and slaves.

As the woman was in charge of civilizing the family, it makes perfect sense that Scheherazade is the main character, as she cures the king of his madness, ostensibly caused by another woman, and teaches readers about the Muslim social code of the time.[8] She outwits the king, true, but she does it by entertaining and charming him. Submission to God, submission to fate, and submission to the ruler dominate rather a large number of the stories; Scheherazade changes the king, but within the dictates of her society.

Since women and tricksters both provoke awe and misgiving, suspicion and deference, a woman trickster is doubly fascinating. The clever heroine is nonviolent, directing the flow of the system from within, rather than destroying it outright. Thus, women move subtly and gently, using wit, love, and the magic of words to change others.

The poem "Needle and Thread" exemplifies this perfectly, contrasting the "delicate footsteps" of women's tools against larger actions of men.

Needle and Thread

Tempered, annealed, the hard essence of autumn metals
finely forged, subtle, yet perdurable and straight,

By nature penetrating deep yet advancing by inches
to span all things yet stitch them up together,

Only needle-and-thread's delicate footsteps
are truly broad-ranging yet without beginning!

"Withdrawing elegantly" to mend a loose thread,
and restore to white silk a lamb's-down purity...

How can those who count pennies calculate their worth?
They may carve monuments yet lack all understanding.[9]

This poem was authored by the only female official historian to the Han Dynasty Imperial Court, Pan Zhao (48–117 C.E.?), the most famous woman scholar of Chinese history. Her poem criticizes the male "monument-builders," who have no appreciation for the subtleties of women's crafts, and especially women's thoughts. Women's wit is tiny and subtle like the needle, but just as sharp and shining. Though their epics lack the slaughter and glory of warrior-tales, there is a quiet heroism in all their acts.

Cross-Dressing

Women fight confinement to the home in many ways, not least of which is forcing the men into the feminine role, generally to decrease their status. This usually is done to proud warriors in order to shame them in their defeat and give them a taste of women's life.

Confederate spy Nancy Hart was captured by a Union leader, who threatened periodically to give her to his troops. Though she escaped unscathed, she reportedly held a particular grudge — the next time she met him, she tethered him to her horse, forced him to don one of her gowns, and spent hours parading her corseted captive around the town.[10]

For one of Hercules' labors, he spent a year as a slave to Queen Omphale of Libya. Reportedly, she made him wear her gowns and hold a basket of wool for her spinning. Thus, in this comic interlude, the strongest mortal man of all time learned humility and came to accept his anima, while the great queen strutted about in his lion skin, brandishing his great club. At last, Omphale freed Hercules and took him as a lover, realizing that she preferred that he wear the "pants," now that they had learned from each other's roles. Omphale's name, connected with the Greek *omphalos,* or naval, suggests a mystical marriage between the hero and the powerful earth goddess of the center of the world, who teaches him the mysteries of feminism.

Macha, a beautiful Irish goddess, forced her persecutors to endure far more of the feminine world than corsets. She arrived at the home of the widower Crunnchu, took over the household duties and finally joined him in his bed. He prospered greatly. However, she put him under a geas never to speak of her. At a party at the King of Ulster's court, Crunnchu unwisely bragged that his wife could outrun the king's horses. The king demanded proof, and Macha was dragged in, heavily pregnant. She begged off, insisting that she was in labor, but the large crowd of spectators insisted. Crunnchu added his voice to theirs, explaining his life was at stake. Macha ran like lightning, winning the race, and then sank down and gave birth to twins right on the field. But for the men of Ulster's callousness to her pain, she proclaimed that whenever Ulster was threatened, the men of Ulster would helplessly suffer the pangs of childbirth.

Forcing Macha to give birth publicly was a source of shame and taboo-breaking for her, allowing the men to share in her secret birth mysteries. Thus, she forced them to pay the price for that knowledge, fully inducting them into the rite. By giving them female abilities, Macha likewise deprived them of the power to make war while they suffer through their "pangs": While they were part of the birth process, they could not cause death.[11]

Lilith

Of course, turmoil occurs when both genders demand equal treatment and power. Jewish legends speak of Lilith, Adam's equal wife, created from the earth as he was. She refused a subservient position, thus necessitating Adam's finding a new wife, the biddable Eve. This originates in the first creation of man in the Bible: "God created man with His image. In the image of God, He created him, male and female He created them."[12] Only later is Eve formed from Adam's rib. This rabbinic legend explains why.

> After God created Adam, who was alone, He said, "It is not good for man to be alone" (Genesis 2:18). He then created a woman for Adam, from the earth, as He had created Adam himself, and called her Lilith. Adam and Lilith immediately began to fight. She said, "I will not lie below," and he said, "I will not lie beneath you, but only on top. For you are fit only to be in the bottom position, while I am to be the superior one." Lilith responded, "We are equal to each other inasmuch as we were both created from the earth." But they would not listen to one another. When Lilith saw this, she pronounced the Ineffable Name and flew away into the air.[13]

Jewish feminists view the rejected Lilith as a paradigm of their struggle, cast into demonic infamy simply for demanding equality. In the 1960s and '70s, many mothers named their daughters Lilith, clinging to this powerful feminist image and disdaining the name Eve. In this way, they found a new perspective on the 8th to 10th-century legend, concentrating on the primal woman they chose to venerate. In folkloric tradition, she functions as a Terrible Mother, devouring babies and seducing men at night. Still, she remains a valued symbol that woman and man were *originally* created equal in the garden.

Finding Balance

This African-American creation story likewise redefines power in the gender struggle: In the first days, man and woman lived together and were equal in all things. Sometimes they'd fight, but they were evenly balanced and neither one could whip the other. One day, man visited God and asked for more strength so he could dominate his wife. God granted his prayer.

The furious woman went straight to God, and asked him to restore things as they had been, but God refused to retract his gifts. The devil suggested that she ask for God's ring of keys, which were hanging on the mantelpiece. God readily granted them to her. Then the devil explained that the keys had more power in them than strength, since with them, she could cut the man off from the kitchen, the bedroom, and the cradle. With his food, sexual pleasure, and future generations withheld, the man would quickly cave.

The man was shocked when he discovered his wife's new power. He asked God for a set of keys, but God wouldn't give him that. Then he offered the woman half his strength if he could borrow the keys, but she decided she liked the current arrangement. So from then on, man had the greater physical strength, but woman ruled the home.[14]

"Most of the recrimination between quarreling lovers or spouses involves the collision of power and love. To give each its due and endure the paradoxical tension is the noblest of all tasks. It is only too easy to embrace one at the expense of the other; but this precludes the synthesis that is the only real answer."[15] Here power and love war, as each spouse struggles for dominance, and finally finds a (perhaps unequal) way to balance. The tale relates how the gender split isn't as clear as many assume — the man may have greater physical strength, but the woman will always rule the home, subtle yet sovereign. Though the title "Why Women Always Take Advantage of Men" suggests women always win, this story was told in a society where men ostensibly ruled over women, as was true throughout 19th-century America.

Many cultures tell similar tales, of how men are solar heroes of strength and power, yet are simultaneously helpless without absorbing the woman's wisdom. "Man's knowledge (Logos) then encounters woman's relatedness (Eros) and their union is represented as the symbolic ritual of a sacred marriage."[16]

The Sacrificed King

The earliest author anywhere to be known by name, the priestess Enheduana (2300 B.C.E.), wrote a great cycle of poetry to her goddess, called the *Exaltation of Inanna*. Archeologists have discovered over 50 clay tablets with the same poem — clearly a best-seller of ancient times. In honor of Inanna's marriage to Dumuzid, Enheduana and a local king would annually enact the sacred marriage in her seventh floor azure room at the top of her elaborate ziggurat.[17] This ancient blending of sexual union and restoration, birth and death, lies at the center of our consciousness.

Even before Jesus and his sacrifice, the dying god has appeared in many incarnations: Baldur, Osiris, Ba'al, Attis, Adonis. The Babylonian Ishtar strips off her finery and descends into death. When her son-lover, the shepherd Tammuz, dies, the goddess mourns. Yet, her priestesses select a new Tammuz each year, celebrating at the marriage rites and mourning at his death.

In this mythic tradition, the king could only rule as the accepted spouse of the goddess or her mortal incarnation, the queen. This was the *hieros gamos*, or sacred marriage, in which man pledged himself to the land and could only reign through the queen. Among the Celts, the king wedded the territorial goddess, and the headmen served as a governing body on her behalf. Even in Africa, a Bahima tribal chief was installed as a ritual union with the goddess Imama. "Kings seldom held office for life. They were frequently replaced, on the theory that the Goddess needed constant revitalization in the form of new lovers: hence the many lovers of such pagan queen figures as Mab, Theodelinda, Hermutrude, and others," notes symbolist Barbara G. Walker.[18] After a year had passed, the king would be sacrificed and a new one chosen, in order to preserve matrilineal succession.

Though this practice is frequent in myth, it's uncertain how much it took place literally rather than symbolically. But as a staple of legend, it shows the transience of the hero and uncontested rulership of the goddess. She was the queen and he, the annoited one chosen by her each year and then replaced.

This struggle for patriarchal dominance is exemplified by Gilgamesh, a Mesopotamian culture-hero who refused his place in the sacred marriage, rejecting the sacrifice. Gilgamesh himself was chosen to be Ishtar's consort. However, as she offered him tribute from field and orchard, and a mighty chariot of lapis and gold, he feared that his life would be included in the bargain, and that he would become another Tammuz to her. He argues his point logically, reciting how each year she chose another lover and then destroyed him.

> Where are your bridegrooms that you keep forever?
> Where is your "Little Shepherd" bird that went up over you!
> See here now, I will recite the list of your lovers.
> …
> Tammuz, the lover of your earliest youth,
> for him you have ordained lamentations year upon year!
> You loved the colorful "Little Shepherd" bird
> and then hit him, breaking his wing, so
> now he stands in the forest crying "My Wing"!
> You loved the supremely mighty lion,
> yet you dug for him seven and again seven pits.
> You loved the stallion, famed in battle,
> yet you ordained for him the whip, the goad, and the lash,
> ordained for him to gallop for seven and seven hours,
> ordained for him drinking from muddled waters,
> you ordained for his mother Silili to wail continually.
> You loved the Shepherd, the Master Herder,
> who continually presented you with bread baked in embers,
> and who daily slaughtered for you a kid.
> Yet you struck him, and turned him into a wolf,
> so his own shepherds now chase him
> and his own dogs snap at his shins.
> …
> And now me! It is me you love, and you will ordain for me as
> for them![19]

Here Gilgamesh, the great king, defies the Sacred Marriage and dying king in favor of patriarchal rule. Still, goddesses don't respond well to refusal, however justified: Ishtar sets the Bull of Heaven on him for his insolence.

Interconnectedness

In seventh century India, mystic texts called *Tantras* promulgated the idea of Shakti — primal, feminine power that enables the gods. This Shakti comes from Mahakali, or Great Kali, protector of the cosmos. One Tantra states, "women are divinity; women are vital breath."[20] In fact, veneration of the Divine Mother with monuments and worship dates back to 8000 B.C.E. and is practiced still. Cave sanctuaries and womblike domes attest the ancient protective powers of the feminine, present as Creator, Preserver, and Destroyer in all life, tiny and great.[21] The Indian Goddess, unlike the quiet presence of the Jewish Shekhina or the sainted Mary, is sexual, powerful, terrible, and generous. In her form as Kali, she is the destroyer of all things, and is often pictured standing on her prone consort Shiva, whose submissive posture may represent complete surrender to the unconscious, to the goddess. Their union is the source of divine power. As the opening words to the hymn *Saundaryalahari* ("Wave of Beauty") relates:

> If Shiva becomes joined with Shakti,
> he is able to be powerful.
> If not, then
> the god is not even able
> to move.[22]

Shakti is the abstract feminine presence, like the Shekhina, which completes the god as his spiritual unconscious side.

In the Indian *Devî Gita* (Song of the Goddess), the Great Goddess explains her role on earth: "When the Dharma (righteousness) declines and the Adharma (unrighteousness) reigns supreme, I then manifest Myself in the world as Sâkambharî, Râma, Krishna and others."[23] These heroes are male warriors, avatars of the feminine goddess. Thus, this Goddess, like the Judeo-Christian God, transcends gender. Each has their sublimated side manifested as the opposite gender, the dash of yin in the yang.

The famed Indian *Kama Sutra* celebrates sex as a way of reaching the divine. It is joined by Sumerian prayers to Inanna, Ugarit ritual dramas, Japanese texts including the *Nihongi* and *Kojiki,* and various Chinese medico-philosophical tracts. Likewise Tantrism, from sixth century Asia, celebrates *kamakala dhyana,* or meditations on the art of love. The devotee, Shiva-like, contemplates desire with the active female goddess — a man undertaking Tantric practice is asked to envision his partner as Shakti and to pay her homage with his entire being, emotional, spiritual, and physical. Such devotion thus leads to the ecstasy of enlightenment.

> The husband
> having joined in intercourse

with his wife,
being an embryo [again],
is born at this time.
This conception [is] the characteristic of a wife,
that he is born again in her.[24]

These texts, rather than prurient or carnally gratifying, celebrate the male and female energy vibrations throughout the universe, and glorify sexual union as a method for breaking down barriers between the human and the creative force. This sanctification of all life and all its activities brings value to both genders, free of shame, fear, and body-hatred. In these texts, women are elevated as the goddess, leading man to a higher spiritual level.

> The erotic enables the surfacing and connecting of our deepest needs while it also allows a basis for sharing with others. In this respect, the erotic is a response to alienation, to the patriarchal separation of mind from body, "life" from "work," love from power. Knowledge of our erotic selves, therefore, is itself an empowering.[25]

In the same way, the Sacred Marriage of ancient Sumeria and Babylon was a pathway for both genders to reach the divine, an attitude almost incomprehensible today. Over the centuries, prostitution became dirty and denigrated, producing fatherless children and "fallen" women. This was not always the prevailing attitude. Merlin Stone, author of *When God Was a Woman*, notes:

> In the worship of the female deity, sex was Her gift to humanity. It was sacred and holy. She was the Goddess of Sexual Love and Procreation. But in the religions of today we find an almost totally reversed attitude. Sex, especially non-marital sex, is considered to be somewhat naughty, dirty, even sinful. Yet rather than calling the earliest religions, which embraced such an open acceptance of all human sexuality, "fertility-cults," we might consider the religions of today as strange in that they seem to associate shame and even sin with the very process of conceiving new human life. Perhaps centuries from now scholars and historians will be classifying them as "sterility-cults."[26]

Ancient mythologies celebrated the otherness of the two genders, acknowledging and valuing their differences, along with their joining. The deities of Hawaii, for example, are portrayed as opposites, though equal in power.

> Ku and Hina, the male and female, the rising upright and the leaning down, are together the deities of all humankind, both those who have already been and those who are to come. Ku is associated with the upright or sharp stone, while Hina is the flat or rounded stone; Ku is the rising of the sun while Hina is the setting of the sun; Ku is the right hand while Hina is the left hand. Ku is the male generative source while Hina is female source of growth and production.[27]

Yin and yang follow this cosmic division, split yet complementary. Yin and yang each contain a dash of the other color for an eye: masculine embedded in the woman and feminine in the man. Without this, neither can be complete in themselves.

> In all things the yang and yin are present. They are not to be separated; nor can they be judged morally as either good or evil. Functioning together, in perpetual interaction, now the one, now the other is uppermost. In man, the yang preponderates, in woman the yin — yet, in each are both.[28]

By valuing both sides of gender for the powers they offer, a mystical marriage appears, combining divine with earthly, animus with anima. Each has qualities to offer, and each demands respect and love in this ever-shifting dance of power, the battle between genders. Once the heroine has embraced this missing part of the self and incorporated its wisdom, she has prepared herself for the death-journey, the pathway to adulthood.

Facing the Self

CHAPTER 11

The Endless Summons: Descent into Darkness

The Myth of Inanna (Sumeria)

From the great heaven and earth which she ruled supreme, the goddess Inanna set her mind on the great below, the dazzling enigma of the underworld. Before embarking, she instructed her loyal minister Nincubura to mourn for her publicly and privately, so the gods would not let her pass from the earth. If she should not return, Nincubura must approach Father Enki and the entire pantheon and beg them to restore her.

With these words, Inanna decked herself in finery: A wig, a necklace of lapis-lazuli, twin egg-shaped beads on her breast, the *pala* garment of ladyship, a pectoral, a golden ring, and lastly, her measuring rod of state.

Inanna arrived at the palace Ganzer; she shoved the gate of the underworld. "Open up, doorman, open up. Open up, Neti, open up. I am all alone and I want to come in."

Neti, the chief doorman of the underworld, answered holy Inanna. "Who are you?"

"I am Inanna going to the east."

"If you are Inanna going to the east, why have you travelled to the land of no return? How did you set your heart on the road whose traveler never returns?"

Holy Inanna answered him. "Because lord Gudgalana, the husband of my elder sister holy Ereshkigal, has died; in order to have his funeral rites observed, she offers generous libations at his wake — that is the reason."

Neti, the chief doorman of the underworld, answered holy Inanna. "Stay here, Inanna. I will speak to my mistress. I will speak to my mistress Ereshkigal and tell her what you have said."

When Ereshkigal heard that Inanna was aggressively banging on her door, she grimaced, slapping her thigh in anger. At last, she ordered that Inanna pass through the gates one by one, in the manner of all supplicants to the underworld.

When Inanna entered the first gate, her stately wig was removed. "What is this?" "Be satisfied, Inanna, a divine power of the underworld has been fulfilled. Inanna, you must not open your mouth against the rites of the underworld."

When she entered the second gate, the necklace of tiny lapis-lazuli beads was removed from her neck. "What is this?" "Be satisfied, Inanna, a divine power of the underworld has been fulfilled. Inanna, you must not open your mouth against the rites of the underworld."

When she entered the third gate, the twin egg-shaped beads were removed from her breast. "What is this?" "Be satisfied, Inanna, a divine power of the underworld has been fulfilled. Inanna, you must not open your mouth against the rites of the underworld."

When she entered the fourth gate, the beautifully seductive pectoral was removed from her breast. "What is this?" "Be satisfied, Inanna, a divine power of the underworld has been fulfilled. Inanna, you must not open your mouth against the rites of the underworld."

When she entered the fifth gate, the golden ring was removed from her hand. "What is this?" "Be satisfied, Inanna, a divine power of the underworld has been fulfilled. Inanna, you must not open your mouth against the rites of the underworld."

When she entered the sixth gate, the lapis-lazuli measuring rod and measuring line were removed from her hand. "What is this?" "Be satisfied, Inanna, a divine power of the underworld has been fulfilled. Inanna, you must not open your mouth against the rites of the underworld."

When she entered the seventh gate, the *pala* dress, the garment of ladyship, was removed from her body. "What is this?" "Be satisfied, Inanna, a divine power of the underworld has been fulfilled. Inanna, you must not open your mouth against the rites of the underworld."

At last, stripped of all her stately ornaments, naked and shivering, Inanna entered the throne room. Firming her stance, she strode up to the throne where her sister Ereshkigal was sitting. She ordered her to step down and sat on the throne herself. Ereshkigal and her seven judges, the Anuna, burned with anger, shouting so loud that Inanna was rendered stone dead. And then Ereshkigal took her sister's body and hung it on a hook outside the door.

After three days and three nights, her minister Nincubura fulfilled Inanna's instructions. She lamented for her mistress in ruined houses, beat the mourning drum loudly in the sanctuary, beat herself within her rooms. And she visited all the gods, begging for help.

Father Enki answered Nincubura's prayers. He removed some dirt from the tip of his right fingernail and created kurjara. He removed some dirt from the tip of his other fingernail and created galatura. To kurjara he gave the life-giving plant. To galatura he gave the life-giving water. Then he sent these tiny clay men to slip into the underworld, passing through the door's cracks like shadows.

They approached where Ereshkigal crouched, perpetually mourning. Overcome with sadness and pain, she clutched herself and sobbed. "Oh, my heart!" she cried. "Oh, my liver!"

The clay figures wept with her. "You are troubled, our mistress, oh your heart. You are troubled, our mistress, oh your liver."

Ereshkigal raised her head, startled. Though she had lost her family and been consigned to the underground, no one had ever sympathized with her. In gratitude, she offered them anything they wished.

They said to her, "Give us the corpse hanging on the hook."

Once she gave it to them without protest, they sprinkled the life-giving plant and the water on her body, restoring Inanna to life.

As she hurried to the gates, the Anuna seized her: "Who has ever ascended unscathed from the underworld? If Inanna is to ascend from the underworld, let her provide a substitute for herself."

So Inanna departed the underworld, but only with a horde of demons restraining her on all sides.

Upon seeing her goddess restored, Nincubura threw herself at her feet. Her clothes were dust and rags from mourning. The demons said to holy Inanna, "Inanna, proceed to your city, we will take her back."

Holy Inanna answered the demons. "This is my minister of fair words, my escort of trustworthy words. She did not forget my instructions. She did not neglect the orders I gave her. She made a lament for me on the ruin mounds. She beat the drum for me in the sanctuaries. She made the rounds of the gods' houses for me." And thus Inanna refused to let Nincubura take her place. Twice more, Inanna's loyal servants greeted them, and twice more, Inanna shielded them for their loyalty.

At last, Inanna entered the great palace where her consort Dumuzid ruled. Once he had been a humble shepherd lad, playing his pipe on the hillside. But after Inanna had invited him to her couch and discovered his sweetness, she crowned him her consort and bestowed uncounted favors upon him. Now she found him wearing a magnificent garment, smiling cheerfully on her throne. The demons seized him.

Inanna gazed at the man who had not even mourned her for a moment. "Take him away."

Dumuzid tried to run. He begged the gods for help, pleading that he was their in-law. He changed into snake and falcon. But the demons caught him and dragged him to the underworld.

Once he was gone, Holy Inanna tore at her hair, ripping it like grass. "You wives who lie in your men's embrace, where is my precious husband? You children who lie in your men's embrace, where is my precious child? Where is my man?"[1]

Dumuzid's sister, Geshtianna, begged to take his place out of love for him. It was then decreed that Dumuzid spend half the year in the underworld and his sister take the other half. When Dumuzid vanished under the earth, the fields died and the world grew hard and chill. But when he re-emerged, he and Inanna would sport in their fields as shepherd and lady, consort and goddess.

Inanna, later known as Ishtar, Astarte, Ma, Anahita, Asherah, and more, was worshipped continuously from 3500 to 500 B.C.E.[2] Her epic poem, "Inanna's Descent to the Nether World," became one of the world's first recorded love stories, illuminating the relationship between sex and death and the meaning of sacrifice.

Here we see Inanna visiting the underworld out of a desire to experience her dark side: death, mourning, loss. Once a unified great goddess, she has been divided into the sunlight lover and her dark sister, split off from the self. The dark sister, buried in so many women, must be faced and confronted in the underworld to which she's been banished. Patricia Reis relates in her article, "The Dark Goddess":

> We must seek her in those dark places where she has been relegated by our patriarchal culture. Medusa banished to the "darkest regions of the world," the "barbarian" origins of Medea, Hecate's cave, Kali's cremation grounds, the Furies sent underground, the dry dusty underworld of Ereshkigal. She lives in our own dark places. We can find her in our dreams, in our suffering, depressions, and rages.[3]

"We first meet Inanna as a woman fearful, anxious about her awakening sensuality and her future responsibilities as queen of the land. As the story unfolds, she discovers her feminine powers, her strength as a leader, her spirituality, and ultimately her wisdom."[4] Though goddess-mighty, her emotions of hubris, humility, comprehension, and betrayal are all too human.

At the start of this tale, Inanna strides proudly to the gate and bangs on it imperiously. Rather than passively dying, she enters the underworld boldly, actively, demanding its secrets. However, the force of death is too potent to meet shielded by grandeur and finery. Thus, Inanna must shed her staff of office, her adornments, her ladylike gown, her accomplishments, her identity, her cities, her temples, and meet her opposite self with no barriers or defenses.

> The Dark Goddess forces us to look at ourselves with utter, naked honesty. For many of us, this is very frightening — to see ourselves stripped of our illusions and false pretensions. Like Inanna, who had to discard an article of clothing or an ornament at each gate of the underworld, when we go down into the darkness we must cast away all that is not true about ourselves and our lives.[5]

This is stripping the layers to reveal the inner self, as Salome does in her sensual dance. By descending thus, Inanna can shed all but her strongest core before facing her vicious otherself, her shadow sister.

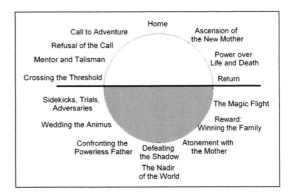

Ereshkigal is Inanna's elder sister, one who once experienced joy and marriage as the Goddess of Grain but now is cast into obscurity as neglected widow. Rather than birthing children for her husband, she must take the souls of the dead into herself by swallowing them. In the dismal Netherworld, she is perpetually cut off from her grain and blossoms above. With only clay to eat and dirty water to drink, she becomes as hopeless and lightless as the miserable kingdom she now rules. She has become a huge, sleeping, black-skinned naked woman living in an empty palace of blue lapis. Sometimes she appears as a savage lion-headed woman suckling cubs, or on a boat, peering wistfully across the river that separates the land of the living from her own realm, called Irkalla, or the House of Dust.

In her article, Elizabeth Barette names Ereshkigal "Goddess of Thankless Tasks and She Who Complains."[6]

> As the Goddess of Thankless Tasks, Ereshkigal looks out for women who hold similar positions: jobs with miserable working conditions, unfair terms, lousy wages; jobs that nobody wants to do but which nevertheless must be done; jobs that are taken for granted by those who don't have to do them. She watches over the women who clean toilets, wrap bloody meat in neat plastic, and slave over greasy machines in hot factories.[7]

And when conditions grow truly intolerable, Ereshkigal is the one who stops them, the one who screams "Enough" in the voice before which all must bow.

In the descent myth, "Ereshkigal is described first as enraged, due to Inanna's invasion of her realm; secondly, as actively destructive; third, as suffering; and finally as grateful and generous," Silvia Brinton Perera comments in *Descent to the Goddess,* her examination of the Inanna myth. "There is a quality of primal rage about her. She is full of fury, greed, the fear of loss, and even of self spite."[8] Though the shadow-self has hidden positive qualities, she shrouds them in loss and rage that the heroine of light must battle through to absorb. The shadow loathes the heroine, who has all the youth, beauty, and advantages of the upper world. Thus her rejection of this lighter self.

At the same time, understanding Ereshkigal and her lessons is vital for the shallow maiden. While she consists primarily of the magical and regenerative

crone, the shadow also contains aspects of mother and maiden "such as independence, assertiveness, sexuality, power, and worldly accomplishment."[9] As
the patriarchy came to fear these qualities, women were persuaded to abandon
them. Thus, heroines descend into the darkness, seeking to reintegrate.

As Ereshkigal describes her sister-goddess in a later version of the myth:

> What has moved her heart [seat of the intellect] what has stirred her liver [seat of
> the emotions]?
> Ho there, does this one wish to dwell with me?
> To eat clay as food, to drink dust as wine?
> I weep for the men who have left their wives.
> I weep for the wives torn from the embrace of their husbands;
> For the little ones cut off before their time.[10]

She is a source of endless misery, trapped in the underworld, unable to feast
with the gods or follow her lover when he abandons her for better things. She
sobs in pain, abandoned by the gods to the lifeless underworld. As Reis notes:

> Ereshkigal, once a mighty and powerful Goddess, was assigned by the new ruling
> gods to the dry, dark realm of the dead as her domain. She suffers there. She eats
> clay and drinks dirty water, she moans, she smites her thighs and sets up great
> lamentations. In the myth, she is portrayed as a woman in labor — a dry labor with
> no birth.[11]

She is indeed Inanna's shadow, reigning alone and unloved in the world's abyss,
as Inanna brings fertility above. Inanna has a husband, a lively kingdom, and
all the world's joys and luxuries. But what of Ereshkigal, confined to the underworld, wailing to be heard?

Inanna, upon a single meeting with Ereshkigal, thinks she has mastered
death, and thus demands the underworld's throne. But Ereshkigal knows better. "I'll make you understand suffering and death," Ereshkigal screams. "You
think the underworld itself will capitulate because of your arrogance? See how
it controls you, destroys you inside and out!" And Inanna perishes.

The little clay figures who rescue her take the opposite tack; they slip
inside rather than pound on the gates. Once inside Ereshkigal's borders, they
sympathize with her rather than bully her, asserting that they know everything.
When kurjara and galatura arrive, Ereshkigal is locked in desperate mourning.
True, she is the unvoiced sorrow of proud, confident Inanna, a queen who never
succumbs to rage, despair, or even self-doubt. But Ereshkigal's pain is deeper
still: She can scarcely bear that she has ordered Inanna's death, as Inanna is part
of herself. Galatura and kurjara moan with Ereshkigal, appeasing her anguish
by the echo of their concern. As Perera notes:

> They affirm her in her suffering. They have been taught by Enki to trust the life
> force even when it sounds its misery. Complaining is one voice of the dark goddess.
> It is a way of expressing life, valid and deep in the feminine soul. It does not, first
> and foremost, seek alleviation, but simply to state the existence of things as they are

felt to be to a sensitive and vulnerable being. It is one of the bases of the feeling function, not to be seen and judged from the stoic-heroic superego perspective as foolish and passive whining, but just as autonomous fact—"that's the way it is." Enki's wisdom teaches us that suffering is part of reverencing.[12]

They validate Ereshkigal's misery and voice Inanna's sublimated pain. They even offer the sympathy (literally together-feeling) that Inanna promised her sister at the gate. In gratitude, Ereshkigal gives them whatever they wish, reintegrating with her joyful half and reviving it.

Inanna, through suffering, has come to understand her sister's loss and misery. Inanna too has suffered death now. She has learned that her impulses and arrogance have consequences. When she embraces Ereshkigal, they reintegrate, each gaining wisdom from the other.

> For the individual, one of the major tasks in the process of psychological development is to recognize, acknowledge, and accept those rejected aspects of the self (the shadow). The process of integration through acknowledging and accepting the shadow aspects of our personalities gives us depth and access to a greater range of expression. Oftentimes the shadow will hold hitherto unknown powers and capabilities.[13]

Though reaching out to her dark-sister side can restore her, Inanna's quest is not yet complete. She cannot master grief and mortality without sacrifice. For her to understand death and still live, someone else must pay the ultimate price.

Above, Dumuzid has clearly begun to relish his position as king more than he cherishes Inanna. But this is more than a lover's quarrel. Having undergone initiation and faced death, Inanna has deepened more than she ever had believed possible. Now Dumuzid with his trappings of power seems childish, unworthy of this new self the goddess has achieved. In fact, Dumuzid literally meant "young son" or "male child."[14] "Be my equal," Inanna challenges him. "Make the descent as I have made and emerge from it stronger, deeper. Grow into a man who has experienced grief and destruction and the inner self, not merely the hedonistic emptiness of the world above. Grow! And thus be my worthy mate." As Perera explains, "Inanna challenges her equal to make the same descent she endured — perhaps to claim the same strength and wisdom."[15]

Dumuzid's attempts at scapegoating and fleeing betray his childishness. Clearly he needs to descend into the underworld himself, where he can bond with an anima whom he can accept nondefensively and revere as his equal. As a child to his goddess-lover, he will never gain maturity. At the same time, Dumuzid weeps, begs, trembles, and bargains to stay out of the underworld, displaying both the primal fear that leads many heroes to be dragged on their journeys and the five stages of grief that psychologists have catalogued today.

Geshtianna, whose name means "vine of heaven," is thought of in the myths as a "wise woman." In service to the human dimension, she does what she can to redeem the one lost to the underworld. Succumbing to the growth cycle her brother resists, she acquiesces to her own cutting down, her own descent: "She does not flee from her fate, nor does she denigrate the goddess of fate as do Gilgamesh and the patriarchy. She volunteers. And in this courageous, conscious acquiescing, she ends the pattern of scapegoating by choosing to confront the underworld herself," Perera adds.[16] Geshtianna's offer moves Inanna as the two sides of the feminine meet — queenship and compassion, willfulness and selfless love. This earthly sister, Geshtianna, completes Inanna's journey on earth, and reconnects her to Dumuzid, her opposite, and so to all of life.

Here appears the Sacred Marriage, in which the priestess representing her goddess would consecrate the divine king. As Elizabeth Prioleau explains in her book on divine seductresses, "The objective was apotheosis, to be remade in the image of the goddess, to channel her divine sex energy and redeem and regenerate the earth."[17]

Yet, within a year, this king must be sacrificed to ensure the blessing of the land and the fields' regeneration, sometimes symbolically and sometimes in fact. This was to ensure to Goddess's unrivaled superiority, disdaining a permanent consort. Thus, Inanna perpetually loses Dumuzid, perpetually finding him once more.

The Great Goddess has no one to match her; her consort, now learned in the mysteries of the unconscious, must die each year. Life cannot remain stagnant and perfect, lover and beloved, static happily ever after — Death and rebirth are the nature of life.

Resisting Pity, Gaining Wisdom

These journeys into darkness represent death — only by completely surrendering to the unknown can the heroine transcend her existence, and learn the wisdom and magic of mortality. In ancient matriarchal mythology, this descent was a desirable initiation made by female seekers of knowledge, as with Inanna. The power of the ancient feminine would guide a woman down to the world of the unconscious, with untold wisdom as a reward. Even the figure of death was not menacing, but welcoming, as the immature anima sought her dark opposite.

As the patriarchal Hellenistic religion took over, the woman's journey and archetypal eagerness for knowledge faded. From this shift in power came the legend of Persephone, an innocent flower princess who must be violently kidnapped to enter the realm of the dead. All eagerness to absorb the underworld's dark secrets vanishes, and a man drags the heroine on her ultimate initiation.[18]

Men are tested by having to endure pain, hunger, and thirst to prove their forbearance — the strength of self all heroes need to overcome their initiation.

Heroines, however, must resist pity, withstanding the claim of what is nearby for the sake of a distant abstract goal.[19] The underworld claims one of Inanna's beloveds, and she must choose: faithful servant, adored child, handsome lover. Like the seed sorting, this is a task of single-mindedness, of willpower. Without it, the heroine can never leave the underworld.

The people of Fujian Province in China had little food or water, and so many died of horrible diseases. Yet rumor told of the fog-shrouded Doonggong Mountain, where magic grasses grew beside a dragon well. Juice from these grasses could cure a hundred diseases and bring fertility back to the land.

Many heroes quested for the grasses, yet none returned. In the village, a girl named Zhiyu watched her two older brothers vanish up the mountain. At last, she picked up a bow and followed. As she climbed, she met an ancient man roasting rice cakes over a fire. "Grandfather, please tell me if this is the path to the dragon well," she said.

"It is, but beware," he said. "You must be steadfast and walk straight ahead, never looking back. Too many heroes have already failed."

She promised to remember, and he gave her a rice cake, adding that she must sprinkle water on all the large rocks she saw. Though puzzled, she promised to do so.

Higher and higher Zhiyu climbed. Behind her, she heard screams and curses, but she didn't look. Then cries turned to sounds of weeping. Still she remained resolute. Then she heard her elder brother crying for help. She shivered. Now she heard her second brother as well. She put her hand over her heart. And there she felt the rice cake. She pinched two pieces off and used them to plug her ears, shutting out the cries. Thus she climbed the mountain to the top.

Awaiting her was a black dragon. She shot arrows into both of its eyes and it vanished into black, greasy smoke. When she gathered the well water and sprinkled it on the grass, it blossomed and produced seeds, which she gathered. On the way down, she poured her flask of well water on all the rocks she saw, and they transformed into her brothers and all the other heroes who had climbed the mountain but looked behind them.

Zhiyu and her brothers returned to earth and sprinkled the grass seed over the barren earth. In no time, the fields bloomed with delicate grasses tufted with soft white hair, so the people named them silver needles. In gratitude, the people named Zhiyu their lucky star, their silver needle lass.[20]

In "Cupid and Psyche," Psyche crosses the River Styx to meet Persephone and bring back "a little of her beauty, enough at least for a single short day"[21] as her final, most difficult task. In the underworld, Psyche must ignore ghosts' cries for help and refuse to speak to them, just as Zhiyu cannot look back. Only through concentration on the distant goal, avoiding immediate distractions, can the heroine rescue her family and all those in need.

When Psyche, newly returned from her ordeal, samples the arch crone Persephone's beauty, she touches the force of death and ultimate wisdom. To become adult she must gain feminine knowledge and face death in order, paradoxically, to give birth.

Psyche, no goddess yet, cannot face the fatal knowledge she carries. Shock overwhelms her as an "infernall sleep ... a black cloud of oblivion throughout her whole body."[22] Psyche then falls to the ground, prostrate as a corpse. Psychologically, this "death" suggests the ending of her old role. Psyche has finished the greatest quest of all, but is she ready? Maybe the best part of her life has ended, she thinks. Or maybe as Cupid's proper wife, she won't be able to handle the responsibility. Even in her greatest triumph, she isn't ready for the awesome, shattering power of adulthood. Joan Gould, author of the fairytale reflection *Spinning Straw into Gold* explains, "The princess isn't strong enough to face transformation yet. But she can't resist or avoid it either...."[23] Thus, Psyche, like Snow White, sinks into a temporary "death." Her old self must perish in order for a new, stronger personality to spring forth.

Now that Psyche has completed Venus's assigned tasks and learned death's secrets, she is fit to be a partner to her husband. She has earned her autonomy and no longer worships her husband as a helpless shut-in. Cupid sweeps her up to Olympus, weds her, and offers her the ambrosia to make her a goddess and his equal throughout eternity. Thus blessed, Psyche gives birth to the child of her new marriage, the girl Pleasure.

CHAPTER 12

I'll Get You, My Pretty!
Confronting the Deadly Mother

Coatlicue (Aztec)

The Great Goddess Coatlicue, mother of all the Aztec deities, had many great temples built in her honor and was revered at altars of volcanic glass. She was the Lady of the Serpent Skirt, living on a high mountain peak over the lost homeland of Aztlan, while her snakes dwelt below in sacred caves. It was Coatlicue who gave all in life and reclaimed all in death. Her necklace of skulls reminded the Aztecs that each must return to her in their time. Someday, all must melt into her lava pools, watching their future lives revealed in mirrors of cool obsidian.

This goddess of the double snake head had 400 sons whom she set in the sky as stars known as the Centzonhuitznahua, and one daughter, the goddess Coyolxanliqui (little bells).

When Coatlicue was sweeping one day, a tuft of feathers fell on her. Hesitating to interrupt her ritual, she tucked the tuft into her waistband and kept sweeping. However, when in her leisure she tried to examine the feathers, she found that they had vanished, leaving her pregnant. "What have you done?" Coyolxanliqui demanded, indignant at her mother's apparent sexual transgression. "Affairs at your age? Have you no shame for the family honor, for your adult children! Who is this lover?"

But Coatlicue had no answer.

Infuriated, Coyolxanliqui sought out her 400 brothers, and incited them to matricide. "Her new children will supplant us, her behavior will shame us," she warned. "This new child will be set above us in the sky. Killing her is our only option."

Her brothers were persuaded, all except the youngest. He hid away, and

127

as the other children plotted, he went to warn his mother. For, he reasoned, if the newest had to perish, the second youngest might be threatened as well, as the older siblings claimed all the inheritance.

The children attacked just as their divine mother was giving birth, when she might be at her weakest. However, forewarned, Coatlicue birthed the divine Huitzilopochtli ("He-who-was-born-on-the-shield"), who emerged fully armed and armored "holding a spear and a blue rod, his face painted, his left leg slender and feathered, his arms and thighs painted blue."[1] Only seconds old, he slaughtered all of his brothers who had plotted to kill his divine mother. Stabbing one after the other with his obsidian knife, he finally reached Coyolxanliqui, and decapitated her.

When Coatlicue witnessed the death of her cherished daughter, she of the golden bells, she was inconsolable. After weeping for many days, she took the shining head of her daughter and set it in the sky, in a place of honor, where it became the moon.[2]

Here the daughter is attempting destruction of the mother for usurping her position ("I'm supposed to be the fertile one! Why are you sleeping around, bearing children? At your age!"). Coatlicue slays her — not with direct combat, but by the woman's life-giving power of birthing the hero. Forced to battle her own children, she represents the conflict of the devouring mother.

To complicate the legend even more, for the glorious sun god Huitzilopochtli to be born, his mother must die. In some legends Coatlicue perishes, while in far more she and her daughter are represented as two sides of the same entity. Destroying her daughter, she divides herself. Here is the truth of the struggle: These two warring goddesses are the same person.

As the patriarchy rejected the Mother Goddess, everything changed. The goddess of all things was demonized, split into sainted virgin and vilified sinner or even death crone. Both lost power, as one was lauded for its weakened state, the other defiled. The Virgin Mary was divine, Mary Magdalene a sinner. Eve was the passive victim, Lilith the vicious child-killer. The Egyptian cat-goddess Bast represented love and fertility, while her lioness counterpart Sekhmet was wrath personified. Persephone was sweet flower maiden, Hecate cackling death-crone. Kali split off from the kindlier Indian goddesses Durga or Parvati as the personification of their wrath. And Coatlicue's daughter rebelled against her sensual, powerful mother.

The virgin goddesses were thrust up into the heavens, and the death goddesses, down to the underworld. The goddess's darker aspects became the demonic: Baba Yaga, the Morrigan, Hel, Hecate, Kali, the Furies, Nemesis, Troma, Mara, Morgan le Fay. She became the wicked witch, mistress of dark spells, lurking in shadow. Thus the cycle of life-death-life was shattered, as the patriarchy believed in clinging to light and life rather than succumbing to death. The dark goddess was only seen as bloodthirsty, engulfing all to fuel her hunger.

> It was the Dark Moon Crone Goddess who took life back into her womb, but the ancients also understood that a New Moon Virgin Goddess would birth life back out again. The Crone was the death-giver as the Virgin was the birth-bringer. Reincarnation was represented by the refertilization of the Crone who became Virgin. The continual interaction of destruction becoming creation is the eternal dance that maintains the cosmos.[3]

However, her cycle shattered, leaving only the wicked witch who brought permanent destruction in her wake, the monstrous villainess who must be punished at the story's end. This schism caused a great fear of death, which was no longer accompanied by resurrection and rebirth.

In this way, the goddess Cihuacóatl personified the Aztec collective hunger for human sacrifice; scholars call her "not so much a woman as the representation of the negative side of the female psyche."[4]

> Cihuacóatl was depicted with her lower face made only of bone and her jaws wide open waiting for victims. Her hair was long and stringy and a pair of knives formed a diadem on her forehead. She was related to evil omens, was savage, and brought misery to men; for it was she who gave men the digging stick and the tump line. She was a night walker, screaming and weeping copiously, but she was also a warrior; on her back she carried the knife of sacrifice swaddled like a child.[5]

Cihuacóatl was demonized, rejected, as the powerfully cruel side of woman, frightening to men, and thus undesired in a patriarchal society.

Women experience the shadow sister as Ereshkigal, depression personified; as Medusa, sublimated rage; as Kali in her frenzied dance; as Cam the fairytale Black Bride; as Medea "who destroys relationships, kills her children and says, 'Let the whole house crash!'"[6] Here we see women's strength, fury, misery, and destructiveness, split off from the anima like Ereshkigal howling in the darkness.

The most powerful and thus frightening aspects of female divinity were relegated to the caves, to the dark corners of the world as chthonic goddesses, contrasted with those ruling from Olympus. "The crucial psychological fact is that all of us, female as well as male, fear the will of woman ... the earliest and profoundest prototype of absolute power."[7] This power is too great for adults to struggle against. "To contain it, to keep it under control and harness it to chosen purposes, is a vital need."[8]

However, it is an even greater need to seek it to discover it, to learn its vital lessons. Those who suppress their dark side are vulnerable to its impulses and desires, yet unable to accept them. It is the people who do not know enough about their own shadow and their own dark side who are most likely to fall victim to evil influences.[9]

> The woman who fights against her father still has the possibility of leading an instinctive, feminine existence, because she rejects only what is alien to her. But when she fights against the mother she may, at the risk of injury to her instincts, attain to greater consciousness, because in repudiating the mother she repudiates all that is obscure, instinctive, ambiguous, and unconscious in her own nature.[10]

Thus the young questor descends into darkness, like Inanna, to meet Ereshkigal and learn her secrets.

The shadow archetype, described by Jung's philosophy, is the characteristics of ourself we most detest, projected onto another person of the same gender, as "the shadow cast by the conscious mind of the individual contains the hidden, repressed, and unfavorable (or nefarious) aspects of the personality."[11] However, more than simply the inverse of the heroine, this shadow has hidden positive qualities as well, often strong and assertive where the heroine is silent and passive. And as the dark mother or witch-queen is the heroine's shadow, the daughter also represents the shadow for the mother — her flaws and unfulfilled desires made manifest. In her battle to achieve a higher consciousness, the heroine pits herself against this shadow, and must integrate it into the self.

To Jungian scholars, though the shadow has been buried in the underworld, it has much to offer the questor.

> Envy, lust, sensuality, deceit, and all known vices are the negative, "dark" aspect of the unconscious, which can manifest itself in two ways. In the positive sense, it appears as a "spirit of nature," creatively animating Man, things, and the world.... In the negative sense, the unconscious (that same spirit) manifests itself as a spirit of evil, as a drive to destroy.[12]

The shadow usually contains values that are needed by consciousness, but that exist in a form that makes it difficult to integrate them into one's life."[13] These are parts of the self that one has been unwilling to look at too closely, made manifest. Today we have crimes and horrors in the news, in fiction, in movies, which give us a place to invest our dark emotions and act out our fantasies outside ourselves. Other, less healthy, relationships involve projecting these dark emotions onto another person: spouse, parent, or child. Others scapegoat a community or person, heaping on them all the world's sins. These buried aspects sometimes surface at inopportune times, a slip of the tongue or a moment's rage which is quickly suppressed and once again buried. But the hero's deepest quest is to stop projecting onto others and triumph over these buried aspects within the self, valuing the rage and fury that can drive one to the greatest heights.

Growing Older

Wolfgang Lederer's *The Fear of Women* speaks of the "uncomfortable and embarrassing truth" that we all believe women can be dangerous. "We do think that women can reject, disown, harm, kill, and even eat their children ... baby girls tend to fare worse than boys; and so the paranoia of women, which Freud attributed to their fear of being killed by their mothers, may have some historical validity."[14] And yet, for Coyolxauhqui, this fear drives her to attempt murder in order to keep her own role as life-giver.

In variants of tales from "Sleeping Beauty" to "The Armless Maiden" to "The Six Swans," the heroine's mother-in-law hides or kills the heroine's child, and then blames the heroine, naming her a witch and smearing her mouth with blood. Just as the heroine represents life-giving and creative power, the witch figure murders and destroys the new life. Worse yet, she seeks to cast her own shadow over the heroine, blaming her for the destructive deed. And yet, this forces the heroine to face her ordeal: to descend into death but also to acknowledge the child-killing, death-dealing rage within her virginal heart. Only by meeting the witch on her own terms can the heroine persevere.

In fairytales, the stepmother and wicked witch "symbolize predatory female sexuality and the adolescent's negative feeling toward the mother."[15] In other words, the enemy is the part of ourselves we most dislike. We see the negative aspects of our mothers in ourselves and reject them, saying, "That's as different from me as possible; that quality belongs to the enemy."

> To accomplish this split from the mother, many young women make their mothers into the image of the archetypal vengeful, possessive, and devouring female whom they must reject to survive. A woman's actual mother may or may not embody these qualities, but the daughter internalizes them as a construct of her inner mother. According to Jung, this inner mother begins to function in us as a shadow figure, an involuntary pattern that is unacceptable to our egos.[16]

She is the fear we won't love our children enough, or will sap their independence, or handle them badly. She is the image of "I won't be like that when I grow up!" Similarity produces a special tyranny, as mother and daughter see their worst qualities reflected in the other and lash out.

Often, this shadow is the Terrible Mother as witch or mother-in-law, furious at being supplanted and relegated to cronehood. "Look at her, trying to arouse my pity through the allurement of her swollen belly, whose glorious offspring is to make me, if you please, a happy grandmother. Happy indeed, to be called grandmother in the flower of my age!"[17] Venus cries. When her adult son marries and is about to have a child, Venus rages.

Her fury stems mostly from the fact that she is to be a grandmother, with pregnant Psyche taking her place as divine mother and goddess. In fact, Venus has always seen Psyche as an enemy because of her youthful beauty. "First the people love her, and name her 'More beautiful than Venus'" she reasons. "Then my son exalts her above me. Soon my entire self will go to her, this girl who is a younger me." Venus cannot accept her changing role, so she demands her son remain a youth. "You, a mere child, actually receive her in your violent adolescent embraces, so that I have to have my enemy as a daughter-in-law. I suppose you think, you odious, good for nothing seducer, that you are the only one fit to breed now that I'm too old to conceive? Let me tell you, I'll bear another son much better than you."[18] With this last threat, Venus clings desperately to her role of matriarch. She can still bear children; she must not be shunted into the role of grandmother! She then confines him in his room.

The Basques tell of a witch who, upon seeing a mother with a beautiful baby, asks to comb the woman's hair. However, she slides a black skull pin into her curls and the young woman transforms into a dove. The witch, in turn, takes the baby and sits with it under a tree, bragging to passersby about her beautiful child. Taking the baby, the witch moves into the young woman's house, where a dove often perches in the garden. The husband tries again and again to catch the dove, and finally succeeds. Upon pulling the pin from her head, his wife returns. When she tells her story, they capture the old witch and burn her in the village square.[19]

This witch clearly craves motherhood, with a husband, fine home, and beautiful child. Fighting her crone state, she absorbs the young woman to take her place.

This is the battle of mother-daughter, heroine and shadow in fairytales. The girl longs to grow up and be queen, while the queen refuses to grow into cronehood, forcing a conflict and reintegration far more profound than the epic battle of father and son.

Separation

As babies, we identify the mother as part of the self— she knows when we're hungry almost as soon as we do, and instantly responds. As long as she's around, the world is safe. At age one-and-a-half or so, however, comes the separation phase. We toddle off independently, eager to explore beyond our mother's arms. It's an exciting, beautiful world and there are so many things other than mother to taste, touch, grab.[20]

Children of both genders idealize the mother, source of endless love and perfect wisdom. In fact, children deliberately avoid any knowledge of the mother's worst qualities: frustration, anger, punishment. Thus the child splits the mother into the "good" one and the "bad" one. Only the bad mother has headaches, yells, gives spankings. And she is temporary. Soon enough, the good mother will reappear. We will await her for years, always convinced that the woman before us, who makes us feel inadequate and angry, is not Mother. Not really.[21]

Snow White is especially desperate for her mother's love, willing to make herself ugly and worn on a regimen of chores, eagerly allowing Mother into the house to lace her till it hurts, to feed her poisoned fruit. She cannot shut the door on her. If her only possible relationship with the woman is that of murderess and victim, so be it. As Betsy Cohen notes in *The Snow White Syndrome*:

> What is fascinating about the Snow White fairy tale is that every mother is like the wicked queen at certain *moments* in her life.... Snow White's real mother, her good mother, dies. It is the stepmother who embodies evil. Repeatedly, Snow White hopes to be cared for by a good mother, but instead she encounters the bad mother. Only after four life-threatening attacks is Snow White forced to accept the facts: "My stepmother has been out to get me."[22]

In her chapter titled "Snow White and Her Shadow," Madonna Kolbenschlag notes, "We come into the world as mirror images of our mother — destined to be not only her reflector, but also her silent inquisitor. The relationship between mother and daughter is the most intimate, most intense, most symbiotic and symmetrical bond known to humans."[23] Mother and daughter start off as a single united set of desires, one that can be challenging for the daughter to reject without rejecting the mother's love, while the mother has an equally hard time accepting the daughter as a distinct individual motivated by her own desires.

Snow White possesses the ultimate competitive, antagonistic shadow. (In the earliest forms of the tale, she is Snow White's biological mother rather than stepmother.) She is clearly threatened by her daughter's beauty and the fear that the daughter will supplant her. "What is stressed is the anger and fear that attend the queen's realization that as she and Snow White both get older, she must lose. This is why the major feeling involved is not jealousy but envy — to make beauty that important is to reduce the world to one in which only two people count."[24] Her questioning "Who is the fairest of them all?" is pure competition, which turns murderous as soon as Snow White takes the lead. In the tale, the Queen looks in the mirror to see the most fair, and sees a reflection that is not her own.

More frightening still is her uncensored demand for Snow White's heart and liver in a little box "boiled for my supper." Eating one's enemy is far more intimate than any other form of possession or mastery. Here, the stepmother wishes to absorb Snow White's youth and beauty and believes consuming her will lead her there. "The queen's desire to eat Snow White's lungs and liver implies only her desire to include Snow White's beauty and power within herself, and whatever sexual feeling is involved in that is included in the original passion to be fairest."[25] Kolbenschlag adds, "When the wicked stepmother devours what she believes to be Snow White's liver and lungs (vital organs), she recaptures a primitive cannibalistic expression of envy, the belief that one acquires the power and characteristics of what one eats."[26] By eating this most central part of Snow White (or desiring to), the stepmother tries to become her younger self once more, fair and desirable, the triumphant new queen.

Freud defined the Oedipus complex as the sexual feelings of the four-, five-, or six-year-old child, directed toward the parent of the opposite sex, accompanied by competitive urges against the parent of the same sex. The girl is trying on her mother's clothes, which are more interesting than her own. Someday, she will be a mother herself, and she and Daddy can live together as the new parents playing house.

But contemporary psychology suggests the girl doesn't actually want Daddy — she wants adulthood. She has to grow up, get out, find her own man. Meanwhile, the mother often struggles to keep everyone in their roles: She as head of household and the daughter content to sweep the floors and wait a while longer to wear her glittering ballgown.

Whatever the mother's motives (usually competition) the daughter instinctively knows that she must break free in order to pursue her journey. Vasilisa, the brave Russian Cinderella, must cunningly escape Baba Yaga, the witch of the woods. Likewise, Cinderella ducks her stepmother's restrictions and makes her debut.

Many women comply with external, harsh demands. They are unwilling to rebel, to "cause a fuss." Cinderella in her many incarnations discovers this solution solves nothing. Offered compliance, the stepmother becomes harsher and more demanding, deepening her opposition in personality to the heroine. As the shadows in Cinderella's psyche, the stepmother and stepsisters personify her doubts. "You're worthless and ugly; no one will marry you. You're only fit to serve," they chant, voicing the fears that lurk inside the heroine. These detractors chip away at the heroine's self-possession until she begins to doubt her desires. She must break out and attend the ball but also must face her stepmother and learn how to dominate a household, give orders, acknowledge her own suppressed cruel streak. She needs the shadow's dark vicious strength, and the shadow craves her innocent happiness. They will have to find a way to reintegrate. Or like Coatlicue, only one will emerge from their conflict, gazing longingly at the distant moon.

CHAPTER 13

Ceasefire with the Self: Healing the Wounded Shadow

"Medusa" by Louise Bogan (America)

I had come to the house, in a cave of trees,
Facing a sheer sky.
Everything moved,— a bell hung ready to strike,
Sun and reflection wheeled by.

When the bare eyes were before me
And the hissing hair,
Held up at a window, seen through a door.
The stiff bald eyes, the serpents on the forehead
Formed in the air.

This is a dead scene forever now.
Nothing will ever stir.
The end will never brighten it more than this,
Nor the rain blur.

The water will always fall, and will not fall,
And the tipped bell make no sound.
The grass will always be growing for hay
Deep on the ground.

And I shall stand here like a shadow
Under the great balanced day,
My eyes on the yellow dust, that was lifting in the wind,
And does not drift away.[1]

Here, the speaker faces Medusa as a dark reflection. At the same time, this furious self is frozen, hidden away in a "cave," unable ever to move. This is a sacred place of feminine fertility, with rain, grass, trees, sky, but this growth and protection come at a price. "In this fantastic realm, the speaker has it both ways, much like the figures adorning Keats's Grecian urn. There is fertility (water, grass, hay) without the corruption of it (the water does not fall, nor the hay get mown)," explains analyst Deborah Pope.[2] This is a realm in which Medusa can be confronted without fear, yet it is a "dead scene forever now." Medusa is frozen, lifeless in the midst of fertility.

The bare eyes and hissing suggest an individual in pain, fleeing to preserve the self in this static environment. The speaker is facing this trauma "like a shadow" in its presence, struggling to reintegrate the self. The speaker both longs for and fears this cut off maternal source, motionless, awaiting the speaker's approach. Here is creative power, femininity, reintegration, but forever frozen, sheltered, until the heroine is prepared to admit it.

The Legend

Medusa was a beautiful young woman, ancient and powerful, the only mortal sister of the three immortal Gorgons, born of ancient marine deities Phorcys and his sister Ceto, and thus a powerful triplicate, like so many maiden-mother-crone paradigms. Hesiod describes "the Gorgons who, beyond the famous stream of Okeanos, live in the utmost place toward night, by the singing Hesperides: they are Sthenno, Euryale, and Medusa, whose fate is a sad one, for she was mortal, but the other two immortal and ageless both alike."[3] Many myths show them dwelling in the far west or in the underworld, just as Athena and the pantheistic goddesses, Zeus's sisters and daughters, dwelt in the sky. There Athena, born motherless from her father's head, wielded her spear, shield, and breastplate, fought in battles, and was the eternal virgin, a creature of intellect, rather than body.

One day Athena entered her temple to find her uncle Poseidon raping the lovely Medusa. As Ovid tells it, Athena "turned away and covered with her shield her virgin's eyes."[4] Athena staggered, overwhelmed with horror at this violation on so many levels. This was her maiden temple, her private sanctum. This innocent girl was young and divine, like herself, one deserving protection. And further, it was her uncle performing this horror, her uncle thrusting her into the world of pain and terror and sexual knowledge through this violation. Revolted, Athena waved her spear and transformed Medusa into such a hideous monster that all who saw her were turned to stone.

On the surface, this is puzzling and easy to dismiss as an Olympian tantrum. Medusa, like Echo, Io, Menthe, Daphne, and so many other lithe nymphs, is the victim here, assaulted by the dominant god. However, the nature of her punishment is the key. Athena's curse cuts Medusa off from the sexual mysteries of the priestess, but also from future rape. Medusa is safe forever in her monster form, safer even than Athena in her armor. This form has defenses:

the venom of the snakes, the banishment to the impenetrable underworld, and the famous petrifying gaze. Medusa's stare is the ultimate power — one that says "No, don't come any closer!" This stare freezes men with its power and stops them in their tracks forever.

Thus Medusa, whose name once meant "the female ruling one," lives cowering in the underworld, a source of feminine power raped by male authority.[5] Medusa's oceanic cavern at the far Western edge of the world parallels the gateway to death, which she guards. She is rage and power and hideousness so great that a single glance turns intruders to stone: "Nothing but terror emanates from Medusa's head."[6]

Her sisters protest this change. How can their beautiful sister be this face of fury, this man-killer? Athena transforms them as well: Better the three sisters protect each other than two remain beautiful and defenseless, prey for the next hungry god to devour. Medusa armors herself against male intruders, she waits, and she destroys any who dare force themselves inside her lair. "She becomes the Unapproachable, who fends off all sexual lust, numbs her enemies with terror, and repels desire."[7] Medusa dwells in the underworld, crouched in the safety of this still half-life, where nothing changes, where no one dies or is born or is harmed.

At last, Perseus penetrates her sanctum endowed with marvelous gifts from Athena and her emissaries: winged sandals, a helm of invisibility, a magic pouch, a sword, the shield-mirror that protects him from her gaze, softening it down to a reflection. But wait! Wings, shoes, cap, bag, and mirror are *feminine* talismans, all except the traditional hero's blade which he will use to slay her. And hasn't Athena done enough to Medusa, who now is tucked out of the way, protected, defended, but no longer likely to succumb to men or bother Athena ever again with frighteningly carnal images?

The truth is that Athena has pushed all the frightened, violated parts of herself away, wrapped them in dangerous barriers, and buried them in the underworld. Medusa is her frightened childself, her rage at the gods and men, the abused self, the wounded part. Now Athena can pretend all is well, be Daddy's girl, host her father's parties, be polite to her uncle (though they were frequently rivals), and never allow anyone to reach the ugly, writhing, bottled up fury that she has hidden away.

Athena dwindles to virginal maiden, goddess of Zeus's intelligence, in service of the male solar ego. She molds men into heroes, teaching them warfare, while she teaches the women crafts of the home. She blatantly rejects all maternal impulses in Aeschylus's *Oresteia*, as she also justifies the priority of men over women, saying, "It is my task to render final judgment here.... There is no mother anywhere who gave me birth ... I am always for the male with all my heart, and strongly on my father's side. So, in a case where the wife has killed her husband, lord of the house, her death shall not mean most to me."[8]

She has become a sexless defender of the patriarchy, as an extension of Zeus, no more. The ancient ode "To Minerva" praises her as

> Daughter of aegis-bearing Jove [Zeus], divine,
> Propitious to thy votaries' prayer incline;
> From thy great father's fount supremely bright,
> Like fire resounding, leaping into light.
> Shield-bearing goddess, hear, to whom belong
> A manly mind, and power to tame the strong!
> Oh, sprung from matchless might, with joyful mind
> Accept this hymn; benevolent and kind![9]

Zeus is alluded to three times in eight lines, while her aspects (fire, light, shield, might, mind) are all shallowly masculine. But as an identity, this is insufficient.

Athena feels part of herself is lacking. In myth, this often prompts a search for the self's younger, weaker aspect, the lost child. At this moment, a young hero prays to her for help — Perseus, child of Zeus like herself, whose mother is threatened with a forced marriage to King Polydectes, who sends Perseus on a quest for Medusa's head to get him out of the way. Clearly, Perseus and his mother Danae need a Medusa, an avatar of women's rage and wisdom and protection all at once to save them from King Polydectes.

Athena does not fly in to save Danae. The truth is, she has confined that part of herself, self-protection and rage and feminine power, down in the underworld. For her to stop this threat, Perseus must find her Medusa side and retrieve it for her. So she arms him. Athena offers the mirrored shield, link to her reflected and banished self so far buried. She can give him a sword and her brother, Zeus's messenger, can give him winged sandals. But though he can reach the underworld, this man will never find Medusa.

He needs invisibility and protection, a helm and a bag, feminine talismans Athena cannot access. She is a solar goddess, so cut off from herself that she cannot approach the underworld with its mysteries, and thus she sends Perseus. She has him petition the Graeae, ancient crone sisters who know all the secrets of the world, to find the nymphs of the Hesperides, and then coax those nymphs in their inner feminine sanctum of treasures to yield their gifts to him. As Demetra George notes in *Mysteries of the Dark Moon: The Healing Power of the Dark Goddess*, Perseus "could not have killed Medusa without the help of another goddess, Athene.... To a large extent, therefore, the hero is a pawn in a celestial game between different aspects of the goddess."[10]

Thus gifted, Perseus slips past the underworld's barriers and approaches Medusa. His helm protects himself from even her divine perception, while his footsteps, winged with the spirituality of birds, draw ever closer. "I am like you, the divine female," Perseus' gifts seem to say. "I am cloaked in your power, the power from which Athena separated herself. Let me in."

Medusa senses someone is there and turns her gaze on him. But he is a victim as she is, cast into the seas by his grandfather, ignored by his father, with mother and self endangered by the patriarchy in the form of King Polydectes. Perseus holds the mirror that to inner self, but more, he *is* Medusa's inner self, the frightened child behind the rage-filled gaze that Medusa cannot outstare.

Reflection — a shallow perception rather than a deep-felt experiencing — becomes a way to master one's fear of the object. This is not a fear of the external, but of the deeply experiential inner self. Confronted with this wounded hero so like herself, Medusa succumbs and allows her barriers to be broken, allows her return to the world above. This, like all growth, requires great pain; Perseus' sword slices Medusa's head from her body. But there is also glorious birth as children, once sired by Poseidon, spring forth: Pegasus, beloved of the Muses, and the golden hero Chrysaor. Walling herself off has resulted in stagnation, isolation, as Medusa rages and nurses her wounds. But until now, she has failed to grow beyond them. With a sword-strike, with a mirror, Perseus opens her to her painful past, forcing her to confront it, accept it, and move forward. Medusa is no longer frozen, unable to give birth to her desires and needs. She can finally return to life.

Though Freud and his cronies view Perseus's act as a castration of the mother, the myth is not so clear-cut.[11] Paradoxically, Medusa's head only gains true aggressive power when decapitated and carried away. In "The Ker as Gorgon," Jane Ellen Harrison argues that "her potency only begins when her head is severed, and that potency resides in the head; she is in a word a mask with a body later appended." In fact, this gorgon head symbol is "a cultus object, a ritual mask misunderstood."[12] In ancient times, it was depicted bodiless, warding men from entering sacred places. Greeks and Romans mounted it on shields making it a weapon as Perseus does.

Perseus, aided by magical bag and sandals, returns to the world above where he finds a sea-monster prepared to devour a young maiden. No more! Armed with Medusa's power, he fixes the monster in Medusa's fierce gaze that will let no monster harm an innocent and petrifies him. He performs the divine marriage with Andromeda, and then returns home to rescue his mother, once more with Medusa's gaze. The essay "For the Love of Medusa" observes, "Perseus went to a lot of trouble to kill a woman and rob her of her terror. But this was all necessary before he could look upon the nude and bejeweled body of a woman and carry off his own mother.... Now she and her son can travel together where they will."[13] Having destroyed the tyrant Polydectes, he likewise kills the grandfather who abandoned him and his mother.

Lastly, he performs the return. The mortal world has been repaired, but Athena is still divided from herself. He offers her Medusa's head that he was sent to find, and she plants it on her aegis, or breastplate, incorporating it into her goddess-identity.

In one unconfirmed tradition, Athena was Libyan, with the Medusa symbol a representation of herself as her destroyer aspect, the goddess Medusa-Metis.[14] As the legend merged with the Greek, the Athena myth became fragmented: she was shallow maiden, Metis was cast as her mother (consort of Zeus before he devoured her and her wisdom), and Medusa as her enemy. Demetra George notes:

> From a sociological perspective this myth marks the ingestion of the feminine warrior wisdom principle to the needs of the new patriarchal order. The patriarchy championed Athena as benevolent, suppressed Metis altogether, and denounced Medusa as evil. Athena and Medusa were then cast as opponents.[15]

This is the split that Athena, bereft of both mother-wisdom and dark side, must conquer in order to reintegrate.

The aegis likewise belonged to the women of Libya, but then became the emblem of divine sovereignty among the Greek gods, usurped by Zeus.[16] As it is explained in the Roman *Astronomica*:

> But when Jupiter [Zeus], confident in his youth, was preparing for war against the Titans, oracular reply was given to him that if he wished to win, he should carry on the war protected with the skin of a goat, aegis, and the head of the Gorgon. The Greeks call this the aegis. When this was done, as we have shown above, Jupiter [Zeus], overcoming the Titans, gained possession of the kingdom.[17]

This royal crimson-dyed goatskin was inscribed with oracular serpents representing the goddess wisdom, and Athena can only place her lost Medusa aspect on it once Perseus reclaims the bag from the Hesperides' magical garden of femininity and Medusa's wisdom from the underworld.

With Perseus's return, Athena reclaims her lost feminine self, the strength of the penetrating protective gaze, the wisdom of the serpent goddess, the knowledge of the underworld. This is Athena's descent by proxy and this is her integration. Perseus also offers her the helmet, with its feminine magic of invisibility and protection, and she dons it, a whole goddess at last.

This status as goddess of women is exemplified by her statue at the Parthenon. "The statue of Athena is upright, with a tunic reaching to the feet, and on her breast the head of Medusa is worked in ivory. She holds a statue of Victory about four cubits high, and in the other hand a spear; at her feet lies a shield and near the spear is a serpent."[18] Here, she is shown surrounded by feminine symbols: the statue of Victory (Nike), the serpent, her Medusa aegis and magical helmet. Her symbol is the owl, the bird of death and regeneration, as well as female wisdom, darkness, night, the moon and mystery. The helm is decorated with griffons and sphinxes, borderlands creatures who offer wisdom and riddles. On the statue base was illustrated the birth of Pandora, the progenitor of the race of women.

Even more powerful is her reclaimed aegis, shining with the power of the underworld. Athena is described wielding devastating power on the battlefield of Troy:

> She donned the stormy Aegis flashing far, adamantine, massy, a marvel to the Gods, whereon was wrought Medusa's ghastly head, fearful: strong serpents breathing forth the blast of ravening fire were on the face thereof. Crashed on the Queen's breast all the Aegis-links.[19]

Thus Athena reclaims her own: virgin and monster in one, clad in the feminine tokens of wisdom.

Sublimated Rage

> The Gorgon is a Western manifestation of the Great Primordial Mother who gives birth to all life and consumes her own creation.... The Gorgon expresses the reality that life feeds on life within cycles of transformation. She is a threshold guardian, a plumed serpent, whose apotropaic visage, with the large eyes of a predator, the grinning mouth of a skull, fangs and protruding tongue, resembles the masks of other wrathful deities and protective ancestors venerated throughout the world. For the ancient Greeks, such cosmic powers in female form were considered threatening to societal order. Her decapitation at the hands of the Greek hero Perseus functioned as a blood ritual for the new male rites of passage.[20]

Medusa, like many bird-women and serpent-women, is a creature of the borderlands, guardian of the threshold and of hidden wisdom. She embodies the fertile young woman combined with the death-crone of the underworld, protector and protected as one. Medusa is often pictured with brass wings, symbolizing her freedom and dynamic movement between realms. Her snakes offer the revered all-seeing eyes.

She is likewise associated with water, as she is the daughter of sea gods. In Ovid's *Metamorphoses*, Perseus lays Medusa's head down to unchain Andromeda, and the head creates the first coral.

> The fresh sea-weed, with living spongy cells, absorbed the monster's power and at its touch hardened, its fronds and branches stiff and strange. The Nymphae Pelagi [Sea-nymphs] tried the magic on more weed and found to their delight it worked the same, and sowed the changeling seeds back on the waves. Coral still keeps that nature; in the air it hardens, what beneath the sea has grown a swaying plant, above it, turns to stone.[21]

Among the ancient Greeks, Medusa's head was a symbol of warning, of driving off evil spirits. It guarded temples and sacred places (always bodiless), with gnashing teeth and protruding tongue.

> In Hesiod's *Theogony* (275 et seq.) and in the *Odyssey* (XI, 633–5), Medusa is the guardian of terrifying places, either the nocturnal borders of the world or the under-

world. She reappears in this role in Dante's *Divine Comedy* (Inferno, IX, 55–7) and Milton's *Paradise Lost* (II, 611). Guarding the doorway to the world of the dead, she prevents the living from entering.[22]

Prometheus Bound likewise describes "the snake-haired Gorgons, loathed of mankind, whom no one of mortal kind shall look upon and still draw breath."[23] These are guardians, barriers for those who mean harm. In ancient Libya, the Medusa head was found on shields, ovens, town walls, and buildings to ward off enemies and malicious spirits.[24]

In modern times, the image of Medusa has regained much of its original power as the face of subsumed female wrath, decapitated by the patriarchy. "Female will is embedded in female power, which is under present conditions the earliest and profoundest prototype of absolute power."[25] As George comments, "Medusa's face reflects her anger over the ways in which the patriarchal mentality has violated, castrated, desexualized, and disempowered her as the queen of the serpent mysteries."[26] In a 1986 article called "Ancient Gorgons: A Face for Contemporary Women's Rage," Emily Erwin Culpepper wrote that "the Amazon Gorgon face is female fury personified. The Gorgon/Medusa image has been rapidly adopted by large numbers of feminists who recognize her as one face of our own rage."[27]

Culpepper speaks of channeling the deep mythic power as protection. She describes fighting off a stranger's attack with a terrible, ferocious stare, the face of fury, the face of the dark goddess: "bursting, contorting with terrible teeth, flaming breath, erupting into ridges and contortions of rage, hair hissing." As she adds, "What I saw in the mirror is a Gorgon, a Medusa, if *ever* there was one."[28]

Medusa is the face of feminine fury, banished to the underworld by frightened mortals. However, this goddess can reemerge in all of us in times of need: "The Gorgon has much vital, literally life-saving information to teach women about anger, rage, power, and the release of the determined aggressiveness sometimes needed for survival."[29]

When women today dream of Medusa, they are seeing this archetypal image of frozen rage, cut off from the self and longing to scream.

> Her unbidden appearance is often experienced by women today as a terrifying and uncontrolled eruption of a certain powerful kind of energy into consciousness. She is one who is present in the fierce struggles faced by many women. Her mythic presence is felt when a woman faces a decision on abortion, an incest memory, rage, child abuse, depression, body dysfunction, or eating disorder. She erupts through the cracks in our psyches during each of these events, and she works her way into our bodies.[30]

The gorgon Medusa was sometimes veiled as the unknowable future, and to look upon her face was to see one's own death, and thus be turned to stone. "Once one fully faces the Medusa, she (or he) is initiated into the realms of the Powers, her entire life and consciousness transmute, and she can never quite go back to the illusions of her former life."[31] Women cannot cower from the future, the raging, frightened self. Instead they must quest for it, learn from it, and integrate it into their own personalities in order to find wholeness.

CHAPTER 14

The Elixir of Life: Reward

The Lion's Whisker (Sudan)

There was once a second wife who married a wealthy man with one son already. The son was rude to her, kicking her and refusing to do a single task to help her, from picking up his clothes to bringing water for the crops. She had to do it all herself. Her husband ordered the boy to behave, and he seemed to obey, but in private, things only grew worse. In desperation, the young wife fled to the village elder. "My stepson hates me!" she cried. "When we're alone together, he calls me names, and flings rocks at my back when no one is looking. What am I to do?"

The elder considered. "What do you want to happen?"

"I want him to love me as part of the family. I want us to be friendly."

"This is powerful magic indeed," said the wiseman. "But it is possible. How much do you desire this?"

"Oh, I will do anything!" the woman vowed.

"Very well. Bring me the whisker of a living lion."

"What!"

"With it, I can construct a potion that will make your stepson love you. But it cannot be made without the whisker."

"Very well." Though her heart was beating like a drum, the young woman straightened proudly. "I will."

The next morning, she carried a huge piece of raw meat down to the river where lions drank. She hid behind a tree and waited. After many hours of nerves and patience, a lion ambled down to the river. He sniffed at the raw meat she had laid there, and then finally gulped it down. He raised his tawny, golden-maned head. The young wife held her breath. Clearly, he knew that she was there, watching. At last, the mighty lion moved slowly back into the forest and disappeared.

For days and then weeks, the young woman repeated this pattern. Each day the lion came. Each day he ate the meat. Every few days, she moved the meat a hair closer to herself and watched and waited, unmoving.

Finally, one day she sat beside the lion as he ate. He ignored her. The next day, willing her hand not to shake, she reached out and gently pulled a whisker from his face with a single light tug. She remained there, quite still, as he shook himself and walked away.

Face aglow, the young woman brought the whisker to the wiseman. "Now you can make the potion!"

He smiled proudly at her. "Ah, but a woman as brave and patient as you needs no potion to charm her stepson. You've already learned how to do it."

So the woman went home and coaxed her stepson with patience, with diligence, with strength to accept her small kindnesses, to talk to her, to share his concerns. And within a year, they had become a happy family, just as she had wished.

"The Lion's Whisker" is interesting for its role reversals, both in the kindly stepmother and the cruel stepson. While these traits appear in fractured fairytales and modern retellings, they are less common in the classic stories themselves. This folktale is also notable for its universality, appearing across Asia and other cultures. In some, the woman must coax a battle-weary husband back to his family and away from his brutal memories of war. Why is this tale so common?

The heroine's goal is to become a complete mother, resplendent with power. If her family is shattered, by either grief or remarriage, she cannot become whole without assembling the pieces. In the case of this tale, the child is not hers until the end. She, likely an untried maiden, has inherited this family. She cannot succeed simply through kindness; she must quest for the wisdom to become a true mother to her stepchild. In so doing, she earns his love with effort and patience in a story reminiscent of our everyday struggles.

Sometimes claiming one's reward is a dramatic moment — seizing Tam Lin off his horse, or claiming the prince in marriage. Other times, it is the quieter love and acceptance which makes one a wife or mother in more than name. The male hero quests to conquer the tyrant, the heroine quests to create a family.

There are many exceptions. Heroes of both genders quest for sacred objects, for wisdom, for answers to riddles and inner growth. But through it all, both heroes are growing toward adulthood and balance.

The questing heroine comes to realize that this is more than the quest for a wedding veil, to be Mrs. Somebody. Absorbing the dark goddess teaches her to defend her children with a wildcat's fury, to stare down fears, Medusa-like, to listen to the aches and pains of whimpering Ereshkigal, deep within herself.

By listening to the whole self, and to others, she becomes a wisewoman and nurturing queen.

Women's capacity to nurture is often exploited, as culture assumes that this is a natural drive, requiring no reciprocation. Thus the mother is cast in the constant role of self-sacrifice. As others take mothering for granted, she does likewise, not realizing how much of the self she's giving up by denying her own needs.

Too many girls marry expecting to become instant wives and instant mothers. "How can the mere signing of a document change a life?" asks Nancy Friday in *My Mother/My Self.* "Young girls imagine being married so long, when reality comes, it seems a dream. It took me time to become a wife, to give up my fantasies of what marriage should be."[1] If the woman is not the perfect mother overnight, she's seen as a failure. Many tales reflect that this is a process of patience and learning, growing through mistakes to find what's needed. As Campbell notes, "The agony of breaking through personal limitations is the agony of spiritual growth. Art, literature, myth and cult, philosophy, and ascetic disciplines are instruments to help the individual past his limiting horizons into spheres of ever-expanding realization."[2]

In the Celtic tale "Fair Exchange," a woman's baby is switched with a changeling. She feels sorry for the crying, sickly child, and cares for it tenderly. Still she is determined to get her own back. After seeking advice from a wisewoman, she snatches the Fairy Queen's bridle as the woman rides past. Cleverly, she offers the queen a gift in the form of the beautiful, healthy child she has raised. Only when the fairy queen accepts does the woman lay down her condition: the fairy queen shall have her son back when the woman's own son is restored. The woman returns home with her own child and the blessings of the fairies on them both.[3]

In this case, as with "The Lion's Whisker," patience, understanding, and love are the keys.

> The full round, the norm of the monomyth, requires that the hero shall now begin the labor of bringing the runes of wisdom, the Golden Fleece, or his sleeping princess, back into the kingdom of humanity, where the boon may rebound to the renewing of the community, the nation, the planet, or the ten thousand worlds.[4]

For the heroine, this is not the king's abstract intellect; it is the nurturing wisdom of the queen, guiding her people through strength, compassion, and love. Sometimes she only brings teachings and the dual knowledge of the underworld. And sometimes she indeed brings the "runes of wisdom" or the water of life that will heal the dying leader.

Gazing down from the heavens, Lia descended to earth and lived among the people of the Goanna tribe of Australia. They had only mudholes for water sources, and life was difficult. When Lia married the chief, she discovered something surprising. He never seemed dry or thirsty, or even dusty. He was always washed and in good spirits, without cracked lips or dust-caked skin.

Each day the men left the village, explaining that they had great responsibilities. Each day, the women dug in the hard ground for roots to feed their families, toiling all day with a single waterskin to share among them all.

Only in the setting sun's light did the men return, carrying one skin of water for the women to drink the following day.

One day, after the men had left, Lia gathered the women. "The Mother made enough water for all," she said. "We must find more for ourselves."

The women hunted through the mountains, but didn't find a drop. When they returned covered in mountain dust, the men blustered and yelled until the women feared for their lives.

The next day, no one would go with her, so Lia went alone. She climbed and climbed, and when she could go no further, she curled up to sleep.

The Tukonee, tiny people of the cave, swarmed around her, and told her to bring all the women up the mountain. The next day, she led all the women up the mountain, and thrust her digging stick into the crevices between boulders, deep enough to touch the mountain's heart.

The entire mountain shook, as the stick sprang from Lia's hands and burrowed deeper into the earth.

Water exploded from the stone and cascaded down the mountainside, down to the dry desert, where it pooled into the Murumbidgee River. The women eagerly drank, water cool in their hot mouth and dry throats. They splashed each other and poured water over their tight, dry skin. They laughed and hugged. They cried tears that blended into the new, life-giving river. And then they crossed the river and built a village of women, and never returned to the stingy men.[5]

Here, Lia saves not one child but all the women of her village, seizing as reward the life-giving water. She, like those who seek the water of life or the medicine that will heal the dying king, is deliverer of the grail, and of her people who see her triumph each day in the flowing water.

CHAPTER 15

Of Carpets and Slippers:
Flight and Return

Baba Yaga (Russia)

Once upon a time, a peasant man lived deep in the Russian woods. He had twin children, a boy and a girl. As his wife had died, he remarried, but the new wife mistreated his two children and fed them only scant scraps. One day, when her husband had left, she decided to do away with them forever. "You're such good children," she said. "Today you must go and help my grandmother, who will give you all manner of treats."

The sister flinched at this sudden kindness. "I don't trust her," she whispered to her brother. "Let's go visit our own grandmother on the way."

"Oh, my dears," their grandmother said when they arrived. "That isn't her grandmother living in the woods; it's Baba Yaga, a terrible witch who feeds on human flesh!"

"What shall we do?" the boy asked.

"I'll pack you some food to keep you safe on the trip. Here's bread, a little meat, and a bottle of milk. Guard yourselves and remember to treat everyone you meet kindly."

As the children ventured deeper into the forest, they came across a hut walking about all on its own, high up on a pair of chicken legs. As they watched, the house settled before them. "Who's there?" a creaky voice called.

Taking their grandmother's advice, the girl replied. "Our stepmother sent us. Is there anything we might do to help you?"

Baba Yaga, bloated and surprisingly large for her immense age, opened the door. Stringy gray hair lay sparsely on her head, and her apron bore suspicious bloodstains. Looking them over, she licked her lips. "Indeed, you must both help me. If you work hard, I'll reward you. Otherwise, you'll go into the cooking pot."

She told the girl to sit by the fire and spin (a task she'd never learned to do) and sent the boy to collect water in a sieve. Then she curled up for a nap on her enormous bed. As the girl combed the wool flat and wondered how to begin, she heard a squeak by her knee. Three tiny mice sniffed about, fruitlessly seeking crumbs. Sympathizing despite her own miserable plight, the girl dropped them the heel of her bread.

"Thank you," the mice squeaked. "Now, wind the wool around the spindle and we'll advise you — we've watched the witch spin here every night, though she's not as kind as you."

"Thank you so much," the girl said. "Can you help me escape?"

"Not us — we're indoor mice. But the cat leaves often enough. You should ask him. Stay outside when you do — we don't want him in here with us."

The girl slipped to the door as Baba Yaga snored. "Cat, are you there?"

"Indeed," said the cat. "And there's such a funny sight, you've no idea. That boy keeps drawing water with a sieve, but it all leaks out before he can walk a step!"

"Oh dear. Brother!" He hurried over from his pointless task. "Stop the holes up with moss," she told him. "It's the only way." He tried this and found he could carry water and fill the witch's cooking pot easily. "You're so wise," she told the cat and gave it the milk.

"You're generous to share your food," the cat said. "The witch only gives me kicks."

"Do you know how I can escape?"

The cat stretched its narrow spine. "I stay close to home. But ask the dog. He may have some advice."

She knelt before the dog, and offered him her piece of meat. "Can you help us escape the witch?"

The dog licked her in thanks for the gift. "Steal her comb and mirror that sit in the sewing chest beside the fire. When she pursues you, cast them behind," he said. "It may slow her." The girl took the comb and mirror, hiding them in her empty pockets.

The next morning, the witch ordered the boy to chop wood for her kettle and the girl to spin. The moment she left, the children took the comb and mirror and ran away as fast as they could. The dog snarled at them but they threw him the last of their meat and he ate quietly. Tree branches tore at them, but the girl tied them back with her hair ribbon.

"Are you spinning?" Baba Yaga called as she walked in.

"Yes, Grandmother," the cat called from where he sat on the spinning wheel.

Baba Yaga walked in and found the cat tangling and snarling the yarn (without the mice helping, the cat couldn't help but make a mess). "The children have run away," she screeched. "Why didn't you stop them?"

"In all my time here, you've never even given me a cheese rind, but the girl fed me milk."

The witch hurried after the children, and came upon the dog, eating. "Why didn't you stop her," she demanded, kicking him.

"In all these years, you haven't given me so much as a bread crust," the dog said. "The children gave me meat."

Baba Yaga glared at the tree. "Why didn't you trap her in your branches?"

"You've never tied so much as a string on me, but the girl wrapped me in a bright ribbon."

So Baba Yaga had to chase the children alone, and she mounted her flying mortar and pestle. The children heard her swishing through the air and threw down the mirror. An enormous lake sprang up behind them. The witch knelt beside the lake and drank and drank until all of it was gone.

Then the girl tossed the comb down and a thicket of thorns rose. Baba Yaga searched and searched for a passage, but there was none to be found, and she had to return to her hut.

At last, the children reached home and told their father what had happened. He banished their stepmother, and they all lived happily from that day on.[1]

In the underworld (or in this case, the witch's hut), the heroine learns all manner of insights. Still, the tricky part is returning to the world of life. Campbell notes:

> All these different mythologies give us the same essential quest. You leave the world that you're in and go into a depth or into a distance or up to a height. There you come to what was missing in your consciousness in the world you formerly inhabited. Then comes the problem either of staying with that, and letting the world drop off, or returning with that boon and trying to hold onto it as you move back into your social world again. That's not an easy thing to do.[2]

The wicked witch or shadow figure can be quite seductive — If the heroine stays, she could learn magic enough to rule the world, magic beyond that which her childself is prepared to absorb. She could live in Baba Yaga's hut forever, crafting potions and cackling to herself. This is why the dark side is so seductive, a self-made prison in which her darker impulses, in the form of the witch, try to trap her.

Baba Yaga is benevolent and terrifying, wisewoman and monster. "Baba" means grandmother, or possibly "pelican," suggesting her birdlike goddess nature. "Yaga," however, connotes "disease," "fright," or "wrath."[3] She offers a wise power the sheltered heroine has never experienced; like shallow Athena confronting Medusa, or Psyche before death's throne, she is mesmerized.

At the same time, tiny voices persuade her to escape. The animal helpers represent the rational, daylight sides of the self, the parts of consciousness who have observed how to spin by watching when the heroine didn't even know it, the tiny glimpse that noted the witch's magical comb and mirror. "Don't keep filling water in a sieve," they say. "Find a way around the problem. Step back and consider your options rather than pouring in more energy. Then you'll find your way." These powers of observation are powerful weapons beneath the heroine's consciousness, which she cultivates while in the underworld. She learns to observe, to make friends, to give of herself and her own sustenance. Only then, as one who mothers others, can she battle free of her own confinement.

Like the Armless Maiden, the fleeing girl saves her childself, in this case the little brother who faithfully follows her through her adventures. The longer she stays in the unconscious, the more risk she will become a deadly witch herself, gleefully feasting on her brother and thus destroying her own innocence. Often the heroine must guard those less fortunate, rescuing loved ones from the dark underworld of despair or confinement. If this lost soul is not her child or young brother, it may be her rationality (father) or her animus and emotional warmth (lover). Sometimes it may be an animal helper, one who offers an outside, thoughtful perspective. In each case, she is not just reuniting her family. She is reuniting her self.

Once a woman wanted a child so badly that she gazed up at the sky. "Master Sun, only give me a child and you may take her back when she turns 12." The sun heard her plea and granted her a lovely girl, whom she named Maroula. When she turned 12, the sun saw her gathering water and whisked her away to his palace, with its beautiful garden. However, Maroula was miserable there. She would cry and tear at her face, and then assure the sun when he returned at night that she had only scratched herself on the rosebushes. At last, she confessed that she wanted her mother. The sun took pity on her and gave her a deer to ride home, and many gold coins.

The deer grew hungry, so Maroula sat in a cypress tree while he grazed. The daughter of a drakaena (ogress) arrived, gathering water. But when the girl bent over the pool, and saw Maroula's reflection from the overhanging tree, she thought it her own. "I'm too pretty to gather water," she told her mother. The younger sisters fared the same. Then the drakaena came out herself to discover what her daughters had seen. When she found Maroula, she decided to eat her for dinner. "Finish baking your bread first," Maroula said. "Then I'll come down." She called the deer and they hurried away. The drakaena gave chase, but they slipped into Maroula's mother's house and slammed the door on the drakaena, though the doe's tail got caught in the door. Her mother sewed the tail back on, and they all lived happily ever after.[4]

In this version, Maroula encourages the ogress to wait, to take things in the proper order — a potent tool that Maroula employs as distraction. She too uses mirror-magic to perplex the enemy and an animal helper to carry her home.

Though enlightened from her adventure, she is still a child, rather than a Beauty or Psyche, ready for love. She returns home with new tools (the deer and the gold) that will aid her when she is ready to venture forth again.

Stonewalling

This story is categorized as Aarne-Thompson 313H: Magic Flight from Witch, but, as with many tales, the familiar elements of the story are just as important as its overall structure. The Motif Index of Folk Literature catalogues in this way, focusing on such elements as the slipper test, the forbidden chamber, or disenchantment with a kiss. An index of these appears at the end of the book, along with selections from the Aarne-Thompson Index.

The escape with tools like comb and mirror is a popular pattern throughout the world, known as Motif D672: The Obstacle Flight. While the tools vary, they are women's symbols — food and drink, circles and cups. Like Athena with helm and aegis, the heroine must prove she has mastered the tools of the goddess and their shapechanging magic in order to snatch power from her enemy.

In the following Italian version of "The Master-Maid," the heroine goes a step further and tricks her ogress mother into giving her the knowledge to carry her and her prince far away.

> After the ogress had eaten, her daughter gave her wine to drink, and made her drunk. Then she said: "My mother, what must I do to get away from here? Not that I want to go, for I wish to stay with you; but I want to know just out of curiosity. Tell me!"
>
> "What you must do to get away from here!" said the ogress. "You must enchant everything that there is here, so that I shall lose time. I shall call, and instead of you, the chair, the cupboard, the chest of drawers, will answer for you. When you do not appear, I will ascend. You must take the seven balls of yarn that I have laid away. When I come and do not find you, I shall pursue you; when you see yourself pursued, throw down the first ball, and then the others. I shall always overtake you until you throw down the last ball."

All this, the daughter did, stalling her mother with the enchanted furniture, which reassured that all was well. At last, however, the ogress was no longer fooled and gave chase.

> When the ogress had nearly overtaken them, Snow-white-fire-red [for that was the maiden's name] threw down the first ball, and suddenly there arose a lofty mountain. The ogress was not disturbed; she climbed and climbed until she almost overtook the two again. Then Snow-white-fire-red, seeing her near at hand, threw down the second ball, and there suddenly appeared a plain covered with razors and knives. The ogress, all cut and torn, followed after the lovers, dripping with blood.
>
> When Snow-white-fire-red saw her near again, she threw down the third ball,

and there arose a terrible river. The ogress threw herself into the river and continued her pursuit, although she was half dead. Then another ball, and there appeared a fountain of vipers, and many other things. At last, dying and worn out, the ogress stopped and cursed Snow-white-fire-red.... Then the ogress could stand it no longer, and died in great anguish.[5]

This is the tale of Snow-white-fire-red, like the Grimms' "The Master Maid," in which the heroine who lives in the ogre's castle advises the prince on how to complete his tasks, and finally escapes with him. The fairytale index names this AT 313 The Girl as Helper in the Hero's Flight. As shown by the Baba Yaga tale (a subset of this one, as AT 313H), the girl is more than helper: she is rescuer, doer, actor. As Jurich notes, "It is the 'helper' who initiates all the plans by which the 'hero' *is saved*; it is *she* who succeeds in that daring and courageous attempt — and frequently succeeding *in spite of* the male's stupid miscomprehension and frustrating interferences."[6] Thus the AT label implies the hero is the central figure, rather than a near-bystander dragged on the heroine's quest to face the dark of the ogre's lair and escape before its dark power engulfs her.

Snow-white-fire-red is poised between maiden and queen, as indicated by her name (the innocence of white snow, the maternal and royal crimson of triumphant mother). As an emerging goddess, she knows she can no longer wait at home while her prince needs rescuing. Snow-white-fire-red tricks the ogress and steals her own knowledge to escape her. As she has absorbed the woman's power, she is free to leave, to become a queen in her own right. The objects used represent the tools of the intellect, women's power of voice, of weaving, of the home. Snow-white-fire-red causes the land itself to battle her mother, as mountain and plains block her passage. Then comes the more potent goddess power of water and the regenerative serpent. With these, the ogress is thwarted.

In the same way, Baba Yaga's heroine steals feminine power from the world of the unconscious: comb and mirror. These feminine symbols become feminine barriers of forest and lake. The lake is a reflection that Baba Yaga must conquer to pass, by drinking it and absorbing her deadly reflective shadow back into herself. The forest, however, is a barrier made up of the heroine's defenses, bolstered by her new supernatural knowledge. It protects her home and loved ones from the witch, using her own power against her. Like Medusa's head, it screams, "Come no closer or I will strike you." Like a dark impulse of the psyche defeated by unrelenting will, Baba Yaga must fade back into the shadows.

One luckless Persian prince named Shapur was captured by the enemy Shah Kisra. He was taken to the women's quarters of the palace, where the women bound his hands and sewed him up in a donkey's skin, whereupon he was cast into a dark dungeon with only bread and water. A beautiful damsel, slave to the Kisra's wife, took pity on him. He begged her to bring him warm milk when she secretly visited, so she could soak the donkeyskin in it and thus render it supple. Though fearful of discovery, the girl faithfully did so. At the end of two weeks, the hide was soft enough for Shapur to emerge. He blessed the girl and vowed to be her slave.

She told him there would be a festival in Rum the next day and promised to have horses waiting. Indeed, they were, along with weapons and jewels, and so the couple stole away together. Safely on the way to Iran, they summoned Shapur's army and thus defeated Kisra. Shapur became one of the greatest of Sasanian rulers, with the damsel always by his side. He called her *Dilāfruz-i-Farrukhpāi,* or "Lucky-footed Luster of the Heart."[7]

One of the most chilling hero-flights is that of Medea, fleeing with her lover Jason and the golden fleece. When her own brother Absyrtus pursues them, she kills him and cuts his body into small pieces. As they sail, she proceeds to leave a trail of pieces behind the ship, forcing her pursuers to stop and retrieve each piece so that Absyrtus might be shown the proper burial rites.

In this act, Medea is abandoning her feminine lineage, in which the mother's family was sacred and the priestess was supreme. Medea literally dismembers this aspect of her life, giving the sacred golden fleece she protects to the solar hero Jason, in return for his marrying her. She betrays her priestesshood and her beliefs, all for love. Thus, his later betrayal, like Theseus's abandonment of Ariadne, is all the crueler.

Refusal

Sometimes the heroine is seduced by the magic and safety of the innermost cave, and can't bear returning to the world of life. In those cases, she may need persuasion or the agency of another to return, like the tiny clay figures who aid Inanna. These are once again aspects of the psyche, parts of the personality that aid in freeing the self from entrapment.

The sun goddess Amaterasu, "Shining Heaven," is still worshiped today as the principal deity of the Japanese Shinto religion. She is the symbol of the Japanese people and their unity, and her emblem, the rising sun, appears on the Japanese flag. In one tale, she quarreled with her brother, the storm god Susano-o. After he destroyed everything around him, she withdrew into a dark cave and let winter descend upon the world. Darkness covered the earth, and demons ruled.

The gods tried all manner of tricks and persuasion to coax her out. All failed. Finally, the goddess Uzume positioned herself at the cave entrance and began dancing erotically. The laughter from the other gods grew so loud that Amaterasu grew curious and tugged back the boulder blocking the cave entrance, just a crack. However, the gods had prepared for this and hung a mirror there.

The sun goddess, who had never beheld herself before, was stunned by the glorious beauty of her own reflected image. While she gazed, awestruck, the other gods reached through the crack and tugged her out, bringing life and hope back to the world.

Here the great goddess undergoes a symbolic "death," by vanishing into a cave. Only the divinity of her own beauty and godliness can restore her to her worshippers, by the gods tugging her through the crack in symbolic rebirth. Cave and mirror play their parts, as Uzume is like the ribald goddess teasing the distraught Demeter, coaxing her to revel once more in the world.

Goddesshood and Wholeness

CHAPTER 16

Forever Cycling: Rebirth

Changing Woman (Navaho)

First Man and First Woman dwelt on earth and were lonely. The world teemed with monsters, and there was no source of protection from them. One day, First Man saw that a great dark cloud had covered Ch'ool'í'í, Giant Spruce Mountain, so he climbed it to see what he would find. At the top, covered in rainbows, lay a tiny girl. He brought her home, and she grew into an adult in just a few days, flickering from girl to woman to crone and then back again. They called her Changing Woman. When Talking God, who dwelt above, saw that she was grown, he garbed her all in white, with a skirt and headdress of glimmering shells.

However, First Man and First Woman left her, and Changing Woman was lonely. One day, as she climbed Ch'ool'í'í, she gazed above and wondered if the sun might be a person like herself. She lay on a flat warm rock for four days, feet to the east and legs comfortably spread, letting the sun's rays warm her. In four more days she gave birth to two boys, who in four days beyond that had grown to the size of 12-year-olds. Talking God came and trained them, and the boys grew fast and strong.

"Who is our father?" they asked one day.

"You have no father," Changing Woman said. "That cactus over there might as well be him. Now here, if you are grown now, you can hunt with these new bows. But don't leave sight of the house or go east."

But the boys headed straight in that direction.

Raven and Buzzard, Magpie and Coyote saw them go, and they told the monsters that two strong young boys were hunting. That day, Yé'iitsoh the Big Giant came to Changing Woman's hut. As she heard him come, she hid the boys under a pile of sticks.

"What a fine-smelling corncake you've baked," Big Giant said.

159

"Go away, by no means is it for you," Changing Woman retorted.

"That's all right, I would rather eat boys. Where are you keeping them?"

"All of you monsters have eaten all the people. There's no one here."

"Then who made the footprints?"

"I made them myself with my hand, to pass the long hours. I pretend that others live here who made the prints, who I can talk to." And she demonstrated in the dust with the side of her hand. Big Giant studied the marks, which seemed quite like the old ones, so he went away.

Changing Woman looked outside and saw more monsters coming. So she cast a set of magical hoops in each direction: white to the east, blue to the south, yellow to the west, black to the north. At once, a great gale surrounded the hut, blowing all directions so fiercely that no monsters could enter.

Inside the hut, the twins knew she had no more hoops to protect them. They felt ashamed that they had disobeyed their mother's orders and brought Naayéé', the Alien Monsters, on her. They stole out of the hut before dawn so the monsters would leave her alone.

They met Spider Woman in her cave, who told them that the Sun Jóhonaa'éí was their father. She instructed them about the four dangerous places they must cross to reach him, and gave them a pair of hoops with eagle feathers as protection.

The boys quested past all the obstacles where they proved themselves to their father and completed their warrior training. He tested them and gifted them with mighty armor and weapons. Then they returned to earth and slew the Naayéé', the four great monsters that had threatened their home. At last they returned to Changing Woman, and she sang with jubilation.

However, hundreds of monsters still remained, and the boys feared that they couldn't defeat them all. They returned to Jóhonaa'éí their father to beg his help a second time. "The first time I helped you for nothing," Jóhonaa'éí said. "But this time, I wish your help in return. I am lonely in the sky, and wish your mother to make a home for me in the west, where I can rest when I am weary."

"Of course," said Monster Slayer, the elder son.

"No!" said Born for Water, the younger. "She must make her own decisions. We will bring her your proposal and beg her to accept it. But the choice is hers."

Jóhonaa'éí went into a curtained chamber and removed five hoops: black, blue, yellow, white, and one multicolored and glittering with mica. He also gave them knives and hailstones in the same colors. "Take these to your mother," he said. "She will know what to do."

Changing Woman did not. "I have no knowledge of these," she said. "And Jóhonaa'éí does not know me." She gazed wistfully at the sky. "Once I dreamed of companionship and lay on the mountain. Once I felt your father's warmth inside me. But since that time, he has never visited me, and I have only known him from afar." And she wept.

At last, she took the hoops and knives and hailstones. She rolled the black hoop to the east, and tossed the black hailstone through it. In the south, she did this with the blue. To the west, the yellow. To the north, the white. The multicolored hoop she threw straight up, and the five knives with it, blowing a mighty breath behind them. Clouds gathered overhead.

The world stormed for four days, a storm so vicious that all the monsters and everyone not in Changing Woman's hut were blown away. The only ones still living were Old Age, Cold, Poverty, and Hunger, but they pled their usefulness, so Monster Slayer let them live. Then Jóhonaa'éí the Sun came to earth to congratulate his children and take back the magic weapons he'd once given them, for now was a time of peace.

Changing Woman made her way to the summit of Ch'ool'í'í, Giant Spruce Mountain, where she had once lain, wishing for a consort, and where she had first felt the sun's warmth penetrate her body. As she sat there recollecting, Jóhonaa'éí the Sun arrived in a blur of heat and sat beside her. He sought to embrace her, but she struggled to free herself. "Why do you molest me? I want no part of you!"

"But I want you," he said. "Come with me to the west and let us make a home there."

"That's not what I want. What right have you to ask?"

"Did I not arm your sons so they could slay Naayéé' the Alien Monsters? Have I not cared for your people?"

"It was not I who asked for these things," Changing Woman said. "You did them of your own will."

And he tried again to embrace her. "When our son Monster Slayer last came, he promised you to me."

"What do I care for another's promise? I am not his to give."

The Sun started to walk away but then turned to face her. "Please?" he said. "Come to the west and make a home with me, for I am lonely. All day I labor alone in the sky. What good is that? What good is male without female or female without male? What good are we parted?"

She paused. "I want my own house in the west," she said. "It must float on shimmering water, away from the shore. And I want shells: white and blue, with soapstone and turquoise, agate, jet. I want elk and buffalo and muskrat and deer and prairie dogs to keep me company while you are gone. Provide me these things and I will come."

"Who are you to demand all this," he asked, "and why should I honor it?"

"I will tell you why," she said.

"You are male and I am female.

"You are of the sky and I am of the earth.

"You are constant in your brightness but I must change with the seasons.

"You move across the heavens while I remain fixed.

"Remember that I allowed your rays within my body. Remember how I endured pain to bear your sons. Remember that I protected them and raised them to defend their people from the Alien Monsters.

"Remember that, dissimilar as we are, we are of one spirit. As unlike as we are, we are of equal worth. There can be no harmony in the universe if we are not at peace.

"If there is to be such unity, my needs are important as yours. My whims matter as yours do. I will give nothing that you do not give also. There is to be nothing less."

This is what Changing Woman said to the Sun on Ch'ool'í'í, Giant Spruce Mountain.

He considered for a long moment and then put his arm around her. And she did not pull away. He promised her all she wished. And together they dwelt in the west, in perfect harmony.[1]

To achieve the greatest success, the heroine becomes a "goddess" herself. In this way she achieves enormous power and becomes a guardian for the next generation. While this acknowledgement in the external world is more important to the male hero, many heroines achieve inner ascendancy and outer recognition together.

In *Diné bahané: The Navaho Creation Story*, Changing Woman ascends to the heavens to become the sun's wife, but only if he gives her autonomy, trust and respect. She becomes protectress of the human race, watching over them from far above as mother figure, guardian of girls' initiations into womanhood.

> When she has become elderly and infirm, she leans upon her curved walking staff and heads toward the east and the rising sun. After a while, she sees her young self approaching from a distance and when the two meet, they join and Changing Woman is reborn. It is this rebirth, given through her to all the Apache, that is celebrated in the ceremony of the Sunrise Dance. She is resiliency and renewal ... the mother of a people.[2]

Today, Changing Woman's tale is evoked in the Navaho and Apache womanhood ceremony, in which a girl "becomes Changing Woman," mother to her people. In a deerskin dress adorned by tinkling metal ornaments, the girl dances with an oak cane hung with feathers and colored ribbons in the four sacred directions, and when she grows old someday she can lean on it. She runs around this cane four times, capturing the four phases of her life and ensuring longevity. She goes about, blessing the infants and the sick; whatever wish is made at that time is certain to come true.[3] As one initiate is described, "Her face was solemn, and she showed none of the fatigue that surely she felt after more than six hours of ceremonial dancing. At these moments all were aware of a powerful presence within the girl — a woman's presence in the body of a young teenager."[4]

Initiation ceremonies are a powerful force throughout the world, guiding newcomers through the entire monomyth cycle from leaving home through death and apotheosis, as Changing Woman experiences. Central to this is the ordeal — the battle with the Self in the dark nadir of the cosmos.

> Again and again we find initiatory ordeals (battles with the monster, apparently insurmountable obstacles, riddles to be solved, impossible tasks, etc.), the descent to Hades or the ascent to Heaven.... [Their] content refers to a terrifyingly serious reality: initiation, that is, passing, by way of a symbolic death and resurrection, from immaturity to the spiritual age of the adult.[5]

This may involve a new family role, like becoming a grandmother, or getting a new job. It may be a significant birthday. For all these, we have small ceremonies — a cake, a shower, a card. Or sometimes we have the great ceremonies: a Quinceañera, Bat Mitzvah, first haircut, graduation. The most fundamental of these divide into separation, *liminality*, and re-incorporation: In an American wedding, the bride is isolated from men and surrounded by women like her bridesmaids. She dresses in white with a protective veil. After the ceremony, she and the groom enter the reception, reintroduced to their community as the new Mr. and Mrs.

Today, many cultures have abandoned initiation ceremonies, or softened them into Hallmark parties. Gone is the mentoring of the wisewomen, who teach young girls the road to adulthood. Still, another psychological gateway exists, sublimated below the surface of consciousness. As Estés notes:

> Because matrilineal lines of initiation — older women teaching younger women certain psychic facts and procedures of the wild feminine — have been fragmented and broken for so many women and over so many years, it is a blessing to have the archeology of the fairytale to learn from.[6]

This is the true meaning of descent and death: losing the old self in place of the new. Whether literal or symbolic isolation, this period offers us the chance to reinvent ourselves in our new form. "In the darkness, we take the risk of being torn apart in order to incorporate new energies, new powers. We risk the death of our old Selves, so that we may be reborn at her hands. [The Dark Goddess] teaches us to 'dis-member' and consciously 're-member' ourselves."[7]

A Different Initiation

Synonymous with initiation is rebirth — a return from death to life. Sometimes, this is symbolic. Eliza in "The Six Swans" sinks down in apparent death as soon as her task is complete, or Persephone returns to her mourning mother. Sometimes, however, this is far more literal as heroines descend into the underworld, returning in triumph and wisdom.

Joseph Campbell notes that this descent is common to all cultures, and to all genders:

> In the first stage of this kind of adventure, the hero leaves the realm of the familiar, over which he has some measure of control, and comes to a threshold, let us say, the edge of a lake or sea, where a monster of the abyss comes to meet him. There are then two possibilities. In a story of the Jonah type, the hero is swallowed and taken into the abyss to be later resurrected — a variant of the death-and-resurrection theme. The conscious personality here has come in touch with a charge of unconscious energy which it is unable to handle and must now suffer all the trials and revelations of a terrifying night-sea journey, while learning how to come to terms with this power of the dark and emerge, at last, to a new way of life.
>
> The other possibility is that the hero, on encountering the power of the dark, may overcome and kill it, as did Siegfried and St. George when they killed the dragon. But as Siegfried learned, he must then taste the dragon blood, in order to take to himself some of that dragon power. When Siegfried has killed the dragon and tasted the blood, he hears the song of nature. He has transcended his humanity and reassociated himself with the powers of nature, which are the powers of our life, and from which our minds remove us.[8]

The Chinook people were experiencing a winter harder than any before. It was time for spring, but snow up to a man's waist still blanketed the ground. Each night more snow fell. After much talk, one of the elders said, "Our grandfathers once said that if someone threw a stone at a bird, the snows would never end. Who has done it?"

At last, a terrified little girl confessed to the crime.

The chief decided she would be given to winter. They set her on a block of ice and floated it out into the current. The people all chanted and prayed for the snows to lift. A warm wind touched the earth, and in a few days, all the snow had melted. After a summer near the salmon stream, the people returned to their winter lodgings. A block of ice floated by, and on it was a dark spot. They dragged the ice block close with poles, and there was the girl! They warmed her with heavy blankets, and she soon awoke, well and healthy. From that day, she could walk barefoot on ice and snow. Thus the people named her Wah-kah-nee, "She drifts."[9]

Many of the Grimms' heroines are killed, but reappear as harps, birds, and magical guardians for their children. Each must risk herself completely on her quest, dying in order to be reborn more powerfully. This ultimate form of initiation answers the most primitive longings inside a woman as she travels from innocence to knowledge, light to darkness, and once again to light.

In a folktale from Kenya, Marwe and her brother were responsible for keeping monkeys from the bean fields. When monkeys ate all the beans, Marwe feared her parents' anger and thus killed herself. She journeyed into the underworld where she met an old woman, who identified herself as Marwe's guide. Marwe lived with the woman for many years, learning and doing chores. When Marwe missed her family above ground, the old woman took her to two pots and asked her whether she preferred hot or cold. "Cold," Marwe said. Her guide dipped her hands and feet into the cold pot and they emerged covered in jewels.

Thus Marwe returned to her overjoyed family. When the neighbors found how rich and beautiful she had become, they all sent their sons to be her suitors. But Marwe was captivated by the ugliest of all, a man named Sawoye who suffered from vicious skin diseases. Her time in the underworld had taught her to read men's hearts, and she knew he was best of all. The two married, and after the wedding night, Sawoye's disease vanished, revealing his handsomeness. The couple lived happily and wealthily with Marwe's jewels to support them both.

One might think their tale had ended, but Marwe's suitors grew jealous and murdered Sawoye one night.

Marwe, however, had already died and knew the underworld's secrets, including how to revive the dead. She recited magic incantations over her husband's body and revived him stronger than ever. He slew all the suitors when they returned to steal Marwe's wealth, and the couple lived happily for the rest of their lives. Since both had already died, they met their deaths without fear.[10]

This story has many lessons. Marwe, unlike her brother, begins the tale by atoning for her mistake. In the underworld she meets her mentor, the wisewoman who offers her supernatural knowledge along with beauty and wealth — Marwe descends a child and arises an adult, having gained mystic knowledge of death and the unconscious. Only thus has she earned adult beauty and a woman's dowry. This deep intuition she's gained teaches her to look beneath the surface and judge character rather than appearance. As with Beauty and the Beast tales, this insight is rewarded with a handsome husband. Marwe has learned to fight death rather than give in to despair, and with this power, she rescues her husband. Finally, they both have learned that death and the unconscious are natural rather than threatening. Thus, this simple fairytale teaches the twin powers of knowledge and faith.

CHAPTER 17

Apotheosis:
Mistress of Both Worlds

Demeter and Persephone (Greece)

Persephone was playing with the deep-bosomed daughters of Oceanus and gathering flowers over a soft meadow, roses and crocuses and beautiful violets, irises also and hyacinths and the narcissus.

As she spied a particularly lovely bloom and reached for it, the earth yawned open there in the plain of Nysa, and Great Hades, the Host of Many, leaped from it on his chariot drawn by immortal horses. He dragged her up onto on his golden car and bore her away lamenting. The heights of the mountains and the depths of the sea rang with her immortal voice, and her queenly mother heard her.

Bitter pain seized Demeter's heart, and she rent the covering upon her divine hair with her dear hands. Her dark cloak she cast down from both her shoulders and sped, like a wild bird, over the firm land and yielding sea, seeking her child. But no one would tell her the truth, neither god nor mortal man; and of the birds of omen none came with true news for her. Then for nine days queenly Demeter wandered the earth with flaming torches in her hands, so grieved that she would not taste ambrosia or the sweet draught of nectar. But when the tenth enlightening dawn had come, Hecate, with a torch, met her, and spoke to her and told her news: "Queenly Demeter, bringer of seasons and giver of good gifts, what god of heaven or what mortal man has rapt away Persephone and pierced with sorrow your dear heart? For I heard her voice, yet saw not with my eyes who it was. But I will tell you truly and shortly all I know."

When Demeter heard that her dark brother Hades had stolen her flower princess, the innocent jewel of her heart, her wrath was unappeasable. She avoided the gathering of the gods on high Olympus, and went to the towns and rich fields of men, disguising herself. And no one of men or deep-bosomed women knew her when they saw her, until she came to the house of wise Celeus who then was lord of fragrant Eleusis. Desperately sad, she sat by the Maiden Well, from which the local women drew water. And to them, she appeared an ancient woman cut off from childbearing and the gifts of Aphrodite. There the daughters of Celeus, son of Eleusis, met her.

They spoke kindly, and she followed them home. Demeter remained sad in the palace, until cheerful Iambe danced a lewd dance and brought a smile to her face.

The goddess became nurse to Demophoon, Celeus' baby son. She grew to love him so that she anointed him with ambrosia and breathed sweetly on him as she held him in her bosom. At night she would hide him like a brand in the heart of the fire, so he might never die. But one night, his mother spied this, and yanked her child from the flames.

Demeter scowled. "I would have made your dear son deathless and unaging all his days, and would have bestowed on him ever-lasting honor, but now he can in no way escape death and the fates. Yet shall unfailing honor always rest upon him, because he lay upon my knees and slept in my arms." As Demeter stood there, she took on her own aspect, beautiful and terrible at once. Beauty spread round about her, and a lovely fragrance wafted from her sweet-smelling robes, and from the divine body of the goddess a light shone afar, while golden tresses spread down over her shoulders, so that the strong house was filled with brightness as with lightning. As she departed, all the people built a great temple to honor her.

Demeter caused a most dreadful and cruel year for humanity; the ground would not make the seed sprout, for the rich-crowned goddess kept it hid. In the fields the oxen drew many a curved plough in vain, and much white barley was cast upon the land without avail.

All the gods pleaded with her to relent, but Demeter stubbornly rejected all their words. She vowed she would never set foot on fragrant Olympus nor let fruit spring from the ground until she beheld her own fair-faced daughter.

Now when all-seeing Zeus heard this, he sent Hermes to win Persephone back from grim Hades. When Hermes descended, he found the lord Hades in his house seated upon a couch, and his shy mate with him, much reluctant, because she yearned for her mother. Hades willingly sent Persephone home, but secretly offered her a pomegranate, and she ate a few of its seeds.

Great was Demeter's rejoicing as she embraced her daughter in the world above. Then bright-coiffed Hecate came near to them, and she too embraced the daughter of holy Demeter; from that time Hecate was minister and companion to Persephone.

However, having tasted the dark mysteries of the underworld, the girl had grown beyond flower-maiden and could not return to her past innocence. But

Demeter would not release her. At last, Zeus, guided by his mother, Rhea, found a compromise: Persephone reigned as queen of the underworld and wife to Hades for part of the year, and in spring she returned to Demeter.[1]

This story, retold from Homer's *Hymn to Demeter*, was reenacted each year as the Eleusinian Mysteries. For 2,000 years, the Greeks celebrated this legend of death and rebirth, as it reflected the cycles in their own lives. Initiates were sworn to secrecy, so we have scattered knowledge today of the rites as they were practiced. While a note of mourning appears in the rites of Demeter, there is also bawdy talk and joking. This ritual is not merely a hope for crops; it acknowledges the cycle of childbirth, marriage and death, with all its apparent hopes and fears.

Initiates were crowned with wreaths of myrtle and carried rods called bacchus, symbols of the ending of the old life and rebirth of the new. When the procession of worshippers reached Eleusis, they would fast, just as Demeter did when grieving over Persephone's abduction. For nine days, reflecting the nine days of Demeter's search, initiates reenacted Demeter's quest, gave sacrifices, and drank her sacred barley-water. Having sipped her holy drink by the site of Demeter's well, initiates filed into the *omphalos,* the cave or navel of the world. This represented the passage to the underworld. As the seekers entered the darkened Telesterion, the Greater Mysteries began. In a mystic drama, the part of the legend dealing with death was imparted. The initiates experienced fear in all its physical symptoms: cold sweats, tremors, and nausea, as the hallucinogenic barley drink coursed through them, and dreadful apparitions howled through the halls.[2]

After this terrible spectacle came a pleasing light, heralding the Goddess's arrival. The Mysteries culminated with the shout, "The queen of the dead herself has given birth in fire to a mighty son!"[3] With the acknowledgment of this birth came the knowledge that death leads to rebirth. The great destroyer, Hades, by giving Persephone a son, became her own and humanity's renewer. Finally, the initiates passed out of the firelit tunnels to reemerge into the meadows for dancing and feasts.

These annual Eleusinian Mysteries attracted thousands, both men and women. What accounts for the popularity of this myth? The mother is questing for a return to her status as fertility goddess and mother, seeking the joy stolen from her. This need echoes within all people who have lost their happiness and seek to reclaim it.

Persephone's dark moon passage carries her from terror and loss to a new sense of self; when she returns in the spring, she often is depicted holding a child. Being impregnated by the creative masculine creates new life in her, and thus, in all she guides through the mysteries.[4] As George notes, "She emerged as Kore, the maiden, carrying the newly-born life essence of a person's old self."[5] The initiates feel release from their fears of death, as they too emerge into life.

Circles

Persephone spends half her time as maiden and flower princess, helping Demeter as fertility goddess of the harvest. For the other half, she rules the dead as a crone. This dichotomy is perplexing, but less so if we understand the message contained here. Persephone is mistress of both life and death, using knowledge from one world to teach in the other. She is a true multifaceted and complete goddess.

In a lesser-known form of the tale, Persephone descends without Hades' brutality. When she, as innocent flower maid, discovers the wandering spirits of the dead, she worries to her mother that no one waits to usher them into the next world and ease their fears. Demeter admits that death is her realm, but adds that she must prioritize growth and the world of life. Upon hearing this, Persephone voluntarily descends to succor the lost souls.

Upon her daughter's departure, Demeter's loneliness pushes her into mourning, and she shrouds the earth with snow. Eventually, her grief immobilizes her, and she can only sit like a statue, waiting.

One day, crocus shoots spring from the ground, whispering among themselves that Persephone is returning. As the maiden arises from the underworld, Demeter greets her flower-princess joyfully, and her renewed energy revives all the plant life.

Each year, the pair reenact this ritual, symbolic of the death and rebirth of the dormant fields. To Demeter, this is a symbol of faith that releasing her daughter will lead to reunification, when her childself and guardian of the dead is ready to return.

In the strictly gender-segregated society of classical Greece, this story would have held special meaning for women. "The special bond of mother and daughter in the women's part of the segregated household must have often been rudely broken by a powerful father who snatched away a beloved daughter into a marriage."[6] This shattering of the family must have been experienced like rape for mother and daughter as the latter was torn wailing away. Demeter responds to this violence by withholding her fertility from the earth, shutting herself away and mourning, and then questing for her lost innocent self. Only when this self has experienced death (and, often, once she has birthed Hades' child) does she return to the world of her childhood, in her endless circle of seasons.

Neumann describes the true mystery of the tale: "The daughter becomes identical with the mother; she becomes a mother and is so transformed into Demeter. Precisely because Demeter and Kore are archetypal poles of the Eternal Womanly, the mature woman and the virgin, the mystery of the Feminine is susceptible of endless renewal."[7]

Estés writes, "This is our meditation practice as women, calling back the dead and dismembered aspects of ourselves, calling back the dead and dismembered aspects of life itself. The one who re-creates from that which has died is always a double-sided archetype. The Creation Mother is always the Death Mother and vice versa."[8] Persephone is maiden and flower-goddess, death-crone and queen of the damned. This duality does not represent a split, but a converging; Persephone returns each spring and dies each autumn because she has mastered both worlds.

In the Homeric hymn, she is always called Kore (maiden), until her return from the underworld, when she is finally called Persephone (destroyer or slayer). There is one exception. When Zeus refers to her annual descent, he names her Kore, reminding her that each pilgrimage requires starting from an innocent state, as an initiate willing to surrender herself to the mysteries. Initiation is a liminal state, outside one's normal experience, and must be repeated throughout a lifetime.[9] Just as the judges over the dead were once mortal men, Persephone uses her wisdom of secrets from the underworld to aid the world above. Her compassion, gained from the earthly world, brings a spark of hope and mercy to the land of death.

Estés concludes by saying, "Because of this dual nature, or double-tasking, the great work before us is to learn to understand what around and about us and what within us must live, and what must die. Our work is to apprehend the timing of both; to allow what must die to die, and what must live to live."[10] Indeed, the final stage of the journey is understanding — both understanding the nature of the world and understanding the mortality that awaits us all. The mistress of both worlds comprehends the delicate balance between innocence and experience, death and life.

Mother of Life and Death

The seven goddesses known as Matrkas, or mothers, are sent by Indra to destroy the child Karttikeya. However, upon seeing him, they are so overcome with tenderness that their breasts flow with milk. The fierce goddess Kali, after slaying the demon Daruka, can likewise only be appeased by suckling a pair of babes, once again linking nurturing and destruction.[11] "Kali's lower right hand, though it ends in bloody talons, makes the gesture of dispelling fear. Her feet symbolize not only conquest, but mercy and protection; her right foot rests over Shiva's heart, so that the picture could be taken to represent the complete surrender of the devotee to God and his constant protection."[12] Thus Kali is defender as well as destroyer.

Throughout the world, the most powerful goddess is birth and death combined, Athena and Medusa reintegrated. Ishtar of Babylonia was the greatest of moon goddesses, spreading through the ancient world as Astarte and Ashtar, until her worship blended into that of the Greek Artemis and Egyptian

Isis. She is the goddess of fertility, for fields, animals, and man. Yet she is also destroyer, depriving just as she gives. Her son, Tammuz, fruit of her body, represents the vegetation of the earth. With the attainment of manhood he becomes her lover; yet, at the blazing summer solstice, she condemns him to death and he sinks to the underworld.[13]

Another goddess, Lakshmi of India, displays this twofold nature. She is the goddess of wealth and generosity, the one who protects her devotees from sorrow. In her avatars of Sita and Radha, she is a devoted consort, gladdening the days of her lover. However, even she has a dark side:

> In time of prosperity
> she is indeed Lakshmi
> bestowing good fortune on the home(s) of men.
> In the same manner,
> she thus becomes Alaksmi
> [and] she comes forth to [cause] destruction.[14]

Here, the *Devi-Mahatmyam*, Glorification of the Great Goddess, shows her as vicious and kindly, changing like all goddesses with the seasons. She is Persephone, both flower-maiden and death crone. And this is the apotheosis of the heroine, becoming life-giver and death-dealer as one.

This was how goddesses existed in the beginning of time, as Tiamat was creatrix and dragon, Freya both fertility goddess and queen of the Valkyries, Gaia the birther of fields and monsters. In this way, the great harvestress of life is the inverse aspect of the fecund earth mother. Even in her demise, she and the life within her continue cycling.

Kalwadi, an Australian goddess, was busy babysitting. However, she conceived an insatiable hunger for babies, and occasionally she would devour one. Her children were furious over their own children's deaths. When Kalwadi vanished, her children tracked her to an underwater lair and killed her. When they cut her open to rescue the babies, they discovered the children were alive in her womb. Australian aborigines celebrated this rebirth in their initiation rituals, as once again, death leads to birth, and the Dark Goddess's womb is a source of new life for those who dare to journey that deeply.[15]

According to the Nahua of ancient Mexico, Cipactli was the first goddess. An alligator swimming through primordial chaos, she harbored the potential for all life within herself. Two serpent gods tore her apart. Her lower body fell and became the earth, and her upper body rose to become the heavens. The Nahua believed they could hear her sobbing at night, wishing for the living beings to die and rejoin with her.[16] Though the hero Marduk slew the dragoness Tiamat and Gaia's grandson Zeus supplanted the great earth goddess, their power still remained: The living earth was fashioned through both their bodies. Tiamat and Cipactli died in the process, but the earth and all its bounties was their legacy — a triumphant act of life-giving even through death.

These stories all emphasize the connection between birth and death. Within the Great Goddess both concepts link, showing the deep understanding ancient people had for the duality of life. The heroine completes her journey by mastering this knowledge, incorporating the death-energies of the underworld into herself and acknowledging their glory. Only thus can she merge with the cycle of life, growing gracefully into mother and wisewoman without fearing death. For it is not an ending but a regenerative spiral. As one life ends, another begins, and on, and on.

❖ Section II ❖

ARCHETYPES

The anthropomorphic representations of the Goddess — the young Maid, the mature Mother, and the old Grandmother or Ancestress, all the way back to the original Creatrix — are, as the Greek philosopher Pythagoras later noted, projections of the various stages of the life of woman.[1]

The now-popular archetype of the triple-goddess, divided into maiden-mother-crone, is a relatively recent theory. It was first postulated by Jane Ellen Harrison, who notes, "We find not only three Gorgons and three Graiae, but three Semnae, three Moirae, three Charites, three Horae, three Agraulids, and, as a multiple of three, nine Muses."[2]

The theory was eagerly adopted by Robert Graves in *The White Goddess*. He depicted the triplicity as Maiden, Mother and Crone, and many neo-pagans revere this imagery. While some scholars attributed this archetype to the lively imagination of the poet, recent archaeology has shown how many "Goddess Triplicities" echo back into antiquity, as the three great Queen Gwenhwyfars who wed King Arthur, the Creatrix-Preserver-Destroyer triad in India, or the Norns who foretold fates in Norse myth.

Women's mythology is all about cycling from larger to smaller, pregnancy to slimness, waxing mother to waning crone. "As the Moon regulated women's menstrual cycles, the ancients worshipped the Moon as Goddess. Her changing faces as she waxes and wanes throughout the month unfold her triple-aspect as Virgin of the New Moon, Mother of the Full Moon, and Crone of the Dark Moon," notes Demetra George on her essay on the Dark Moon mysteries.[3] For a few days each month, the moon vanishes. This is like the woman's withdrawal and rest during her cycle of menstruation.

Once, the whole Goddess reflected this entire spectrum: kindly and terrible, as the awesome Mother Earth. However, the conquering patriarchy split her into her three aspects. Although patriarchal cultures could find a place for the virgin and mother energies, they could find no such use for the old woman.[4] The young virgin could represent stored energy, and she maintained some sacredness for that reason. The mother transmitted energy, gave it to others. The old woman, however, only had knowledge; this could be threatening, and was increasingly trivialized by the discriminating patriarchy. Thus the crone was frequently divorced from the pantheon. Just as Athena, Artemis, Demeter, and Hera were respected goddesses, the Furies and their mistress Hecate were relegated to the underworld, demonized, discarded. Powerful wisewomen from Medusa to the sphinx became monsters the heroes slew.

Other mythologists split the feminine archetype in different ways. Campbell, like Harrison, perceives woman as mother and maiden, both divided into positive and negative aspects: Benevolent nature goddess or wicked stepmother, innocent princess or crafty seductress. However, Campbell, in the tradition of Jung and many others, categorizes the female only as influence on the male protagonist.

Antonia Wolff, longtime mistress of Carl Jung, formulated four feminine archetypes: Mother, Hetaera, Amazon, and Mystic.[5] Her theories provide women with a unique model of development. While her archetypes are contained in a short and somewhat unsystematic paper that has not been widely distributed, they offer an intriguing twist on the triple goddess archetype.

The Amazon wants to win, no matter the cost. Quintessentially virginal, she is Daddy's girl, and looks to him for approval, for the animus that completes her. "Achieving, accomplishing, and winning laurels for herself" matter most.[6] She is Athena competing with Arachne in a weaving contest, and, upon losing, destroying her competitor. The Amazon is a comrade and rival of men.[7]

The Hetaera (sacred prostitute) discovers her inner sensuality by relating to her consort. She is his mistress, his bride, his inspiration, his anima. The Hetaera's instinct "is directed towards the individual contents of a relationship in herself as well as in the man."[8] In her more primitive form, she is Aphrodite, hopping between beds. The more mature Hetaera is Isis or Tam Lin's Janet, defending her lover at all costs. When spurned, however, she becomes the murderous Medea or Circe.

The Mother is the source of bounty, archetyped as Mother-Goddess birthing the trees and oceans. Her counter is the devouring mother who swallows her children, or through her indifference, starves them. Demeter and Gaia embody these roles, providing or destroying as they desire. The instinct of the Mother reacts to "all that in man is in the process of becoming or is undeveloped, in need of protection, in danger, or must be tended, cared for and assisted."[9]

The Medium bridges between the living and the dead, interpreting visions and aiding souls to cross. She and her sisters are shamans, witch-priestesses, seers, oracles, medicine women.[10] The Medium must consciously manage her access to the unconscious, through art, spirituality, or contemplation. Thus she humanizes and masters the hidden world. In her negative aspect, she distorts the future, as the oracle who misleads Oedipus by telling partial truths, or as Mara, goddess of illusions.[11]

WOLFF'S ARCHETYPES				
	As creator	*As destroyer*	*Power*	*Animus*
Amazon	Competitor, hard worker, builder	Fighter and death-dealer	Man's world of war and intellect	Father
Hetaera	Inspiratrice, lover, enabler	Femme fatale	Woman's world of relationships and self-knowledge	Lover
Mother	Nurturer, protector, teacher	Devouring mother	Life, birth, and creation	Son
Medium	Seer, magician, wisewoman	Deceiver and distorter of the future	Death, rebirth, and the future	Wiseman

Toni Wolff's archetypes provide a valuable counterpoint to Jung's four psychological functions, viewing women for themselves rather than as the mysterious Other or anima on the hero's adventure. Jung perpetually links woman with nature as the terrifying wildness man must conquer and tame in order to incorporate into the self. Thus woman must struggle in a culture that considers her a minority. Woman often considers her needs inessential because women's identity is perceived and defined by men. To woman, struggling to discover the Self, centuries of literature and symbolism that consider her man's helpmeet and support undermine her journey. As Simone de Beauvoir notes, "What peculiarly signalizes the situation of woman is that she — a free and autonomous being like all the human creatures — nevertheless finds herself living in a world where men compel her to assume the status of the Other."[12]

Woman, whose reproductive abilities have her spending more time involved with the species' life than the male, inevitably becomes linked with the symbolism of nature. The nine months in which she swells with life reflect spring's planting stretching to autumn's harvest. Likewise, as she nurses and cares for the unsocialized children, she is seen as the bridge between wildness and man. In male stories, she is the Other, a projection of the wilderness like a tree nymph or siren. How then, reading these tales, can she form a true identity? Who is she when she tries existence as the self, rather than as the hero's shallow anima?

For my own list of archetypes, I decided to mimic the moon's phases, not clearly discernable as absolute stages, but expanding and contracting from wax-ing to full to waning. Thus maiden-mother-crone becomes a progression. The bereft, questing mother swells into the triumphant matriarch, and then wanes into the destructive child-killer as she sinks toward cronehood. A fourth phase echoes within this cycle: The dark of the moon in which the goddess, like her moon coun-terpart, vanishes from the world and is reborn. This is the life cycle that comprises many heroine's journeys — Maiden to Mother, Mother to Crone, Crone to Spirit Guardian, Death to Rebirth and a new cycle.

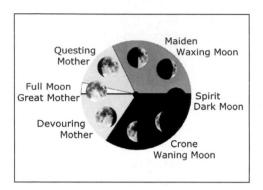

Reflections

The heroine's journey takes her from birth through the world of life. This can also be called the external world of society and manners, the world of com-mon day, one of homework and agendas and crying babies and muddy floors. By contrast, the underworld below the horizontal split is the realm of the unconscious, of magic, of desires made manifest with a wish, and, yes, of death. This is the woman's traditional sphere of power — the world of emotion and spirit. Yet too long a stay will transform princess to death-crone, Kore to Perse-phone. Thus the heroine must finally ascend, richer for her underworld knowl-edge, and yet committed to the world of life.

When these archetypes are placed in a circle, patterns appear. It is most important to note that each archetype's shadow, or direct opposite, appears clearly across the circle. This is the missing or sublimated self that the questor must meet and absorb in order to triumph. For the questing heroine inno-cently embarking on her journey, it is the Terrible Mother, who has completed her own life journey and hovers on the cusp of destructive cronehood. At the apex of life and the light world sits the princess. However, innocent goodness can be equated to powerlessness, as, like Snow White or Iphigenia, she is the prey for dark forces. When the powerful ruler tries to destroy her, she can only kneel on the ground and beg him to stop. The Divine Whore, or her coun-terpart the elderly Trickster have more power, but it is that of deceit, of flout-ing society's rules, of acting shamefully. She defies convention, often taking power from the men whom she will not let ignore her. Eventually, the independent heroine grows to wife and mother, the self-sacrificer who risks her life to save her family and will manage to feed them, whatever the cost. Her shadow is the widow. With husband divorced or gone, children grown, she finally manages to reconnect with herself and explore her own desires, rather than those of others.

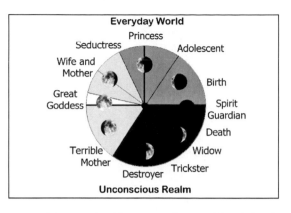

Finally, she ascends to the great goddess, poised between the worlds of death and life, the embodiment of the earth and all it contains. Her consciousness, reflected by earth, sea, and triumphant full moon, has expanded to contain the entire world. Her shadow is the new moon goddess, who withdraws completely into the self until not even a glimmer remains. She is the vanished goddess, soon to be reborn as a fragile sliver of a child and recommence the cycle.

Thus the heroine's journey is mirrored by the shadow's journey, as the Terrible Mother descends into the darkest realm of the self and ascends to cronehood as the fairy godmother, who gracefully ages until she passes into the realm of the spirit, the greatest power of all.

Rising Moon: Maiden

"In the triple emanation of the Goddess as New, Full, and Dark phase Moons, she manifests on three levels — as Creatrix, Preserver, and Destroyer, as Virgin, Mother and Crone; and as young maiden, mother/wife, and old woman/widow."[1] In this context, however, "virgin" is not about sex, but is more accurately defined as "beholden to no man." She is growing in life as the moon grows in size, free to play and celebrate her life, free of responsibilities.

Aphrodite and Inanna, for example, were maiden goddesses. "Virginity was to these ancients in their wisdom a grace not lost but perpetually renewed, hence the immortal maidenhood of Aphrodite."[2] She, in particular, was known for re-virginizing herself each year after a bath in her sacred spring.

> The wanderings of the goddess carried her far, yet each spring she returned with Her doves to Cypress for her sacred bath at Paphos. There She was attended by her Graces: Flowering, Growth, Beauty, Joy, and Radiance. They crowned Her with myrtle and lay a path of rose petals at Her feet. Aphrodite walked into the sea, into the pulsing moon rhythms of the tide. When She emerged with Her spirit renewed, spring blossomed fully, and all beings felt her joy.[3]

The image of Aphrodite surrounded by other women, renewing her virginity and wholeness, reflects women's yearly pilgrimage to a place of renewal, be it spa or retreat. This is her time to be alone, to concentrate on herself and find wholeness. In Through the Goddess: A Woman's Way of Healing, *Patricia Reis asks:*

> How much more meaningful it would be if women were able to understand this need consciously, incorporating times of "virginity" in their daily lives. Indeed, anytime we are not engaged sexually is ours alone, to be virginal, complete unto ourselves. Then, each time we consent to open ourselves to another sexually can be "the first time."[4]

Thus, the virgin is the person "at one with herself." She is independent, striving toward a relationship with her goddess rather than a man.[5] In fact, she is fiercest when protecting women's mysteries — The power of her untapped sexuality makes her invincible. She is warrior-maid, seductress, questor, both chaste innocence and wild instinct.

179

CHAPTER 18

Smart Girls Rule!
The Adolescent Questor

Golden Lotus (China)

Gum Lin, or Golden Lotus, grew up in a Chinese village short of water, where the families cried from thirst. Every day she wandered the mountains seeking water, and at last she discovered a small, still lake. Eagerly, she gathered all the bamboo stalks surrounding the water and carried them home. The next morning, she tied them into a long, water-bearing tube, and climbed the mountain to dig a trench for her water-pipe, to bear the water close to the village.

She climbed straight, since she knew the pipe would need a simple downhill path. Every few feet she stopped and dug her careful channel, lining it with another piece of her dwindling bamboo supply. Sweating and filthy as she was, Gum Lin knew she had almost reached her goal. Then she stopped, amazed. She could see the lake ahead, sparkling in the sun and teaming with waterbirds. But blocking her from the water stood a high stone gate, firmly shut.

She tugged at the cold stone, and pried with her shovel, but it wouldn't budge. Then a soft, grey swan floated close to the gate. A voice echoed in Gum Lim's head: "Find the gate key, and the waters is yours." Gum Lin stared. Had the swan spoken to her? Before she could ask, it swam away.

She circled the lake, seeking an entrance, seeking a clue, seeking the mysterious key. She finally made her way to the far side of the lake, where she'd once gathered bamboo. Her face fell. She had stripped away most of the strong, healthy plants, and there weren't enough to build a pipe this far. All of her work wasted! And the poor villagers below were still scratching at the dry earth and praying. "Ask the daughter of the dragon," chirped three brightly-colored songbirds overhead. "Sing your people's song on the banks," a peacock whispered. And so Gum Lim did.

181

Kneeling there on the muddy bank, Gum Lin sang. She sang the songs of the rice field workers, whose fields were dry and barren. She sang the lullabies that mothers sang to their hungry babes at night. And at last, Loy Yi Lung, the dragon's daughter, rose from the lake. Her gown was peacock silk, and her black hair sparkled like loose droplets. "Please, may I have the key to the stone gate?" Gum Lin asked politely. "My village is desperate for the water."

"I will help if I can," Loy Yi Lung said. "But my father keeps it in a cave under the water, and guards it jealously. His guards would kill even me for trying to steal it." She thought matters over, perfect brow furrowing. "Often when I sing, my father swims to the cave entrance to listen. Perhaps if we sing together, he will come. Then you can slip past him and find the key."

Together they sang like the songbirds themselves, and perhaps the birds lent them a touch of sweetness. When the dragon surfaced to hear their clear voices, Gum Lin slipped into the water. Loy Yi Lung sang even louder to cover her splashing, and the birds twittered with joy. Underwater, Gum Lin swam to the cave and crept inside. Golden coins and jewels sparkled in piles, heaped against every wall. She itched to stuff her pockets, but she knew her village needed water for planting more than anything.

Her lungs ached, and she longed to snatch some jewels and go, but she knew that wouldn't save her village. She beat with her feet, pushing herself to the cave bottom so she could search. Digging through the heavy, water-cold jewels, she only found more. Wait, was that something smooth and warm? Or was she drowning, hallucinating from lack of air? Gum Lin lunged and clutched ivory in her groping fingers. She tugged forth the key, topped with a jeweled swan. Lungs bursting, she propelled herself to the surface, where she swam to the stone gate, and carefully unlocked it.

Water gushed down the path she'd carved, straight down the mountain and into the village streambeds. It flooded the thirsty rice paddies and seeped into the wells.

The village greeted Gum Lin as a hero, and welcomed the dragon's daughter, too, as she moved into the village streams to be close to her new friend. Each day, the two girls would lift their voices in beautiful harmony.

To this day, women near Wild Swan Lake sing of the daring of Gum Lin. And when they sing, those who listen carefully can hear a soft, echoing harmony in the river.[1]

Here is the traditional heroine — the simple, good-hearted girl carrying food through the forest or outwitting demons and kings. The majority of fairy-tale heroines are brave and clever, using their generosity and compassion rather than swords and axes. They quest to protect those they love, and their kindness wins them help from the birds of the forest themselves. But whether they need to gather fleece from fire-breathing sheep, hold a beast-lover close, or dive under the waves until their lungs burst, these gentle heroines have the fortitude of bedrock.

Succeeding in a Man's World

Among the great United States folk heroes, such as Paul Bunyan, Pecos Bill, and Mike Fink, pioneers and frontiersmen of legend were predominantly male. There were folk heroines such as Belle Starr, Annie Oakley, and Calamity Jane, but these were real people, not giants or babes raised by coyotes. As folklorist Robert D. San Souci explains:

> In the past, American society expected women to limit their concerns to home and family — not to put themselves forward as explorers, hunters, warriors, or rulers. Though real-life women claimed these roles, most storytellers (the majority of them men), whether creating with pen and paper or spinning a yarn around a campfire, portrayed female characters — even the "outsize" wives of such figures as [the giant] Paul Bunyan — as pretty much content to stick close to home.[2]

The oppressed minority cultures of America needed tales of subtlety, of patience, of quiet heroics, but the American philosophy of the white man settling the West into a gender-specific paradise had little room for spunky women. Though the Native Americans had powerful female deities, like the Zuni Rabbit Huntress or Navajo Changing Woman, and African Americans had tricksters like Molly Cottontail, Anglo settlers bragged almost exclusively of male heroism, even as pioneers of both sexes crossed the continent side by side. Through extensive research, San Souci managed to discover a few female folk heroes, less publicized, but just as legendary as their counterparts. One of these is retold below.

Mike Fink, the legendary riverboatman and folk hero, had a daughter named Sal, who was just as rambunctious as he. Best known as the "Mississippi screamer" for her high-spirited roaring, she once killed a ferocious mother bear with just her hands. One day, she was captured by pirates with a grudge against her father. When the pirates fell asleep, Sal, grimacing at her harsh treatment, burst her bonds as if they were no more than apron strings. After helping herself to their knives and pistols, she tied the men's feet together all around the campfire. With one of her ferocious yells, she yanked the rope's loose end, catapulting them all straight into the embers. As the men howled, she gathered up all their pelts and a chest of gold "in payment fur th' inconvenience!" and with another triumphant whoop, she was off![3]

Though Sal Fink is clearly acquainted with weaponry, she instead uses subtlety, waiting for the men to fall asleep and dragging them into the fire to make their escape. She remains spunky, strong, and feminine at the same time.

Among the strong heroines of Native American legend, Spider Grandmother of the Hopi rules as creatrix, shapechanger, magician, mentor and leader, guiding heroes and heroines alike. In one episode from *The Fourth World of the Hopis*, the chief of Tikuvi village challenged the people of Payupki to a footrace. The Payupki village was small, and only had one runner at all, though he was eager to try. As the Tikuvi were discussing what to wager on the race, they heard a tapping at their kiva.

It was Spider Grandmother. "Hello," she said. "I have medicines I can rub on your runners' legs to help them win."

"Go away, old woman," said the proud young men. "We can win without your help."

So Spider Grandmother went to the Payupki, who welcomed her. She rubbed medicines on the boy's legs, and he won the race. With it came an enormous pile of gifts the Tikuvi had wagered: bows, belts, moccasins, and baskets. That night, the Payupki chief sent for the boy. "You ran well, but they will want a rematch. So you must run even faster." The boy started training the next morning. When he returned home, his sister was grinding corn. "Look how you're panting," she said. "You'll have to do better than that."

"All you know about is grinding corn."

"I'll come with you tomorrow, then. There's something you should see." The next day, the boy and girl raced all the way to the sand hole and back. She quickly outdistanced him. When the boy reached the hut, he found his sister quietly grinding corn, not even a bit winded. So the boy went to the chief and told him his sister was far faster.

The Tikuvi sent for Spider Grandmother to help them, but since they couldn't find her, they found another sorcerer. Spider Grandmother shook her head as she rubbed medicine into the girl's legs. "The Tikuvi are bad-hearted and will cheat," she said. "I will shrink myself down into my spider form and help you tomorrow."

The Tikuvi men gathered, and their women too, because a girl was running. The race began, and the girl won easily, and then a second race, third, and fourth. Each time she won a great pile of goods until the Tikuvi had nothing left. The men wanted to give up, but the Tikuvi women scowled at all their work wagered away, and wagered that they would live with the Payupki if their champion lost the final race.

The Payupki girl ran like fire, with Spider Grandmother sitting on her shoulder crying, "Run, daughter, run!" Suddenly, a white dove flew past her. "The other runner has transformed!" Spider Grandmother looked up and saw a hawk overhead. "Dive, hawk!" The hawk flew at the dove and knocked it to the ground. Twice more this happened, and so the girl won the race.

The Tikuvi women followed the Payupki back to their village. "Treat them like family," Spider Grandmother said. So each family took in one or two of the women and treated them well. And across the lake, the proud young men of the Tikuvi had to grind the corn and make the pots, for all the women had left them.

Here the "proud young men" discount many women: Spider Grandmother with her magic, the girl runner, their own women who spent so long crafting all the goods they were wagering. The women's wagering themselves seems like sense: they would rather live with a tribe that respects girl runners and Spider Grandmother than make a new pile of goods for their men to wager away. Once they leave, the men will learn to value hard work as they do the women's chores themselves.[4]

Taking Charge

This "spunky" spirit of the Hopi runner girl or Sal Fink characterizes many beloved heroines before they were softened into childish figures who spinelessly await their true loves. The Cinderella of Perrault and Disney, of course, is known for meekness, doing housework and obeying orders. But many other Cinderellas are more resourceful. Stories like "Vasilisa the Beautiful" and "Tattercoats" see the heroines questing, tricking wicked witches, and defying their treacherous fathers. The Grimm Brothers' Ash-Girl plants and nurtures a tree on her mother's grave, thus turning the mourning and tragedy of her mother's early death into a force for creation. Giambattista Basile's Italian "Cat Cinderella," published in Naples in 1634, is probably the oldest Western version of the tale. In it, a governess actually instructs the lovely Zezolla on how to murder her stepmother! Zezolla does so, and the governess marries her father, only to become an even worse stepmother, propelling Zezolla into the familiar legend. This heroine gains the aid of fairies and wins the prince through her cleverness and trickery, showing that not all Cinderellas win through passive sweetness.[5]

Molly Whuppie, though a girl, has her own Jack and the Beanstalk tale. Like Jack, she breaks into the giant's house three times and carries off his treasures. Crossing the bridge of one hair, each time she turns and taunts him. On the third time, however, he catches her. "If I had caused you all this trouble, what would you do?" he asks gleefully.

Molly says, "I would put you into a sack, and I'd put the cat inside wi' you, and the dog aside you, and a needle and thread and shears, and I'd hang you up upon the wall, and I'd go to the wood, and choose the thickest stick I could get, and I would come home, and take you down, and bang you till you were dead."[6]

The giant laughs and proposes to do just this. While he's out choosing a stick, Molly sings out, "Oh, if ye saw what I see."

"Oh," says the giant's wife, "What do you see, Molly?"

But Molly never said a word but, "Oh, if ye saw what I see!"[7]

Thus she persuades the giant's wife to trade places with her. She cuts her way from the sack and sews it back up with the needle and thread, sealing the giant's wife inside. The giant comes back and starts thrashing the sack with all his might, but the cat and dog's yowls drown out his wife's protests.

Even in the Bible, women were once celebrated for their feminine potency, in a way that modern tradition has in many ways forgotten. Judith sneaked into an enemy camp in her finest clothes and, seducing the enemy general with her flattering words, decapitated him. Miriam protected her brother Moses while he was floating down the Nile River, and reunited him with both his mother and his Jewish heritage, ensuring that he would save the Hebrew people. Their many spiritual sisters, like Tamar, Rebecca, Deborah, Rahab, and Jael, likewise seize their destinies and preserve their people.

Accounts from the Bible also suggest Jesus showed inclusiveness towards women, valuing them among his followers. His partnership with Mary Magdalene especially enriched both of their spiritual journeys. Mary Magdalene, waiting by Jesus' tomb, was the first person to speak to him on Easter Sunday.[8] Nowhere in the Bible is she identified as a prostitute, but rather as a valued disciple.

In Mark 14: 3–4, Mary of Bethany (often identified as Mary Magdalene) anoints Jesus from an alabaster jar. In Biblical times, a sacred daughter would do such a thing to anoint a king, or a sacrificed king of the sacred marriage. When Jesus utters, "She is come aforehand to anoint my body to the burying," he acknowledges the act's significance.[9] Thus Mary confronts mortality in the form of the crucifixion and overcomes it. After, with her love and faith outweighing death, she is the first to see her resurrected teacher in a vision.[10] Mary is the first to report Christ's rising, just as pagan priestesses announced the resurrection of Dionysus, Attis, and Osiris each year. Through this initiation, Mary becomes "a woman who has realized the marriage of the masculine and the feminine within herself, thus becoming a true *anthropos*, like her teacher."[11] Mary Magdalene "had to become truly woman, in all the sexual dimensions of her femininity, accepting and integrating her masculine nature as well before realizing her status as speaker and knower."[12]

In "The Finn King's Daughter," from Norway, the father fears his daughter will marry the serving boy, so he confines her in an earthen cave before he rides off to war. When the king fails to return, the daughter digs herself out, bare-handed, and roams the forest, finally crossing a river on wolfback. She seeks work as a castle kitchen maid in the next kingdom, and saves the prince there from marrying a troll-hag. Having survived the wilderness and mastered hearth-craft, she must best the troll princess at creating poetry, the words of creativity itself, to win her groom.[13]

Here is the heroine's task: pure creativity and life-force, wielding craft, magic, and devotion as weapons to accomplish her goals. Often, like Scheherazade, she is a brilliant orator and storyteller, bending the world to her will. Other times, she uses the simple magic of loyalty and fearlessness to save those in need.

Greek Antigone learns her brother's body has been left to rot as a traitor, and King Creon has promised stoning to any who bury him. Ismene, Antigone's spineless sister, remarks, "Nay, we must remember, first, that we were born women, as who should not strive with men; next, that we are ruled of the stronger, so that we must obey in these things."[14] Antigone rejects this protest, retorting that she wouldn't have Ismene's help if the girl offered it, after that speech. By burying the body (a mundane, feminine action), she defies Creon and makes him appear a fool and a bully to his own people. All the while, she displays piety to the gods and loyalty to her dead brother. In the end, Antigone dies for her defiance, but her actions prove that even in ancient times women used common actions to indeed "strive with men."

In burying her brother, Antigone saves his ghost and comes to terms with her own mortality. Facing death, acknowledging its power and inevitability, is part of the heroine's journey, as is saving one's loved one from its grip. The death faced may be symbolic, as with the following story, but the faith and courage required to redeem a lover remain constant.

In the territory of Irman, between Iran and Turan, the people were being ravaged by wild boars. A brave youth named Bizhan offered to slay them, and accompanied by his lieutenant, Gurgin, he completed the task. Gurgin was filled with envy for the fame his friend would receive and so, plotting Bizhan's downfall, he described the beauty of Manizha, daughter of King Afrasiyab, and urged him to go see her in Turan. There, Bizhan spied the princess feasting with her handmaidens under a cypress tree and was instantly besotted.

Manizha, likewise entranced, invited him into her tent, and finally drugged him, dressed him in women's clothing, and conveyed him back to her apartments so they could stay together. When King Afrasiyab discovered his daughter was harboring a man, he condemned Bizhan to death, a sentence he finally commuted to imprisonment. Confining him in a dark, gloomy pit in a neighboring forest, he shut the opening with a heavy stone. He then banished Manizha from the palace.

The girl begged at doors for scraps, which she lowered to her imprisoned lover through a crevice. When she heard of a visiting merchant from Iran, she placed her sorrowful tale before him and entreated his help. The merchant offered her food for the prisoner, including a fine roasted bird with a signet ring concealed within. When Bizhan found the ring, he knew the merchant was the great warrior Rustam, come to rescue him. When Manizha returned to the merchant, he told her to light a beacon fire at night to guide him to the pit. This she did. Rustam and his warriors removed the rock and carried them both to Iran, where the king heaped jewels and fine garments on Manizha in recognition of her heroism. She and Bizhan remained together for the rest of their lives.[15]

Here Manizha is her lover's savior. Perhaps she is not chained in the pit herself, but her acts of feeding him each day link her with the descent, as she guards this trapped part of herself from further harm. Like Eliza of "The Six Swans," she is powerless, voiceless, toiling in anonymity until she succeeds and earns her reward.

> One of the commonest dream symbols for this type of release through transcendence is the theme of the lonely journey or pilgrimage, which somehow seems to be a spiritual pilgrimage on which the initiate becomes acquainted with the nature of death. But this is not death as a last judgment or other initiatory trial of strength; it is a journey of release, renunciation, and atonement, presided over and fostered by some spirit of compassion.[16]

This spirit is generally a mistress rather than a master.

CHAPTER 19

Don't Bet on the Princess: The Prize

The Tale of Déirdre (Ireland)

Once a girl was born as shining as the sun, and all the people of Ulster rejoiced. But the Druid of Ulster shook his head and warned that many hurts and losses should come to the province of Ulster on account of the girl that was there born. When the nobles of Ulster heard, they intended to kill the child, but King Connor refused. "We cannot defy fate," he said. "And it would be an even worse pity to destroy so lovely a child. I will take the girl under my own protection and wed her myself when she's grown.

He raised her in a fortress without a single window, save those that looked out on the sheltered courtyard and its orchard. Déirdre, as she was called, had every luxury and the finest education, for she was to marry the king. But he penned her in so no other man might approach her. A high wall, not easy to surmount, surrounded that spacious habitation, and four savage man-hounds were on constant guard there, and his life were in peril for the man who should venture to approach it.

When Déirdre had reached marriageable age, she stood at her window, watching her nurse slaughter a calf. Its blood dripped on the snow, and a raven landed to eat from what remained. "Now there is what I must have," Déirdre said. "The blackness of the raven, the redness of the blood, and the whiteness of the snow."

She fashioned snowmen and drew pictures of a man with those colors, despite her nurse's scolding. One day, she discovered that there was a chink in the fortress behind a curtain; there she beheld the men training outside, most especially the hero Naisi. His hair was black like a raven's wings, his lips were red and his teeth white.

189

The nurse's heart softened at Déirdre's pleadings, and she snuck him into the fortress. When Naisi beheld Déirdre's splendor, love crashed over him in a great flood. Déirdre beseeched him to take her and escape to Alba. Though Naisi feared King Connor, he agreed at last.

Déirdre poisoned the dogs and Naisi crept to the castle with his two brothers. They lifted the girl across the walls, through every rough impediment, so that her mantle and the extremity of her dress were all torn to pieces, and he set her upon a steed's back, and no stop was made by them until they reached the harbor. That same night they departed, three times 50 warriors, and the same number of women and dogs and servants, and Déirdre went with them. For a long time they wandered about Ireland, in homage to this man or that, and often Connor sought to slay them, either by ambuscade or by treachery. Often they slept in rude houses out in the fields, so no men would behold and covet Déirdre's incomparable beauty.

Now one day, the high-steward of the local king went out in the early morning, and he saw Naisi and Déirdre asleep. He hurried back to the king and awakened him. "We have," said he, "up to this day found no wife of like dignity to thyself. Naisi the son of Usnach hath a wife of worth sufficient for the emperor of the western world! Let Naisi be slain, and you can wed her."

"No!" said the king, "But visit her each day and woo her for me secretly." When Déirdre rebuffed the king's advances, he sent the sons of Usnach into the most dangerous battles. Déirdre and her friends fled again, and word of this reached Connor.

The men of Ulster thought it a great pity that the sons of Usnach should die in the land of foes for the sake of a woman. They prevailed on Connor to send the messanger Fergus to make truce with them, and he agreed. However, a treacherous band of Ulstermen rejected the proposed truce. Their leader, Eogan the son of Durthacht, greeted Naisi with a mighty thrust of his spear. Naisi fell to the ground, dead. The Ulstermen fell on the sons of Usnach and killed them all, together with their servants, and spared only Déirdre, whom they bound and brought to Connor.

Déirdre lived on for a year in the household of Connor; and during all that time she never smiled nor laughed, nor raised her head from her knee. Connor wooed her with gifts and gentle words, but Déirdre could only respond:

> Ah Connor! what of thee! I naught can do!
> Lament and sorrow on my life have passed:
> The ill you fashioned lives my whole life through;
> A little time your love for me would last.

> The man to me most fair beneath the sky,
> The man I loved, in death away you tore:
> The crime you did was great; for, till I die,
> That face I loved I never shall see more.

That he is gone is all my sorrow still;
Before me looms the shape of Usna's son;
Though o'er his body white is yon dark hill,
There's much I'd lavish, if but him I won.

I see his cheeks, with meadow's blush they glow;
Black as a beetle, runs his eyebrows' line;
His lips are red; and, white as noble snow
I see his teeth, like pearls they seem to shine.

Well have I known the splendid garb he bears,
Oft among Alba's warriors seen of old:
A crimson mantle, such as courtier wears,
And edged with border wrought of ruddy gold.

Of silk his tunic; great its costly price;
For full one hundred pearls thereon are sewn;
Stitched with findruine, bright with strange device,
Full fifty ounces weighed those threads alone.

Gold-hilted in his hand I see his sword;
Two spears he holds, with spear-heads grim and green;
Around his shield the yellow gold is poured,
And in its midst a silver boss is seen.

Fair Fergus ruin on us all hath brought!
We crossed the ocean, and to him gave heed:
His honor by a cup of ale was bought;
From him hath passed the fame of each high deed.

If Ulster on this plain were gathered here
Before king Connor; and those troops he'd give,
I'd lose them all, nor think the bargain dear,
If I with Naisi, Usna's son, could live.

Break not, O king, my heart to day in me;
For soon, though young, I come my grave unto:
My grief is stronger than the strength of sea;
Thou, Connor, knowest well my word is true.

"Do you truly hate me beyond all others?" Connor asked.

"The only one I hate more is Eogan, the son of Durthacht."

"Then," said Connor, "you must dwell with Eogan for a year. After this, you shall like me better."

The next day they drove away over the plain of Macha, and Déirdre sat behind Eogan in the chariot, and beside her was Connor, and the two who were with her were the two men whom she would never willingly have seen together upon the earth. As she looked upon them, "Ha, Déirdre," said Connor, "you are like a ewe pressed between two rams. You'll soon soften to one of us!" Now the chariot was passing a great rock, and Déirdre twisted her head from the chariot and struck her head upon that stone, and she shattered her head, and so she died.[1]

This story is an episode in the Irish *Táin Bó Cúalnge*, epic saga of a cattle raid and its warrior hero Cúchulainn. As with all heroic epics, there are battles, valiant warriors, and sweet princesses of surpassing loveliness. Déirdre is no exception. So striking that every man who sees her desires her, her beauty is cursed. She is trapped in a men's story, one in which the heroes all seek their anima, the helpless princess chained in a dragon's lair. It's no wonder she's doomed from the onset.

Déirdre has dreams for herself: she desires love and growth, movement along the goddess path. When she dreams up her hero, all black, red, and white, she is creating her animus, giving birth to her vision.

The three original sacred colors were white, red, and black, signifying the goddess as maiden, mother, and crone: purity, maternity, and wisdom. Upheld by Indian and Greek legend, these colors were later adopted by the Christians as symbols of faith: virginity, martyrdom, and death.[2] These colors appear prominently in Snow White, as her mother conjures up a sacred daughter by means of the spilled blood. "If only I had a child as white as snow, as red as blood, and as black as coal."[3] White, red, and black are goddess colors: young moon, full moon, and new moon. "White was the color of death, of ice and bone and the snows of winter; black was the color of earth, of the darkness of the womb, of gestation; red was the color of blood, birth, menstruation, and life."[4] Yet the power of these colors has faded, and they remain a rote phrase embedded in this and other ancient tales.

Naisi is the ideal romantic animus, fulfilling Déirdre's every desire and abandoning honor, rules, and logic, all for love. They dwell in the borderlands, or in the wild unconscious of the forest, where they can surrender completely to each other. This is Déirdre's idyll, her perfect world.

However, like all idylls, this one, as artificial refuge, is doomed. "We are waiting for Déirdre to make one decision, any decision, that would free her from the fearful web in which she is entangled."[5] Her story is especially poignant as she struggles against her fate and finally succumbs to it. Déirdre is like the highest aspirations of the soul. She cannot be won by the greedy Connor, but only the self-sacrificing Naisi. Déirdre manages to outwit Connor in that he "gets no joy" of her, and she joins her love in death. However, like Shakespeare's Juliet, this is the only triumph she can manage.

Findabair, daughter of the Irish queen Maeve, fared even worse as a prize. Her mother secretly named each of her warriors her champion and promised them her daughter's hand. Hundreds were killed when they discovered the plot and made war with one another.

Brünnhild, by contrast, may be a prize, but she sets the stakes for herself, pitting *herself* against the suitors in contests. As told in the medieval rendition of her tale, *The Nibelungenlied*:

Over the sea there dwelt a queen whose like was never known, for she was of great strength and surpassing beauty. With her love as the prize, she vied with brave warriors at throwing the javelin, and the noble lady also hurled the weight to a great distance and followed with a long leap; and whoever aspired to her love had, without fail, to win these three tests against her, or else, if he lost but one, he forfeited his head.[6]

Across the seas, would-be husbands would arrive in crowds when a princess of India came of marriageable age. The greatest epic heroines, Sita in the *Ramayana* and Draupadi in the *Mahabharata*, selected their own suitors, garlanding them in the *svayamvara* (own choice) ceremony. Their suitors, Rama and Arjuna respectively, had proven themselves best through physical prowess, but it was the princess's job to choose and wed the final victor.

When Arjuna and Princess Draupadi returned home, Arjuna's mother made him promise to share his winnings equally among himself and his four brothers, the Pandavas — so Draupadi ended up with five husbands! They lived happily together, but the eldest brother, Yudhishthira, was tricked into reckless gambling by his cousin, Prince Duryodhana of the Kaurava brothers. Losing consistently, Yudhishthira wagered all his brothers, then himself, and finally Draupadi. Once again, she was the spoils, but this time, no longer of her choice.

When Draupadi heard that she had been lost in gambling, she protested, quite logically, on several levels: Her husband Yudhishthira had already lost himself, and thus could not stake anything further. Further, staking one's wife is immoral. "What prince is there who playeth staking his wife? The king was certainly intoxicated with dice."[7] Lastly, she insisted that all participants consider the right course of action.

> Morality, however, it hath been said, is the one highest object in the world. If cherished, that will certainly dispense blessings to us. Let not that morality now abandon the Kauravas. Going back to those that are present in that assembly, repeat these my words consonant with morality. I am ready to do what those elderly and virtuous persons conversant with morality will definitely tell me.[8]

Yudhishthira, however, insisted that Draupadi come before the princes, "although she was attired in one piece of cloth with her navel itself exposed, in consequence of her season having come" (in other words she was menstruating).[9] Draupadi tried to run away, but Prince Dussasana (Duryodhana's younger brother) seized the queen by her long hair.

> And Dussasana dragging Krishna [Draupadi] of long long locks unto the presence of the assembly — as if she were helpless though having powerful protectors — and pulling at her, made her tremble like the banana plant in a storm. And dragged by him, with body bent, she faintly cried — "Wretch! It ill behoveth thee to take me before the assembly. My season hath come, and I am now clad in one piece of attire." But Dussasana dragging Draupadi forcibly by her black locks while she was praying piteously unto Krishna and Vishnu who were Narayana and Nara (on earth), said unto her — "Whether thy season hath come or not, whether thou art attired in

one piece of cloth or entirely naked, when thou hast been won at dice and made our slave, thou art to live amongst our serving-women as thou pleasest."[10]

Draupadi protested that it showed disrespect for her to be dressed so incompletely before the princes, that her husbands would seek revenge (though so far they were offended yet compliant), and that the elders had lost all virtue to allow this treatment.

After some argument, Prince Dussasana insisted that the Pandavas, rightfully won, should remove their upper garments as proof of servitude. Further, Dussasana, forcibly seizing Draupadi's sari before the eyes of all, began to drag it off her. Desperate, Draupadi prayed to all the gods for protection, and miraculously, her sari grew and grew so no matter how much Dussasana tore off her, Draupadi remained modestly covered.

King Dhritarashtra sympathetically ruled that Draupadi was free and innocent; moreover, he offered her a boon. She forgivingly requested that her husbands be freed from slavery as well, beginning with Yudhishthira. However, this insult to their wife incited the Pandavas into the war of the *Mahabharata*.

Through this demeaning incident, Draupadi behaves modestly and genteelly, asking the princes to examine their wisdom and morality to rule on how she is treated. Likewise, she channels faith and devotion to the gods, as they reward her with protection. Her logic and pleas, unfortunately, are met with brutish violence. Secluded as is appropriate for a chaste married woman, a princess, and a woman in menstruation, Draupadi has been humiliated before the court, victimized, her privacy and rights violated. Draupadi's five husbands ride off to war, determined to revenge her honor, and her moment of shame causes an epic battle as great as Helen's Trojan War.

Happily Ever After?

In tales, the clichéd princess abandons her identity in order to marry and take on that of her husband. Queen Esther of the Bible must leave behind much of her Jewish heritage when she weds the king. Snow White is obviously heir to her father's kingdom, which she abandons while riding off with the prince. In this way, the rescued princess loses more of her self than she gains. The quest for identity and knowledge cannot end successfully if the heroine completely abandons all identity simply to marry. Without a man who can be animus to her anima and offer her what she's missing, the blissful marriage and "happily ever after" are foredoomed to failure.

Hera, queen goddess of marriage, is most often depicted as the villainess of Greek mythology. However, she was once a primal ruling goddess, queen of the earth and guardian of female sexuality. In her honor, the ancient Greeks celebrated the Heraea, precursor to the Olympic Games, racing bare-breasted in three age groups to represent her three life stages: maiden, mother, and crone. However, this goddess's time eventually faded. As Zeus ascended, Hera became no more than his diminished wife, raging with jealousy and hurt at her loss.[11]

The new Hera of classic myth is spiteful and vengeance-driven, a nagging, cruel figure who torments Zeus on every occasion. She persecutes Io and Leto, Zeus's paramours, and tortures Heracles with madness, shifting the blame to Zeus's victims, whom he deceived or frequently raped.

At the same time, Hera has few weapons at her disposal. Raped by Zeus in his form of a pitiable cuckoo seeing shelter, Hera weds him to restore her divine dignity. She does not indulge in affairs — this is suitable for a god but not a married goddess. Zeus, however, has plenty of consorts and even births his daughter Athena out of his head, clearly demonstrating how he doesn't require a wife even to perform that function. Thus denigrated, it's no wonder she turns hostile.

For the "princess" figure, the goal in life is happy, successful marriage. Thus, she makes herself into the ultimate anima for all men. She "adapts herself to his wishes, makes herself beautiful in his eyes, charms him, pleases him."[12] She displays few signs of self-awareness, concentrating only on how to best reflect her animus "like a many-sided crystal," with no volition, no identity, only surrender. The young lady spends hours daydreaming about the perfect man, then meets him and falls instantly in love.[13]

The princess is devoted to keeping her marriage alive, even through obstacles. The king in "The Wild Swans" believes Eliza guilty of witchcraft and orders her burned at the stake. Eliza dotingly forgives him at the end, and they resume their happy ending. Psyche and Persephone are abducted, yet they both find love and embrace the concept of marriage. When kings exile their queens, those loyal wives quest unceasingly to be reinstated.

The princess craves the perfect husband — one who is powerful and handsome, a strong provider for her children. When offered a choice, she instantly picks the "best" man and ends the decision right there. But generally their fathers choose for them, or circumstances dictate the choice. Cinderella, Juliet, and dozens of other heroines meet their prince's eyes across a ballroom and the mutual decision is irrevocable. The little mermaid has a similar moment, but her experience is tragically one-sided. Many other princesses wait on the man's quest as a prize, even when they are the protagonists. After Zeus has tricked his way to Hera, after the prince has battled thorns to waken Sleeping Beauty, after Ivan has leaped miles on a magic horse, what is there to do but say yes?

In the Swahili "A Woman for a Hundred Cattle," a married woman is so poor that she must promise her favors to a would-be suitor for a side of beef, which she wishes to serve her visiting father. Her family's poverty comes from the immense bride-price of 100 cattle that the husband once paid the father, thus beggaring himself. During the meal, the seducer bursts in, impatient for his reward. The heroine sits them all down to prove their unreasonableness: the husband has paid far too much for a bride beyond his means, while her father demanded 100 cows when he already possessed thousands, thus beggaring his daughter. Far more foolish, however, is the suitor for presuming he could have a woman once purchased for a hundred cattle with just a side of beef. Humbled, the seducer leaves, and the father sends her 300 cows.[14]

Many cultures saw the brides leaving permanently and the sons staying with their parents' household, supporting them in old age. Thus, sons were more prized as a permanent asset to the household. Likewise, bride-prices (which went in different directions among different communities) had a way of turning the daughter into a commodity, valued for her youth, virginity, and beauty over education and wisdom. In the Swahili tale, the heroine criticizes the ludicrous system and the men who have foolishly bought into it. She maintains her own self-worth, even in the face of this treatment and thus goads the men into positive action to amend their mistakes.

Most of these fairytales conclude with the marriage. The prince has elevated the princess to the role of queen; nothing else need happen after the blissful Hollywood wedding. The marriages that continue after the story's end, however, have disturbing twists. Persephone's husband is dour and grim, with a number of indiscretions. Bluebeard's wife finds her handsome, rich husband plans to murder her. In the Grimms' Sleeping Beauty, Beauty's ogre-mother-in-law swallows her children and frames her for their deaths.

As victims, these passive, loving heroines are often blamed for the catastrophes that befall them. In the Indian *Ramayana,* Princess Sita is kidnapped by the evil Ravana, until her husband Rama can rescue her. She is a source of strength as well as wifely devotion, warning Ravana that she could burn him to ashes with the fire of her chastity. However, after rescuing her, Rama accuses Sita of infidelity while she was Ravana's captive and banishes her, pregnant, to the forest. There she dwells until, twins in hand, she meets Rama several years later. She assures him she is innocent, crying, "Mother Earth, if I have been faithful to Rama, take me home, hide me!"[15] The earth swallows her, proving her innocence, but, no matter how much he demands her return, Rama has lost his wife forever. He has a golden image of her fashioned, which sits beside him in place of his wife thereafter.

Sita must sacrifice her life on earth to assure Rama of her fidelity, just as the Armless Maiden and many others flee unjust accusations and come to discover themselves in the forest. For many questing heroines, this is only the beginning of the tale. But Déirdre, Juliet, the little mermaid, and far too many other passive princesses end in tragedy.

CHAPTER 20

Mu Lan's Sisterhood: The Warrior Woman

The Rabbit Huntress (Zuni)

Long ago, a maiden lived in the American Southwest. She and her parents dwelt alone, since her twin brothers had died in a hunt many years before. During the summer, they could gather beans and corn, squash and melons. But in the winter they had little to eat besides dried beans. Most families hunted game during the winter; even the maiden's family had axes and rabbit sticks hanging on the walls. However, her father was too old to hunt, and girls were supposed to stay at home, not wield weapons in the depths of the forest.

One day, as the maiden watched the hunters return from the valley beyond the pueblo, arms laden with rabbits, she determined to follow them. After all, she had hunted with her brothers as a child, and her family desperately needed the meat. That evening, she asked her parents for permission.

Her mother looked away. "We lost your brothers in a hunt. Must we lose you as well? Stay home; we will manage without."

"If you truly wish this, I will help you," her father said. He took a deer-skin and sewed the maiden a pair of long, warm leggings to protect her from the snow. He sharpened his old stone axe and gathered the strongest rabbit sticks. Her mother made a stack of corncakes studded with hot peppers, and strung them all on a yucca fiber to hang around her daughter's neck.

The daughter took all these gifts and set out on her journey. Carefully, she clambered down the cliffs and into the river valley. There the snow spread lightly and evenly over the ground, patterned by the tracks of many rabbits. She followed the tracks eagerly from one hollow to another. Her trapping skills were clumsy at first, but she grew sure with practice, as she remembered her brothers' lessons. Soon she had collected a vast pile of rabbits for her family.

197

As it grew dark, she didn't notice the falling snow or the whistling wind. She wanted to catch another rabbit, and then another. When she finally looked about her, snow had wiped out her trail.

"That's all right," she told herself. "I can shelter in a cave and find my way home in the morning." She searched among the rocks until she found a narrow opening. After carefully checking the area for wild animals, she unstrung her load of rabbits and gathered sticks to start a small fire. She cleaned one of the rabbits and roasted it over the flames. Together with her corncakes, it made a luxurious meal. At last, she curled up on the cave floor and drifted toward sleep.

From outside the cave came a long, drawn-out cry. "Who is it?" she called.

She heard twigs crunch and crackle outside the cave. A huge, shadowy figure filled the entrance. "Oh ho, look what I've found," it said.

The maiden froze. Huge red eyes glared at her, filling up the creature's entire face. The body was as large as three whole people. It was a cannibal demon, which had haunted the world since ancient times. She raced to the back of the cave and crouched behind an outcropping of rock.

The demon tried to squeeze through the cave mouth, but it was too enormous. "Let me in!" it shouted.

The girl said nothing.

"At least bring me something to eat; I'm very hungry," it roared.

"I ate all my food."

"Bring out your rabbits; I can smell them."

In desperation, the girl threw it a rabbit. The demon seized it in its talons and swallowed it in a gulp.

"More!"

The girl threw it another rabbit. Another gulp.

"More!"

The girl grew angry. At this rate, she would have none to bring home. "I have no more. Go away."

"Throw me your clothes, then!"

She tossed her jacket and leggings, and the demon gobbled those too.

"I'm coming in there to eat you and your rabbits," the demon roared. He raised a massive stick and shattered the stone of the cave mouth.

"You won't get in unless you strike a great deal harder," the girl shouted, trying to conceal her fear.

"Easily done!" the demon roared, and he shattered half the entrance in his fury.

"Still not hard enough," she said, starting to tremble.

With a roar, he gave the cave mouth a truly massive strike and the entire front of the cave smashed. Just as he started to walk inside, a voice boomed, "Hold! Cannibal Demon, you must be causing trouble again. You're making so much noise, we could hear you all the way on Thunder Mountain."

Two war gods appeared. Each swung his war club once, and the demon fell down dead. "You can sleep safe now, hunter maiden," one called. "We will watch over your cave tonight."

In the morning, the gods told the maiden much about how to hunt, for they were impressed with her bravery. The maiden bowed low and breathed on their hands to thank them. She returned to her village, laden with her strings of rabbits. Everyone stared in wonder. Never had they seen a maiden hunter before, and she had caught more than any of them. The maiden, however, did not stop, but hurried home to her parents.

When she arrived, her parents cried with joy to find her unharmed.

"Now we have food," she said. "I'll make rabbit stew tonight, and every night this winter."

"You've done well, daughter ... and hunter maiden," her father said. "You will hunt for our family from this day forth, and your brothers' axes are yours."[1]

The warrior maiden differs from other heroines in that she associates herself with the hero's journey, not the heroine's — Disguising herself in men's clothing, she battles the evil overlord, mystic sword in hand, male mentor advising her in the ways of combat. Despite or perhaps as a consequence of her gender-spanning state, she is the "strong woman" most readers visualize. She is the one who dresses as a boy and rides to war, the one who says, "If a man can do this task, I can do it too." Although she divorces herself from many aspects of femininity, she still follows the same journey as her quieter sisters.

The warrior woman is a powerful protector, rescuing helpless women from rape and murder. The Rabbit Huntress, for example, becomes a supernatural figure, the keeper of game for the Zuni people.[2] At the same time, the warrior is a committed virgin, slaying suitors with her hunting dogs or bows. Such is Daphne from Greek myth, who flees the ardent Apollo and transforms into a laurel tree rather than submit to him. Other warrior women are less desperate but just as determined, refusing men and leading them on a merry chase if they persist.

Gurdafrid was the daughter of Iranian chief Gazhdaham. Suhrab, a young Turanian hero, laid siege to their castle, so Gurdafrid donned armor and took to the field. She met Suhrab in single combat and during their fight she lost her helmet, exposing her flowing hair. Spellbound, Suhrab begged her to stop fighting, and she did, warning him of the ridicule he'd receive if he admitted to pleading for mercy from a girl. Apparently moved by his loving words, she vowed to surrender the castle to him. That night, she and her father escaped through a secret passage. They left him the empty castle, but to Suhrab it was worthless, as it held no trace of the brave warrior-maid.[3]

Upon defeat by the demon Mahisa, who prophesized that only a woman could slay him, the gods of India combined their fiery wrath. This primal fury solidified into the beautiful Durga, whose splendor filled the universe. Each of the male deities gave her a weapon: Shiva's trident, Vishnu's discus, Vayu's bow, and so forth. Thus equipped, the newly-formed goddess mounted a lion and rode into battle. Though a male creation, Durga herself creates female warriors, like Kali and the Matrakas, and wins battles handily without male support. Unlike traditional Hindu women, she is not subordinate, nor does she perform household duties. "She excels at what is traditionally a male function — fighting in battle. As an independent warrior who can hold her own against any male on the battlefield, she reverses the normal role for females and therefore stands outside normal society."[4] Though suitors court her, she defeats them all and thus remains independent.

A similar archetypal warrior is the moon goddess Artemis. She saves the helpless Iphigenia from sacrifice and defends her own mother with drawn bow, protecting mothers in childbirth and lost children alike. At the same time, she rejects romance, swearing her forest nymphs to chastity and punishing them for the slightest transgression: Bolen notes that she is filled with contradictions. "On the one hand, she rescues women and feminist values from the patriarchy, which devalues or oppresses both. On the other, with her intense focus on goals she can also require that a woman sacrifice and devalue what has traditionally been considered feminine."[5] Her virginity becomes a weapon as she slaughters men in its defense, and punishes her dryads mercilessly for any breech of celibacy. She is the girl dancing with her dryads. She is the independent virgin, uncatchable by man. She is the huntress, famed for tearing the spying Actaeon into shreds with his own hunting dogs.

Artemis greatly admired her aunt Athena, who also took vows of chastity and excelled in the masculine worlds of warfare, adventure, and politics. She remained unapproachable, even asexual, but "this very inapproachability, this stubborn sexual independence, permits her to be spiritually, psychologically, even physically close to the male heroes she champions."[6] Athena allies herself with men based on skill and knowledge alone. She is the goddess of wisdom: crafter, inventor, tactician. But while she is devoted to the mind, she has completely divorced herself from the physical. "Living in her head, the Athena woman misses the experience of being fully in her body. She knows little about sensuality and about what it feels like to push her body to its limits."[7] She cares for companions but distances herself from maternal or procreative demands to dwell completely in a "man's world."

Homer notes that three hearts are proof against Aphrodite's love magic.

> First is the daughter of Zeus who holds the aegis, bright-eyed Athena; for she has no pleasure in the deeds of golden Aphrodite, but delights in wars and in the work of Ares, in strifes and battles and in preparing famous crafts. She first taught earthly craftsmen to make chariots of war and cars variously wrought with bronze, and she, too, teaches tender maidens in the house and puts knowledge of goodly arts in each

one's mind. Nor does laughter-loving Aphrodite ever tame in love Artemis, the huntress with shafts of gold; for she loves archery and the slaying of wild beasts in the mountains, the lyre also and dancing and thrilling cries and shady woods and the cities of upright men.

Hestia, too, determined to be "a maiden all her days."

So Zeus the Father gave her a high honor instead of marriage, and she has her place in the midst of the house and has the richest portion. In all the temples of the gods she has a share of honor, and among all mortal men she is chief of the goddesses."[8]

Hestia, later the Roman Vesta, was chief of the Vestal Virgins, daughters of the foremost citizens of Rome, and a strong political force. These maiden goddesses were elevated and revered for their choices, ever representing the untamed maiden archetype.

The Hero's Path

No section on warrior women would be complete without acknowledging Joan of Arc, the 13-year-old who heard a message from St. Michael and rushed to crown the Dauphin and then break the siege at Orleans. She succeeded in both her goals in 1429, but was captured and subjected to English interrogation within a year. Though she refused to recant her belief that she was appointed by God, she was finally excommunicated and burned at the stake.[9]

Showing the warrior woman's fearsome independence as a fighter for freedom, God, and king, she considered her vow of virginity essential, pledging to remain virgin "for as long as it should be pleasing to God."[10] Her guiding saints directed her to a marvelous sword buried behind the altar in the Church of St. Catherine de Fierbois. Though it was quite old, the rust fell off with no effort, evidence of its divine magic.[11] Joan also garbed herself as a knight with horse, male clothing, and weapons. This step into androgyny horrified the judges at her trial, who called her cross-dressing "an abomination before God."[12]

Even as she dressed as a boy, Joan obeyed her feminine side by submitting to the will of her "voices," the saints that bestowed on her divine mission. When questioned, Joan replied humbly "that she was only a poor woman who knew nothing of riding or making war."[13] The judges at her trial urged Joan to abandon her feminine faith and perception, the evidence of her senses, in favor of the masculine adherence to law, but she would not recant. Though she was executed for her actions, she was later sainted for her faith and adherence to divine will.

The warrior woman travels through androgyny, disguising herself as a man and riding to war. In fact, her path is often indistinguishable from the hero's quest, as she leaves behind all trappings of the feminine. Still, she seeks balance, trying to reconcile her growing perception with the skills of battle.

Tsiek tsiek and again *tsiek tsiek,*
Mu-lan weaves, facing the door.
You don't hear the shuttle's sound,
You only hear Daughter's sighs.
They ask Daughter who's in her heart,
They ask Daughter who's on her mind.
"No one is on Daughter's heart,
No one is on Daughter's mind.
Last night I saw the draft posters,
The Khan is calling many troops,
The army list is in twelve scrolls,
On every scroll there's Father's name.
Father has no grown-up son,
Mu-lan has no elder brother.
I want to buy a saddle and horse,
And serve in the army in Father's place."

In the East Market she buys a spirited horse,
In the West Market she buys a saddle,
In the South Market she buys a bridle,
In the North Market she buys a long whip.
At dawn she takes leave of Father and Mother,
In the evening camps on the Yellow River's bank.
She doesn't hear the sound of Father and Mother calling,
She only hears the Yellow River's flowing water cry *tsien tsien.*

At dawn she takes leave of the Yellow River,
In the evening she arrives at Black Mountain.
She doesn't hear the sound of Father and Mother calling,
She only hears Mount Yen's nomad horses cry *tsiu tsiu.*
She goes ten thousand miles on the business of war,
She crosses passes and mountains like flying.
Northern gusts carry the rattle of army pots,
Chilly light shines on iron armor.
Generals die in a hundred battles,
Stout soldiers return after ten years.

On her return she sees the Son of Heaven,
The Son of Heaven sits in the Splendid Hall.
He gives out promotions in twelve ranks
And prizes of a hundred thousand and more.
The Khan asks her what she desires.
"Mu-lan has no use for a minister's post.
I wish to ride a swift mount
To take me back to my home."

When Father and Mother hear Daughter is coming
They go outside the wall to meet her, leaning on each other.
When Elder Sister hears Younger Sister is coming

She fixes her rouge, facing the door.
When Little Brother hears Elder Sister is coming
He whets the knife, quick quick, for pig and sheep.
"I open the door to my east chamber,
I sit on my couch in the west room,
I take off my wartime gown
And put on my old-time clothes."
Facing the window she fixes her cloudlike hair,
Hanging up a mirror she dabs on yellow flower powder
She goes out the door and sees her comrades.
Her comrades are all amazed and perplexed.
Traveling together for twelve years
They didn't know Mu-lan was a girl.
"The he-hare's feet go hop and skip,
The she-hare's eyes are muddled and fuddled.
Two hares running side by side close to the ground,
How can they tell if I am he or she?"[14]

This epic poem from the fifth or sixth century describes Mu Lan's quest in the army. Though she begins the tale weaving, Mu Lan is quick to cast her feminine trappings aside. She excels in battle and impresses all who see her. However, in the end, she refuses a minister's post and requests the heroine's goal — reunification with her family and a triumphant return to the home.

When Mu Lan returns from her adventure, her family greets her as a male hero, cooking a feast and running to the door. She settles sedately into the home life she desires, referred to only as "daughter" and surrounded by family.

Confucian philosopher Lü K'un wrote that women can and should serve as models for men, as moral integrity far outweighs one's gender. He called Mu Lan his "teacher" for her independent spirit, so powerful that her goodness supersedes the rule that men and women should remain separate.[15] She is famed for fidelity and courage, a paragon to heroes as well as to warrior-heroines.

CHAPTER 21

Sword and Shield:
The Warrior Lover

Anat and Ba'al (Ugarit)

Anat, the maiden, was daughter to the father-god El. Goddess of war, the hunt, and savagery, she slew Yam-Nahar, the seven-headed serpent, with her deadly arrows. One day, her brother Ba'al invited her to his home, and, laying out many delicacies for her, confided how he longed for a great palace. Thus he hoped to establish his supremacy over the earth, using his powers of wind and rain to grow the fields. Anat felt her warrior blood surge at the thought of challenging their father. Her eyes went red and she could feel the brush of every sharp fingernail against her palms. She faced her brother, and told him she would visit El.

> I shall trample him like a lamb to the ground,
> I shall bring down his hoary head with blood to the grave,
> The grey hair of his old age with his gore.[1]

Anat stamped her foot and rose into the sky, into the domain of El, Father of the Years. As she slammed open the gates, the bases of the pavilions quaked. She came before El, armed like a warrior, not a supplicant, and he hid himself in seven chambers inside eight enclosures. She pounded on the door so that the entire building trembled. "El, I bring a request," she cried. "And you must grant it."

> [Or] I shall seize thy curls with my right hand,
> thy locks with the great power of my hand,
> I shall pluck out the hair of thy pate.
> I shall bring down thy hoary head with blood to the grave,
> the grey hair of thine old age with thy gore.[2]

From within seven chambers inside eight enclosures, El answered her:

204

"I know thee, my daughter, that thou art invincible
That it is impossible to withstand the goddesses."[3]

Thus he hastily gave Ba'al and Anat all they desired.

As Anat traveled the land in search of her next adventure, she spied a light-ning flash from across the ocean. This was the hero Aqhat, wielding his divine bow and arrows. Anat instantly coveted them. Rushing to Aqhat's side, she eyed the bow with its string of flashing lightning.

Hear, I beseech you, O hero Aqhat,
Ask silver and I will give it you,
Gold and I will bestow it on you;
but give your bow to Anat,
let the sister-in-law of peoples take your arrows.[4]

Aqhat refused, and Anat, in desperation, offered him eternal life, but Aqhat shook his head.

A bow is the weapon of warriors;
shall now womenfolk hunt with it?[5]

Anat glared. Refusal to surrender his bow was all very well, but this was a strike at her deepest, most glorious self. She summoned her flock of eagles, which struck him over and over and slew him. The beautiful bow tumbled to the ocean below, shattering as it impacted, and Anat tumbled down beside it, sobbing. For she would have granted this handsome warrior eternal life and all it could offer, but now he had died for only a broken bow.

This encounter with death was merely a precursor, however, to a far more devastating loss. Ba'al invited his fellow god Mot to a feast, but served only bread and wine. Now Mot, god of the underworld, hungered constantly for human flesh. Infuriated by Ba'al's weak hospitality, Mot threatened to drag him down to the underworld and devour him. Ba'al trembled with fear, racing across the land to do fertility rituals and purify himself. However, it was all to no avail, and Mot slew him.

Anat shook with horror. Her beautiful brother, darling of the gods, had perished. And their father El lay helpless, rolling in ashes, sobbing, and gash-ing his face in mourning. The earth swallowed up its bounty and the fields baked in the desert sun.

Anat searched for Ba'al across the land. At last she discovered his body in the lovely fields of the shore of Death. There she covered her loins with sack-cloth. She scored her skin with a stone knife, and gashed her cheeks and chin and raked her body. Then she hoisted Ba'al's corpse onto her shoulders and carried it to the Heights of Tsaphon of the North. She bewailed him and finally buried him there. She slaughtered goats and bulls, deer and sheep, 70 of each in Ba'al's honor.

> Then she descended into the underworld and killed Mot.
> She seized divine Mot
> with a sword she split him,
> with a sieve she winnowed him,
> with fire she burnt him,
> with mill-stones she ground him,
> in a field she scattered him;
> his flesh indeed the birds ate,
> his limbs indeed the sparrows consumed.
> Flesh cried out to flesh.[6]

She cleaved him with her blade, burned his body with fire, ground him up with a hand-mill, and scattered his remains like corn over a field, returning him to the land. As she bound the undying god in the cycle of nature, enacting the rebirth that comes after death, Ba'al revived. He threw himself at Mot and they gored each other like oxen, bit like serpents, tugged like greyhounds, until Mot cried that the kingdom should be Ba'al's. Thus the kingdom was restored, and the divine pantheon dwelt together on high, with Anat fiercely defending her family and her people.

The Ugarit culture flourished on the Syrian coast between 1500 and 1200 B.C.E.[7] El the sky god and Asherah of the Sea headed its pantheon, together with their children Ba'al and Anat. These latter two reflect the Greek Artemis and Apollo in a number of ways. Both gods represent the sky, while their sisters are mystic archers. The goddesses are maidens, succumbing occasionally to affairs but never to marriage. They are devoted protectors of their brothers, as Anat defeats all of Ba'al's enemies, from the sea dragon Tannin to his rival god Yam. When Ba'al complains that unlike the other gods, he lacks a fine house, Anat vows to intercede with their father, El, and thrash him if he will not comply. These brother-sister partners have complementary skills; they are both warriors, but fulfill each other in many ways as animus-anima.

When Ba'al went hunting, Anat followed, and copulated with him in the form of a cow. "He did lie with her seven and seventy times, she allowed him to mount eight and eighty times" as token of his status as fertility god.[8] She remained virgin, however, unwed and unconquered. She too was a goddess of life and the growing earth, despite her dreadful cruelty toward her foes. After hosting a feast at Ba'al's palace to celebrate his victory over Yam, she adorned herself in rouge and henna, traveled to two nearby towns, and slaughtered the inhabitants:

> And lo, Anat
> gives battle in the valley; Mightily she cuts in pieces the people of
> the two cities; She slaughters the people of the Western Shore;
> She destroys the men of the Eastern Sunrise.
> Beneath her like balls roll heads,

above her like locusts fly palms of hands; like avenging grasshoppers
are the hands of the quick warriors. She hangs
heads on her back; she binds
hands to her belt. Up to her knees she wades
in blood of the swift soldiers, to her thighs in the gore
of quick warriors. With her shafts she drives out
the enemies; with her bow-string the foes.[9]

Anat, like the Greek Eris [Discord], or her Roman counterpart Bellona, twin sister to the war god Ares/Mars, is the counterpart and supporter of her brother, egging him on and realizing his desires. "Anat is violent and war-loving, yet she also establishes conditions of peace in the land. She is imperious yet fiercely loyal to her beloved Ba'al. She is sexual and brings forth offspring without ever ceasing to be a maiden. She is not Ba'al's wife but his companion."[10] Thus she has evolved beyond virgin huntress and into a partner with her animus.

However, the warrior's passion for an equal is often doomed. It is difficult to be lover and independent entity, even more so if one's love offers only identical skills and desires. What gifts of the psyche can Ba'al offer that Anat doesn't already have?

This also becomes a mother-child relationship, as Ba'al's demands for help prompt Anat to defend him over and over. She defeats his enemies, orders his palace built, and finally retrieves him from death. He needs rescue and each time, she complies. Ba'al's desires overwhelm her, forcing her to release him into death and go questing in order to discover her independent identity. He is the sacrificed god so common in myth, and she is the sacrificer, who must prune away the demands of the son-lover in order to grow.

Other Warriors

While these archetypal warriors like Anat and Artemis are guardians of maidenhood everywhere, their status is rarely considered the end of the journey. The warrior is questing for her animus and her future, often discarding her confirmed maidenhood and growing beyond it, like any other heroine.

Gurdya was the sister of Bahram Chubina, chief captain in the city of Rai. He and a few of his chiefs were plotting to overthrow the king, when Gurdya suddenly appeared from behind the curtain, warning her brother to not let his greed outweigh his wisdom. He resented her advice and continued his plotting. By Gurdya's second warning, Bahram relented, but by that point, war was certain. Bahram defeated his enemy twice, but the third engagement left him mortally wounded. Gurdya held him as he died, and, inconsolable, she laid him in a silver coffin. Immediately after, the Khan of Chin (China or Chinese

Turkistan) proposed marriage. She responded that his offer was ill-timed and he should give her four months before expecting a reply. She selected eleven hundred and three score troops, donned her brother's armor, and led the troops to war. The Khan heard of this and dispatched an army of 6,000, warning her that unless she accepted him in marriage, she would be taken prisoner. Gurdya doffed her helmet and identified herself, and then slew the army's chief and many of its soldiers. The king heard of Gurdya's valor, and, remembering the loyalty she had always shown, he requested her hand. She became both his queen, and as warrior, overseer of the royal bower.[11] She was warrior as needed during wartime. But after, she became a fully feminine reigning queen.

Thus even the independent warrior woman may settle down, or simply take a lover, one suited to her stages in the quest. However, keeping him — especially if his competitive warrior nature matches her own — can prove exceptionally difficult.

Artemis was enamored of the hunter Orion. They hunted together through all the forests, until Grandmother Gaia feared all the animals would be killed. Thus she (encouraged perhaps by a jealous Apollo) sent a giant scorpion to slay Orion. Devastated, Artemis set him in the skies as the constellation Orion the Hunter. A perpetual womanizer, he chases the Pleiades through the heavens and hunts Taurus, the bull, with Cancer ever nipping at his heels.

"Paralleling the myth of Artemis and Orion, an Artemis woman may fall in love with a strong man and may then be unable to keep a competitive element out of the relationship, which kills it," Bolen notes.[12] Orion and Artemis competed in hunting until the forests lay near extinction and the other relationships of Artemis's life, like those with her nymphs and brother, went neglected. Like Ba'al, who was consuming Anat's sense of self, Orion had to die for the balance to be restored.

This man is less of a completing animus and more of a soul twin: a mirror reflection of the heroine with the same desire for action. This pair makes a perfect team, but tragically often ends in death and parting. The warrior's lover may compete with her and feel jealous of her success. But even if they remain in accord, they are too similar. Neither brings the melding of opposites who join in a perfect relationship as animus and anima. She may regard him fondly, even love him, but he offers her no potential for growth. Each constantly mirrors the other, offering support and acceptance, but no change.

The virgin huntress or intellectual shies from men. She is aloof because she cannot let down her guard or allow herself to be vulnerable to the Other. Thus Artemis destroys Actaeon, the hunter who dares behold her bathing in a vulnerable moment. "Part of her clings to the lower innocence of the unconscious virgin; part of her yearns for the higher innocence of the mature virgin who is confident enough to be consciously vulnerable."[13] The invulnerable warrior cannot evoke this tender state in her; for this, the warrior requires a different sort of man, who is drawn to her strength of will and independent spirit as qualities he craves but that are underdeveloped in himself.

Artemis, in her night-sky travels, beheld the beautiful shepherd-boy, Endymion, fast asleep under the stars. She visited him in a dream, which he enjoyed so much that he prayed Zeus to let him sleep forever. To this, Artemis added her wish for his eternal youth. Rather than another warrior, Artemis found herself loving the most passive of all mortals, a nurturing shepherd boy confined to eternal sleep, longing only to worship the moon-goddess above. So Endymion slept forever under the stars and evoked tenderness in the fierce-hearted Artemis, who bore him 50 daughters called the Menae.

Here the non-threatening, gentle lover touches the huntress's heart, where a competitive warrior will fail in this quest. Endymion is the true animus for the moon goddess, gentle and sweet in his unceasing dreams. This is the source of the woman's ultimate growth: the sensitive scholar who represents the missing side of the warrior woman's personality. He teaches her compassion, reminding her that "she doesn't need to be so tough all the time." While he supports her goals and willingly submits, he wakens the sensitive side that she lacks. He tempts her towards marriage and motherhood, unlike the fellow warrior, who is happy to remain in a single partnership of equals forever.

Another example is Deborah from the Bible. Though she rides to battle at the head of the army, she afterwards returns to judging, seated on her hill of olive trees. She is described as "the wife of Lapidoth" (Judges 4:4), though he doesn't feature in the story. Clearly, he remains at home, unsuited to the world of battle. However, Deborah has chosen this man to complete her, rather than Barak, her warrior partner. Deborah and Barak are both leaders, both likeminded; she summons him and takes charge without a hint of romance between them. "Up; for this is the day in which the Lord hath delivered Sisera into thine hand: is not the Lord gone out before thee?" she cries.[14] And Barak leads 10,000 men down Mount Tabor at her word.

Barak's famed request that Deborah lead the battle beside him is not truly a cowardly request — she is the general here.

> Barak said unto her, If thou wilt go with me, then I will go: but if thou wilt not go with me, then I will not go. And she said, I will surely go with thee: notwithstanding the journey that thou takest shall not be for thine honor; for the LORD shall sell Sisera into the hand of a woman" [Judges 4:8–9].

This woman who defeats General Sisera is not in fact Deborah, but Jael, who lulls Sisera to sleep and then slays him with a tent peg, a weapon of the home. Deborah recognizes Jael's accomplishments as winning the battle by the hearthside in a way she and Barak couldn't, and names her "Blessed among Women."[15] For Deborah, the valor does not go to the mighty warrior woman, nor the respect to General Barak; there is valor in slaying the enemy as a quiet woman hidden in her tent, just as there is merit in her quietly-laboring husband. Deborah gracefully retires back to her olive tree, where she, as the only female judge of the Bible, governs and protects her village and family.

The wiser warrior women fight when needed, but then progress to protector of the family, resuming their place as leader rather than warrior. Thus Deborah, like Mu Lan, returns home when battle no longer demands her presence.

The Indian goddess Minaksi, born to the local Pandyan king, was notable for her third breast, which, as prophecy foretold, would vanish when she met her future husband. Meanwhile, the virgin princess became an invincible warrior, subduing all she encountered. But when she reached the Himalayas and met the god Shiva, the third breast vanished along with her belligerence, transforming her into an ideal bride.[16]

The quintessential warrior woman of Greek mythology is Atalanta. Abandoned in the hills of Arcadia (ironically, because her father had wanted a son) and raised by bears, Atalanta lived wild and free. By chance, she encountered Prince Meleager, a famed hunter whom she nearly killed for slaying her adopted bear brother. Meleager reasoned with her, and she finally became his hunting partner and lover. They roamed the hills for years, killing and celebrating their triumphs with the future Argonauts. When the terrible Calydon Boar began ravaging the land, Meleager and Atalanta slew it together, and he presented her with the valuable hide. His jealous uncles demanded he rethink his generosity, and when they began insulting Atalanta, Meleager killed them both with a stroke of his sword.

His horrified mother, Althea, stormed home in fury; her son, slayer of her dear brothers, would never marry a nameless hussy from the mountains! She opened a locked chest and withdrew a charred stick of wood. Years ago, the three Fates had promised her that her son's life would last as long as the stick remained unburnt. With a single toss, Althea threw the stick into the fire and ended her son's life. He died in Atalanta's arms.

After her tragic loss, Atalanta returned home, where her father was delighted at his warrior daughter. Nonetheless, he decided to marry her off. In true folkloric fashion, Atalanta challenged suitors to a footrace, and had them beheaded when they lost. Hippomenes, a young man of little athletic skill, longed to win her and coax her into marriage. Refusing to compete with her directly, Hippomenes instead dropped golden apples, gifts from Aphrodite. Each time one fell, she chased it, lured by its dazzling beauty. Thus his coaxing her with generous gifts won her hand, and, in time, her heart.

Atalanta is an Athena figure, comfortable in the men's world and shrugging off her sensitive side as proverbial women's weakness. "Atalanta is very much like our modern heroines — ambitious and accomplished, and comfortable in the world of men. The trouble is, she has no training in the art of relationship."[17] Thus Hippomenes plays things carefully; by tempting her with gifts of love that she has to chase, rather than beating her outright, he succeeds. Hippomenes is the sensitive man, the one who is the warrior's true animus. He is kind where she is brisk, gentle and loving where she is standoffish. He is the one who urges her to commit to marriage and children, while she favors wildness and independence. Yet, her surrender is rarely treated as a loss. No matter who takes the aggressive leader's role, "the function of the gentle animus is the same — to bring up issues that a woman ignores or neglects in her life" as A.B. Chinen tells it.[18] By accepting the gentle suitor, the warrior woman grows into a strong, balanced person who defends her young with a wildcat's tenacity.

CHAPTER 22

Sisters: Lesbianism in Folklore

Bearskin Woman and Grizzly Woman (Blackfoot)

When Bearskin Woman dreamed of Double Moon Woman, she knew she was fated to be a *kwame*, or lesbian. She ventured into the forest and met a bear, Grizzly Woman, and the two speedily fell in love. Bearskin Woman made an amulet that let her take on bear-shape, and they dwelt together happily in a cave.

When her father and brother discovered the relationship, they were far less happy. Gathering some warriors, they surrounded the cave, but the two bears emerged and slaughtered all who had planned to harm them. Bearskin Woman only ceased her destruction when she spied her sister, Sinopa, standing nearby.

Bearskin Woman retook her own form and clutched Sinopa's hand. "Tell the village that I have dreamed of Double Moon Woman, and found my love out here in the forest. Grizzly Woman and I are happy here, and we are holy women, who can bring good luck to all of us if we are left in peace."

The tribe, upon hearing this, was happy to have them living nearby in the forest. But Bearskin Woman's six brothers fumed because the women had defeated them and killed many of their friends.

They gathered piles of prickly pears and strewed them in the cave entrance, and then yelled piercing war cries. Startled, Bearskin Woman and Grizzly Woman rushed outside, fierce and growling. When the prickly pear stickers pierced their paws they howled with pain, but they kept running.

Sinopa, who hated the fighting, had followed her brothers. She shot a magic arrow over their heads, which pushed the brothers to safety, far from the angry bears. But the two bears still pursued them. Whenever their pierced paws brushed the earth, the blood turned to trees. Wherever they dug in their claws, lakes appeared.

The six brothers all hurried up a tree, and huddled there, afraid to descend. Below, the bears licked their paws and waited. But Sinopa shot her arrows over her brothers' heads, propelling the men into the sky one by one, where they became stars. Then Sinopa rode the bow up into the sky where it became the crescent moon and she the queen star of her six brothers. Those seven stars in their cluster are still visible today.

Now free to dwell near their tribe, Bearskin Woman and Grizzly Woman lived happily for many years. When they died, they became the Two Bears of Heaven, who still chase the six star-brothers round and round the sky.[1]

Homosexuality is frequent in the ancient world; Zeus and Apollo fight over the male cupbearer Ganymede, and Achilles, greatest hero of the Trojan War, wears female clothing and then takes his best friend Patrocles as his lover. The famed *Kama Sutra* of India addresses homosexual acts, though it spends far more time and emphasis on heterosexual ones. Though the Judeo-Christian Bible is less tolerant, it is important to note that there is no prohibition against homosexuality, only male homosexual intercourse, mostly because of the perceived violation of others' rights or the association with sexual assault or idolatry. There is no Biblical condemnation of lesbianism.

Throughout the world, lesbianism has always been prevalent but understated, rarely acknowledged or brought to the attention of male writers. In the West, particularly Medieval Europe, writings about lesbian relationships are extremely limited:

> Europeans had long found it difficult to accept that women could actually be attracted to other women. Their view of human sexuality was phallocentric — women might be attracted to men and men might be attracted to men, but there was nothing in a woman that could long sustain the sexual desires of another woman. In law, in medicine, and in the public mind, sexual relations between women were therefore ignored.[2]

Thus, these gynocentric relationships only existed in the private sphere of the home — understood and acknowledged, but rarely a matter for literature or history.

Other cultures acknowledged a variety of relationships, and mixed these tales into their lexicon, albeit sometimes in a joking manner.

Coyote, as a joke, dresses herself as a male, complete with stuffed trousers. While disguised, she plans to seduce Fox, a trumped-up female who is forever grooming her pelt and bragging about her cleverness. The joke is on Coyote, who discovers she enjoys sex with her own gender, just as Fox actually welcomes the opportunity. Coyote discovers her new lesbian interests and heads off to more cross-dressing encounters.[3]

In some African tribes, the publicly acknowledged *baghuru* ritual was used to cement friendships built on pledges of mutual assistance and support,

particularly among wives of the chief. These relationships often involved a sexual dimension, though this aspect was kept below the notice of the husband.
Among the Nyakyusa, the Mongo, the Nupe of Nigeria, the Tswana of southern Africa, and the Azande of the southern Sudan, reciprocal relationships
among adult women are particularly common among the polygamous households, which provide limited attention from their husbands.[4]

As with the African tribes, Chinese polygamy led to a women's community inside the household, with a plentitude of wives waiting to be seen by the
possibly elderly husband. Likewise, brothels, with their close female communities, were havens for female relationships.

> The predatory power nexus of masculine-feminine interaction is absent, many les-
> bians argue, because the male is absent. And with him goes the penis-as-weapon;
> the aggressive, rapist encounter; the denial of female eroticism and gratification;
> and the pain of relational incongruity. The entire baggage of patriarchy is thrown
> out, leaving women free to weave ties of passion and compassion among themselves.[5]

In China, lesbian relationships were regarded with indifference or occasionally
delight by the male chroniclers. Pao Yu, hero of the famed Ch'ing dynasty
novel, *Dream of the Red Chamber*, is quite charmed when he walks in on an
intimate moment between two young women, one of whom is a nun. Indeed,
as Buddhism gained popularity in the Ming dynasty, lesbianism in nunneries
became a popular literary theme, as writers assumed the women had taken vows
to avoid procreative obligations.[6]

Notable is a Chinese play by Li Yü (1611–1680) called *Pitying the Fragrant
Companion*. In a Buddhist convent, a young married woman falls in love with
a woman two years her junior. They take vows as lovers before the Buddha
image. Unlike the bittersweet ending of Bear Woman, this story ends in triumph, as the married woman convinces her husband to take the lover into the
household as a second wife.[7]

Many experts on the Chinese theories of Yin-Yang see heterosexuality as
the most harmonious balance. At the same time, they assert that "a double yin
energy can be harmonious, as yin is yielding," and thus women can care for
each other in a highly mutual relationship.[8] While we have limited knowledge
of Mayan private life, their cosmology offers fascinating insights. In the *Popol
Vuh*, the divine grandparents Xmucané and Xpiyacoc create the world. But the
Mayan "x" suggests "woman," casting our creator couple as Grandmother of
the Sun and Grandmother of the Light. This remains a tantalizing linguistic
theory only, as the Spanish transcribers (all male clergy) edited and censored
the Mayan legends they recorded.[9]

Japanese sexual attitudes are described as "permissive," as homosexuality
and promiscuity are less condemned than in Western Culture. Samurai were
known for homosexual relationships; since these militaristic areas of the culture only valued women as breeders, women turned to lesbian relationships.

Ukiyo-e woodblock prints, especially, feature explicit relationships among nuns.[10] Homoerotic relationships likewise occurred between a mentor and her young student in the youth hostels known as *musume yado*, where pubescent girls learned about sex and courtship.[11]

Japanese Shintoism offers the texts of the *Record of Ancient Things (Kojiki)* and the *Chronicles of Japan (Nihongi)*. Both, like the Western Bible, contain stories of historical record, along with frequent sexual behavior. Unlike the Bible, however, there is little moral condemnation from a deity or his earthly representatives. In the *Nihongi*, the emperor pursues a young woman, and eventually seduces her. However, she remains distant. "The way of husband and wife is the prevailing rule now and of old time. But for me it is not convenient," she explains. "Thy handmaiden's disposition is adverse to the way of conjugal intercourse." Convinced by her honesty, the emperor weds her sister instead.[12]

Two-Spirits

A long time ago, in the Native American Winnebago tribe, a warrior band returned with several captive Sioux, including a chief. Normally, the Warrior clan of the Hawk took charge of prisoners, but in this case, only two members of that clan remained, a grandmother and a boy. Since the only male Hawk was a child, the grandmother dressed in a man's leathers and made the ruling: the leader would not be harmed, but he would have to live in their village for the rest of his days, living, dressing, and working as a woman.

This is one of the many origin myths about the creation of Two-spirits, a minority group within many Native American tribes, now almost purged from modern society. Pedro de Magalhaes de Gandavo described them in 1576:

> There are some Indian women who determine to remain chaste: they have no commerce with men in any manner, nor would they consent to it even if refusal meant death. They give up all the duties of women and imitate men, and follow men's pursuits as if they were not women. They wear the hair cut in the same way as the men, and go to war with bows and arrows and purse game, always in company with men; each has a woman to serve her, to whom she says she is married, and they treat each other and speak with each other as man and wife.[13]

These women are following the hero's quest, with male mentors and weapons, but they take it a step further, wedding women and permanently abandoning their feminine natures. These are tales of transitions, of people who embrace their sublimated side to such an extent that they invoke that other gender, permanently taking on its role. The grandmother of the tale is not a warrior by birth: she has married into the tribe. In the same way, she is not a man by birth, but she has assumed a man's duties along with a warrior's. The Sioux chief, too, was born a man, but will no longer fight.

In fact, Two-spirits were considered a third gender, properly able to marry men or women, but not other Two-spirits. For this reason, the term "gay marriage" does not properly apply. The term Two-spirit originated in 1990 in Winnipeg, Canada, during the third annual intertribal Native American/First Nations gay and lesbian conference. This literal translation of the Ojibwa phrase *niizh manidoowag* (two spirits) was chosen to distance Native/First Nations people from non-natives as well as from the inappropriately used "berdache" and "gay."[14]

Some tribes believed gender (including this third one) was determined before birth, and raised their children as they felt their destinies suggested. Among the Kaska Tribe of western Canada, some parents would decide to raise their daughter as a son, and tie dried bear ovaries around her belt to prevent her from becoming fertile. They would then raise her as a hunter.[15]

A young man became a Two-spirit if and only if during his vision quest he received a dream telling him that this was his destiny. Among the Hočąk, a young man would become this *teją 'čowįga,* "blue ocean woman," as they called it, if the Moon appeared and blessed him. If it told him to "take up the skirt," and he did not, the Moon would take his life. This blessing offered him the powers to see the future and excel at women's duties beyond anyone in the tribe. Thus, the Two-spirits had the reputation of being clever and lucky beyond others, much prized in the tribe or in matrimony.[16] Some spouses even believed the Two-spirits could give them magical powers.

While the Two-spirit men often became second or third wives to warriors, and were permitted to adopt children (famed Lakota warrior Crazy Horse had two Two-spirit wives), Two-spirit women were more frequently monogamous, as the head of the household. Among the Lakota, it was important that the *koskalaka* ("young man" or "woman who does not want to marry") be ritually bound to her wife with the blessing of the goddess Double Woman, binding them together with a rope baby, like tying off their fertility.[17]

The Navaho believe that *nadle,* as they call Two-spirits, existed in the third world of creation. As they consider our current world to be the fifth, *nadle* are treasured as an enduring legacy from that revered past. The twin heroes, White Shell Girl and Turquoise Boy, the first *nadle,* introduced pottery making and many tools. When their world was no longer livable, they ushered their followers into the fourth world.[18] These *nadle* were relied on to bless the tribe. As one Navaho representative explained:

> If there were no *nadle,* the country would change. They are responsible for all the wealth in the country. If there were no more left, the horses, sheep, and Navaho would all go. They are leaders just like President Roosevelt. A *nadle* around the *hogan* will bring good luck and riches. They have charge of all the riches. It does a great deal for the country if you have *nadle* around.[19]

Other tribes of the world carried on similar traditions of allowing children to switch gender. The South Asian hijra are a similar "third gender," mostly born male, who take on more feminine roles, joining a hijra family as the first step of socialization. They perform religious ceremonies believed to bring about luck and fertility. In a Cretan myth, the woman Iphis was raised as a boy, since her father planned to kill any daughters he produced. Iphis grew into a beautiful youth, with whom the woman Ianthe fell in love. In time, Iphis returned her affections and prayed Isis to transform her into a man, which was done.

In one famous tale, repeated across many cultures, a girl was brought up as a boy. When she grew up, she rescued and married a princess, and the deception wasn't discovered until after the wedding. The king decided to send his new "son" on a dangerous mission to find a magical horse. However, the "prince" poured wine into the fountain, dizzying the horse so it succumbed easily. Next the king demanded taxes from the demons, whom the prince tricked. Growing ever more frustrated, the king finally demanded his father's rosary, stolen by the demon queen. The prince snatched it as the queen slept, but she awoke and rode after him in fury. "My curse upon you," she shrieked. "If thou be woman, be thou man; if thou be man, be thou woman." And thus the prince became a man, and spent his days with the princess he loved.[20]

Here we see early myths of gender-transformation, in which the princess loves and marries a woman. The court is distressed by this turn of events and gives her tasks they hope will kill her, until she receives her dearest wish and becomes the man she has always appeared. Thus she completes her transformation and finds acceptance at court.

Sappho

> Although they are
> only breath, words
> which I command
> are immortal.[21]

So wrote Sappho, who addressed so many poems to love and the arts of poetry and dance. From this Greek poetess who made her home on the isle of Lesbos originates the modern word "lesbian."

> By far, most of her themes concern erotic love in some respect: calling on deities associated with love and celebrating both love between women and love in marriage. The fact that much of her love poetry is homoerotic, written for women and celebrating love between women, has evoked great controversy. Her name and island have become synonymous with female homosexuality.[22]

Unfortunately most of her poems, including those most controversial ones, have not survived to the modern day. Most of the fragments we possess are single lines quoted in others' books as examples of poetic techniques.

"I shall be a virgin always," she writes in one tantalizing line, perhaps acknowledging desire that transcended traditional marriage.[23]

> The night is now
> half-gone; youth
> goes; I am
> in bed alone.[24]

She was, in fact, widowed, with a daughter named Kleis about whom she bragged lovingly. Born around 620 B.C.E., she welcomed accomplished women from Greece and Asia Minor to Lesbos, where they joined in an artistic commune. This school was dedicated to Aphrodite, Sappho's muse, and was, as she called it, a *moisopolon domos,* house of those who cultivated the Muses.[25] There, her many protégés, such as the celebrated Damophila, composed their own lyric poems.[26] She nurtured these women, writing many poems of love and affection to them:

> Be kind to me
> Gongyla; I ask only
> that you wear the cream
> white dress when you come
>
> Desire darts about your
> loveliness, drawn down in
> circling flight at the sight of it.[27]

At last, many would depart for advantageous marriages, with Sappho singing their marriage songs. To Anactoria, she wrote

> Go, and be happy
> but remember (you know
> well) whom you leave shackled by love
>
> If you forget me, think
> of all our gifts to Aphrodite
> and all the loveliness we shared
>
> All the violet tiaras,
> Braided rosebuds, dill and
> crocus twined around your young neck.[28]

In 1871, Thomas Wentworth Higginson's essay envisioned Sappho's idyllic school of women, saying:

Let us now turn and look upon her in her later abode of Mitylene; either in some garden of orange and myrtle, such as once skirted the city, or in that marble house which she called the dwelling of the Muses. Let us call around her, in fancy, the maidens who have come from different parts of Greece to learn of her. Anactoria is here from Miletus, Eunica from Salamis, Gongyla from Colophon, and others from Pamphylia and the isle of Telos. Erinna and Damophyla study together the complex Sapphic metres; Atthis learns how to strike the harp with the plectron,

Sappho's invention; Mnasidica embroiders a sacred robe for the temple. The teacher meanwhile corrects the measures of one, the notes of another, the stitches of a third, then summons all from their work to rehearse together some sacred chorus or temple ritual; then stops to read a verse of her own, or — must I say it? — to denounce a rival preceptress. For if the too fascinating Andromeda has beguiled away some favorite pupil to one of those rival feminine academies that not only exist in Lesbos, but have spread as far as illiterate Sparta, then Sappho may at least wish to remark that Andromeda does not know how to dress herself. "And what woman ever charmed thy mind," she says to the vacillating pupil, "who wore a vulgar and tasteless dress, or did not know how to draw her garments close about her ankles?"[29]

Sappho's own descriptions reveal a dance, filled only with women, enjoying the joys of sisterhood:

> And their feet move
>
> Rhythmically, as tender
> feet of Cretan girls
> danced one around an
>
> altar of love, crushing
> a circle in the soft
> smooth flowering grass.[30]

There they lived in a haven, women alone, celebrating the arts. Sappho was their guide and mentor, as she describes it, "like a mother with all her daughters around her."[31] Perhaps they were a cult of Aphrodite, forming a female-only *thiasos* of devotees bound by ritual as well as fellowship.[32] Perhaps they only numbered among the extraordinarily predominant female poets of the time, training with the most celebrated lyricist of their day.

Though classicists often idealized (and censored!) Sappho into a headmistress of a women's school bare of improprieties, she has long been known as a depicter of homosexual ideals. The third-century Roman Maximus Tyrius drew a parallel between the instruction given by Socrates to men and that afforded by Sappho to women. "Each," he says, "appears to me to deal with the same kind of love, the one as subsisting among males, the other among females."[33]

She wrote in a style that was unusually personal for her time, and was one of the first Greek poets to write in first person. Her works in her lifetime were sung and quoted extensively; she appears on Roman coins and vases, attesting to her great popularity. Sappho composed her own music and refined the prevailing lyric meter to a point that it is now known as Sapphic meter. Plato named her "the tenth Muse."

Today, many make pilgrimages to Lesbos, exploring Sappho's world and paying homage to this first of lesbian writers. But lesbianism has always existed in the world, among the women's communities where male chroniclers dared not set foot.

CHAPTER 23

The Right to Choose: The Seductress

The Marriage of Aphrodite (Greece)

I will sing of stately Aphrodite, gold-crowned and beautiful, whose dominion is the walled cities of all sea-set Cyprus. There the moist breath of the western wind wafted her over the waves of the loud-moaning sea in soft foam, and there the gold-filleted Hours welcomed her joyously. They clothed her with heavenly garments: on her head they put a fine, well-wrought crown of gold, and in her pierced ears they hung ornaments of orichalc and precious gold, and adorned her with golden necklaces over her soft neck and snow-white breasts, jewels which the gold-filleted Hours wear themselves whenever they go to their father's house to join the lovely dances of the gods. And when they had fully decked her, they brought her to the gods, who welcomed her when they saw her, giving her their hands. Each one of them prayed that he might lead her home to be his wedded wife, so greatly were they amazed at the beauty of violet-crowned Cytherea.[1]

Aphrodite was the only member of Zeus's pantheon not descended from the Olympians. Born from the foam of their grandfather Uranus's murder, she floated to the island of Cypress, wafted on the moist breath of Zephyrus, the western wind. She wandered ashore, heady blossoms sprouting under her bare feet and birds serenading her with adoration. There the Hours and Graces adorned her in swan-soft robes, and bore her up to Olympus.

She stood like a queen before the Olympians, diffusing the scent of cinnamon and bedewing the air with balsam. The gods wordlessly offered her their hands and hearts, so dazzled were they at her glory.

Queen Hera's eyes narrowed, and she hastily nudged Zeus. "She must be married off!"

Zeus blinked. "Of course. I will stand as her father here: Let the gods press their suits."

"Be mine," Apollo said, amber locks blazing like the sun he ruled. "Command the gentle Muses as your handmaidens and sit on a throne of gold beside my own."

"Wed me," Poseidon said. "I offer you treasures: shipwrecks and sea-gems, sunken islands and hidden coves. Whales will sing for you, and seals dance. All the mysteries and secrets of the waters shall be yours. Be my queen."

Hera gripped the lame smith Hephaestus by the shoulders and propelled him forward. "Say what I told you," she hissed.

Hephaestus, filthy and stunted, gazed up at the loveliest of goddesses. "I'd be a good husband for you. I work late."

Aphrodite drew his chin up and kissed him. That night, the two wedded in a glorious Olympian fete.

Hephaestus was Hera's son, but she had flung him off Olympus when he was born deformed and twisted. He only took his place among the gods by gifting her with a jeweled throne that imprisoned her with mechanical arms until she relented. Now Hera gave him Aphrodite, whom he coveted beyond all things. But she knew what a torment this marriage would be.

Ares, god of war, gave Aphrodite many gifts, and she invited him to dally with her in her husband's bed. But Helios, the sun's charioteer, saw them and told Hephaestus. Brooding revenge, Hephaestus stalked to his forge and hammered out a bronze net, so light as to be invisible, and yet so strong no god could shatter it. He hung it all around the bedposts and roof beams, and then pretended to set off for the isle of Lemnos.

When Ares and Aphrodite retired to bed, the net held them fast and immobile. Then Hephaestus retuned, and proclaimed in a voice loud enough for all Olympus to hear:

> "Father Jove," he cried, "and all you other blessed gods who live for ever, come here and see the ridiculous and disgraceful sight that I will show you. Jove's daughter Venus [Aphrodite] is always dishonoring me because I am lame. She is in love with Mars [Ares], who is handsome and clean built, whereas I am a cripple — but my parents are to blame for that, not I; they ought never to have begotten me. Come and see the pair together asleep on my bed. It makes me furious to look at them. They are very fond of one another, but I do not think they will lie there longer than they can help, nor do I think that they will sleep much; there, however, they shall stay till her father has repaid me the sum I gave him for his baggage of a daughter, who is fair but not honest."[2]

All the gods came to witness the spectacle, though the goddesses were too modest, and remained at home. The gods laughed at the sight, and, glancing stealthily at one another, each silently acknowledged that the slow, crippled smith had beaten the mighty god of war. "I would not be caught thus for anything," Hermes said.

"I would, to lie in fair Aphrodite's arms," Dionysus retorted.

Aphrodite turned tearful eyes at the watching gods. She smiled hopefully at her furious husband, and it was as if the sun had come out after a long rain.

"Let them go," Poseidon said. "I will stand surety that Ares will pay what penalty you ask for this transgression. Tie me in your net if he does not." The other gods were likewise charmed by Aphrodite, and begged for clemency.

Hephaestus, much moved, released the lovers.

Though Aphrodite wandered where she willed, Hephaestus forgave her and loved her time and again. She was the ultimate chooser of her fate, ever majestic and autonomous, a goddess whose power could ensnare even the other Olympians. Fairest of goddesses, she carried herself like a queen, whether dancing on Cypress with her maidens or blessing mortals with the gifts of love.

Aphrodite (Venus to the Romans) is the ultimate goddess, the most beautiful and sensual of all her pantheon. She is "the almighty Lady of Everything — cosmic totality, death and rebirth, and the sex energy of existence."[3] Firstborn among the Olympians from the sky father and earth mother themselves, she rises from the patriarch Uranus's murder, thus melding death and fertility indelibly in the minds of her followers. Rather than wedding a potential equal such as Poseidon, she commits to the crippled little smith, Hephaestus. Part of this is a desire for dalliances. As the unconfinable goddess of fertility, she had many children, with many fathers: Phobos and Deimos (Ares), Harmonia (Ares), Hermaphroditus (Hermes), Rhodos (Poseidon), Priapus (Dionysus), Aeneas (Prince Ankhises of Troy), and Eros (Zeus or Ares or spontaneous generation). "Not only is Aphrodite sexually powerful, she is sexually generous. In some myths she is said to be married to Hephaestus, but this relationship in no way limits or fulfils her sexual expression."[4]

Yet she never stays long with Ares or Hermes, instead preferring to return to her husband. Hephaestus is the artist and craftsman, the ultimate builder. Aphrodite wields a force to which even Zeus falls victim. However, the Great Goddess requires her opposite, powerless and shy yet committed and indescribably creative, to complete her.

Aphrodite was the untamable wanderer, born of the sea. Unlike the Olympians, she traces her identity back to Inanna, Ishtar, and Astarte, the supreme goddess with the subordinate son-lover. Her lover Adonis, as the god of corn and vegetation, must perish to be reborn each year, while the goddess, as continuous principle of life, remains behind, watching over the earth. The boar that slays him exemplifies the male aspect of the great mother as fertile pig sacrificing the lover that he may be reborn as the son.[5] Even Eros, with his tiny hunter's bow, could be viewed as another of Aphrodite's son-lovers.[6]

As goddess of love and beauty, Aphrodite was ever dazzling, ever divine. She also had the power to make others irresistible, which occurred in one memorable moment of *The Iliad*.

Juno ... turned her eyes to Jove [Jupiter] as he sat on the topmost crests of many-fountained Ida, and loathed him. She set herself to think how she might hoodwink him, and in the end she deemed that it would be best for her to go to Ida and array herself in rich attire, in the hope that Jove might become enamored of her, and wish to embrace her.[7]

Arraying herself with ambrosia and scented olive oil,

she plaited the fair ambrosial locks that flowed in a stream of golden tresses from her immortal head. She put on the wondrous robe which Minerva had worked for her with consummate art, and had embroidered with manifold devices; she fastened it about her bosom with golden clasps, and she girded herself with a girdle that had a hundred tassels: then she fastened her earrings, three brilliant pendants that glistened most beautifully, through the pierced lobes of her ears, and threw a lovely new veil over her head.[8]

She then borrowed the legendary girdle of Venus, which could make all women irresistible. In this moment, Juno is evoking the Aphrodite within herself, becoming vibrant and young and dazzling — sex goddess rather than queen mother. In this form, she seduces her husband, thus keeping his eyes from the Trojan War.

Aphrodite was endlessly versatile, known by many epithets. She was the Golden One, goddess of beauty; mother of Aeneas, darling of gods and men; Aphrodite the Persuasive; Smile-loving; goddess of the Serene Sea; and Aphrodite the Slayer of Men.[9]

Seductive goddesses often seem soft to modern readers, inconsequential prostitutes who belong as far from the battlefield as possible. But these femme fatales are ignored at the hero's risk. They are the sirens and mermaids who dash men against the rocks with their sweet songs. They are Circe, who transforms men into pigs. Ishtar, of the inexorable wrath, Delilah, Judith, and Salome, who charmingly murder. Or they are Déirdre and Helen, luring men to battle over their unconscious beauty.

Rarely endowed with independent money or position, force or military might, women throughout history have often resorted to the cleverness men have always found intoxicating. This involved wisdom of the body as well as the mind, as these women relished their femininity, rather than suppressed it. As seductresses, they displayed a confidence, body-knowledge, and allure that others found irresistible. As Elinor W. Gadon explains in *The Once and Future Goddess*, "Our bodies *are* ourselves. We are sensuous beings who know the world through our senses, who know ourselves through physical intimacy."[10]

The king's mistress, such as Madame de Pompadour or Diane de Poitiers, was often more influential than the politically-chosen queen. Her spiritual sisters, the courtesans of Venice and other parts of 17th and 18th-century Europe, wielded significant political power. Often poets, performers, and artists, the courtesans were expected to be skilled courtiers (the original meaning of courtesan), educated entertainers, delightful conversationalists, and perfect companions. Across the world, Japanese Geishas (literally artists) learned music, dance, the tea ceremony, literature, and poetry. The similarly-roled hetaerae of Greece were scholars and leading public figures, such as Plato's students Lashena of Mantua and Axiothea.[11] The hetaerae were the only women who took part in the Symposia.

Femme Fatales

Mythical seductresses likewise employed irresistible wit and charm. In one of King Topa's campaigns, the Inca built a town before the fortified hilltop they were besieging. The village women danced so provocatively that they lured the enemy guards down to join them, at which point the Inca conquered the fort.[12]

Large-wombed Freya was the Norse goddess of dance, song, laughter, love-making, and other generally fertile aspects of life. Coveting a finely-crafted necklace four dwarves had just completed, Freya offered them gold and silver, but they demanded four nights, one spent with each of them. Freya agreed, but gained more than the magical necklace. Each dwarf represented a compass point along with its corresponding element, and as she visited them, she assimilated their wisdom.

The Irish queen Macha made war on one uncle and wedded the other in order to claim her father's kingdom. But the uncle she had slain, Dithorb, had five sons who schemed against her. One night, the five young men were cooking venison by the fire. Macha appeared to them one by one, and lured them seductively into the forest. As each lowered his guard, she bound him tightly. At last, she slung all five on her back and carried them home, where she forced them to build her fortress of Emain Macha.[13]

One of the most famous seductresses is Biblical Salome, whose dance of the seven veils won her a murderous boon from King Herod:

> When Herod's birthday was kept, the daughter of Herodias danced before them, and pleased Herod. Whereupon he promised with an oath to give her whatsoever she would ask. And she, being before instructed of her mother, said, "Give me here John Baptist's head in a charger." And the king was sorry: nevertheless for the oath's sake, and them which sat with him at meat, he commanded it to be given her. And he sent, and beheaded John in the prison. And his head was brought in a charger, and given to the damsel: and she brought it to her mother [Matthew 14:6–11].

Though the Bible doesn't go into detail, Salome's seductive dance has been portrayed in film, opera, and ballet, as well as in the famed play by Oscar Wilde. She is the embodiment of an Aphrodite woman as she spins and arcs, luring the king into submission. The novel *À Rebours* by Joris-Karl Huysmans offers these fevered imaginings, describing a painting of Salome:

> No longer was she merely the dancing-girl who extorts a cry of lust and lechery from an old man by the lascivious movements of her loins; who saps the morale and breaks the will of a king with the heaving of her breasts, the twitching of her belly, the quivering of her thighs. She had become, as it were, the symbolic incarnation of undying Lust, the goddess of immortal Hysteria, the accursed Beauty exalted above all other beauties by the catalepsy that hardens her flesh and steels her muscles, the monstrous Beast, indifferent, irresponsible, insensible, poisoning, like the Helen of ancient myth, everything that approaches her, everything that sees her, everything that she touches.[14]

As with Freya's enlightenment, Salome gains strength and magic through her dance, evolving from woman to something far more menacing. The seven veils she sheds are like the veils of Inanna, discarded at each of the underworld gates. This stripping is not merely exhibitionist. It is a way of connecting more deeply to the self by shedding barriers against the outside world. Though we consider the erotic a way to influence others, it is also a means to connect with the self, to savor sensation and relish one's own body. Audre Lorde describes this in "Uses of the Erotic: The Erotic as Power":

> When we begin to live ... in touch with the power of the erotic within ourselves, and allowing that power to inform and illuminate our actions upon the world around us, then we begin to be responsible to ourselves in the deepest sense. For as we begin to recognize our deepest feelings, we begin to give up, of necessity, being satisfied with suffering, and self-negation, and with the numbness which so often seems like their only alternative in our society. Our acts against oppression become integral with self, motivated and empowered from within.[15]

Lorde adds, "That creative energy empowered, the knowledge and use of which we are now reclaiming in our language, our history, our dancing, our loving, our work, our lives."[16] Through the dance, Salome is not just swaying the king; she is learning herself, as she makes the descent into her body-knowledge, and with it, self-knowledge. "It is the pure feminine energy that allows a woman to be in love with her body ... unprocessed and unpossessing, its strength is vulnerability, vulnerable to life, to love, to otherness."[17]

And yet, Salome uses her influence to deal death, like Aphrodite or Ishtar, enraged and murderous. Across the world, beauty and savagery, love and death meld, and the most beautiful of seductresses may strike down the unwary.

Morgiana, of "Ali Baba and the Forty Thieves" warns her master repeatedly that he is harboring the king of thieves as his honored guest. Frustrated at Ali Baba's oblivious naïveté, she finally dances provocatively for the thief, and then stabs him with a hidden dagger. A grateful Ali Baba frees her and weds the clever girl to his son.

Another seductive dancer is Mohini (Delusive), a feminine aspect of the

Indian god Vishnu. When she meets the demon Bhasma, whose touch turns everything to ash, she beguiles him, and promises to yield her favors if he will dance with her. She raises her left arm and then her right, watching as he imitates her gestures. Then she places her hand on her head, and he does likewise, destroying himself.

Throughout literature, the archetypal temptress is a "fallen woman" who discards conventional morality and behavior. She is the murderous succubus, the Morgan le Fay or Circe who brings down kingdoms. Is this the only role allowed her?

Pre-Raphaelite painters glorified femme fatales from Eve to Delilah as lush, sensual, and vibrant. John Keats, like other romantics, wove lyric images of "La Belle Dame sans Merci" and "Lamia" in his poems. Likewise, the Marquis de Sade's novel *Juliette* showed the femme fatale triumphing, symbolizing not evil, but all the best qualities of women. Modern writers too are beginning to embrace the courtesan as heroine, crafting the movies *Dangerous Beauty* or *Moulin Rouge!* and books such as the bestselling *Memoirs of a Geisha* or *Kushiel's Dart*. These tales offer fascinating glimpses into the hidden world of danger and eroticism.

Still, the courtesan as protagonist is not as new a concept as readers may imagine. For every Morgan le Fay who seduces the innocent Arthur, another woman embraces her feminine sensuality to prosper in a male-oriented world.

Sexual Autonomy

Lady Ragnell, or the Loathly Lady, arranges her own marriage to Sir Gawain in exchange for saving King Arthur's life. Though hideous to behold, the lady controls her own marriage and destiny. After the wedding, she transforms into a beauty, but warns Gawain that their wedding has broken only part of the spell. The transformation will only be permanent if Gawain answers correctly: Should she be ugly at night, when they are alone together, or day, when in view of the court? He solves the riddle when he gives her the right to choose for herself. In literature, assertiveness in women is often reflected by a monstrous or demonic form. However, Lady Ragnell is rewarded with socially pleasing beauty at her tale's end, indicating that her independent nature has its place in society. Only Lady Ragnell's self-determination, the right to choose, can lead to happiness for both partners.

Queen Maeve of Irish legend was another such independent lady. She was made queen of Connaught by her father and she had many husbands and lovers whom she divorced or even assassinated when they proved troublesome. Before each relationship, she explained that she required that her consort be generous in gift-giving, courageous in battle, and trusting in the bedroom. She was upfront about her frequent affairs, adding, "Should he be jealous, the husband with whom I live, that too would not suit me, for there was never a time that I had not my paramour."[18] She was sovereign always, instigating the battle of the *Táin Bó Cúalnge* so she might claim the prize bull that would make her equal in all things to her husband Aillil. Leading the battle in all her finery, she is a fierce warrior and quick thinker, fueled by determination. She knows her own worth, even offering "the friendship of her thighs" in exchange for the bull. The fact that most of her lovers die paints her as a font of mind-altering, intoxicating love that transcends mortal power to withstand. She is like the fairy queen, stealing young men and using them up.

History's most famed seductress, Cleopatra, likewise claimed independence through the tools available to her. Her every move was calculated to impress, to seduce, to entice — Plutarch saw her as "a *femme fatale*, with grace, charm, and unusual appeal."[19] Though strong co-ruler of Egypt with her brother-husband, she smuggled herself to Julius Caesar's bedroom rolled in a carpet, and persuaded him to back her independent rule under Rome. In 45 B.C., an enamored Caesar presented her to Rome as the goddess Isis-Venus.

After his death, Cleopatra determined to ally herself with Mark Antony, Caesar's successor in Egypt. She met him on her floating palace, with sails of purple and deck piled with roses. Her hands were scented with kyphi, a rare mix of violets and other flowers, while her feet were anointed with egyptium, almond oil with orange blossoms, and cinnamon.[20] In Shakespeare's lavish description:

> The barge she sat in, like a burnish'd throne,
> Burn'd on the water. The poop was beaten gold;
> Purple the sails, and so perfumed that
> The winds were love-sick with them; the oars were silver,
> Which to the tune of flutes kept stroke, and made
> The water which they beat to follow faster,
> As amorous of their strokes. For her own person,
> It beggar'd all description. She did lie
> In her pavilion, cloth-of-gold, of tissue,
> O'erpicturing that Venus where we see
> The fancy out-work nature. On each side her
> Stood pretty dimpled boys, like smiling Cupids,
> With divers-colour'd fans, whose wind did seem
> To glow the delicate cheeks which they did cool,
> And what they undid did.[21]

Antony was instantly beguiled.

Both he and Caesar appalled the Roman people when they submitted to her adulterous personal and political desires. Yet Cleopatra used her talents as tools. She was seduction personified but also boldness and self-determinism, embracing her femininity to rule as triple queen.

Shakespeare knew instinctively what any student of the Cleopatra legend quickly learns: that the queen is no longer a person whose character can be re-created. She is the stateswoman, the fatal lady, the harlot, the martyr, a "dream walking" all at once, a heroine who long before 1607 had assumed a thousand faces, a thousand complexions, a thousand personalities. We can't see her, we can't describe her, we can't label her — because she has dwelled too long in too many minds. But we all know what Cleopatra is. Cleopatra is ancient sex, *la différence*.[22]

Her final, noble suicide with a basket of sacred asps, to avoid humiliation at Caesar Octavian's hand, marks her as the ultimate chooser of her own fate. "She transcended gender roles, rose to the highest distinction as sovereign, and molded the destinies of the two greatest men of the world, all with Eros and queenship working in perfect concert."[23]

Blessed Seductress

Trickster goddesses perform bawdy skits and display their private parts, generally shocking the audience into laughter. This is a celebration of the female body and a defiance of those in authority who try to keep women, and their bodies, under wraps. Thus, in the feminist realm, "women's erotic-reproductive capacities become rich sources of meaning, no longer tragic forms of oppression.... Releasing erotic impulses and using them as a ground for living transforms the point of repression — the life instincts — into a force for liberation."[24] In a Mexican tale, a girl lifts her skirt in front of a boy and he faints (not the other way around!). A Pueblo woman leads warriors into battle; before the attack, she lifts her skirt four times, exposing herself, and then defeats the enemy.[25] Heroines across the world flip up their skirts, defiantly displaying their gender and breaking society's conventions. This is a source of energy and magic rather than shame. As Gadon notes in *The Once and Future Goddess*, "When women deny all those parts of themselves said to be like nature — the relational, the carnal, the body processes and rhythms — they are denying their bodily, sensate selves."[26]

In the *Tain*, the great warrior Cúchulainn was so filled with masculine energy that he rushed upon his own countrymen, weapons drawn. Quickly, King Conchobar gave orders

to let out the womenfolk to meet the youth, namely, thrice fifty women, even ten and seven-score bold, stark-naked women, at one and the same time, and their chieftainess, Scannlach ("the Wanton") before them, to discover their persons and their shame to him. Thereupon the young women all arose and marched out, and they discovered their nakedness and all their shame to him. The lad hid his face from them and turned his gaze on the chariot, that he might not see the nakedness or the shame of the women.[27]

Embarrassed, Cúchulainn looked away and his battle-rage broke: "A man may thus comfortably face one naked woman at a time, at least when he is in control of the situation; but a crowd of uncontrolled naked women constitutes a plethora of concentrated sexuality, and the ancient hero could not stand up to so much energy."[28]

Radha, lover of the young god Krishna, is both his devotee and his equal, abandoning herself to passion and thus reaching a higher spiritual level: "Oh where has this Radha learned such proficiency/ In the ways of love/ That she has conquered the unconquerable?" scripture asks.[29] Thus she earns the "invincible lord's" devotion as he has earned hers. She is married, but her passion for Krishna is too natural and divinely ordained to resist. "The conviction of Radha and Krishna that each is the life of the other may correspondingly be interpreted as hinting at their metaphysical equality as well as affirming their intimate interdependence."[30] Her love and acknowledgement of it makes Radha holy. Thus Radha, who succumbs with all her heart to sacred passion, is a model for lovers everywhere.

Surrendering to one's feelings, and even the needs of one's body, has been considered sacred throughout history, in contrast with today's denigration of sexual acts. "Rather than repress our bodily needs, which later return as a dirty fascination or morbid rejection of the body itself in the persona of female-mother flesh, we should integrate and accept the body's pleasures as well as its pains," comments Trask in *Eros and Power*.[31]

The oldest recorded story, *The Epic of Gilgamesh*, focuses on the culture-hero Gilgamesh's need for a companion, and the taming of the wild beast-man, Enkidu. More interesting is the method of taming, as Gilgamesh tells the harlot Shamhat to seduce him. Shamhat is considered an artist, skilled enough at her profession that she can domesticate Enkidu into a rational being. She is revered as a powerful destroyer and tamer, much like Aphrodite, exercising her influence. Gilgamesh instructs her,

> "That is he, Shamhat! Release your clenched arms,
> expose your sex so he can take in your voluptuousness.
> Do not be restrained — take his energy!
> When he sees you he will draw near to you.
> Spread out your robe so he can lie upon you,
> and perform for this primitive the task of womankind!
> His animals, who grew up in his wilderness, will become alien to him,
> and his lust will groan over you."[32]

The *hieros gamos*, or sacred marriage, was performed by women in ancient Sumeria, Babylon, Anatolia, Carthage, and Canaan. Ritually, the woman would prostitute herself to a stranger, pledging her body to the goddess's higher purpose. This submission to instinct was truly a religious act, exploring the spiritual not as connecting with the man but as connecting with the self. By offering herself to a stranger, rather than a husband or lover, the supplicant could experience the male aspect of the visiting god and incorporate it. Unconnected with love, this was sex as experience of the universal masculine.

The permanent temple prostitutes were likewise revered as symbols of the goddess, offering ancient man his link with the anima.[33] Well-educated and allowed to inherit property, the prostitutes were generally considered equal to men. In Akkadian they were known as *qadishtu*, sanctified women. Others called them "sacred women" or "the undefiled."[34]

For a man, this sacred marriage represented more than pleasure; it was an essential contact with the mysterious life-creating magic of the woman's body. The sacred marriage between king and priestess was a similar experience, representing king and goddess, or king and earth. He wedded the land in order to be bound to it forever.

The sacred marriage was often considered a way of uniting civilizations, as Zeus wedded local mother-goddesses such as Europa, Io, Semele, Maia, Leto, Dione, Leda, Metis, and even Hera. As Greek legends evolved, these Great Goddesses of night and earth softened into mortal women or forgotten titanesses only notable for their divine children. Hera's jealous rages at Zeus, for which she is most famed, may be a reflection of the tension between censoring pantheistic religion and sensual mother-goddess worship in the ancient Greek world, as the sexual, powerful mother goddess dwindled to a scattering of patriarchal consorts.

Full Moon: Mother

Throughout the world, the earliest goddess was always the mother: She is Gaia, with all life springing up from her body. Nyx, who laid the cosmic egg out of which the world was born, Cybele, the Roman/Anatolian Magna Mater. She is Devi, the imaginative force throughout the world.

As Campbell explains, "When you have the goddess as creator, it's her own body that is the universe. She is identical with the universe."[1] The Goddess Nut of Egypt encompasses all the heavens, and the goddess Tiamat is the world embodied, until the Babylonian hero Marduk tears her open to create a world of male-centered power. The Goddess represents the full moon and the color red, brimming with the blood of life and birth. She nourishes and shelters the world with her awesome cosmic nature. No longer resorting to seductions or schemes, she is life incarnate, triumphant in her role. She is queen above her subordinate son, the king, reigning on a throne of gold. This is the goddess's fullest stage, shining like the moon her counterpart.

According to Jung, the Mother Goddess as the world and entire source of life comes from pre-birth, during which, for an infant, this is literally true. After birth, this concept is reinforced, as the child depends entirely on her for food, warmth, and safety. As such, the infant is overwhelmed by the mother's importance, and, as she develops into comforter and punisher, the child's split view of the terrible and divine mothers emerges. The heroine's journey is the quest to reintegrate terrible and benevolent mother into a single individual—the self.[2]

She may struggle through obstacles or blocks to achieve her maternal status: if death steals her child, she, like Demeter, must quest for the girl's return. Only then can she resume her role as queen. And darker trials loom ahead. As the Goddess's full, glorious beauty begins to wane, she may turn deadly, slaying her daughters rather than letting them supplant her. Here appears Venus, the Terrible Stepmother, furious at demotion. From there, only a short road remains to Destroyer or Dealer of Death.

231

CHAPTER 24

The Other Right to Choose: The Thwarted Mother

Crystal the Wise (Chile)

There once was a gentleman who had quite a daughter. Whatever her teachers gave her to learn, she gobbled up. Foreign languages, geography, astronomy — all were unspeakably easy for her. And mathematics! She could add up columns of figures far better than her father's accountants could. Before long, she had taken their place.

When Crystal (for so she was called) grew a bit older, the neighboring children came over to ask her to explain the problems their tutors had set. Soon everyone came to learn from her. In time, word of this reached the king. He wrote to the young woman, saying, "My son is nearly grown, but my daughter has trouble with her lessons, and needs a teacher who could make her understand. Will you come and stay with us for a few months?"

Crystal was delighted to do so. When she arrived at the palace, the king, queen, and princess greeted her warmly. The prince, however, sulked like a little child. He had offered to tutor the princess himself, but the king had said, "You're too impatient. I have found someone else who can do a better job than you can."

Over the next few weeks, the prince sat in the back of the classroom and contradicted Crystal whenever she spoke. His interruptions grew more and more frequent. Still, Crystal continued to teach, because she liked the little princess and wanted her to do well. Tired of being ignored, the prince stood up one day and said, "This isn't how I learned it. Everything you're teaching my sister is wrong." Crystal walked right up and slapped him! After that, the prince kept away from her lessons.

When the time came for Crystal to leave, the prince went to his parents.

"I'm grateful for all Crystal taught me, and after all, she's the cleverest woman in the kingdom. May I have your permission to marry her?" The king and queen eagerly agreed, and Crystal also accepted.

After the wedding, the prince took his bride to a secluded cottage deep in the forest. As she was changing into her nightclothes, he came in and said, "Well, Crystal, are you ready to apologize for slapping me?"

"Apologize? I was right to slap you! And I'll do it again if you keep on about it."

"Is that so?" the prince snarled. He dragged her down to the cellar, where he thrust her through a trapdoor, into a little cell under the floorboards. There was a chair and a table and almost nothing else. In the morning, he asked her if she'd changed her mind, but she said no. Every day he came down and demanded she repent. Every day she refused.

Crystal grew weary of her imprisonment, but there was no way she would apologize. One day, she noticed a corner of her cell was damp. Upon breaking through the dirt, she discovered a rushing underground stream. She dug a hole big enough to squeeze through, and swam all the way to her father's house.

Her father was appalled to find out how she'd been treated. "I'll see the king immediately."

"Oh, no, don't," Crystal said. "Just dig a tunnel into my cell and bring me some decent food, and of course, my books. The prince only lowers bread and water." And Crystal swam back to her cell with the prince none the wiser.

At last, he grew tired of her refusals and called down, "I'm going to Paris to enjoy myself. I'll have a servant feed you while I'm having fun."

"Go ahead," she called back cheerfully.

As soon as the prince had left, she bribed the servant to stop lowering bread and water. She ran to her father and, with plenty of money from him, hurried to Paris. There she disguised herself and rented a palace alongside her husband's.

Each day, she drove out in her carriage behind four white horses. Her gown was thick with embroidery, and her fan was trimmed with delicate lace. When the prince saw her, he was dazzled by her beauty, though he didn't recognize her in Parisian fashions. He began courting her, and wedded her inside a month, never mentioning, of course, that he had another wife back home. Nine months later, she gave birth to twins, a girl and a boy. Since Crystal had learned a bit, she made the prince sign a contract, vowing the children would be his heirs. Three years passed. Then the prince told her he had been summoned home for his sister's marriage. He didn't mention how his family had also written how much they longed to see Crystal.

Returning home, the prince hurried to the cottage but discovered the cell empty. The servant told him Crystal had died of loneliness, so the prince had no choice but to go to his parents and tell them Crystal had perished.

His family, of course, was devastated. They reminded the prince how brilliant and caring she had been, until he truly felt ashamed of his actions. Then the prince heard a footstep behind him. He turned to see a veiled woman, his children following. She raised her veil, and he saw that Crystal was alive after all. Stunned to see his doubly-wed wife, the prince knelt down before the court and begged her forgiveness. And after that, they lived quite happily, together with their family.[1]

I have a particular affection for this story, as I saw it performed on stage when I was a small child, and then never came across it again until I began my research. It's a rather romantic tale, as the lady seduces her husband over and over again. He, of course, is a disloyal playboy, though I doubt he'd have the courage to stray after her complicated revenge. The play version I saw had an Italian flavor, unsurprising, since this tale also appears in Italo Calvino's famed collection as Aarne-Thompson 891 The Man Who Deserts His Wife and Sets Her the Task of Bearing Him a Child. When the smart young lady is locked in her cage, she instructs her father to dig a tunnel.

"So I can rescue you?" he asks.

"No, so I can have fresh gowns and my maid can do my hair and bring me her famous desserts," she replies sedately. In this version, the wife has three children while disguised as three different women, all meant to entrap her husband, which she succeeds in doing. In this tale "the heroine deprecates male tyranny and shows that female insistence on truth and freedom accomplishes good, here in the form of generation and rejoicing. The husband comes to appreciate that feminine wisdom."[2]

She claims the ultimate right to choose, yet she stays within the confines of marriage by confining her conquests to her husband.

As previously discussed, marriage is not enough for the heroine. She must grow into a triumphant mother figure, with children to carry on after her. Sometimes, especially in Bluebeard tales, the antagonist is not the witch, but the husband, particularly a neglectful one.

Śakuntalā, daughter of the nature goddess Menaka, must likewise seek her husband through struggle and adversity. This epic play, *Śakuntalā and the Ring of Recollection*, hails from India, written by the fourth to fifth century scholar, Kalidasa. Raised as an ascetic by her adoptive father, a priest, Śakuntalā falls in love with the visiting King Dusyanta. However, thanks to a traveling monk's curse, her husband forgets all knowledge of her until he can see his royal ring, now lost in the river Ganges. When she arrives at the palace, pregnant with his warrior son, her friends remonstrate the king for not keeping his promise and summoning her. The king protests that he never married her, and cannot possibly now wed this pregnant stranger.

Copying the act of the more famous Sita (from the *Ramayana*), Śakuntalā calls upon the spirits of nature to hide her away. In both epics, the heroine stipulates, "Protect me if I've been a true wife," and this divine protection becomes proof of innocence. She invokes earth-goddess magic and calls on her mother-archetype to protect her in place of her doubting husband, taking refuge with the universal anima.

A fisherman finds the ring in the Ganges. When it reaches the king, he remembers marrying Śakuntalā. Through his blindness, he has lost his pregnant love of all loves, the only one likely to produce a son. The nymph Sanumati, sent by the heroine's mother, spies on the king and sees his remorse. In the end, the king travels up to the god Indra's domain, where he finds his wife and son. When he meets Śakuntalā, he falls at her feet, saying:

> May the pain of my rejection
> Vanish from your heart;
> Delusion clouded my weak mind
> And darkness obscured good fortune —
> A blind man tears off a garland,
> Fearing the bite of a snake.[3]

Blaming the traveling monk for his curse, the gods reunite Śakuntalā with her husband, and promise that their son will become Bharata, a mighty king destined to turn the wheel of his father's empire.[4]

Here, the ring symbolizes the king's forgotten promise, just as Śakuntalā's half-divine birth marks her as the hero of the tale. In this love story, she must regain her husband and force him to acknowledge her. When he honors his promise, she and her son can return to earth with their newfound wisdom.

A popular folktale found from Egypt to Ireland is AT 875: The Clever Peasant Girl Who Solves the King's Riddles. The king, determined to wed a clever wife, sets the girl riddles and tasks varying from "take a coin and produce meat, a mirror, a map, and the same coin again" to "come to the palace neither dressed nor naked, neither walking nor riding, bearing a gift that is not a gift." The clever yet poor maiden solves the first puzzle by buying a sheep and knitting its wool into a portrait of the king (a mirror) surrounded by the map. She butchers the sheep, sells the meat for a coin, and presents the king with its heart. For the second riddle, she dresses in a fishing net, comes riding a goat so short her feet drag, and offers the king a bird that promptly flies away.

The delighted king promptly marries her, but is not prepared for the depth of her cleverness; he makes a faulty judgment, and she helps the plaintiff achieve justice. Angrily, the king demands his wife leave, taking only the one thing she loves best. In true witty style, she feeds him a sleeping potion. When he wakes the next morning in her parents' house, she explains that she has simply taken what she loves best — him. Undone by her cleverness, he reinstates her as queen.[5]

This story focuses on separation of power between the genders — if the king marries an equal, like Crystal, he must prepare for her wit to entrap him as well as support him. This exchange of clever barbs and marital spats will remind many readers of their own marriages in the early days of silliness and courtship. Yet this tale only emerges when dealing with a clever, assertive wife so determined to create her own fate that she kidnaps her husband in a brilliant reversal of gender roles.

In an Iraqi version of this tale, the clever peasant girl arouses the sultan's interest by offering a series of provocative riddles rather than solving his. Before the marriage's consummation, he rides off to battle, leaving her alone in the palace. Undaunted, she assembles an army, dresses as a man and rides after him. Pitching tents opposite his army, as if to an enemy, the girl challenges her opponent to a game of chess. She wins his dagger in a wager, and then in turn wagers a "beautiful Kurdish virgin." She substitutes herself for the slave girl and conceives a son. She does this twice more, following her husband around the country, wagering her disguised favors, and bearing three children. After three years, with his first marriage (as he thinks) unconsummated, the sultan decides to set aside his original wife and wed his highborn cousin. The clever girl sends her three children to the wedding, bearing the dagger and other tokens of proof, and thus wins him back.[6]

As with Śakuntalā, the heroine here craves legitimacy. Her marriage must be consummated, children acknowledged, herself proclaimed true wife to her husband. These clever heroines realize that moping at home while the husband adventures is not security, but inequity. She has already won her husband by great or clever deed. However, to own more than an empty title, to be queen in more than name, the heroine must travel on his adventures, experience his triumphs and losses, share a life with him. If he puts her aside, she follows nonetheless.

Shakespeare's *All's Well That Ends Well* echoes this familiar tale. Helena, an orphan, loves her foster-brother, Count Bertram. By saving the king's life, she earns the right to marry her sweetheart, but not his love. He coldly writes to his mother after the wedding:

> I have sent you a daughter-in-law: she hath recover'd the king, and undone me. I have wedded her, not bedded her; and sworn to make the "not" eternal. You shall hear I am run away: know it before the report come. If there be breadth enough in the world, I will hold a long distance.[7]

His mother is not amused at his treating "a maid too virtuous/ For the contempt of empire!" so harshly.[8] She fulfils the role of mentor and councilor to Helena, encouraging the girl to seek her estranged husband.

Meanwhile, Bertram writes Helena a sharp note: "When thou canst get the ring upon my finger, which never shall come off, and show me a child begotten of thy body that I am father to, then call me husband; but in such a 'then'

I write a 'never.'"[9] Helena is a doctor's daughter, with enough knowledge of her father's craft to battle death and save the suffering king. Still, her greatest trial is gaining the oath-breaking Bertram's love, through subterfuge, ingenuity and perseverance.

Helena boldly follows her husband, but, not having Crystal's talent with disguise, has the young virgin Diana seduce him and wheedle away his ring. At night, Helena takes Diana's place in Shakespeare's famous "bed trick," and conceives a child. Once again, the ring symbolizes the man's promise and compliance.

Several folktales use the famous "bed trick," such as "Iktome Sleeps with his Wife by Mistake." In this Native American tale, an older woman suspected her husband of being attracted to girls half her age. When she heard her husband, Iktome, proposition one of them, she quickly concocted a plan. She changed clothes and tipis with the girl, so that the husband snuck into his wife's bed late at night. While Iktome had previously mocked his wife's body, he praised the one he was cuddling. "Ah, how nice it is to fondle a firm young breast, not a sagging one like my wife's," he said. And then, "Oh pretty one! How full of fire you are! How ardently you make love, not just lying there like dead, like my old woman does it." At each of his compliments, his wife merely giggled girlishly.

The next morning, his wife managed to outrace him to their tent, whereupon he walked in and demanded breakfast. But she seized a cooking spoon and started beating him; with each whack, she reminded him of his insults. "So I'm not a hot one, you say. I just lie there like dead!" She picked up her turnip digger and resumed the beating, as he turned and ran out of the tent, as fast as he could.[10]

"The Garbage Girl Who Married the King" (AT 873: "The King Discovers his Unknown Son") echoes this, though with happier results. The king is getting married, but the wife-to-be is secretly in labor with another man's child. Her mother cleans up the local garbage girl and substitutes her in the ceremony. The king places a pair of bracelets on her wrists and they spend three days together. At the end, the bride's mother meets the garbage girl, ostensibly to pay her and to switch the women back. Instead, she tears the fine gown from the garbage girl and throws her out. The garbage girl gives birth to fine twin boys, and raises them alone, poverty-stricken for many years. At last, she takes them to the king's palace and has them kick at anyone entering or leaving, saying that the palace is theirs. When the king sees that they wear the bracelets, he summons the garbage girl, who refuses to come until he sends a fine gown to her. Thus acknowledged, she tells him her story. The king banishes his false wife and marries the garbage girl.[11]

Here we have the true Cinderella "rags to riches" story. At the same time, we have the true wife, fertile and faithful, and her treacherous shadow, as the

True Bride and the False Bride. Once again, a piece of jewelry symbolizes a legitimate pledge and marriage given, functioning the same as the signet rings of the other tales. Only when the king sees the token does he comprehend the identity of his true wife.

In this set of tales, the lady, though an abandoned wife, is smart and self-motivated. She wants her husband back and succeeds through cleverness and perseverance. Her husband is the childish one, not valuing her, holding on to petty grievances. Thus in the end, the wife not only bears children, but also coaxes her husband to mature and accept his role. In this way, she creates a family by fashioning a husband, not just giving birth.

CHAPTER 25

Strength and Honor Clothe Her: The Wife

Isis and Osiris (Egypt)

Isis, whose name means knowledge, was wife to Osiris, god-king of Egypt. In hieroglyphics, Osiris was represented by the eye and scepter, his name itself signifying "many-eyed," as he was ever-watchful.

Isis and Osiris were twins, born of the earth god Geb and of Nut, goddess of the overarching sky. Having a mutual affection, they enjoyed each other in their mother's womb before they were born, and from this communion sprang the god Horus.

Osiris became king of Egypt and applied himself to civilizing his countrymen. He taught them to plant and sow, and he gave them a body of laws. With the same kindliness, he travelled over the rest of the world, persuading the people to yield to intellect and unite.

During the absence of Osiris from his kingdom, Isis protected it, keeping extremely vigilant and always on her guard. Set, sometimes called Typhon, desired to tear down all Osiris had built. He bided his time, however, until the god's return.

Persuading 72 lords to join him in the conspiracy, together with a certain queen of Ethiopia called Aso, Set formed a crafty plot. He held a great banquet, and in its midst, he revealed a beautiful chest, highly decorated with rare gems.

This was greatly admired by all who were present, and Set, as if in jest, promised to present it to the man whose body would best fit within it. The whole company, one after the other, lay in the chest, but could not fit.

Last of all tried Osiris, and behold, the chest fit perfectly. Thereupon all the conspirators ran to the chest, and clapped on the cover, and then they fastened it down with nails on the outside, and poured melted lead all over. Carrying the chest to the Nile River, they all flung it in.

As soon as report of this reached Isis, she sliced off a lock of her hair and draped herself in mourning apparel. She wandered the country, distraught, searching and inquiring of every person she met where her husband's coffin might lie.

At length Isis learned that the chest had been carried by the waves of the sea to the coast of Byblos, and there gently lodged in the branches of a tamarisk bush, which in a short time had surged up into a large and beautiful tree, and had grown round the chest and enclosed it completely on every side. The local king, amazed at its unusual size, had hewed the tree down, and made that part of the trunk wherein the chest was concealed into a support pillar for his house.

Isis hurried to Byblos, where, setting herself down by the side of a fountain, she refused to speak to anybody except the queen's women. These, however, she saluted and caressed in the kindest manner possible, plaiting their hair, and transmitting into them part of her own wonderful odor. When the queen breathed her maidens' scent, she greatly desired to meet the stranger. Sending for Isis, she made her nurse to her infant son.

Isis nursed the child by giving it her finger to suck instead of the breast. Each night she placed him in the fire in order to consume his mortal part, while, having transformed herself into a swallow, she circled round the pillar and bemoaned her sad fate. One night the queen witnessed her child in the flames and cried out, thereby depriving him of the immortality the affectionate goddess had been creating in him. Great Isis then revealed herself in all her majesty, and asked that the pillar which contained Osiris be given to her. When this was done, Isis opened the pillar and threw herself upon the chest, and made at the same time such loud and terrible cries of lamentation, that the younger of the king's sons who heard her was frightened out of his life.

She sailed away with the coffin and hid it in a remote place. One night, however, when Set was hunting by the light of the moon, he came upon it by chance, and recognizing the body of Osiris, tore it into 14 pieces and scattered them.

When Isis discovered what had been done, she set out in a boat made of papyrus. Wherever Isis found a part of Osiris's body, there she buried it and built a royal sepulcher. After Isis had found and paid honor to all Osiris's parts, Osiris returned from the other world, and told his son Horus to destroy Set.

The great battle lasted many days, but Horus was at length victorious, and Set was taken prisoner. He was delivered into the custody of Isis, who, instead of putting him to death, compassionately loosed his fetters and set him free. This incensed Horus to such a degree that he seized his mother and yanked the royal crown off her head, but the god Thoth came forward, and set upon her head the horns of a fertile cow, which she wore forever after as a helmet.

Thus Horus was made king of the gods, with Isis, the Mother of the Gods and the Living One, ever defending him.[1]

Isis is the great goddess, the divine mother, the mistress of enchantments. She is described in the chants and hymns as "a clever woman. Her heart was craftier than a million men; she was choicer than a million gods; she was more discerning than a million of the noble dead. There was nothing she did not know in heaven and earth."[2] "Isis is typified in many forms, but was especially revered as the goddess of procreation, Universal Mother of the living, and protectress of the spirits of the dead."[3] Her symbol was the cow, and she is usually depicted wearing cow's horns, and between them the orb of the moon. The cow, of course, suggests fertility and life-giving milk, just as the crown Horus claims represents divinity. As life incarnate, who revived her dead husband and protected her ailing son, she was most often depicted as the mother suckling her child.

Osiris is more than her husband; he is her masculine side, dead and submerged as she is live and nurturing. In *The Book of the Dead*, one of the oldest surviving Egyptian texts, he is compared with her brother, husband, son, and even herself: "He is Isis, he himself is found as he spreads her hair over him, I scatter it upon his forehead. Conceived was he in Isis."[4]

This was the most powerful and universal myth of the Egyptian New Kingdom (16th to 11th century B.C.E.), admittedly echoing the Demeter-Persephone myth from the same period. Isis, as goddess of fertility, must restore her husband to life. Her quest to reunite his pieces is like restoring fragments of herself, reconstructing her animus and driving out Set, the source of dark impulses. In some versions, Isis reassembles 13 parts, but cannot find the fourteenth, her husband's genitals. "Through the intensity of her love, she creates an *image* of what is missing and that consecrated image becomes phallos through which she conceives a son ... what was a phallus — power, erection — becomes phallos — love, resurrection."[5] As Isis throws herself on her dead husband's body in a paroxysm of love, she unites with the newly created phallos and brings forth the divine child Horus.

This is one of the most striking features of the myth, reminding devotees that Isis was fertility incarnate. She was also the creator of the pharaoh, as indicated by the throne she often wore on her crown and used as her hieroglyph. She bore him and nurtured him throughout his life. When the old pharaoh died, she preserved his divine essence and passed it to the new pharaoh. "Isis acts as both the psychopomp who guides the dead pharaoh to the land of the dead, granting him immortality there, and the one who, through love, persistence, and patience, saves a germ of the pharaoh's divinity to renourish and mold into the next mature ruler."[6] Thus she impregnates herself with Osiris's corpse and raises Horus to be the next pharaoh, continuing her husband's legacy.

She was goddess of wedlock, presiding over betrothals in her temples. In the beginning, Isis had willed that "men and women should anchor together," and so created the magic that attracted men and women to each other.[7] It was her ordinance that children should obey and love their parents, and that the incumbent husband should make a solemn contract to obey his wife. She also taught the domestic arts, such as spinning, weaving, and cooking, and watched over women during childbirth.[8] Wielding magic rather than warfare, she was mistress of the universe's secrets, which she passed to her child the king.

Women of Valor

Wives throughout myth are known for virtue and loyalty, like Isis, like Penelope, like Śakuntalā. Another wife who stands out for her virtue is Gandhari, wife to King Dhritarashtra in the Indian epic of *The Mahabharata*. Her husband was blind from birth, so Gandhari, upon first meeting him, donned a blindfold that she wore for the rest of her life, so that she would be forever equal to her husband and share his condition. She dwelt with him all her life and perished beside him, as they died together in a forest fire.

On one memorable occasion, she showed hospitality to the sage and avatar Vyasa, who offered her a boon. She requested a hundred sons, and, after two years of pregnancy, gave birth to a lump of flesh. Vyasa divided the mass into 101 pieces, placing them in jars. In time, these pieces grew into 100 sons (including the famed warrior Duryodhana) and a daughter, Duhsala. These children came to be known as the Kauravas.

Gandhari clearly understood the perfect joining of animus and anima, in which the two must bond in equal support, neither above the other. Her unity with her husband and extraordinary progeny make her an exemplary figure in Indian legend.

While successful motherhood is often the heroine's central goal, she also defends her husband. This, too, is the unification of the family.

> When King Conrad III defeated the Duke of Welf (in the year 1140) and placed Weinsberg under siege, the wives of the besieged castle negotiated a surrender which granted them the right to leave with whatever they could carry on their shoulders. The king allowed them that much. Leaving everything else aside, each woman took her own husband on her shoulders and carried him out. When the king's people saw what was happening, many of them said that that was not what had been meant and wanted to put a stop to it. But the king laughed and accepted the women's clever trick. "A king" he said, "should always stand by his word."[9]

Likewise, Biblical Abigail, wed to the wealthy but surly Nabal, stands out as an exemplary wife. David, then in exile, sent a message pleasantly asking for hospitality, since he had protected Nabal's flocks in the past. Nabal sneeringly refused, and David led an army of 400 men toward Nabal's gate. When Abigail heard of Nabal's refusal, she rushed to gather food: 200 loaves of bread, two skins of wine, five dressed sheep, five bushels of roasted grain, 100 cakes of raisins and 200 cakes of pressed figs. Without telling her husband, she rode straight to David, and, bowing before him, explained that her husband was a fool and that she regretted not receiving David's message herself. Upon hearing this, David accepted her gift and blessed her for saving him from bloodshed. When Nabal heard what she had done, his heart failed and God struck him down. Noting Abigail's cleverness and virtue, David proposed marriage and she accepted. She was ever after known as the cleverest of David's wives, and a confidante and source of support for the entire family.[10]

When the husband is immature or churlish, as with those in the previous chapter, the heroine must employ extraordinary cleverness to steer him toward adulthood, bidding him accept his responsibilities. These acts of wisdom and generosity win these women husbands who trust them and rely on them forever.

Anait, heroine of a Russian-Armenian tale, vows to marry no man who does not have a trade. Upon meeting her, Prince Vachegan is enamored, and gladly learns weaving to meet her condition. After the marriage, the prince goes traveling and is taken hostage. He manages to weave an embroidered cry for help and smuggle it to his wife.[11] Thus, his knowledge of weaving, a traditional feminine power, saves him, as he can cry for help through his craft, like Philomela of Greek myth. His status as prince is nothing without his wife's hearthcraft and wisdom.

Through much of the world, the wife was an equal partner, protector and healer of the husband. Tacitus notes how among Germanic warriors, "The soldier brings his wounds to mother and wife, who shrink not from counting or even demanding them and who administer food and encouragement to the combatants.... [The husbands] even believe that the sex has a certain sanctity and prescience, and they do not despise their counsels, or make light of their answers."[12]

Central to Celtic lore is the motif is that women hold the destiny of men in their hands. In the Arthurian stories, all of the Grail Knights are supported and empowered by women, whether wives like Blanchefleur and Guinevere or sorceresses like the Lady of the Lake and Morgan le Fay. In fact, throughout the Celtic legends, there are women of great strength and stamina, compassion and reasoning. In *The Tain*, Emer, the wife of the great hero Cúchulainn, is his greatest strength. She rules her own household, often advising her husband. Emer supports Cúchulainn even as he strays into the world of the Sidhe with Emer's ethereal rival, Fand; Emer knows her husband will always return to her side. Even past his death she refuses to leave him, climbing into his grave, sharing her strength with him as he passes into the Other World.

Other wives descend into death itself to reclaim their loved ones, making the great journey of suffering and self-discovery in order to return enlightened.

In an Irish tale, Marie's husband tells her that her mother can't stay with them any longer. She agrees to send the woman away and then stalls for seven years while weaving her a traveling dress and coat. At last, the clothes are finished, and so, without a word to her husband, Marie and her mother start their journey.

At last they find a house where Marie can work for their keep. There, she meets a young man who persuades her to move into his room with him and keep his presence secret for a year and a day. The two have a child. However, before the time elapses, the mistress of the house discovers them and reveals that the young man is her dead son. Crestfallen, he explains that since he has been discovered, he must serve out his sentence in hell.

Determined to save him, Marie dons a magic belt and takes her new husband's magic ring, which will provide her with sustenance. Bidding her mother and child farewell, she generously takes her husband's place in hell. She remains there for seven years, and in payment, Lucifer allows her to carry a number of souls up to heaven, including her first husband.

When she returns to earth, she discovers her faithless husband has forgotten her and is about to remarry. However, she drops his magic ring in his wineglass and wins him back.[13]

Her visit to hell is not treated as sacrifice. She wins a great boon of souls for her act, along with knowledge and power. At the same time, she is rescuing her helpless husband and then winning him back to her in soul, body, and heart. This resurrection can also be read symbolically, as the lover breathes new life into the beloved's soul. Here, Marie undergoes the great cycle of the heroine's journey: Setting forth, descending into death, and resurrecting, followed by a loving family circle of child and husband.

CHAPTER 26

Don't Heroines Get a Break from Those 3 a.m. Feedings? The Triumphant Mother

The Female Shaman (Siberia)

A summons came from across the lake: "Our son is dying: We need the shaman to come sing for him and save him." Weighed down under her load of gathered herbs, carefully sorted into bundles and baskets, the shaman hesitated. Her own son was also sick, and now was a bad time to leave. Still, she couldn't neglect her duty. She tied on her boots of waterproof reindeer hide and prepared to leave.

"What a bad mother you are," her husband chided. "Your only son is suffering and you go to help another?"

"Their son is suffering too," the shaman said, and she left. When she arrived, the tribe across the lake told her the boy had died.

"What will you give me if I restore him?" she asked.

"Two reindeer teams, spotted white and black."

So the shaman sat in the clearing and beat her drum over and over, chanting with the rhythm. Through her drum she channeled the beat of the forest, the thrum of the seasons, of the earth-womb itself. The boy's corpse choked and gasped, and started again to breathe.

When she returned home, she called to her husband, "Bring out our son, so I may show him my fine new reindeer teams!"

The husband shook his head. "He's sleeping."

"Well, wake him."

"I cannot."

And then the shaman knew her son was dead. She went and gazed at his body, lying so still and cold on his sleeping mat. "I want to have a rest."

"How can you rest — you're the shaman!" her husband said. "You need to save our son."

So she sat and she beat her drum for hours, but nothing happened. The shaman hung her head. "It's useless to keep trying this way. I cannot find his soul. You should kill me."

"I won't kill you," her husband said.

"No, you must. For these reindeer were gifts from a boy who died, and I can ride them into the underworld."

So the husband killed both her and her reindeer and bound her to the sleigh. The shaman's spirit rose into the sky, and there she met a raven. "What a beautiful reindeer team," he said.

"You can have it if you help me."

Then she met an eagle. "What a fine team," he said.

"If you help me, I'll give you the one just as fine that I left at home."

The eagle cocked his head. "Let me give you something in return. A demoness carried off your boy and shut him in her hut. You can find him at the bottom of the hill."

Abandoning her sleigh, the shaman ran to house and peeped down the vent-hole. There was her dear boy's soul, arms tied to a pole. "Mama, why are you here?"

"I came to fetch you home."

"But Mama, we'll both be killed."

"In this realm, I do not fear death." Painstakingly, she squeezed herself through the smoke hole and dropped to the floor far below. She sliced her son's bonds away with her ritual knife and carried him off.

When the demoness found the boy gone, she chased after them, determined to break all their bones. From over his mother's shoulder, the boy spied her, jaws open, wings flapping in the twilight stillness. "Leave me," he cried. "We're too slow."

"I will not. Let her kill us both together," said the shaman. She raised her head. "Spirits, help us now!"

Two guardian spirits came, hers and the boy's. "Watch the sky," they said. "If we can manage to kill the demoness, her blood will spill and redden the clouds." And they flew into battle. She and her son kept running.

After a while, the sky reddened like a bucket of berries, and the shaman and her boy knew they were safe. She slowed, but kept walking until she arrived home with her son's soul clutched in her arms. She knelt before her drum and beat it until Raven and Eagle came. Each sat on one side of her son's body. She drummed some more. Through her drum she channeled the beat of the forest, the thrum of the seasons, of the earth-womb itself. At last, she thrust the soul into her son's body and said, "Wake up, you've slept long enough."

The boy awoke. The shaman ordered the reindeer she had brought back from the underworld slaughtered. One team was to be given to Raven and one to Eagle. Then she finally went to sleep.[1]

This Shaman is "supermom" — she takes a second job and protects her child and the children of others. "I need to sleep," she tells her husband.

"You're a bad mother, and you don't need rest," he retorts. As she rushes from work to daycare, he criticizes her for not doing enough all at once, demanding that she put her family first while still doing her job. Therefore, she lets herself be killed and snatches her son from the demoness, all before she takes a moment for herself.[2]

Fairytale fiends quickly learn to avoid the enraged mother defending her babes. Here is a ferocity beyond the hero's sword or the demon's devouring teeth. Mothers have performed astonishing feats of strength and adrenaline, defied the strongest of villains, and fearlessly battled society's laws, all to protect their children.

A Baltic deity, Saule Meite, or "Little Sun," was raped by her father the moon. Her mother Saule, the sun, slashed the moon's face, permanently scarring him. Then she banished him from the daylight sky.

Cyrus the Great died on a military campaign, but few books record the details. Tomyris was queen of the Massagetae, a Scytian tribe often associated with the Amazons. When Cyrus's imperialism led him to invade Tomyris's land, she tried to negotiate. He refused, and when she unleashed her son against him, Cyrus took the young man prisoner. Furious, Tomyris warned that she would give Cyrus his fill of blood if he didn't return the boy. Cyrus ignored her, and Tomyris's son committed suicide out of shame at being a hostage. Thereupon, Tomyris defeated Cyrus and his army. Flaying and beheading his corpse, she dropped the head in a bowl of blood, commanding him to drink all he could.

Alas, Motherhood is irrevocably linked with the heroine's descent into the underworld, as mortality rates were historically high for both new infants and birthing mothers. The valuable ring or gift offered to a Northern European bride after consummation was considered a sort of wergild, as her life might be forfeit. Despite the joys of the wedding, expectant mothers knew that death might be the price of the new life welling inside them. For this reason, many ancient civilizations equated women in childbirth to warriors, equally honored in life or death.

The Aztec Cihuateteo were five celestial priestesses, women honored for dying in childbirth. They dwelt in the west, in Cihuatlampa, the region of women, where they helped the sun to set each night, bearing it on a litter of quetzal feathers.[3] In ancient Spartan society, as Plutarch related, "it was forbidden to inscribe the names of the dead upon their tombstones, except for men who had fallen in war and women who had died in childbirth.[4] Likewise, Irish women dying in childbed were considered equal with men before the law and were permitted to swear oaths.[5] There was a clear understanding of equal risk between warriors and expectant mothers, both hazarding their lives for the growth of their tribe.

In the heroine's journey, this struggle to emerge from death alive with a healthy child is reflected in individual quests, questing in the Otherworld for a stolen child, or, as a less traumatic substitute, a stolen sibling. For mother-goddesses, the stolen child is echoed in the mother's own lost fertility: the land turns barren or animals refuse to mate. Only with the restoration of the mother's status can spring return.

One of the most famous "mother's journeys" of Western culture is Demeter's search for her kidnapped daughter Persephone. Without Persephone, the world turns to winter for the first time in existence, as Demeter's fruitfulness changes to barrenness. Kore, meaning maiden, also means sprout, casting her as a "shoot" of her mother, both the same plant, as Persephone sinks into the ground and then revitalizes in spring. These figures are so similar-looking in ancient art that they could be considered the same goddess. Thus mother and daughter are a dual entity, one venturing below while the other wanders above, like Inanna and her handmaiden. This is not just a story of a mother seeking her daughter: These goddesses, birth and earth, are the double aspect: One cannot exist without the other.

While to a woman the birth of the divine son signifies a renewal of her animus, the birth of the divine daughter represents a still more central process, relevant to the woman's self and wholeness. "The transcendent birth of the daughter, which actually surpasses the myth itself, suggests a corner of inner feminine experience which defies description and almost defies understanding, although it is manifested time and time again as the determining borderline experience of the psyche and of psychic life."[6]

Woman grows up nurtured by her mother, a relationship which functions as a model for her own adulthood. While the man models his traditionally absent and emotionally distant father, the woman links unconditional love and bonding with her role in life. Thus, she mothers her lover as well as her children, sheltering and protecting them as her mother once did her.

> Her face is the first whose expression changes reciprocally with its own. Her voice introduces it to speech.... She comes when it feels anxious or bored and provides the sense of being cared for. In the earliest stage, the baby cannot distinguish itself and its needs from the mother. The baby cannot yet realize its desires; when it feels discomfort, the mother requites it. This can cause reciprocation from her: her needs become subsumed into the child's. This is a desire for love and closeness as well as for sustenance: this warmth and care provides the glow of intimate oneness in this most primal of relationships.[7]

As the mother cares for the infant, she comes to understand the nature of the body, with its vulnerabilities and desires, and thus reaches a greater understanding of the self. As she nurtures, she learns. "Woman does not merely convert the infant into the person, she guarantees the transmission of culture, language, love, and community."[8] At the same time, as she teaches the baby, the baby teaches her. They are a single entity, and pain will accompany any separation.

Willing Sacrifice

Many tales focus on the hero's death and rebirth, but not on the mother who must part with her son, the sacrificed god-king who was born each year only to love the goddess and then perish. The female deity was lover and mother combined, but did not enact the inferior role of a daughter. Her consort, by contrast, was son, lover, and husband all as one. He died periodically, sometimes because of her wrath, while she reigned eternal. As Merlin Stone notes, "The male chosen held his royal rights for a specific period of time. At the end of this time ... this youth was then ritually sacrificed."[9] This reinforced the temporary nature of the king, and the permanent rulership of the queen. Thus, Ishtar became the appointer of the king, "she who endowed him with prestige." In one inscription, she was "Counselor of All Rulers, She Who Holds the Reigns of Kings." In another, "She who gives the scepter, the throne, the year reign to all kings."[10]

In most myths the earth goddess was portrayed as placing nature's needs above her own, and suffering greatly for the loss of her son-lover. She wept eternally for the holy child whom she had sacrificed for the salvation of humanity.

The mourning mother appears in artwork throughout the world, especially as the pietà statues of the mourning Virgin cradling her crucified son. The most famous of these is Michelangelo's *Pietà* in St. Peter's Basilica in Rome. Mary, who according to scripture was present at the Crucifixion (John 19: 25–27), may have watched his death, or cradled her son's broken body before his burial. Often she is depicted elderly and sorrowing, awaiting regeneration and rebirth.

Inanna echoes this mourning in her own lament. Kneeling before Enlil in his temple, she demands answers to her pitiful queries:

> The bird has its nesting place, but I — my young are dispersed;
> The fish lies in calm waters, but I — my resting place exists now.
> The dog kneels at the threshold but I — I have no threshold;
> The ox has its stall, but I — I have no stall;
> The cow has a place to lie down, but I — I have no place to lie down;
> The ewe has its fold, but I — I have no fold;
> The beasts have a place to sleep, but I — I have no place to sleep.
> ...

> The comely spouse has been carried off by the enemy;
> The comely son has been carried off by the enemy.[11]

As Inanna laments her lost family, she has become the bereft crone who sits wailing in the dark — her dark sister Ereshkigal. Though the spouse isn't named here, it is certainly Dumuzid, the son-lover Inanna has banished to the underworld.

Birth and death are indelibly linked. Birthing represents a separation between mother and child, a severing of the bond that has spent nine months growing. After birth, they will exist as two organisms, separate in their skins.

For, in fact, the grown hero is sacrificed, not through the mother's neglect, but through her willing consent. Attis castrated and killed himself because he was driven mad by his mother, Cybele. Aphrodite's beloved Adonis was gored by a boar (her sacred symbol); Horus was critically wounded by Set, the god his mother Isis refused to slay. Gaia fashioned a sickle, symbol of the harvest, and gave it to her son Cronus, so he could slay his father Uranus. Dumuzid, Gilgamesh, Tammuz, Osiris, "one after the other," as Campbell puts it.[12] On Crete, even Zeus was considered the dying god, subordinate to his mother Rhea. These godly deaths and resurrections cycle like the monthly death and resurrection of the moon, and thus, the feminine principle.[13]

The son-lover was often castrated, as in the cases of Uranus, Osiris, Attis, and Adonis. "The castrated and/or dying youthful consort, a vestige of the times in which the high priestess held the divine right to the throne, is often ignored or misunderstood," notes Merlin Stone in *When God was a Woman*. This was a voluntary sacrifice, a way to destroy a part of the self rather than the whole, and a way of evoking the man's dormant anima. Thus men could supplant the priestess roles as connectors with the divine.[14]

In this phase the goddess is dual: One side is filled with maternal compassion, but the other, darker, side is fierce and terrible, pushing away her son's childish dependence. "For his softness and clinging undermine her, just as her oversolicitude undermines him. His childish need appeals too intimately to her own desire to mother him."[15] The mother has become too identified with the son. His accomplishments are her pride, his needs are hers, to such a point that she cannot separate them into two entities. At the heart, this is egoism — she cannot say no to him because she cannot say no to herself. Her inability to accept that she cannot fix others' lives is the true inability to accept unmendable flaws in herself.

While this seems natural, the child must learn limits and learn to separate himself from the mother if he wishes to grow to independence. The mother, too, must surrender the child to move beyond the stage where she sacrifices too much, helplessly mothering all around her.

The mother defines herself by her child's perception of her — she fears being too harsh with him, or spoiling him, or being less than perfect. With each perceived error, she sees herself reflected in the baby's eyes as lacking the goddess-like perfection that baby expects from her. This substitute for her true childself is actually stifling her — she defines herself by her child's values, not her own.

When the mother manages to deny the "need need need" voice of the child, to say no to his demands, to steel herself against his sobs, she has sacrificed their single nature into a split of two individuals set on different paths. Thus, each can grow: The son can begin his own mythic quest for identity, starting with separation from home and culminating in the descent into death and regeneration. The mother grows as well, expanding from the archetypal madonna of Isis, cradling and feeding her child, to the independent Athena, the goddess at one with herself. She becomes "the fatal goddess, the Goddess of Fate, and often therefore the inexorable one, the goddess of death whom even the efforts and entreaties of her son cannot mollify."[16]

A famous and tragic mother is Frigga, wife of the Norse god Odin (Wotan). Her son Baldur, handsomest and kindest of the gods, was plagued by nightmares and dark fears. Upon investigating, Odin discovered that mead had been poured for his son in the hall of Hel, and his death was imminent. Frigga straightened. Her prefect son could not die! She walked throughout creation, asking everything, both living and inanimate, to vow never to harm her son. Everything pledged, but Frigga forgot the apparently-harmless mistletoe. The mischievous god Loki fashioned a dart from the plant, and persuaded Baldur's well-meaning brother to throw it. Baldur was slain. Devastated, Frigga took charge and sent a message to Hel, asking how her son might be recovered. She discovered that Baldur might live if every living thing wept for him, and thus she embarked on a second journey. Unfortunately, Loki disguised himself as an old witch and refused to weep other than "waterless tears," thus condemning Baldur to permanent death. For his crimes, Loki was bound against a cliff with a snake dripping poison on his face for all the ages of the world. But this could not console Frigga, whose bright son now dwelt among the dead.

In Euripides' *The Bacchae,* Queen Agave and her wild sisters the Maenads have been celebrating feminine rites deep in the woods, rites that prohibit any male intrusion. This is a chance to connect with nature, unbinding the proper hairstyles of civilization, breast-feeding young animals in a shaking-off of rules and proprieties, releasing their animal sides, drinking from the earth's springs and crowning themselves with leaves:

> And up they started to their feet, brushing from their eyes sleep's quickening dew, a wondrous sight of grace and modesty, young and old and maidens yet unwed. First o'er their shoulders they let stream their hair; then all did gird their fawn-skins up, who hitherto had left the fastenings loose, girdling the dappled hides with snakes that licked their cheeks. Others fondled in their arms gazelles or savage whelps of wolves, and suckled them — young mothers these with babes at home, whose breasts

were still full of milk; crowns they wore of ivy or of oak or blossoming convolvulus. And one took her thyrsus [ivy-wound staff] and struck it into the earth, and forth there gushed a limpid spring; and another plunged her wand into the lap of earth and there the god sent up a fount of wine; and all who wished for draughts of milk had but to scratch the soil with their finger-tips and there they had it in abundance, while from every ivy-wreathed staff sweet rills of honey trickled.[17]

The queen's son, Pentheus, spies on these rites, like Agave's intrusive masculine side, holding her back from her wild dancing and encouraging rationalism. The maddened Agave tears her son Pentheus to pieces and parades the parts through the street, dancing wildly as she celebrates. She has been liberated as pure female, unfettered by her inner rational side.

While these legends generally end with the son's reconstitution, this tale does not, leaving Agave tragically "on the brink of transformation, her maenadic initiation incomplete."[18]

In initiation, psychic dismemberment is necessary. The animus, the side that makes the heroine rigid and controlled, is holding her back. She cannot make decisions based solely on rules, as her choices need to be heartfelt. This animus must be torn apart piece by piece in order to let the heroine reconstitute herself as female, without her earlier dependence on the masculine side. Thus she learns to stand alone.

Once the misplaced phallic energy has been dismantled, the woman must confront the deep layers of repressed female aggression that are rising to the surface. She must learn how to gather the pieces as Isis does, confronting the fragments and nursing them back to life. She must suffer the pain of separation before the joys of rebirth. But for the mother with clinging child, this psychic dismemberment leads to a new life.

CHAPTER 27

Earth and Sea Incarnate: The Great Goddess

Pele and Hi'iaka (Hawaii)

The great goddess Pele visited Kauai in the midst of a hula festival. Disguising herself as a mortal woman, Pele approached the rustic hall, and everyone turned to admire the beautiful stranger who had appeared so unexpectedly and whose person exhaled such a fragrance, like sweet plumeria garlands.

Instinctively, the wondering multitude parted and offered a lane for her to enter the halau. But drummers and *kaekeeke* players — the entire audience — became petrified and silent at the sight of Pele, as she advanced step by step, her eyes fixed on the handsome prince Lohiau.

He, in turn, laid down his *pahu* drum, yielding it to another so he could sit beside the beautiful enchantress. Seating her beside him, he offered her the best of everything, but Lohiau himself could not eat. His mind was churning; his eyes stuck fast on the woman at his side.

When they rose from the table he led her willingly to his house, where they lay side by side. But she would favor him only with kisses. In his growing passion he forgot his need of food, his fondness for the hula, the obligations that rested upon him as a host. For three days and three nights, he lay at her side, struggling to overcome her resistance. But she would grant him only kisses.

And, on the third night, as morning approached, Pele told him, "I am about to return to my place, to Puna, the land of the sunrise. I will prepare a habitation for us, and when all is ready I will send for you. Then, for five days and five nights you and I will take our fill of pleasure. After that you will be free to go with another woman." For Pele cared for men, but took no permanent lover. After she had said all this, Pele plunged into the ocean and vanished.

All this time, as Pele courted Lohiau on Kauai, she was only there in spirit — her body rested with her sisters, deep in a trance under a *hala* tree at Lau-pahoehoe. It had been many days since Pele had lain down to sleep, and her sisters sobbed, frightened she had left them forever. Of them all, Hi'iaka-i-ka-poli-o-Pele (Hi'iaka in the Bosom of Pele), the youngest and most affectionate, believed Pele was well, and prepared to wake her. Hi'iaka sang:

> Awake now, awake, awake!
> Wake, Goddess of multiple god-power!
> Wake, Goddess of essence most godlike!
> Wake, Queen of the lightning shaft,
> The piercing fourth eye of heaven!
> Awake; I pray thee awake!

Pele's bosom heaved, color flooded her face. She sighed, stretched herself and sat up. She was herself again.

She begged her sisters to bring Lohiau to Kauai, but they declined. At last, Hi'iaka accepted the mission; but, knowing her sister's cruel temper, she strove to obtain from Pele a guarantee that her own forests and the life of her bosom friend Hopoe should be safeguarded during her absence. Pele granted this, and bestowed on Hi'iaka great power over the elements. "Nothing shall avail to block your road," she said. "Yours is the power of woman; the power of man is nothing to that."

Accompanied by Wahine-oma'o, a woman of wisdom and prudence whom Pele had selected, Hi'iaka arrived at Kauai. There she discovered Lohiau had killed himself from grief at losing the strange woman who had so captivated him. He lay in state in the royal mansion, shrouded in many folds of *kapa*. The goddesses entered the room where he lay, and after ten days of prayer and incantation Hi'iaka had the satisfaction of seeing the body of Lohiau warmed and animated by the reentrance of the spirit. His people celebrated with feasts and sacrifices, until Lohiau announced that he must leave them to visit Pele. He left his friend Chief Paoa in charge, and they soon departed for Kilauea. Lohiau expressed his gratitude to Hi'iaka over and over, but she refused to carry their mutual affection beyond kind words, out of loyalty to her sister.

Meanwhile, Hi'iaka took so long on her errand that Pele was moved to unreasonable jealousy and, regardless of her promise to her faithful sister, she burned down Hi'iaka's forest parks and turned Hi'iaka's bosom friend, the innocent and beautiful Hopoe, into a pillar of stone.

When Hi'iaka and Lohiau arrived at Kilauea, and discovered what Pele had done, Hi'iaka swore vengeance. "I have scrupulously observed the compact solemnly entered into between us, and this is the way she repays me for all my labor! All this time, I have treated the handsome Lohiau as the property of Pele, for I thought she would protect my own forests just as loyally. Our agreement is off: I am free to treat Lohiau as my lover, if I so please."

There, in open view of Pele's court, Hi'iaka invited and received from Lohiau the kisses and dalliance which up to that time she had repelled. Pele pretended not to care. But when Hi'iaka and Lohiau sank to the earth wrapped in each other's arms, the women of Pele's court raised the cry, "For shame! They kiss; they embrace!"

At this, Pele, in a frenzy of passion, convulsed within Mount Kilauea. Earth and sea trembled with her, as her flames engulfed the pair and smothered them in molten lava. Hi'iaka's divine body could not be hurt, but Lohiau was consumed and turned to stone.

Far away, the chief Paoa dreamed that his friend Lohiau needed his help. He only arrived at Kilauea in time to collect his body, but he presented himself to Pele and revealed how loyal Hi'iaka had been, restoring Lohiau to life and keeping him safe. Pele was touched and forgave her sister.

Paoa's impassioned loyalty was incredibly attractive to Pele, but she wanted to be sure of him. She tested the hero by disguising herself as an old crone, but Paoa managed to recognize her with one touch of her burning hand. And the two became lovers for as long as Paoa visited the island.

While Pele dallied, Hi'iaka dug through the earth after Lohiau, passing through the ten layers of death. But at the final layer she was turned back, lest she allow the air of the mortal realm to touch the underworld. Lohiau's spirit fluttered from her clutching fingers and flew overseas. There, the god Kanemilohai found him and reunited him with his stone body. Lohiau returned to life only to find himself standing before Pele. He knelt and begged her forgiveness, but she only said, "Fear me no longer; I have been unjust to you as well as to Hi'iaka. After what I have done, I cannot expect your love. Find Hi'iaka and give it to her."

So Kanemilohai sent the restored Lohiau in quest of Hi'iaka in a beautiful boat of pink and pearl. He sailed to the harbor at Leahi, on the isle of Oahu. When he entered the village there, he learned to his great joy that Hi'iaka and Paoa were visiting there. That evening, there was a great entertainment proposed in honor of Hi'iaka's visit. The guests, crowned with leaves and blossoms, sang and danced in praise of the visiting goddess. Then Hi'iaka sang of Lohiau, mentioning his name with tenderness, and Lohiau, disguised with his cloak of royal yellow reversed and his hair loose over his face, suddenly began harmonizing with her.

Casting off his concealment, Lohiau stood before the guests and dancers. Hi'iaka rushed into his arms and Paoa wept with joy. Soon they all departed together for Kauai, amid great joy and celebration.[1]

The goddess archetype is often a peripheral character, rarely growing or changing. Thus Pele rules her island, but it is her smaller sister-self Hi'iaka "in the Bosom of Pele" that she casts forth like her heart on a string. In the book-length epic of *Pele and Hi'iaka*, Hi'iaka symbolizes a new emerging order in favor of humanity, dynamic instead of majestic, growing and adapting rather than ruling:

> The younger, approaching order is that of the human race which is now peopling the land that Pele made. Hi'iaka is very much this younger, more humane state, despite her familial connections with the fire goddess. The coming together of Hi'-iaka and Lohiau in a traditional happy ending, as the final stage of a long journey, is described as the blending together of the opposing components of male and female, while Pele symbolizes the powerful forces which had kept them apart.[2]

Though Pele may represent the declining old ways, or even the Terrible Mother, she remains ever ruling, ever vibrant and beautiful, as supplicants even today leave offerings on her volcano.

The Great Mother

> I will sing of well-founded Earth, mother of all, eldest of all beings. She feeds all creatures that are in the world, all that go upon the goodly land, and all that are in the paths of the seas, and all that fly: all these are fed of her store. Through you, O queen, men are blessed in their children and blessed in their harvests, and to you it belongs to give means of life to mortal men and to take it away. Happy is the man whom you delight to honor! He has all things abundantly: his fruitful land is laden with corn, his pastures are covered with cattle, and his house is filled with good things. Such men rule orderly in their cities of fair women: great riches and wealth follow them: their sons exult with ever-fresh delight, and their daughters in flower-laden bands play and skip merrily over the soft flowers of the field. Thus is it with those whom you honor O holy goddess, bountiful spirit.[3]

Homer's hymn "To Earth the Mother of All" exemplifies the emotions man felt for the Great Mother: She provided all those living with food, she birthed gods and monsters, crops and oceans. All of her rhythms were cycles and circles, and she encompassed both life and death. Endlessly caring and protective, she glowed with divine power in all her beautiful and terrible aspects. As the *Devi-Mahatmyam* proclaims, "You are the great knowledge, the great illusion, the great insight, the great memory and the great delusion, the great Goddess (mahadevi), the great Demoness (mahasuri)."[4]

The Great Goddess describes herself with awesome effect in the epic by Apuleius:

> I, mother of the universe, mistress of all the elements, first born of the ages, high-est of the gods, queen of the shades, first of those who dwell in heaven, represent-ing in one shape all the gods and goddesses.
>
> My will controls the shining heights of heaven, the health-giving sea-winds, and the mournful silence of hell; the entire world worships my single godhead in a thousand shapes, with diverse rites, and under many different names.[5]

From the very beginning, women have appeared divine — those who can bleed without injury, those who produce life and sustenance from their bodies. A child's mother as world is the most primal and lasting image. From this perspective emerged the Great Goddess that ruled the ancient world before the Great Sky God ever claimed the heavens. Before the patriarchy split her into impotent goddess of light and vilified goddess of dark, she was the universe incarnate.

Even the shallow Juno was queen of heaven and housebound Vesta ruled the powerful Vestal Virgins of Rome. On earth, the women raised and taught children of both genders impressing their societies' values. The matriarch was owner of the house and head of the household, an archetype that still echoes within us today.[6] *The crucial psychological fact is that all of us, female as well as male, fear the will of woman. Man's dominion over what we think of as the world rests on a terror that we all feel: the terror of sinking back wholly into the helplessness of infancy.*"[7]

We've discovered hundreds of early European Neolithic goddess figures, but hardly any representation of the masculine.[8] These ancient stone goddess figures, faceless, with exaggerated hips, breasts, and pregnant bellies abound in ancient temples and ruins: the Indus Valley, the royal tombs of Ur, Neolithic ruins in present-day Turkey.[9] Particularly notable is the Venus of Willendorf, created 22,000–24,000 years ago in present-day Austria. Carved with exquisite care from non-native limestone, she is blatantly nude, with exaggerated breasts and naval, enormous belly, and intricately detailed vulva. Though faceless, she has intricate braids of hair wrapped around her head.[10]

Though male-centric modern civilization was reluctant to accept goddesses until the latter half of the 20th century, it was even more reluctant to accept female sculptors of the pieces. However, in 1996, art professor LeRoy McDermott pointed out that the distorted belly, overly-elongated navel, and tiny feet would reflect a pregnant woman's view, while the facelessness is explained by the lack of mirrors for this ancient self-portrait. As he added:

> Since all the earliest, best-preserved, and most refined pieces appear to be analog representations of women looking down on their changing biological selves, I conclude that the first tradition of human image making probably emerged as an adaptive response to the unique physical concerns of women and that, whatever else these representations may have symbolized to the society which created them, their existence signified an advance in women's self-conscious control over the material conditions of their reproductive lives.[11]

Rather than pornographic statuettes carved by lonely male hunters, these figures represented knowledge and control over the changing self, a perspective that elevated goddesses to supremacy.

Our knowledge of the ancient Great Mother is limited — her rituals were either too well-known to be recorded, or too secretive — imparted only to initiates.[12] "The unmanifest Great Goddess is depicted as transcendent and unmarried, clearly superior to the male gods who are merely her devotees and remain dependent on her invigorating power (sakti) to perform even the simplest task."[13] She is like the queen bee, directing drones and warriors. Thus the queen of the world, like the warrior woman, seeks a submissive partner for her complementary animus: Demeter lying on a thrice-plowed field with the youth Iasion, whom Zeus later sacrificed; the Fairy Queen and her bard, Thomas the Rhymer; Artemis visiting drowsing Endymion; Kali dancing on prone Shiva, Venus and Cupid; Anat and Ba'al; Gaia and Uranus; Isis and Horus. However, this partner is not completely helpless. He entertains and supports the queen, encouraging her to listen to her emotional side. In other words, the consort is her heart.

At the same time, he is the questing warrior, while she rules from her throne:

> The relation of these early matriarchal, husbandless goddesses, whether Mother or Maid, to the male figures that accompany them is ... half-way between Mother and Lover, with a touch of the patron saint. Aloof from achievement themselves, they choose a local hero for their own to inspire and protect. They ask of him, not that he should love or adore, but that he should do great deeds. Hera has Jason, Athene, Perseus, Herakles and Theseus, Demeter and Kore Triptolemos. And as their glory is in the hero's high deeds, so their grace is his guerdon.[14]

CHAPTER 28

Divorcing Anima:
The Goddess Sublimated

Izanagi and Izanami (Japan)

The primordial deities in the sky ordered the twins kami Izanagi no Mikoto and Izanami no Mikoto to descend to earth. Standing on the floating bridge of heaven, the pair gazed down but saw nothing below. Izanagi thrust his jewel-spear of heaven down into the ocean and stirred. With a curdling sound, he churned up the ocean, and when he lifted the spear, the brine coagulated and dripped. It soon hardened and formed the Japanese island of Onogoro ("spontaneously-congealing").

After settling there, Izanagi invited Izanami to describe how her body was formed. She said, "My body in its thriving grows, but there is one part that does not grow together."

Izanagi replied, "My body in its thriving also grows, but there is one part that grows in excess. Therefore, would it not seem proper that I should introduce the part of my body in excess into the part of your body that does not grow together, and so procreate territories?"

Izanami said, "It would be well."

Izanagi and Izanami proceeded to perform a marriage ritual in which they walked around a pillar, he moving to the left and she to the right. When they met on the other side, Izanami spoke first, saying: "Ah! What a fair and lovely youth!"

To which Izanagi replied: "Ah! What a fair and lovely maiden!"

They consummated their relationship, and Izanami gave birth to a leech-like child. Disgusted, they set him in a basket and released it onto the ocean.

Izanagi was convinced that their first child had turned out so because of Izanami's breach of proper decorum in that she had spoken first. The divine

260

couple conferred with the Heavenly Kami above and confirmed that this failure was indeed because Izanami had spoken first.

They returned to the central pillar on the island of Onogoro and repeated the marriage ceremony. This time Izanagi began, saying, "Ah! What a fair and lovely maiden!"

To which Izanami appropriately replied, "Ah! What a fair and lovely youth!" After this new exchange Izanagi and Izanami gave birth to 14 islands and 35 kami.

Delivering Kagu-Tsuchi-no-Kami, the fire god, Izanami was so badly burned that she died, the first instance of death in the world. Izanagi was devastated and exclaimed, "Oh! Thine Augustness my lovely younger sister! Oh! That I should have exchanged thee for this single child!" He buried her on Mount Hiba, on the boundary between the Land of Izumo and the Land of Hahaki.

Izanagi was desperate to find Izanami, so he followed her into the land of Yomi-no-kuni, the underworld. When Izanagi finally discovered her in Yomi, he greeted her with excitement, saying, "Thine Augustness my lovely younger sister! The lands that I and thou made are not yet finished making; so come back."

Izanami hesitated over returning to the upper world since she had already eaten the food of Yomi. She asked for time to consult with the deities of the underworld, and made him promise not to follow or look upon her. For a long time Izanagi waited. But at last he could bear it no longer and sought her. Eventually, he found his wife in one of the darkest regions of Yomi, but he backed away in shock. Her body was decomposing!

"Nay! I have come unawares to a hideous and polluted land," he cried.

And she replied, "Why didst thou not observe that which I charged thee? Now I am put to shame." Furious at this ultimate humiliation, Izanami starting chasing Izanagi through the vast corridors of the underworld.

He ran from the cave and Izanami sent the eight Ugly Females of Yomi to destroy him. Izanagi, while running, tore off his black headdress and threw it on the ground. It turned into a bunch of grapes that the females stopped to feast on. This delayed them somewhat, but when they had finished eating they resumed the chase. Izanagi threw his comb, which turned into bamboo shoots, and then threw three peaches. Each time, the females stopped to eat.

At last Izanagi burst through the Even Pass of Yomi. Snatching a boulder, he blocked the path with it. Then he faced Izanami on the other side of the barrier and proclaimed the words of divorce.

Enraged, Izanami declared that she would kill a thousand people daily in the land above. From behind his barrier, Izanagi replied, "Thine Augustness! If thou do this, I will in one day set up a thousand and five hundred parturition houses [for giving birth]. In this manner each day a thousand people would surely be born." Thus the primordial balance between births and deaths among mortal people came into being.

Feeling distraught and ashamed at what he had done, Izanagi purified himself. He cleansed his left eye, thereby producing the deity Amaterasu Omi-Kami. Following that, he washed his right eye and produced the deity Tsukiyomi no Mikoto. Finally, he washed his nose, creating Susano-o no Mikoto.

After the purification process Izanagi was ecstatic. He rejoiced and said, "I, begetting child after child, have at my final begetting gotten three illustrious children." However, Susano-o no Mikoto was always sobbing out of despair. When Izanagi asked why he was continually crying, Susano-o said that he missed his mother and wished to follow her into the land of Yomi. Izanagi became angry and said, "Go, even as thy heart bids thee," driving Susano-o away.

Thus, though he had lost his soul mate, Izanagi's divine task had finally been accomplished. He withdrew from the world and built himself an "abode of gloom" in Ahaji, where he was forever encompassed in silence as a hermit.[1]

This story originates in the *Kojiki* (*Record of Ancient Matters*), dated 712 C.E., and its companion, the *Nihongi* (*Chronicles of Japan*) from 720 C.E. As with Adam and Eve, this story shows taboo-breaking as the reason death and entropy entered the world. Izanami, like Eve, errs, in this case by speaking first, which suggests she is supposed to be subservient to her husband.

The male Izanagi similarly violates his wife's prohibition by witnessing her vulnerable, decaying state. This underworld retreat is a sacred moment, not meant for the eyes of husbands. Thus, Izanami, spied upon, grows menacing. She appears monstrous, frightening, like the underworld she represents.

Taboo-breaking occurs when men witness breast-feeding, birthing, cooking, weaving, or other archetypal female pursuits. These are "products that women draw from themselves at their expense, for in folk tales and myths they often die as a result of having given too much of themselves."[2] This is female magic, a power man risks his life to interrupt. As with selkies and swan wives, the husband's breaking of the taboo results in his losing his wife forever. Even Izanagi's beautiful new children will not coax Izanami from the underworld.

Later in the *Kojiki*, the princess Toyo-tama-bime is giving birth, and forbids her husband to watch. He peeks into her parturition hut and sees that his wife has become a sea monster. Ashamed, Toyo-tama leaves the child with her husband and closes the sea-border behind herself as she departs.

In derivations of the story of Orpheus from New Zealand and Japan, the lost wife is transformed into a vengeful female who not only refuses to return to the upper world but also continues to wreak havoc from the otherworld.[3] Thus, the great mother goddess becomes the goddess of death. Unlike Eve, who was created to keep Adam company, these two kami start on equal footing;

they create the world together, and each breaks a central taboo — neither knows how to act in a relationship.

Men and women in ancient times needed each other to survive, but both were wrapped in taboos of uncleanliness and threats to their sacredness from inappropriate contact. The trick was to balance these two worlds and explore the foreign gender, while remaining on the safe side of taboo and ritual.

> Men who have not made peace with Medusa in themselves will see feminine sexuality as something that fascinates them, but also as the source of their self-undoing. As they try to protect themselves against its frightening power by destroying the monster, they will unconsciously incite the Medusa woman in their lives to retaliate by castrating them physically and psychologically. A man who desires a positive relationship to women's dark moon sexuality must make the descent into his unconscious, listen to the wailing agony of his decapitated Medusa, reach out in sympathy to her pain, heal the wounds of her rejection, and return whole-within-himself to the upper world. After the hero has proved his separation from his mother, he must reestablish a loving relationship to his inner dark feminine. Until he can do this he will remain trapped in a web of destructive sexual relationships.[4]

Izanagi loses his wife through ignoring her wishes, crossing the unbreakable line of taboo and privacy. Thus the world begins fractured, death-filled, seeking a healing that will never come.

Too many patriarchal cultures put the blame for the world's evils centrally on the woman, resulting in millennia of degradation based allegedly on Eve's sin. Notably, the *Qur'an* offers a different picture of Eden, free of Eve's original sin and the several millennia of blame placed solely on her skinny shoulders:

> But Satan whispered to him, saying: "Adam, shall I show you the Tree of Immortality and an imperishable kingdom?" *They both ate of its fruit*, so that they saw their shameful parts and began to cover themselves with the leaves from the Garden. Thus did *Adam disobey his Lord*, and stray from the right path[5] [italics added].

They both ate: they are both blamed. Thus Adam and Eve of the *Qur'an* are cast into the world as equals.

Jewish tradition is hazier on the blame for Eden: According to Biblical commentary (*Midrashim*), along with close reading of the text, Adam lied to Eve, instructing her that even a brush against the tree would kill her. As she naively explained, "Of the fruit of the tree that is in the middle of the garden, God said, 'Do not eat it, and do not touch it, or else you will die.'"[6] When the snake pushed her against the tree and she wasn't harmed, Eve assumed that the rest of the proscription was equally suspect. Thus Adam's lie to his wife condemned them both, just as Eve's temptation did.

Pandora of the Greeks was said to have released all the evils into the world through her fatal curiosity, opening a forbidden jar. Zeus calls Pandora, the first woman, "an evil thing in which they [men] may all be glad of heart while they embrace their own destruction."[7] Thus the first woman was both gift and curse.

She was called "The giver of all," or "Endowed with everything," as each god gave her gifts: beauty, crafts, grace, wisdom. Ironically, she did indeed carry everything — the curses of humanity as well as the beauty and charm which made her so irresistible. After Zeus offered her a stoppered jar, Hermes gave her curiosity, reaffirming that she was a trap, a gift designed to punish mankind. As Hesiod tells in *Works and Days*:

> For ere this the tribes of men lived on earth remote and free from ills and hard toil and heavy sickness which bring the Keres (Fates) upon men; for in misery men grow old quickly. But the woman took off the great lid of the jar with her hands and scattered all these and her thought caused sorrow and mischief to men. Only Elpis (Hope) remained there in an unbreakable home within under the rim of the great jar, and did not fly out at the door.[8]

Hope remained, a single blessing to succor humankind through its suffering.

This may be the cruelest, most sexist creation story. For Eve was created as Adam's loving companion, but Pandora was created for man's destruction. In pre–Hellenic Greece, Pandora, the all-gifted, was a title of Mother Rhea, with her symbol, the great vase, as source of all things.[9] In the wave of patriarchal reimagining, however, Hesiod's anti-feminist fable converted Rhea's all-giving vase into the source of mankind's ills. As he describes man's fate:

> Zeus who thunders on high made women to be an evil to mortal men, with a nature to do evil. And he gave them a second evil to be the price for the good they had: whoever avoids marriage and the sorrows that women cause, and will not wed, reaches deadly old age without anyone to tend his years.... And as for the man who chooses the lot of marriage and takes a good wife suited to his mind, evil continually contends with good; for whoever happens to have mischievous children, lives always with unceasing grief in his spirit and heart within him; and this evil cannot be healed. So it is not possible to deceive or go beyond the will of Zeus.[10]

From the early inception of patriarchal religion, the goddess became sublimated, and her human incarnations morphed into a force of evil and entropy. Across the world, the Judeo-Christian God created the world through words, establishing creation as a solely masculine act, like Izanagi's giving birth. Zeus became king of the gods, with his patricide of Cronus sublimating the legend of Gaia and her son-lover Uranus. With the gods controlling creation, wisdom, and birth, the Earth Mother dwindled quietly into Grandmother Gaia, content to allow the younger gods supremacy.

The serpent was the symbol, perhaps even the instrument, of divine counsel in the religion of the Goddess, particularly that of Asherah, a goddess in a polytheistic religion whose worship competed with early Judaism. It was surely intended in Adam and Eve "that a serpent, as the familiar counselor of women, be seen as a source of evil."[11] When Eve obeys the serpent, she is disobeying the masculine god by succumbing to the Goddess religion. The tree of knowledge, which she must not touch on pain of expulsion from the patriarchal paradise, represents the sacred sycamore fig tree of the Goddess, which stood beside Asherah's temples. As Stone comments, "According to Egyptian texts, to eat of this fruit was to eat of the flesh and the fluid of the Goddess, the patroness of sexual pleasure and reproduction. According to the Bible story, the forbidden fruit caused the couple's conscious comprehension of sexuality."[12] Thus, Eve introduces Adam to the Goddess religion, sinning in the sight of God. This image of Eve as temptress warned Hebrew men to stay away from seductive temple women.

Athena and Eve are both associated with the snake, and thus, with the ancient serpent wisdom of the Great Goddess. However, the snake becomes a scheming force of evil and trickery. How better to punish the snake, cast down from its ruling temple to the dust of the road, than by having it found the monotheistic religion that would supplant it? Both Athena and Eve are born from men, Athena from Zeus's head, and Eve from Adam's rib: "In both myths, Mother Nature is depotentiated, and her birth-giving powers are taken over by the male," as the authors of *The Myth of the Goddess* explain.[13]

Today's civilization has been cut loose from the essential roots that formed humanity — these roots reach deep into the sacred universe, the domain of spirit where male and female energies balance perfectly and the interconnectivity and unity of all beings is revealed. "In today's world the power of the feminine — the most potent, loving and creative of forces on earth   is severely suppressed, and if not again honored, the imbalance of male and female energies could cause the destruction of humanity, if not Earth itself."[14]

Jesus and Mary

Throughout history Christianity has fixated on the masculine, sublimating, abandoning, or even condemning the feminine. In the Bible, Jesus grows and learns, teaches and tells stories. By contrast, Mary's actions are virginal and divine, without variation. She nurtures Jesus, protects him, and mourns his death. Thus, she is portrayed as an idealized mother rather than a person. In art, Jesus appears on the lap of his mother (often crowning her) or with female sinners at his feet, but never side by side with a female in equality.

Western Europe emphasized Holy Mother Mary's passive receptivity, as her virginity guided men toward spirituality without carnality — without, in fact, imperfect, real women. "The pale, plastered Maid of Nazareth who eventually supplanted the great Theotokos icons of the early centuries was a pale shadow of the vital, autonomous feminine principle."[15] Mary is upheld as paradigm, but as virgin devoted to the needs of males surrounding her. In this way, Mother Mary becomes shallow and innocent, a two-dimensional guardian who lacks the ferocity of a Kali or Tiamat. The medieval image of Mary, especially, lacks the deeper instinct of older goddesses, while her immaculate conception places her outside nature. She is born sinlessly, she conceives asexually, she is carried up to heaven without dying: "The virginity of Mary has above all a negative value: that through which the flesh has been redeemed is not carnal: it has not been touched or possessed."[16]

> Thus official Mariology validates the twin obsessions of male fantasies toward woman; the urge to both reduce the female to the perfect vehicle of male demands, the instrument of male ascent, and at the same time to repudiate the female as the source of all that pulls him down into bodiliness, sin and death. Mariology exalts the virginal, obedient, spiritual feminine and fears all real women in the flesh.[17]

Most female Catholic saints are virgins, martyrs, widows, or celibate married women. As Mary Condren notes in *The Serpent and the Goddess*, "Women have been identified with Eve, the symbol of evil, and can only attain sanctity by identifying with the Virgin Mary, the opposite of Eve."[18] But this is impossible, as Mary was conceived and gave birth immaculately. "To reach full sanctity then, women must renounce their sexuality, symbol of their role as Temptress and the means by which they drag men down from their lofty heights."[19] Virgin martyrs were paradigms of virtue and honor, figures to be emulated. Some include Saints Katherine, Margaret, Lucy, Christina, Cecelia, Dorothy, Agnes, Barbara, and Agatha. All were noble and wealthy. Sought by powerful pagan suitors, they desired to maintain their virginity and Christianity. Thrown into prison, tortured, and killed, these teenage girls were held up as ideals for young women.[20]

However, these young women are revered for rejecting their feminine nature, turning their backs on marriage and sometimes slicing off their hair and even their breasts to appear less attractive. All die as defeminized teenagers, unable to become mothers, lovers, or wisewomen; thus the feminine is once again devalued. "If she renounces the flesh, she is God's creature, redeemed by the savior, no less than is man,"[21] Simone de Beauvoir criticizes. Thus woman is forced to deny her physical nature to seek the divine, taking oaths of chastity and self-denial. This is no feminine role model. As Patricia Reis explains in *Through the Goddess: A Woman's Way of Healing*, "Whenever a woman attempts to contain her premenstrual anger, or perfume her monthly bleeding with deodorized tampons, or 'freshen' herself after sex with fragrant douches, she is caught in the old collision between Sky-Gods and ancient Goddesses."[22] She is trying to hide her "sinful feminine nature," a part of herself that was once celebrated with feasts and initiation ceremonies.

We can be virgin or whore, Athena or Aphrodite, but nevermore woman who is whole in herself, who exudes all these aspects and values them.

> We have tended either to become our bodies — blindly, slavishly, in obedience to male theories about us — or to try to exist in spite of them.... Many women see any appeal to the physical as a denial of mind. We have been perceived for too many

centuries as pure Nature, exploited and raped like the earth and the solar system; small wonder if we now long to become Culture: pure spirit, mind. Yet it is precisely this culture and its political institutions which have split us off from itself.[23]

In ancient Coptic texts, Mary Magdalene appears to a dreamer claiming to be one with the virgin: making up a dual-sided goddess both carnal and saintly.[24] However, she and Mother Mary are perpetually divided into saint and sinner, preserver and temptress. One to be emulated, and the other to be sublimated, until only her whisper exists.

This practice in which woman were denunciated and degraded as corrupt continued through medieval times. Eve's apple-eating sin was held up as condemnation for her entire sex, and women were whores, witches, and scolds, fit only for procreation. Many popes and future saints questioned their purpose of existence, and even whether they had souls. As Saint Augustine put it:

> I cannot see for what help to man woman was created, unless it were toward the goal of procreation. And I do not understand why one would exclude this finality. If woman were not given to man for the goal of engendering children, then for what other help? So they could till the earth together? If this were the help needed, then another man would have been more useful. One could say the same as regards comfort in his solitude. Cohabitation between two friends is so much more agreeable than that between a man and a woman.[25]

Here is a true misogynist, who sees no value toward romantic love or heterosexual companionship (as was often the view in his time). This one-sidedness led to unequal relationships. By devaluing women in worship, public, and private life, men cut themselves off from the spiritual, the unconscious, the emotional. Sex was condemned for both genders, except for procreation, and that was accepted only reluctantly. Both genders, therefore, suffered guilt and self-hatred for any feelings of love, tenderness or desire.

From here came women's confinement to the home: If women had the power of birth, unlike the men, well, let them do that and nothing else. As God warned womankind, "In sorrow thou shalt bring forth children; and thy desire shall be to thy husband, and he shall rule over thee."[26] Women were crafty temptresses needing to keep to their place, virtuous only if they wedded properly and served their husbands.

Chapter 29

Double Double:
The Terrible Mother

La Llorona (Mexico)

Once in a poor Mexican village, there lived a young maiden. She was proud of her great beauty and refused every man in the village when they begged to marry her.

One day, a Spanish officer with a sharp uniform and gleaming mustache rode into the village, leading a battalion of soldiers from Mexico. All the young women decided he was the handsomest, most noble man they had ever seen.

The officer, in turn, could not take his eyes from the proud young woman and her astounding beauty. He courted her, and, in time, they married. Together they had two children whom the Indian woman valued above everything.

The soldier rode away on long journeys, leaving his wife to care for the children. One day, he rode into town in a carriage. Seated beside him was a Spanish señorita, elegant and young. His Indian wife ran up to the side of the carriage and demanded to know who the woman was. To her devastation, the soldier replied that she was the woman he intended to marry.

When the Indian woman demanded he honor his vows to her, he replied that a marriage between a Spanish man and an Indian woman was not a true union. The children were bastards, and he would soon marry properly. Overcome with rage, the Indian woman plotted how she could injure him the most: In a fit of rage bordering on madness, she hurled her two children into the river.

As soon as she threw them, she realized her terrible mistake and leapt in to save them. However, the children had already drowned. After that, she walked along the river at night, weeping and moaning for her babes to return. Her anguished wails echoed through the village like a tortured soul's. The people there hid their own children in their houses when they heard her, as they feared she would steal them to replace her own.

For all eternity, the Llorona is destined to walk along the riverbank, weeping for her children, her terrible cry mingling with the sound of wind over the river.[1]

Throughout myth, the woman who slaughters her own children is the worst of villainesses. This is a perversion of the deepest, most instinctual type of love, sacrificing it for revenge, which must be considered a lesser cause. The Llorona, like Medea of Greek legend, kills her children in order to spite their father. To her, they are symbols of a broken promise, a social inferiority, a hindrance.[2]

Just as the "good mother" is the life giver, the wicked stepmother or "Terrible Mother" takes life from the most innocent, her own children whom she should cherish. Yet this viciousness can sometimes be a response to patriarchy, in a world in which women are most valued for youth, beauty and fertility.

The Sorceress Enraged

Medea begins her tale as guardian of the Golden Fleece of Colchis (modern-day Georgia), symbolic of agricultural prosperity, fertility, and royal authority. She is princess and priestess both, young and fertile, her heart inflamed with passion for the Greek hero Jason. She is also a witch of the dark moon, disciple of the crone goddess Hecate.

She conquers the dragon guarding the fleece with a magic potion and aids Jason in all his tasks, escaping with him and brutally cutting up and scattering her brother Absyrtus's body to delay pursuit. She offers her magical cauldron to restore Jason's usurper uncle to youth, but actually tricks his own daughters into boiling him alive. With the throne restored, she weds Jason and bears him two sons.

After all she has given, he turns from her, finding her foreign magic frightening beside the youth and innocence of a neighboring princess. Medea's fury rivals Hera's at Zeus's infidelities: Jason has forgotten the value of Medea's magic and sees her only as the threatening death-goddess. Thereupon, she slays his fiancée with a poisoned robe and crown but also murders her own two children to take the cruelest revenge she can imagine.

As she proclaims in Euripides' famous play:

> He shall never from this day see his children by me alive, nor will he beget children by his new bride since that wretch must die a wretched death by my poisons. Let no one think me weak, contemptible, untroublesome. No, quite the opposite, hurtful to foes, to friends kindly. Such persons live a life of greatest glory.[3]

She has betrayed her father and brother and her sacred trust as priestess, stealing the golden fleece and offering it, along with herself, to Jason. Now she has given him all she has. As she asks, "What do I gain by living? I have no fatherland, no house and no means to turn aside misfortune."[4] She decides she must kill her two children, though it will cut her cruelly, as "it is the way to hurt my husband most."[5]

Through literature and myth, Medea is infamous as the murderess of children, disciple of Hecate the death-crone, niece of the wicked Circe. But she has few choices once her husband spends all his love on her as comely maiden and loving mother, and then abandons the older death-crone in favor of a sweet, young second wife. Just as Medea is gaining her mature strength, a spineless princess supplants her. Jason will give this new wife his children to raise, and leave Medea bereft, without family or country. He has betrayed her. As she demands of him, "What god or power above will listen to you, who broke your oath and deceived a stranger?"[6]

Jason's cruelty demands a single response. With her magic and supremacy denied, Medea unleashes them in full force: If Jason had thought he feared her before, that is only a grain of sand before her towering wind of fury. She is now the wicked stepmother, the one forced from her motherhood before she was prepared. She takes it even further: If she cannot be Jason's wife, he will have no wife, no children. No other woman will raise her darlings. Thus, she strikes out with her only weapon.

"You are a she-lion, not a woman, with a nature more savage than Scylla the Tuscan monster," Jason cries.[7] It is true. He has challenged the primal nature of femininity, crueler and more terrible than he ever suspected, and he has paid its price. He ends the play lamenting, bereft of all family, with only an empty old age awaiting him, such as he tried to force on Medea.

"Now all is enmity, and love's bonds are diseased."[8] As Jason is the king, his foresworn oaths to Medea imbalance the land, as so often occurs when the male and female powers are imbalanced. His betrayal is destroying the country, a macrocosm of his shattered family.

Meanwhile, Medea soars away on her dragon chariot, abandoning her helpless husband. Her next episode sees her wedding the elderly King Aegeus and attempting to murder her stepson Theseus so her own child can claim the throne. In a world where her husband can steal her sons and replace her and them with other heirs, she strikes back in defense of her family. Medea's ascensions to wife, queen, and death-crone are each linked to a murder, likely expressing her frustration at the patriarchy supplanting her and her goddess's power. In Seneca's *Medea*, she ends her torments of the men who betray her and withdraws from their world, questing for her lost virginity and Colchian origins.

Cannibal Queens

A South American woman with a two-year-old baby was waiting for her husband to return. Though the husband didn't arrive, a lovely woman in a white jacket did. The mother invited her in, and let her hold the baby while she cooked dinner. The baby wouldn't stop screaming. The fire wouldn't light and the baby was only growing louder. "Give him back and I'll feed him," said the mother.

"I have him, he's all right," said the lady in white. After a while, the cries stopped. The mother looked over and saw the woman's mouth was smeared with blood, and half her baby had been eaten. Then the mother knew that her visitor was a condenado: a beautiful shapechanger who disguised herself as a loved one and preyed on human life. The mother was frightened and ran out and hid among the cows. But when night fell, she had turned into a condenado herself. They stayed up until dawn, the two of them, eating the baby.[9]

This is the dark side of the shapechanger-lover. A beloved spouse reveals a hidden side, grows violent or murderous. The victim can transfer the blame to the condenado, like shifting a vicious mother into a stepmother: "My beloved would never act this way. She must be a demon, stealing her shape."

In this case, the condenado is the mother's repressed side. The mother invites her in, offers her food, gives her the baby. By doing so, she is succumbing to her evil impulses, allowing them to subsume her normal personality. It's natural to be frustrated and angry, to fantasize, even to lash out. "The same woman who may be willing to place her body between her child and a runaway truck will often resent the day-by-day sacrifice the child unknowingly demands of her time, sexuality, and self-development."[10] But a strong person battles her dark impulses, acknowledges them, and conquers them. Perhaps she makes time for herself each week, or punches a pillow. Ignoring these hidden desires can be self-destructive, but succumbing to them is far worse.

By contrast, the cannibalism in Hansel and Gretel goes two ways: It is the children tearing at the witch's house, eating the roof over her head. The witch, worn from childbearing, from suckling babies, stares at her skinny body — can children take any more from her? Infuriated, she wants to swallow them back into her belly from which they came. She longs to feast on their youth until her limbs take the strength of theirs and her cheeks plump, to regress back through motherhood and into her stolen youth.[11]

Hansel and Gretel is only one in a myriad of cannibalism tales. In a Kaffir folktale, two children visited their cannibal mother deep in the forest. When they arrived, their father hid them under a pile of skins, but the mother sniffed the air. "There's something here. How nice it smells!" She uncovered the children and cooked them dinner, eating a corpse herself. That night, the children ran away, but their mother chased them, axe in hand. For a little while, the daughter's song drove her off, but just outside the village, the mother swallowed them both, and then all the villagers and their cattle. As she headed home, a bird as big as a hut landed before her and sang, "I am a pretty bird of the valley; you come to make a disturbance at my place." The bird sliced off both her arms and then tore open her stomach. Everyone poured out, still alive. Though the mother tried to catch them and swallow them, she soon died.[12] This odd and grotesque story is all about reciprocation: the mother feeds the children then eats them. The singing daughter is killed; the singing bird kills the mother. Even dying the mother keeps eating, as if determined to keep all the world bottled within herself.

"The Juniper Tree" likewise features the stepmother feasting on her stepchild. The real mother here and in "Snow White" died in childbirth, and so the stepmother reciprocates by killing the child. "From the child's point of view, the first two principal episodes of the tale enact the syntactical inversion of 'I killed you' into 'You killed me,'" if "you" is the mother and "I" is the child.[13] The child caused his mother's death, but her stepmother alter ego causes his. Even if the mother did not literally die, her giving birth represents a type of psychic death. As Adrienne Rich points out, in childbirth "the mother's life is exchanged for the child's; her autonomy as a separate being seems fated to conflict with the infant she will bear."[14]

Babies feed on time and energy and beauty as well as milk, leading to maternal frustration. "I've gotten stretch marks and sleepless nights for you," a tiny voice inside the mother whispers. "And now you get to go to the ball, to be young and beautiful? It's not fair!" Cannibalism thus becomes her logical conclusion: To consume something is to gain its youth and power.

Houmea, wife of Maori hunter Tangaroa, was a true devouring mother. When her husband returned from fishing, she would go down to his canoe and gulp down all the fish before her family could eat. She then pretended sea fairies had devoured everything. Worse yet, she finally swallowed her two sons. Her husband restored them to life with a ritual chant, loaded them in his canoe, and fled. But Houmea turned herself into a cormorant and pursued them, mouth gaping. They fed her hot stones and escaped as she died, but her spirit lived on in the cormorant's form.[15]

The cormorant has an incredible ability to swallow fish, casting it appropriately as the great devourer. Likewise, women are frequently associated with the water and the terrifying unconscious, forcing the men to escape through wit and handmade tools.

The devouring mother knows her child is a part of herself, the one to whom she's closest in all the world. And yet the daughter is breaking away, perhaps forever, as she resists following her mother's career choice, her decisions, her relationships. The mother, sensing the loss of this part of herself, knows it's time to let go, but often clings tighter or rages. The daughter senses this turmoil, and, like the girl in Baba Yaga's tale, must flee the competitive witch before she dies or becomes her.

And yet, the desire to grow in power, to consume the world and take its strength, is greatly compelling. This is the lesson Baba Yaga teaches as she crouches in her traveling forest hut on gnarled chicken legs. All who enter her hut face devouring, either in her cannibalistic pot or in a deeper form. She is the wise crone, wielder of the feminine magic. When children enter Baba Yaga's hut, their old selves are "consumed" and they emerge as adults. And as adults who've learned the lesson of the Terrible Mother, they are prepared to face the destroyer herself. The witch is a personification of evil that eventually consumes itself. The trick is to escape without being consumed by the obsession that drags the witch into ruin.

Wicked Witches

According to Jewish legend, Lilith, the first woman, refused to be subservient to Adam, or to lie under him (as quoted in Chapter 10). Whereupon, she uttered the name of God, and with its power, she fled.

> Adam stood in prayer before his Creator: "Sovereign of the universe!" he said. "The woman you gave me has run away." At once, the Holy One, blessed be He, sent these three angels to bring her back.
>
> "Said the Holy One to Adam, "If she agrees to come back, fine. If not, she must permit one hundred of her children to die every day." The angels left God and pursued Lilith, whom they overtook in the midst of the sea, in the mighty waters wherein the Egyptians were destined to drown. They told her God's word, but she did not wish to return. The angels said, "We shall drown you in the sea."
>
> "Leave me!" she said. "I was created only to cause sickness to infants. If the infant is male, I have dominion over him for eight days after his birth, and if female, for twenty days."
>
> "When the angels heard Lilith's words, they insisted she go back. But she swore to them by the name of the living and eternal God: "Whenever I see you or your names or your forms in an amulet, I will have no power over that infant." She also agreed to have one hundred of her children die every day. Accordingly, every day one hundred demons perish, and for the same reason, we write the angels' names on the amulets of young children. When Lilith sees their names, she remembers her oath, and the child recovers."[16]

Today, Lilith is viewed as a paragon of the feminist movement, equal to Adam and unblamed for Eve's sin. She withdrew from the garden because she valued her own freedom and independence above all. Yet, in medieval times, Lilith was feared and reviled as a demoness. She was, like all Terrible Mothers, a slayer of children, and new mothers used bowls and amulets bearing the angels' names to ward off her presence. Mothers would inscribe these vessels with the words "Out Lilith" and keep a constant watch on the child, particularly in the first vulnerable eight days.[17] Meanwhile, a number of folktales show virtuous midwives and clever mothers defeating Lilith and saving their babies. Frequently, they shut Lilith in a sealed jar, refusing to let her out unless she promises to shower the mother and baby with gifts instead of harm.

Men saw her differently, however, as a succubus who visits them in erotic dreams. From these liaisons, she gives birth to half-human, half-demon monstrosities. Even when men escaped her in the tales, she would continue to hold power over them, as a male-invented incarnation of fantasy, lust, and fear. She spent her time as a life-destroyer, subverting the holy act of intercourse and its design in creating children.

Lilith was endlessly fertile, endlessly wrathful at her own children's death. Thus, as she birthed children who quickly died, she maintained the balance of the world. Outside the normal bonds of creation, she became the defiant one, the destroyer like Izanami crouched in the underworld. Without equality, she would destroy earth's infants, its healthy relationships, in payment for her own perished children. She is the buried rage of Kali, Ereshkigal, Medusa, crouching outside the world and demanding it pay.

In another country, the Persian queen Sudabeh conceived a passion for her stepson, Prince Seyavash, and when he refused her, she pretended he had assaulted her. However, his story rang truer, so the king took no action. Upon this, Sudabeh went to her friend, a witch enduring a difficult pregnancy, and encouraged her to abort her twins. The woman agreed, and gave birth to "two ugly devil's spawn."[18] Sudabeh pretended to be in labor that night. Her maids came running at her groans, and found the two dead misshapen babes that Sudabeh had laid nearby. Sudabeh said that the children were hers, miscarried because of Prince Seyavash's assault. As a result, Seyavash had to undergo trial by fire to clear his name. Sudabeh was finally executed, but only after her machinations caused the prince's death.[19]

Sudabeh kills two unborn children and uses their deaths to implicate her stepson. Though the babies aren't hers (or human), she is another child-killer. Moreover, a marriage has been arranged between her daughter and Prince Seyavash. Like Snow White's stepmother, she is competing with her child, refusing to accept aging. "Come, in secret, just once, make me happy again, give me back my desirability for a moment," she coaxes Seyavash.[20] She clings to youth and beauty, murdering children to achieve her desires.

Waning Moon: Crone

The crone is glorious Hecate, the waning moon, who dwells in the land of death and instructs her young disciple, Medea, in magic. She is the widowed Ereshkigal, demanding respect. She is fiery-breathed Nephthys, sister-wife of Set. Cerridwen, goddess of dark prophetic powers, keeper of the cauldron of the underworld, in which inspiration and divine knowledge are brewed. Hel, half white and half black, who will lead her army of the dead in Ragnarok and destroy all the worlds. She is the screeching Banshee, forewarning mortality. She is Kali, the destroyer. She is the one who heals and kills, she who presides over birth and lays out the dead for burial.

Many cultures believed that by retaining menstrual blood within, the crone claimed power over her magical energy and became an awesome figure. Heroes as well as heroines sought her wisdom: Cúchulainn trained with the Druidess Scathach, while Monster Slayer of the Navajo entreated Spider Woman's guidance. Oedipus faced the Delphic Oracle and the Sphinx, seeking wisdom. These hidden sisters, like the Fates and the Furies, are repositories of the ancient wisdom, the forgotten lore, the ways of magic: The crones are mentors or soothsayers, prophesying the triumphs of kings and the downfall of kingdoms.

In the war of mother-daughter, the crone has wisely retired, understanding the cycle of life, but in many ways transcending it: Her next stage is ascension to the spirit realm as a divine protector. She carries her disciples through the harvest and respite of life, the dark moon of the self, and ushers them through the death-passage transition. The funerary priestess of the soul, she extinguishes the old cycle, and, as midwife, births the new. "As we begin to rehonor the Dark Goddess of menopause, her teachings will help to liberate us from our fears of change and transition, aging and death," Demetra George writes.[1] She is the destroyer, but beyond destruction lies resurrection, for those with the wisdom to welcome her.

Whether we see the Dark Goddess as dancing ecstatically in a swirl of red flames, or enveloped in mist gazing into the inner pools of her psychic awareness, or throbbing with her orgasmic magical-creative energy, or embracing us in our grief, or furiously raging, screaming, crying, or desperately withdrawing into a stupor of denial or numbness, her ultimate purpose in each one of these guises is the same. She destroys in order to renew. The Dark Goddess of the Dark Moon is the mistress of transformation, and she exists everywhere there is change.[2]

CHAPTER 30

Knives in the Dark: The Destroyer

The Birth of Kali (India)

The great Devi, shining Durga, born from the wrath of the gods, was sitting on a tree in the Himalaya Mountains. Just then there came by chance Chanda and Munda, the bodyguards of Sumbha, King of the demonic Rakshasas. They ran to their king and said, "Oh Lord! There is a wonderful thing in the Himalayas. No man can explain that wonder. There is an extremely beautiful woman when compared to whom all your queens are mere worms only. All your wealth is nothing. Your glory is nothing. Your valor is nothing. Your kingdom is nothing. Your pride is nothing. She is more than all this. Go there and bring Her."

Sumbha sent his ambassador to court celestial Durga as his queen, to brag of his wealth and power.

Durga smiled. "He is indeed rich and mighty. But what am I to do? Through ignorance I have taken a vow, how can I override it? Whoever conquers Me in battle, whoever subdues My pride, whoever is a match for Me in power, he should become My husband. Let, therefore, your lord come here and subdue Me, and then very easily obtain My hand."

The messenger would have none of it, and ordered Her to come or "you will shortly witness yourself being dragged by force by your bundle of hairs like a pitiable victim."

Again Durga refused.

Sumbha burned with rage and sent 60,000 soldiers to subdue Durga. The divine Devi produced a sound of "HUM" from inside Her and reduced the general to ashes. She poured a rain of arrows on the Asura army, and the lion of Devi fell on them all like burning fire on a dried forest. The heads of the Asuras

277

were cut off with axes that showered from the Devi's hands, and there was no end to the havoc caused to the Asuras by Her vehicle, the lion. The lion drank the blood of the Asuras, who all were lying dead on the ground. In a moment, there was not a single Asura to be seen.

This news reached the ears of king Sumbha and his anger knew no bounds. He began to bite his lips and ordered his faithful colleagues, Chanda and Munda, thus: "O Chanda! O Munda! Go there at once! Collect a large army. Bring her to me. Do not delay much. Quick, quick! Drag her by the hair, or tie her with ropes, or if not possible at least kill her in battle."

The army, led by the able Chanda and Munda, marched with raised arms towards Durga. They tried to catch hold of Her in all ways. They began to use their bows, discs and swords, and came near to Her. Rage flooded Durga, and Her face turned black like ink. From the middle of Her forehead emerged forth a feminine form of dreadful nature with horrible kinds of weapons in Her hands.

She was Kali with fearful face, with a garland of heads of Rakshasas around Her neck. She had two severed heads for her earrings, a string of skulls as necklace, and a girdle made of human hands as her clothing. Her tongue protruded from her mouth, her eyes glowed red, and her face and breasts were sullied with blood.

Kali roared and the army began to tremble. She fell upon them and began to destroy them in thousands at a stretch. She caught hold of thousands of Rakshasas in one grip and thrust them all into Her wide mouth. Chariots after chariots were entering Her mouth. Elephants after elephants were being churned to powder by Her teeth. She caught hold of some by the hair, some by the neck, some were tossed and kicked by Her feet. Their weapons, and the arrows sent by them, She sportfully swallowed as well. In the twinkling of an eye, the entire army of the Rakshasas was destroyed.

Seeing this terrible scene, Chanda ran towards Kali with great force. He faced Her with discuses, axes, swords, nooses, tridents, all thousands in number. Then Munda also came running with a shower of arrows on Kali on all sides. It looked as if clouds were covering the sun in dense form. Kali, with great rage, thundered violently with Her awe-inspiring face and the fiery tongue. She rushed forth towards Chanda, caught hold of his hair and cut off his head with Her sword. Then Munda came running to Her in anger on seeing his brother killed in battle. She rolled him on the ground and threw off his head with the cut of Her sword. The remaining army, seeing both Chanda and Munda lying dead on the ground, took to its heels and ran in all directions. Durga blessed Kali and named her Chamundi, slayer of Chanda and Munda.[1]

Though She had won, Kali was so much involved in the killing spree that She heedlessly continued, destroying everything in sight. To stop her, Lord Shiva, the destroyer-god, threw Himself under Her feet. Shocked at this sight, Kali stuck out Her tongue, and ended Her homicidal rampage. She is often depicted this way in her mêlée mood, standing with one foot on prone Shiva's chest, Her enormous tongue protruding. She holds a bloody cleaver and a severed human head in her upper arms. Her lower arms offer succor, however, making the signs of "fear not" and blessing.

Kali then took up residence in a forest, terrorizing the area with Her fierce companions and wild dancing. A devotee of Shiva prayed for Him to intercede, so Shiva appeared and challenged Kali to a dance contest. Though His dance defeated Hers, She claimed Him as consort, joining Him in his destructive cosmic dance through the rest of time.

Thus Kali is born from rage in the *Devi-Māhātmyam,* or *Glorification of the Great Goddess,* authored in 400–500 C.E. Kali appears dominant in her iconic representation with Shiva, often dancing on his prone body, her feet on his thighs and chest. She is a force of chaos, more likely to incite her consort to reckless behavior than to subdue him. Their wild cosmic ballet is heedless, frenzied, frightening, a force capable of destroying the world. But whereas Shiva's dance takes place in the cosmic realm, Kali's is in this world. She merges her earth power with that of Shiva, the sky god, and thus sustains the universe.

During this dance, Shiva's other wife, Parvati, watches silently, in fright. She reflects Kali, supplementing her wild nature with a gentler one and calming Shiva's destructive tendencies. She guides him within the domestic sphere, and gentles his destructive tandava dance.[2] Kali is a union of opposites:

> A paradoxical deity who combines within herself the poles of creation and destruction, birth and death, love and fear. This dual aspect of her character is implied by her epithet "Terrible Mother." The emphasis on Kali as a coincidence of opposites is understandable, given the feminist critique of attitudes that deny the earthier, more bodily and sexual side of existence.[3]

Though Kali apparently represents physical killing, she actually exemplifies the death of ego and the regenerative power of the sexual mysteries. The blood Kali sheds is not merely destructive force: it is "the primal matter of both life and death, which can be transmuted by divine alchemy into a new being. In purging the world of evil, the goddess is also preparing the space for the new generation or race which follows all cataclysms and peoples the world afresh."[4]

> In the ancient world, Chaos *is* Tiamat and Chaos *is* Kali. These goddesses were metaphor who expressed their culture's awareness of the universal Powers of Chaos. They represented the original churning womb or Crone-stirred cauldron or birth, death, and transmutation — the gaping Hole or spiraling Eye associated with the primordial female Powers in which all of us originate and to which all of us will return, to change once more.[5]

Kali had an ambiguous relationship to the world. On the one hand, she destroyed demons and thus brought order. However, she also served as a representation of forces that threatened social order and stability by her blood drunkenness and subsequent frenzied activity.

> She is adorned with several arms as a girdle, freshly cut heads as a necklace, children's corpses as earrings, and serpents as bracelets. She has long, sharp fangs, is often depicted as having clawlike hands with long nails, and is often said to have blood smeared on Her lips. Her favorite haunts heighten Her fearsome nature. She is usually shown on the battlefield, where She is a furious combatant who gets drunk on the hot blood of Her victims, or in a cremation ground, where She sits on a corpse surrounded by jackals and goblins.[6]

She is the great goddess "whose stomach is a void and so can never be filled and whose womb is giving birth forever to all things."[7] While Kali's acts appear wantonly destructive, her role is to protect the cosmic order by destroying demons. Like Medusa, she is the face of rage, thrust forth from the woman as a protector. She defends Durga from forcible marriage and enforces her sovereignty, emphasizing this independence as she dances on the prone, worshipful Shiva. As a modern symbol of female empowerment, Kali returns to women the three virtues they have historically been most denied: strength, intellect, and sexual sovereignty.[8]

> The image of Kali has become important in contemporary feminist consciousness in an attempt to recover imagery more compatible with the reality of female power, anger, and assertion.... Kali's reminder of the dark, avenging side of life, and the power of rage, readied for action, poised against the contemporary backdrop of a plundered and wounded earth, is a vision of spiritually energizing female power far removed from the benevolent mercy and accepting patience of Lakshmi or Mary.[9]

Shyama-Kali is the tender dispenser of boons and dispeller of fear, worshipped in households. She is Raksha-Kali, the protectress, in times of famine or earthquake.[10] Her worshippers understand that destruction brings creation and new life. As Sri Ramakrishna describes in his gospel:

> After the destruction of the universe, at the end of the great cycle, the Divine Mother garners the seeds for the next creation. She is like the elderly mistress of the house, who has a hotchpotch-pot in which she keeps different articles for household use.... After the destruction of the universe, my Divine Mother, the Embodiment of Brahman, gathers together the seeds for the next creation. After the creation this Primal Power dwells in the universe itself. She brings forth this phenomenal world and pervades it.[11]

Kali became the dominant deity within Tantric Hinduism, where she was praised as the original form of things and the origin of all that exists. She was termed Creatrix, Protectress, and Destroyer. In Tantra, the way of salvation was through the sensual delights usually forbidden to a devout Hindu, such as alcohol and sex. Kali represented the ultimate forbidden realities, and thus her worshippers absorbed her into the self and overcame her terrible nature in what amounted to a ritual of salvation. She taught that life fed on death, that death was inevitable, and that in the acceptance of these truths there was liberation. Kali, like many vampire-deities, symbolized the constant chaos of the universe: Life was ultimately untamable and unpredictable.[12]

Fear of the Anima

The Polynesian culture hero Maui dies as he crawls inside the vagina of the great goddess Hine-nui-te-po, hoping to be unnaturally reborn out of her mouth. When men interfere with the women's sphere of birth, the results are terrifying and often fatal. These myths convey a subtle fear of the feminine, as many Maori myth-women end up being terrible monsters.

Many men feared women would devour them: In Alaska, a hunter realized that all who kayaked east never returned. When he followed their path, he found a woman who invited him in to dine. However, the ornaments on her walls were actually the skins of the vanished hunters! Forewarned, the hunter remained awake at night and managed to defeat the cannibal woman with a magic word.[13]

Likewise, some of the most famous "man eaters" in myth are the Amazons, an entirely female race said to come from Libya or Scythia. They were nomadic warrior-horsewomen who cauterized a single breast (hence their name, "breastless") to facilitate firing their bows. When they wanted to conceive daughters, they would kidnap men, impregnate themselves, and (like black widows) kill the victims. Male offspring they likewise killed. Most myths with Amazons feature their being subdued, conquered, or killed at the hands of heroes like Theseus and Achilles.[14]

Though these young warriors can be intimidating, the old woman, even conquered, is a terrifying figure. Though ostensibly powerless, she hoards an infinite well of magic she can tap, often for the forces of destruction, as in the following Creole tale:

As a slaver ship sailed over the ocean, three sailors dropped dead, all with dried up guavas where their hearts should have been. Upon searching, the captain discovered an old slave woman no one had seen before, who pointed a finger at him, white with infinite malediction. He ordered her whipped to death. The sailors did so and flung her corpse over the side, where the sharks veered away without touching it.

That night, the captain could not sleep, and the next night, he felt his memories fading away. The third, "his blood thickened into a sugar as dense as carbon, clotting around his suddenly dried-up heart."[15] As the crew panicked, the ship ran aground and plummeted to the bottom of the ocean, surfacing only in the company of other phantom vessels, and warning the sleepless slave traders of the human ferocity secreted in the hearts of their rotting holds.[16]

Some cultures, particularly in Latin America, offer stories of women with the vagina dentata, or toothed vagina. Kalapolo Amazonian narratives detail a shapechanging (and sex-changing!) goddess named Nafigi who rapes men until they die. She is a succubus, men's fears of women incarnate. While she is sexually crazed and even venomous, the worse threat comes from her genitals, as her vagina contains a poisonous caterpillar, a tiny piranha, and a stinging ant.[17] This threat is a type of castration anxiety, as well as a set of cautionary tales of avoiding rape and encounters with foreign women. The poisoned woman is also a common trend in folklore, the femme fatale with whom a first night will be a man's last.

This is the harmful, destructive side of the anima: the devouring or Terrible Mother. "In this guise the anima is as cold and reckless as certain uncanny aspects of nature itself."[18] Men who have not reconciled themselves with this side of the personality see the other as threatening, something to be pushed away like Lilith, condemned like Eve, or destroyed, as with King Shahriyar of *One Thousand and One Nights*.

Great Destroyers

In our denial of death, we avoid confrontation with a basic reality. We conceal the ravaged face of death with cosmetics and bury our dead in costly metal boxes outfitted with luxurious bedding to provide comfort and security and to ignore the inevitable decay of the flesh into a pile of bones. In our avoidance of the reality of death, we do not face our fears of the great unknown. In separating death from life, we have severed our connection to the universal chain of being in which plants and animals, the earth and its atmosphere, the planets and galaxies are united in a never-ending cycle of life, death, and rebirth.[19]

Thus culture becomes a death-culture, sterile and split off from sensuality, experience, growth. This split is a danger to male and female alike: How can we be at one with the universe if we reject destruction, death, and suffering? Only through entering death with loving trust can we pass through the supreme ordeal and emerge triumphant.

The Australian ancestress Kalwadi is an important figure in male initiations. Boys are bloodied and placed in a hole in the ground, known as Kalwadi's womb. She is described as swallowing boys and regurgitating them as men, though she also has a reputation as a cannibal. Men once searched for her and killed her, but upon slitting her open, they discovered the children she had swallowed were not in her stomach, but had traveled to her womb, awaiting rebirth. Here, once again, the great goddess melds birth and eternal life with death and destruction. In this tale, she is the ultimate devourer, combining rebirth with insatiable appetite as she devours all she captures. In this way she is a great primal force of nature, ever seeking, ever ravenous.

Tlazolteotl of the Aztecs was known as "the filth eater." One could place every unclean work before her, every vanity and degradation, no matter how grave. The people exposed all, and Tlazolteotl cleansed them of it, purging their shame and replacing it with new growth.[20]

The ancient creation epic the *Enuma Elish* features the dragon-goddess Tiamat. Once beneficent creatrix, she turns monstrous, birthing monsters to defend herself:

> Ummu-Hubur [Tiamat] who formed all things,
> Made in addition weapons invincible; she spawned monster-serpents,
> Sharp of tooth, and merciless of fang;
> With poison, instead of blood, she filled their bodies.
> Fierce monster-vipers she clothed with terror,
> With splendor she decked them, she made them of lofty stature.
> Whoever beheld them, terror overcame him,
> Their bodies reared up and none could withstand their attack.
> She set up vipers and dragons, and the monster Lahamu,
> And hurricanes, and raging hounds, and scorpion-men,
> And mighty tempests, and fish-men, and rams;
> They bore cruel weapons, without fear of the fight.
> Her commands were mighty, none could resist them.[21]

Finally dying at the hands of the solar hero Marduk, Tiamat turns from birther of monsters and destroyer to creator, as her body becomes the earth.

The Destroyer-goddess throughout myth is a cannibal like Kalwadi, devourer of babes like Lilith. She is the "Veiled One," Caillech, the pre–Celtic Goddess of Winter, shrouding the earth in snow. Yet she is also the wise counselor who ushers spirits out of this world and into the next. The death goddess is the divine mother who "even in death can be counted on to take her children back into her cosmic womb."[22]

Russian lore sees Vasilisa the Beautiful, a Cinderella-like heroine, entering the deep forest on an errand for her stepmother. Though she is afraid to approach the frightening witch-crone Baba Yaga and beg a lit coal for her stepmother's fire, she is polite and humble. She listens to her magic wooden doll, which advises her how to charm Baba Yaga with politeness, and how to do all the errands she demands. The doll protects her, and Vasilisa returns home with a burning skull that destroys her stepfamily as soon as they behold it. Yet this is a fairytale: Free of the wicked stepfamily, Vasilisa lives modestly at home until a prince claims her, and they live happily ever after.

The confrontation with Baba Yaga, cannibalistic witch and mistress of nature, is replete with symbolism. Her hut roams the forest on chicken legs, evocative of a monster and a more atavistic time: The reptilian legs may represent our primitive origins, not yet evolved into mammals. Many stories add that her hut is always turning to face the darkest part of the forest.[23] If the forest represents the feminine unconscious, then Baba Yaga lives in its deepest reaches.

In fact, this dark forest is the land of death, another way of seeing the unconscious. As such, Baba Yaga is Persephone, the crone goddess and mistress of the underworld. "In appearance, she is tall, bony legged, pestle headed, and has a long nose and disheveled hair. At times she is a young woman; at other times she appears as two sisters, one young, one old."[24] The ancient taletellers wisely realized that the goddess who provides flowers and growth in summer likewise takes back the gift of life in winter, descending to the realm of the dead.

Other cultures echo this balance between life and death in their goddesses. Athena kills on the battlefield, but also teaches agriculture and healing. Demeter brings the crops or withholds them as she wishes. The Morrigan could be seen washing the shrouds of warriors who were going to die in battle. At these times she appeared as a great hag, wading in a river of blood. Yet she was also mentor and advisor to heroes. These two sides, comfort and harm, death and sustenance, exemplify the double nature of the terrible goddess of death and rebirth.

In this way, Baba Yaga is both a provider of food and a devourer of people. The mortar and pestle in which she rides is both for creating food and for grinding up corn (and other living things) to begin anew. The Slavic inhabitants of Eastern Europe believed that she lived in the last sheaf of grain bound each year and that whichever woman bound it would bear a child.[25] As time progressed, she transformed from a goddess of harvest and rebirth to a witch of legend and nightmare. This blending of birth and death may remind readers of Mother Nature herself, sometimes generous and nurturing, sometimes cruel. She is the mistress of life and death, but people must not forget the latter role: "From death and decomposition come the fertile substance that ensures and vitalizes new life. In her emanation as age, change, deterioration, and death, she finds the seeds for new life in the composting heap of decomposing forms."[26]

CHAPTER 31

Source of All Answers: The Wisewoman

The Old Woman and the Devil (Palestine)

In Palestine, an old woman and the devil decided to place bets on who could create more discord. The two went to the market, where the devil inflamed a quarrel, goading a seller and buyer until the butcher struck the man with his cleaver and killed him. "Observe my power," he bragged. "For I have sent one soul to death and corrupted the other."

"That's nothing," the woman said. With the devil, she went to a cloth seller. "I need a length of very fine cloth for a dress," she said. "My son is having an affair with a married woman and must bring her gifts. I know it's a sin, but he'll beat me if I don't buy these things for him." She bought the cloth and then went straight to the merchant's home and knocked on the door. His young wife answered. "I'm so sorry to impose," the old woman said. "But it's time for prayers and my house is so far! May I pray here?"

The young woman assented and led her to the bedroom. Once alone there, the old woman hid the cloth in the clothes basket, prayed, and departed. "Now," she told the devil outside. "Let's see what happens."

When the cloth merchant came home, he found the cloth and accused his wife of adultery. Though she protested her innocence, he beat her and sent her back to her parents.

The next day, the old woman visited the cloth seller's shop. "I need more cloth," she said. "I stopped by a kind young woman's house to pray yesterday and I must have left my package there."

Stunned, the cloth-seller returned the fabric to her and rushed off to make amends to his wife. "You see," the old woman told the devil. "While you cannot repair the great damage you caused, I can." And the devil conceded the contest.[1]

In the 1980s a study was conducted on women aged 35 to 55. It found "instead of the expected decline of mental health with age, that most women experienced a sense of resurgence of revitalization, a new sense of self and self-worth that gave them great confidence." The key here was flexibility to change, as the study showed "women who *combined* marriage, motherhood, and work were in the greatest state of psychological well-being."[2]

Menopause offers new directions and opportunities for the woman no longer burdened with young children. She becomes the vivacious grandmother who cooks amazing ethnic foods, crafts beautiful fashion accessories, leads the family, and comforts her grandchildren. She can explore careers or creative projects, offering a flexibility that was even more significant in the past, as the elders were revered as the keepers of life's stages: "In many primitive societies, old women are specialists in those critical moments when the designs of culture are threatened by a breakthrough of nature — birth, illness, and death — moments when we are reminded of our animal origins and human limits." Now androgynous, the wisewoman, like the two-spirit, has become shaman. In ancient cultures, she was the only class of female to assist with the hunt and male rituals.[3] Long ago, the elderly were a rarity, believed to be blessed with supernatural abilities, which they might use to help or harm.

> The ancient wisewoman crone was the Dark Goddess's earthly representative to society. She was venerated as elder sought out for advice, as seer called upon for prophecy, and as healer asked to tend the ill. The crone acted to bridge the transition from the dark to the new moon; she was the funerary priestess who helped the old to die and the midwife who assisted the new to be born.[4]

A similar flexibility arrives for the man, who, unpressured by career and household duties if he has retired, can explore his softer, sublimated side: "In age, the man can reclaim his 'feminine' side, which had to be repressed to allow him to protect his young as a warrior; the woman can reclaim her assertive, aggressive masculine side, which had to be repressed for her to stay close to the young she must nurture."[5] These elders can explore their suppressed abilities, thus integrating the community.

But today, aging is viewed as fearful and shaming, rather than as a passage to psychic maturation. Many women live in "empty nests," with grown children gone, and the husband perhaps dead or divorced. This may seem a time of abandonment. Post-menopausal and post-maternal, she has fewer responsibilities than she has had in decades.

Mother-daughter relationships can grow complex or hostile, as some mothers resent their daughters' youth and beauty, while others seek to relive their youths vicariously; perhaps the mother selects the son-in-law who represents the husband she has always dreamed of.

The mother-in-law who began by cherishing her son-in-law then becomes hostile; she groans over human ingratitude, poses as a martyr; she becomes in her turn an inimical mother.... A mother needs a rare combination of generosity and detachment in order to find enrichment in her children's lives without becoming their tyrant or making them her tormentors.[6]

The transition to grandmother and wisewoman is a major shift, now matriarch, but no longer nurse. If the grandmother does not feel supplanted as mother, she can "play the privileged role of guardian angel," as Simone de Beauvoir notes in *The Second Sex*.[7] No longer responsible for discipline and education, she can enjoy providing love and guidance. Likewise, some women become godmothers and teachers, nurturing the next generation though they aren't bound by blood.

Our culture associates femininity with sexual procreativity, thus treating menopause as the end of women's sexual identities. Advertisements for beauty products all offer to hold back aging, keeping women clinging to youthful looks by the tips of their artificial fingertips. Facelifts and collagen likewise offer the appearance of youth and smoothness. Meanwhile, men in their fifties are seen as powerful and authoritative. As Demetra George notes:

By removing the layers of patriarchal distortion from a woman's own inner images of herself as crone, she can come to see the inherent beauty of the natural unfoldment of her aging body and of the power it continues to hold for her. Women can then let go of all the artificial cosmetics and operations whose purpose is to conceal rather than enhance the true face of the crone. In this way we all can reconnect with the magical, mystical, and mysterious third phase of a woman's life.[8]

Unbridled Power

In Jung's psychology, he saw the child transition from viewing the mother as ineffable goddess to viewing her as human. At this point, "all the fabulous and mysterious qualities attaching to her image begin to fall away, and are transferred to the person closest to her, for instance, the grandmother."[9] Thus the grandmother becomes a font of unearthly wisdom. "Not infrequently she assumes the attributes of wisdom as well as those of a witch. For the further the archetype recedes from consciousness and the clearer the latter becomes, the more distinctly does the archetype assume mythological features."[10] In the child's vision, the grandmother can be a blend: presider over the mysteries, monster, wisewoman, and crone. This image led to patriarchal terror of her stature.

"The patriarchy feared the feminine in connection with her role in birthing and dying even more than in her association with sex. The wise crone transformed into the ugly hag, the death-snatcher."[11] From here we get the perception of the old woman who is "dried up" or "useless," a repulsive creature who must be hidden from sight.

> Significantly, the presence of the Crone is vehemently banished in a culture both terrified of death and in thrall to horror and socially-manufactured megadeath. This same culture fetishizes youth, progress, and the "future," encourages rapid obsolescence and turnover, and emits a continuing parade of pseudoscience or that which is "new." Age, organic change, darkness, decay, and death are radically denied.[12]

To the patriarchy, death is the cutoff to ambition and rule, the final "debt" that robs men of all they possess. Thus they cringe from the crone, who is associated with great age, entropy, death, and even doomsday.

Though crones may appear to be mundanely spinning or cooking, their cauldrons and spindles offer immense power over life's cycle: The three fates of Greek myth spin, measure, and cut the threads of life, controlling all the living through this feminine craft. Their Norse counterparts, the Norns, are called lawmakers as well as the arbiters of fate, ever virginal, ever spinning:

> Thence come maidens
> three,
> having knowledge of many things...
> Urth one is called;
> the second Verthandi...
> Skuld the third.
> They laid down laws,
> they chose life
> for the children of people;
> they tell fates.[13]

The crone's dark space is often symbolized by the cauldron — a place of transformation, where new is cooked from disparate ingredients. Brigid's cauldron revives the dead, and Medea's can bring youth or destruction to the elderly and feeble. This is the death-womb, which regenerates humanity through the Goddess's cyclic nature. The crone bent over her churning cauldron is Wisdom, the "Organizing Principle" that knows the recipe, that can be trusted to deliver from deep within. This is a cauldron of creativity, reshaping deep fears, volatile emotion, crippling sadness. As Patricia Reis reflects:

> Whenever I have felt the Dark Goddess' consciousness filling me there is always an accompanying dread. I know my life will never be the same. I know that I am being initiated into a new aspect of myself, a new part of my journey, which exists separate from my relationships to anyone else. And yet there is also a sureness, a firmness, a resoluteness, as in a re-solution.[14]

As the Catholic Church gained power, the local priestesses and followers of "pagan" ways were reviled and hunted down. Innocent household tools such as cauldrons and brooms became the province of witches. Women who displayed outspokenness, independence or other traits "undesirable" to the new authority found themselves killed.

> The story of the witches, or the genocide of women healers, is one of those epochs in human history so devastating and beyond comprehension that it has scarcely been touched by historians. Scholars are still not in agreement as to how many women were put to violent death; estimates range from one hundred thousand to nine million.[15]

The Inquisition persecuted witches (literally wise women), who had always been bastions of advice and cures for the village. Many of their remedies had a psychic component, leaving them open to accusations of magic. These women were natural leaders of the encroaching economy, first feudal and then industrial, and thus Church and State combined to target them as obstacles. These witches were accused of casting spells, having intercourse with the devil, cursing men and animals, and (rather tellingly) causing impotence or painless childbirth. Women were meant to suffer, and men to be virile and rule the household; any attack on that status quo was deemed deviltry. Of course, those who claimed innocence were generally tortured to death, while only those who pled guilty were allowed to do appropriate "penance." The infamous water test in which women could only drown or affirm their guilt by floating was one in a series of grisly devices employed to rid the earth of wise women.

Death-Dealer

The crone in her role as death-goddess is a terrible figure:

> Over his head is shrieking
> A lean hag, quickly hopping
> Over the points of their weapons and shields —
> She is the gray-haired *Morrigu*.[16]

This goddess of prophecy and war advised and guarded the great hero Cúchulainn: She "intensifies the hero, nerves his arm for the cast, and guides the course of the unerring lance."[17] At the same time, she is a menacing figure who warns Cúchulainn, "I guard your death."

Resistance to female participation in battle stems from a fear of the mythic potency of the warrior crone, according to Jane Caputi, author of *Gossips, Gorgons, and Crones*. Lurking beneath chivalrous refusal to allow women in combat is

> A terror that if the symbol of the female warrior were reactivated in a feminist context, it would awaken the need for female authority over war and peace, require a redefinition of war, and undermine the authority of patriarchal "civilization." With the mythic warrior Crone as our model, women might once again hone those arts of prophetic warfare and practice those ancient female Powers.[18]

The wisewoman is mistress of mortality, the final judge against whom there is no appeal. As such, her presence on the field is too frightening, too devastating, when she wields magic and mysteries in the service of death.

The Greeks revered Hecate in this role, acknowledging her wisdom even as they cowered before her might. The *Theogony* relates:

> Whom she will she greatly aids and advances: she sits by worshipful kings in judgment, and in the assembly whom she will is distinguished among the people. And when men arm themselves for the battle that destroys men, then the goddess is at hand to give victory and grant glory.[19]

Hecate, originating in Nubia, and traveling through Egypt to the Black Sea, was the goddess of the dark side of the moon, often viewed as the shadow of Artemis or Persephone. Hers was the magic of the borderland, the pathway, the graveyard. Dogs were her servants, and the cauldron her tool. At crossroads she was portrayed as triple maiden with key, rope, and dagger: The key opens the gates to the Underworld and its Mysteries, the rope represents the umbilical cord of rebirth and renewal, and the dagger or sacrificial Athame slices away delusion. She was the queen of witches, the hidden one, sacred and terrible. She held life and death in her hand, offering bounty or famine as she willed:

> To those whose business is in the grey discomfortable sea, and who pray to Hecate and the loud-crashing Earth-Shaker, easily the glorious goddess gives great catch, and easily she takes it away as soon as seen, if so she will. She is good in the byre with Hermes to increase the stock. The droves of kine and wide herds of goats and flocks of fleecy sheep, if she will, she increases from a few, or makes many to be less.[20]

She gifted those who honored her with inspiration and vision; her shadow side of pale Persephone (the maiden) was stagnation and stupor as the underworld's unwilling captive. She gloried in magic and wisdom, gateway to the unconscious mysteries. Greek women understood that acknowledging Great Hecate and embracing her teachings, as modern Wiccans do, was a pathway to understanding death, rather than dreading it.

She was "crone" in its original meaning, from Greek *cronos*, meaning time. Like Kali (from Sanskrit *kala*, also meaning time), she is mistress of the life cycle and of prophecy. The Dark Mother, the third of the trinity, is often seen as Time the Destroyer. She inhales all the worlds at the end and exhales them at time's beginning. She is beyond time and space and the whole of manifestation. She is called "dark" because she is mysterious — we, as mortal, time- and space-bound creatures cannot really conceive of Her.

> One has to give something to the death dealing mother, acknowledge her presence, leave a candle at her crossroads, admit your shadow side to view. If you give a part of yourself to lunacy, she will permit you to pass to and from the realm of the moon's dark phase. Otherwise she will detain you and stupor and blackness will possess you.[21]

For many, this mistress of death is too powerful, too frightening, as she demands sacrifice and loss in return for her wisdom. Thus, the great wise-woman/destroyer, the double-sided archetype, has been irrevocably split in fairytales. She is whittled to a shadow of herself, a fairy godmother singing of mice and ballgowns, as she pulls grandmotherly treats of illusion and artifice from her dainty wand.

Thought-Magic

The old wise woman offers "assistance in times of difficult passage. As midwife to the psyche she is constellated in 'emergency' situations where a spirit, a song, an alternative, a new being is emerging."[22] She is the passage to creativity, to death of an old life, or way of thinking, in favor of the new. Her tool is frequently the imagination or voice, so vital to fairytale heroines, so threatening that the "scold's bridle" was invented to keep her from using it.

She is the 12 helpful fairies at Sleeping Beauty's christening, but also the 13th elderly and wizened, thrust into the cold. She is the apple-seller or beggar at the crossroads, wheedling bread from the heroine as a character test. All offer prophecy and wish, blessing and curse. All come true. Too often, fairytale heroes ignore the old woman's warning and are punished, as she is a fairy or goddess in disguise. These wisewomen offer implacable, unappeasable potency that the wise hero will not discount, on forfeit of his life.

In an Armenian tale, a king had the presumption to laugh at a little old woman scurrying about. "She looks like a she-devil from the bottom of a well," he laughed.

She scowled at him up in his palace window. "We'll see which of us laughs last!"

But the king kept laughing whenever he saw her.

The old woman had the power of transformation, so she changed herself into a young, pretty girl and got herself appointed as the queen's maid. But as soon as she set a brush to the queen's hair, the queen turned into a hideous old woman. When the queen saw herself in the mirror, she screamed and screamed. With that, the old woman vanished.

Back in her own form, the woman went to see the king. "Clear off, you horrid old creature!" the guards laughed.

"Let her in," the king commanded.

"So, you've guessed that I transformed your wife," the old woman said.

"Please change her back! I'll give you anything!"

"Well, I feel sorry for her, if not for you." She changed the queen back into her old form, and never again did the king mock his subjects.[23]

Here, the crone teaches the king a valuable lesson — don't discount little old ladies! Likewise, he foresees his wife's evolution from queen mother to dark goddess. He mocks her at his own risk, as this is a natural, unstoppable process, a frightening glimpse forward as warning of the ineffable and the inevitable.

According to the Laguna Pueblo Tribe, Spider Grandmother, or Thought Woman, created the world through imagination. Spider dwelt alone and complete, but she longed for someone to share the perfection of her songdream, a magic "like the power of dream, but more pure. Like the spirit of vision, but more clear."[24] As she envisioned land coalescing, like a web from a single silken thread, the earth rippled into life, with spidery lines of power folded and enfolded into a tightly moving shape, cradling the power of the universe within itself. Thus walnuts, cacti, and all manner of things grow wrinkled as they mature, as do people, to celebrate Spider's wrinkling and enfolding of the world.

She sang a pair of bundles into being, and they began to sing, to echo her song, to join it. Each of the two new singers also carried a bundle, and in each bundle the life of the universe rested, waiting until it was sung into life. As they sang their heart's song that mirrored hers, the music deepened. Spider Grandmother named the pair of beings Ic'sts'ity and Nau'ts'ity. They, her daughter-creators, echoed her chants and created new ones, and so they brought about a great spiral of stars and planets and all the universe.[25]

This story is notable because Spider Grandmother does not birth the world but, wrinkled and enfolded on herself as her creations, she harnesses thought and imagination to weave the world. It, like her, grows wrinkled in its wiscom. Spider Grandmother spins the world into being with what she imagines, with the stories she tells. This gift she passes on to others, creating through thought, the primal essence of the self.

No longer creating gods through birth-magic, the crone goddess has become a figure of prophecy, whose very words carry the power of life. As Barbara Walker notes in her insightful article, "Witches Past and Present":

> The Greeks' principal Goddess of oracular powers, magic, and midwifery was Hecate, derived from the Egyptian pre-dynastic term for a tribal matriarch, hek, which meant a wise-woman versed in the hekau or "words of power." This was a woman having the authority of the logos, the creative word. She could make things happen just by speaking-as witches, centuries later, were supposed to make things happen by speaking their curses or spells. Logos power was later usurped by male gods such as Yahweh, who claimed to bring things into being by saying them. But long before the Bible, hekau were the material of all creative word magic, spells, charms, prayers, invocations, exorcisms, chants, liturgies, and every other mystic verbal practice of our ever-verbalizing species.[26]

Today, modern Wiccans evoke this power of Hecate, casting spells with word and ritual that echo the magical power of birth. "In ritual magic, the energy raised is directed by willpower. Women who celebrate in Goddess circles believe they can achieve their wills in the world."[27] This need not be chanting or ritual: Woman today can project her will on the world though writings, demonstrations, speeches, gatherings.

These tools make the wisewoman more than a mentor for young heroines: They cast her as creatrix, the thinker or elder who solves the problems of the entire village. She is the shaman who solves riddles, the clever one who defeats monsters.

Inner Growth

There are things the Old Woman can do, say, and think which the Woman cannot do, say, or think. The Woman has to give up her menstrual periods before she can do, say, or think them. She has got to change her life.... The woman who is willing to make that change must become pregnant with herself, at last. She must bear herself, her third self, her old age, with travail and alone. Not many will help her with that birth. Certainly no male obstetrician will time her contractions, inject her with sedatives, stand ready with forceps, and neatly stitch up the torn membranes. It's hard even to find an old-fashioned midwife, these days. That pregnancy is long, that labor hard. Only one is harder, and that's the final one, the one which men also suffer and perform.[28]

This is the explanation of the crone stage by Ursula K. Le Guin, one of the most influential writers of feminist science fiction. The Crone is primarily in relationship with All-That-Is (where Virgin is primarily with Self, and Mother is with Other). Achieving the status of Crone means moving back into the great sentience out of which all arises, thus she sees into the elements behind form. She is often depicted with wide open eyes; often associated with the gaze of owl or snake — and knowledge of the dark. A sudden transition such as widowhood has pushed the woman into sacred space. In an altered state of consciousness, with her ego weakened, she can directly connect with the deep unconscious. Often she takes refuge in the underworld, an isolation hut, a veil, which provides a chrysalis in which she can transform into a new self.[29]

When women understand the true power of the final stage, they can move from focusing on their children to focusing on themselves and their own creativity. Cronehood, like maidenhood, is a function of spirit as well as biology. When Demeter was mourning her stolen daughter she felt she had lost all that made her fertility goddess and mother. She was "like an old woman, born long ago, who is excluded from childbearing and the gifts of garland-loving Aphrodite.[30] She pressed her barrenness further, inflicting it on the entire earth.

Rather than marking it through menopause, for some women, this begins the day the last child heads for college, or the day the first grandchild is born. The woman no longer needs to place her family, relationship, or career before her own needs and growth. This can be cause for celebration rather than mourning: At last, she can fill the time as she wishes — with a class, a new job, volunteer work, a pet project that's waited all these years.

Becoming the family matriarch or retiring likewise can signal a new phase of life. This is "a psychological frame of mind, when a woman begins to reap the harvest of wisdom that arises from all her varied life experiences."[31] Before this, she was too busy changing babies, running errands, cooking for a squabbling family. Now is a new kind of quiet, one that allows her to look deeper, to savor the moments around her. The woman who has been self-sacrificing, neglecting of her own desires, is most overwhelmed by this change. "Dislodged from her sheltering occupations, her plans disrupted, she finds herself suddenly, without recourse, put face to face with herself."[32] It is she is who has flexibility, projects to fall back on, who welcomes this new phase of life.

The male perspective may view success as life's goal, and thus death as a failure to hang on longer, to climb one final mountain: Hamlet may contemplate suicide out of despair, Gilgamesh race all his life to outwit death, Achilles only accept it in return for immortal glory. But the feminine perspective is that of Isis and Demeter summoning the crops each year, of Ishtar and Inanna mourning their dead boy-kings, only to welcome them the following season. Life is cyclical, regenerating in an unending spiral of faith and acceptance. With each generation comes new talents and knowledge, new streams branching from life's churning river.

CHAPTER 32

Mrs. Fox and Her Cronies:
The Trickster

A Woman of Valor (Persia)

In a city in Persia, there lived a Jewish porter named Hassan who could barely support his family. Every evening, he went to the forest to collect kindling to sell for extra money. Even with the double income, he could not even afford a blanket for himself, but had to cover himself with his donkey's blanket at night. The townsfolk treated him roughly and ordered him around when they saw him.

The only thing of any value they owned was a tiny square of land adjoining the river. Their rich neighbor had often asked them to sell, but Hassan's wife always refused.

One night, a group of rich merchants had been drinking heavily. They stopped by Hassan's house and loudly banged on the door, calling for him to bring them water. "Hassan, we want Hassan!"

The wife answered the door. "You mean *Hawaja* (Master) Hassan, do you not?"

"What are you talking about?" one merchant asked. "Where's Hassan, you know, the porter?"

"I must ask you not to speak so irreverently of my master." She curtsied. "Please wait a moment and I will ask my mistress if he is home."

The wife ran straight to her rich neighbor and banged on the door. When he arrived, she made him this offer: "I will give you my land, which you have desired for so long, on one condition. Lend me your house and everything in it for a week, starting this minute." The neighbor promptly agreed.

The wife returned to the waiting merchants. "I am afraid my master is not here. Please, the lady of the house asks that you come inside his house and wait for him." And she led them next door into the rich neighbor's house. Inside, thick carpets covered the floors and shelves groaned under the weight of costly trinkets. The merchants looked around in astonishment. Could Hassan truly live in such a place?

The wife served them delicacies from the kitchen and bade them rest on expensive sofas. When the men had finished eating and drinking, the wife refused to let them leave. "Hawaja Hassan will be insulted if you leave without seeing him."

While the men ate the excellent dinner she had served them, the wife rushed to find her husband. As always, he came trudging out of the forest, a thin bundle of sticks laid across his donkey's back. She pressed on her astonished husband a fine suit she had borrowed from the mansion. "Quick, husband. Take what money you have and go to the bathhouse. Make sure you get a good wash and a shave. Then put these clothes on and go to our neighbor's house. Hurry. I'll take care of the donkey." And her husband did so.

When Hassan reached the mansion, he found the men being entertained by musicians his wife had hired. "My master has just returned from a long day in town," she explained as her husband seated himself on the silk cushions as if they belonged to him. "He likes to work as a porter now and then, to better understand the poor classes." The merchants exchanged agonized glances. How could they have treated him so abysmally?

His wife instructed Hassan to offer the men use of the enormous pool, the gardens, and every other luxury of the house. Although the men insisted they must get home to their families, Hassan delayed them longer and longer with feasts and entertainment, until they had stayed three days and three nights. With every new luxury, the merchants winced at how brusque and insulting they had been to such a wealthy man.

Then Hassan's wife ordered her husband to ride his neighbor's donkey with all his servants attending him. "Go to the market and buy a great many goods. Promise to pay in a week." Of course, by this point, his reputation had swelled to the point where none would refuse him. The wife sold those goods at a profit, and then bought more goods for her husband to sell. As this continued, he grew richer and richer until he could buy himself a fine house not far from his neighbor's.

And so, Hassan the lowly porter became *Hawaja* Hassan, and all because of his wife. A woman of valor is the crown of her husband.[1]

This Persian Jewish tale falls under the twin headings of AT 859E: Poor Suitor Pretends to Wealth and AT 545B: Puss in Boots. In this tale, the female trickster is natural and believable, as she uses her craftiness to increase the status of her family. She follows the heroine's journey through guile and subterfuge, but comes across as a clever, enterprising figure rather than a malicious one.

Most folklorists would characterize the archetypal trickster as masculine. Loki, Maui, Hermes, Puck, Gwydion, Jacob, Robin Hood, and Odysseus himself all are male. Even animal tricksters such as Puss in Boots, Renart the Fox, Anansi, Brer Rabbit, Coyote, and Raven have a predominant masculine flavor. Some commentators point out the patriarchal nature of most pantheons. Others argue that trickster is a wanderer, earthy and sexual. Historically, women have needed to bear and raise the children, and so are less likely to desire trickster's roving sexual escapades.[2] Tribal girls are expected to be modest and controlled, rather than "loose, sexually promiscuous, and lacking in self-discipline."[3] However, male anthropologists from outside cultures are unlikely to view the private world of women.

The French fabliaux were 13th to 14th-century stories in verse concentrating on body parts and bodily functions. In their private salons, women retold these tales, which were highly popular and highly obscene.[4]

Likewise, the unrecorded feminine rituals of the Eleusinian Mysteries offer us Baubo, goddess of belly laughs and suggestive stories, as women told ribald jokes to awaken the earth to fertility.[5] When Demeter sits weeping by a fountain in Eleusis, Baubo boldly lifts up her skirts and prances around, fully exposing herself to the goddess. Demeter is forced to laugh at her antics and the earth begins to thaw, heralding Persephone's return.[6] She is sometimes known as Iambe, goddess of indecent speech, for she entertains all Olympus with her antics. Homer's *Hymn to Demeter* relates:

> A long time she [Demeter] sat upon the stool without speaking because of her sorrow, and greeted no one by word or by sign, but rested, never smiling, and tasting neither food nor drinks because she pined with longing for her deep-bosomed daughter, until careful Iambe — who pleased her moods in aftertime also — moved the holy lady with many a quip and jest to smile and laugh and cheer her heart.[7]

Only the Orphic version carries a more uncensored view of events, saying "She [drew] aside her robes and showed a sight of shame."[8]

A similar incident appears in the Japanese tale "The Mother and the Demon." A mother and a daughter jump in a boat to flee from a demon. When he drinks up the lake, destroying the font of feminine power that preserves them, they instantly retaliate. They flip up their skirts, in other versions breaking wind or pounding spoons on their hips: The outrageous physical act makes the demon laugh and spew up the lake.[9]

These dirty goddesses offer a sacred sexuality and with it something even more precious: laughter. Thus Baubo teases Demeter out of her mourning and Ama No Uzume evokes curiosity in Amaterasu. At the same time, laughter fills the entire body, making it shake beyond control. It is healing, revitalizing, overpowering, like the upset and reversal that mark creation. Many creators are tricksters, and vice versa. Thus these goddesses, with their taboo-crossing and rule breaking, offer unmitigated pleasure mixed with joy and creative energy.

Tricksters are frequently older women, sometimes mentors, sometimes wanderers, but always fonts of wisdom. In a Basque tale, a young man met an entrancingly beautiful Lamia and longed to marry her. She agreed, but only if he could correctly guess her age. He asked an old neighbor woman for help, and she concocted a plan. She traveled to the Lamia's cave and bent over, back to it, so that her face peeked between her own legs. The Lamia arrived, and, startled, declared, "In my 105 years, I've never seen such a sight!" And thus the boy could marry her.[10]

Many of these trickster women act as mentors, as in the tale above, where the elderly woman solves the mystery, and allows the hero to reach his heart's desire. Often too old to procreate, the crone's task is to further the fertility and quests of her descendents, most often her granddaughters, either biological or surrogate: Han mane'ak su, "woman who plays the wedding," is a necessary inclusion at every Rotuman (located in the South Pacific) wedding ceremony. This elderly woman mocks all the guests, and questions the bride's chastity, the groom's virility, and everything else she can think of. This silliness helps to bring the two separate families together.[11]

Tricksters are marginalized figures, as are women, so the two combine well into the outsider, the one determined to wreck the status quo. While she need not overturn society permanently, she calls attention to its flaws, superficialities, and ego-driven powerful figures, asserting her own dominance. "She seeks to expose and protest oppression and create social and political justice for both genders," explains Marilyn Jurich in *Scheherazade's Sisters: Trickster Heroines and Their Stories in World Literature.*[12]

The trickster rarely grows or changes: he/she has a simple goal and spends the story trying to achieve it. As Lewis Hyde said in *Trickster Makes This World*, "He doesn't win the way the big guys do, but he doesn't suffer the way they do, either, and he enjoys pleasures they find too risky."[13] Trickster stories offer a laugh, a bright moment in a dull world. Women are more likely to steal husbands and lovers than property and money.[14] They particularly enjoy stealing male dignity and pride.

In a tale from *Arabian Nights*, a naughty wife plots to cook geese for her lover without her husband getting even a bite. She insists that her husband kill two birds and invite a guest for dinner. When the husband only brings one guest, she insists he go find some more. Then she whispers to the guest that her husband plans to make him a eunuch and cut off his testicles. When he runs off in a frantic hurry, she hides the geese and tells her husband that the guest stole them. The husband runs after him yelling, "Just let me have one of them," but the guest runs even faster. In a less sensational version of the same type 1741 tale, Clever Gretel from the Grimms lies similarly to steal a pair of chickens for her dinner, and warns the guest that her master will cut off his ears if he stays.

The trickster represents the lighter qualities of the shadow, subverting rules and ignoring authority. She glides effortlessly through society's conventions as if they don't exist. She is sexual, lifting her skirt to provoke laughter or distraction. Trickster is a creature of impulse, outside morality, outside convention. Deceit is practiced, not as falsehood, but to assure a sense of personal difference and independence from society.[15] The female trickster "embraces such contrarieties and the oppositions are more certain, more apparent for her, being a woman. Her very nature is considered contrary by the traditional male-ordered society. She has been regarded as life and death, goddess and witch, beauty and virtue coupled with the abominations of mortality and degeneration."[16] As the less threatening figure, she has less need than a male to fear reprisals. The female trickster must "wriggle through the distorted images, slide under the preconceptions in order to recover and reclaim her identity."[17] This she does while remaining wholly feminine vivacious and clever.

Kamdaak Waneng of Papua New Guinea is a shapeshifting trickster; she breaks all sex taboos and social rules to seduce whomever she wishes, especially male relatives. She also snares men into her garden, where she wields total power. Her male counterpart, Gabruurtan, is frequently at her side, though she plays tricks on him as well, such as feeding him women's food, thus making him break a taboo and pollute himself. (In Papua New Guinea, male and female roles are clearly defined in many areas.)[18]

Unencumbered by children, husband or titles, the trickster is nonetheless wise beyond words, using her mercurial powers for others or merely for amusement. She is like the shameless old woman who can say anything at a party. Thus, she is a catalyst for transformation in others: When the old self dies of shame, the new self can emerge. And she is the Dark Goddess, a power men should not discount. As Vicki Noble, author of *Shakti Woman*, writes:

> The Dark Goddess is no lightweight. She promises trouble, an end to form as we have known it, the death of the ego.... She is transformation in the extreme, and her power is regenerative and healing. Like a trickster, she frees us from the trappings that bind us to our tiny personal worlds; like a knife she cuts away all that is unessential and not truthful. She shatters structures, disintegrates the personality, destroys form. She liberates and saves, heals and frees.[19]

In the Caroline Islands of Micronesia, there lived an octopus goddess named Hit. Her daughter had an affair with a married sky god, and the god's wife gave chase. Hit began dancing lewdly. So lewdly, in fact, that the sky woman fainted from arousal and had to be carried home. Each time she followed, Hit danced and distracted her, allowing her daughter to give birth to the hero Olifat.

There are far more tricksters in tales, from the Female Coyote to the Japanese kitsune, or fox-woman. In the *Popol Vuh*, the previously mentioned heroine Blood Woman, and the seductresses Lust Woman and Wailing Woman are all called "k'axtok,'" tricksters attempting to fool someone.[20] Most "smart girls" are tricksters, from Scheherazade to the clever peasant girl unraveling the king's riddles, to British Molly Whuppie and Kate Crackernuts. Female tricksters identified by Jurich include the disguised Tattercoats and performers of the "bed trick" like Crystal the Wise, seductresses like Cleopatra, and assertive questors, storytellers, and riddle-solvers throughout the world.

Even in the Bible, Jacob's wife Rachel proves his equal in craftiness. After stealing all her father's idols, she stuffs them in her camel's saddle and sits on them. When her father comes looking, Rachel explains she can't stand up and greet him "for the custom of women is upon me" (i.e., she's menstruating).[21] Her father quickly withdraws.

A last trickster is Mrs. Molly Cotton Tail. She hails from African-American stories, and though she is married to Mr. Hare, there's no chance she'll go by "Mrs. Hare." In fact, she makes him stay home with the children now and then. In a charming tale (one of several), Molly and Mr. Fox visit Mr. Fox's brother, Hungry Billy. At night, Molly digs up the butter crock and eats every drop, then reburies the empty container in the stream. When Hungry Billy accuses them both, Molly suggests that he watch her and Mr. Fox. In the hottest part of the day, stolen grease will sweat out of the butter thief's stomach. Molly smears the sleeping Mr. Fox's stomach with butter and escapes in perfect freedom.[22]

"As nurturer and protector, the traditional roles allotted to her, woman seeks to benefit those for whom she cares and tries to improve her community."[23] Using her keen moral sense, she forces justice on those in power, by guile if necessary. Just as heroines are as prevalent as heroes but less showy, less noticed, trickster heroines have their own traditions, taking on roles of Puss or Coyote, yet remaining fully feminine, earthy, and colorful.

New Moon: Spirit Guardian

"When the veil between the worlds is most transparent, the Crone Goddess is honored as gatekeeper to the realms of spirit."[1] This shadow goddess wanes, dwindling from destroyer to godmother, blessing the next generation with her wisdom. She is the repository of the tribe's secret lore, guiding her followers through the mysteries and initiations of the intermediary passageway between death and new life.

In the dark of the moon, when she withdraws, she births herself, transforming from ancient to infant, awaiting new life in her new form. As the Bhagavad Gita states, "As a man abandons his worn-out clothes and acquires new ones, so when the body is worn out a new one is acquired by the Self who lives within."[2]

She will pass on her spirit to a new infant, who will bloom into a questing maiden on her own heroine's journey, and then descend into darkness as the sacrificing mother. From there, she will become a wisewoman herself, passing on her own grandmother's lore and perpetuating the cycle, through untold generations, through infinite cycling eternity.

CHAPTER 33

Unearthly Guardian:
The Protector

The Witch in the Stone Boat (Iceland)

Prince Sigurd went questing for a bride and found a princess of surpassing kindness and beauty. They wed and dwelt awhile in her father's court. In time, Sigurd's father died, and he set sail for home, along with his family. While his wife and infant son were playing on deck, a fearful witch sailed up alongside them in a boat made entirely of stone. She snatched the child from the queen's arms, and, stripping off the queen's finery, donned it herself. She then forced the queen into the stone boat and commanded it to sail all the way to the underworld.

In the underworld, a three-headed giant greeted the true queen and entreated her hand in marriage. When she refused, he locked her away.

"No, you must let me return to my family," she cried.

"You may see your son three times, but then you must be my bride."

Seeing no other choice, the young queen agreed.

In the world above, the witch took on the queen's appearance, though the baby never failed to cry when she held him. Sigurd noticed a change as well, as his wife seemed cruel and quarrelsome for the rest of the voyage. When they arrived home, she hid herself in her quarters for many hours each day.

One night, as the child's nurse entered his room, she beheld the floor parting. A beautiful woman in white emerged through the gap, with a thick iron chain descending from her waist into the floor. She picked up the baby and held him close, and then replaced him in his cradle and vanished. The next evening, the woman returned as before, but this time she murmured "Only once more."

The nurse told the king, who was determined to investigate. That afternoon, he peered through the crack in the queen's chamber wall, and he heard her say, quite plainly, "When I yawn a little, then I am a nice little maiden; when I yawn halfway, then I am half a troll; and when I yawn fully, then I am a troll altogether." She yawned tremendously, and a dark mist seeped from her skin, changing her into a troll. The floor opened before her and a three-headed giant brought her an enormous trough of meat, which she devoured. Then she resumed her human shape.

That night, the king hid in the baby's chamber. When the woman in white arrived, he recognized his wife, and, seizing his sword, hacked apart her iron chain. A great weight fell crashing beneath her, as the three-headed giant who had kept the queen so close tumbled to his death. The king executed the false queen, and he and his family were united at last.[1]

After the perfect wedding, the story isn't complete, despite what Lang, Perrault, and Disney would suggest. Like the Vietnamese Cinderella, Tam, even joyously wedded heroines must withdraw from the world, regress, reincorporate the fragments of themselves they've abandoned before they can take their place as queen.

The mother in "The Witch in the Stone Boat" has her happily ever after, the royal marriage and baby the princess or White Bride desired above all. But now she's leaving her home, the baby won't stop crying, her husband's nice but doesn't understand her anxiety. She sails along the transformative waters, and feels her mood shift to something as hard and unnatural as a stone boat floating on the water. "I want independence, not a husband and baby and kingship," her subconscious cries. At this moment, the White Bride withdraws into the underworld, on her own Psyche quest for growth and understanding. Taking her place is the snarling Black Bride, who makes the baby cry, who wears her smiling face like a mask. (See chapter 3 for more on AT 403: The Black and White Bride).

> This is the essence of the Matron's story: The Maiden, who used to consider herself single in every sense, finds herself doubled, split, fragmented when she weds (or acquires a partner), exiled from her native home, subject to fits of temper and exhaustion, followed by spasms of guilt or regret.[2]

In many pagan and Catholic "downfall" myths, the male god is stripped of his full former powers by being sent "earthward," the female, by being sent "skyward."[3] Lucifer rules hell, as does the powerless Pluto. Odin wanders the earth as a mortal. By contrast, Psyche labors painfully in Venus's heavenly abode, and many abused goddesses flee to the moon. Zhiyu, the silver needle lass, struggles up a mountain, and Brünnhild slumbers helplessly atop another.

Up above, there is only surface beauty from the glorious wedding and happy boat trip. In the underworld, however, the young queen gains understanding. The underworld is the source of feminine power from which the witch emerges, and where the giant teaches the questing queen to master her strength and return, through her own magic, to her child. The everyday world of king and country pales against it.

As she faces the triple giant, like the Beast in his castle, she accepts his ugliness. He is her husband's shadow: the twisted gigantic side that demands attention from her, that wants her all to himself. This is the other side of marriage, inseparable from the handsome prince despite its burial below the conscious world.

As she shifts from caring for her husband and child to reintegrating, a change appears. Dwelling on herself as she has been, the shadow queen is "cruel and quarrelsome," uncomfortable with the baby, peering beneath her perfect marriage to its jagged edges and moods concealed within. She must become the perfect queen, powerful and unsympathetic to gain the household's respect. At the same time, her Madonna side craves to cuddle her baby, and so she does, in the dead of night so no one will see. At last her husband finds her thus. "You're not a scary monster," he muses. "Sure, you've been angry, snarling at me and withdrawing to your room with a headache. But you're still you. You're the woman I married, sweet and maternal, the fair princess I courted. Underneath your anger and moods, you're still my true love." Recognizing and accepting her darkness, he slices away the rope that's weighing her down: The fears that bind her to the snarling giant. She is free. And she, having descended into the depths of her subconscious and faced the monstrous fears there — the giant or ogre her husband may be, the witch she may become — feels herself again. She smiles at her husband and all is well.

Swan-Maidens

While the fairytale heroine slowly discovers her Beast-husband is a prince, the male hero encounters the opposite: his fairy wife's hidden monstrous side. These patterns reflect the common fears and conflicts between men and women as women leave home to wed frightening enigmas, and sweet, pretty wives grow into dominant crones shrouded in women's mysteries.

Selkie tales of seal-women are popular from Canada to Scotland, prompting beautiful ballads such as "The Great Silkie of Sule Skerry." If a hunter steals her skin, she marries him, but when she finds it once more, she always vanishes into the sea. Sometimes, she reappears as a seal, to guide fish into her grown sons' nets, but she remains the magical creature of the life-giving ocean that she was born to be.

Related tales feature swan maidens in Sweden, frog wives in China and Tibet, porpoise girls in Micronesia, bear women in North America, peries (fairies) in Persian folklore, and apsaras (celestial nymphs) in Hindu myth.[4] These women are beautiful, magical, and as animal as they are human. They are provocative, seductive, unnatural, disturbing. From the male teller's point of view, this type of romance reflects a desire to connect with the world of nature, and particularly the threshold to the magical world, as heroes court nymphs of the wild feminine oceans, streams, forests and skies — women who are half-divine, half-animal — a bridge from the human world to that of the unconscious.

From the woman's perspective, the stories speak differently: The man may tame the fairy bride, but not for every moment of her life. Though she loves him and her children, she must depart to her magical home. The sealskin or swanskin represents the woman's untamable magical nature: When she wears it, she feels completely herself, able to swim and fly as well as tend the fire. Like the animal she imitates, she becomes completely unselfconscious, wholly in tune with the forces around her. Even while she is married, the skin waits in a chest or closet, set aside but awaiting her desire.

"The woman is hungry for intimacy but thirsty for silence, which is her original self gliding through the sea. How can she give up one or the other?" Joan Gould asks of the selkie wife.[5] Many times each day as she balances her art and her children, her beauty parlor appointment and their playdates, she crosses and recrosses the borderline between intimacy and solitude, embracing others and embracing the self.

This unending cycle of going and returning is natural for the women, a way to feel completely themselves "within their skins." Withdrawal may be a short respite, time taken for herself each day to read the newspaper or do yoga. This may be a vacation, like Aphrodite's annual sacred bath, from which the mother returns, rested and ready to resume her family roles. Or it may be a new career, a return to independence, a seeking of the autonomy she once had before creating a family.

Never Goodbye

Even when the mother leaves forever, like the selkie, her protection hasn't ended, nor has her love. The Grimms' Cinderella has the tree over her mother's grave, which provides her with her ballgown. Vasilisa the Beautiful, the Russian Cinderella, has her mother's doll, which advises her how to act. The Goose Girl's handkerchief with a few drops of her mother's blood likewise speaks to her and gives advice. The message is clear: Death cannot destroy love. Like the Little Mermaid, these absent mothers ascend into higher selves, glowing with the energy of the spirit world. Only thus do they become mighty enough to protect those below.

A Vietnamese man named Trong Qui was so fond of gambling that he lost all his possessions, and, thus bereft, put his wife up as stakes. When Tu Nhi Khanh heard she had been lost this way, she was sick with horror, as she knew she would be unable to fend off the rich man's advances. She clasped her children close and bid them farewell: "My little ones, I must abandon you, but it will not be to live with another man, whatever may be the wrongs of your father."[6] Then she committed suicide.

This act brought Trong Qui to his senses, and he foreswore gambling, keeping to a better life from that day forward. One day, as he was visiting the Temple of Trong Vuong, his wife appeared to him. "After my death, the Emperor of Jade took pity on me and accepted me into his service," she said. "Now I carry rain and messages throughout the land."

Trong Qui begged her forgiveness, and they spoke all night in the temple. Before leaving, Tu Nhi Khanh warned him that war was coming and that only a righteous one of the Le family could save them. She asked him to raise their sons wisely and to follow this hero, whatever he asked. Trong Qui did as she had said, and their sons rose to be privy counselors to the Great King.[7]

In this tale, the risen spirit appears to her sorrowing husband, advising him how to protect the family in her absence. Reincarnated as the highest form of consciousness, the soul, the departed mentor feels a tug from the mortals of the earth. The spirit "always appears in a situation where insight, understanding, good advice, planning, etc. are needed but cannot be mustered on one's own resources."[8] She appears especially to helpless children, who are closest to animals with their needs and drives, and endlessly faithful in their beliefs. To them she offers gifts and guidance, until she must pass away, leaving them with the deeper spirituality she has cultivated. Becoming a spirit guardian is thus regarded as a triumph, an ascension into a more powerful self.

In a Brothers Grimm tale, a dying mother asked to be buried under a nearby juniper tree. In time, the father remarried a woman with a little daughter named Marlene. Though she was stepsister to the father's little boy, the children loved each other dearly. The cruel stepmother, however, killed the boy and served him to her husband for supper.

Marlene gathered all the bones from beneath the table, tied them up in her best silk scarf, and then carried them outside, crying tears of blood. She laid them down beneath the juniper tree on the green grass, and after she had put them there, she suddenly felt better and did not cry anymore.

> Then the juniper tree began to move. The branches moved apart, then moved together again, just as if someone were rejoicing and clapping his hands. At the same time a mist seemed to rise from the tree, and in the center of this mist it burned like a fire, and a beautiful bird flew out of the fire singing magnificently, and it flew high into the air, and when it was gone, the juniper tree was just as it had been before, and the cloth with the bones was no longer there. Marlene, however, was as happy and contented as if her brother were still alive. And she went merrily into the house, sat down at the table, and ate.

Then the bird flew away and lit on a goldsmith's house, and began to sing:

> My mother, she killed me,
> My father, he ate me,
> My sister Marlene,
> Gathered all my bones,
> Tied them in a silken scarf,
> Laid them beneath the juniper tree,
> Tweet, tweet, what a beautiful bird am I.

The goldsmith gave it a golden chain to keep singing, as the shoemaker gave it a pair of red slippers, and the miller a millstone. The bird flew home and dropped the gold chain around his father's neck, and the slippers to his sister as he sang. With a great crash, he dropped the millstone on his stepmother and killed her. This broke the spell and he turned back into a child.[9]

  This is a tale of life, death, and resurrection: Birth and death occur in the story's first scene and are "doubled and repeated as rebirth and murder in the body of the tale," notes Maria Tatar.[10] The mother dies and becomes the juniper tree, evergreen and eternally growing, deepening into the earth and living for herself. The boy is chopped up for stew, like the dismemberment of Osiris or other sacrificed heroes, followed by his transformation and spiritual ascension.

  We see the juniper tree restore her child to life out of scattered bones, a power reserved for the divine. Since the spirit is immaterial and yet immeasurably potent, it exists in a higher state, able to perform actions mortals can only imagine. It is an ascended being, a force of incalculable magic. As Jung notes:

> Spirit, we say, is the principle that stands in opposition to matter. By this we understand an immaterial substance or form of existence which on the highest and most universal level is called "God." We imagine this immaterial substance or form of existence also as the vehicle of psychic phenomena or even of life itself.[11]

In this way, the juniper tree is a source of protection and blessing for the child, ever present in his life. The bird, a representation of the soul, flies out of the tree in a symbol of literal rebirth, like Tam reappearing as nightingale and tree.

> Death is not the final ending, but a step in the cycle. After death comes the other
> world, the spirit world, a resting place of learning before rebirth.
> Those who are dead are never gone:
> they are there in the thickening shadow.
> The dead are not under the earth:
> they are there in the tree that rustles,
> they are in the wood that groans,
> they are in the water that runs...
>   [African Traditional. Birago Diop, "Mali Poem"].[12]

  Unfortunately, this lore has left our stories: the unconquered mother, reborn as tree, has been replaced by the frivolous fairy godmother. The princess's encounter with the dragon is discarded in favor of her rescue by the handsome prince. We flee the darkness and cling to the superficial light, afraid of shadows, afraid of feminine power.

> Today we are afraid of many of the dark moon teachings, such as alchemy, astrology, and other spiritual or psychological disciplines, which reveal information about the unconscious or subtle dimensions of being.... Yet it is these teachings, based on the timing of cyclical patterns, that give us the guidance that enables us to pass through the dark nonphysical dimensions of being — of death and rebirth, endings and new beginnings, or spontaneous healings — with clarity and confidence instead of panic and terror.[13]

We have lost the lore from ages past that promised that the crops that died in winter would come again in spring. We cling to youth, fleeing entropy with all our technology. And yet, letting go carries its own lore, in the wisdom of deeper possibilities below the surface.

CHAPTER 34

Coming Full Circle: Rebirth

Copper Woman
(Nuu-chah-nulth, Vancouver Island)

Copper Woman was born from death, one might say. Twelve women sailed with her from their dying tribe, preserving all the wisdom of the ages within themselves. Each day, the 12 women pretended to sip and nibble from their dwindling stores, but in truth they saved it all for her of the gleaming skin, the youngest. When they finally drifted to the haven of a deserted island, only she remained alive.

The girl who would become Copper Woman sipped from a beachside stream and swallowed raw mussels until strength returned to her shrunken stomach. Then she built a pyre for her companions and, weeping, set it alight, sending them home. She dwelt in a cave, gathering fish and oysters, berries and eggs, and so survived year after lonely year. She became a woman and yet had no ceremony in which the priests danced for her and offered themselves to her, whichever she desired. She remained alone.

At last, three elderly women paddling a canoe arrived. They had dreamed of this girl, face glowing with the green eyes that meant a soul was reborn within her. Now they had come to teach her the ancient mysteries, the lore passed from the elders when the time was right. Copper Woman, starved for companionship, drank in every word, and learned the teachings of a lifetime in only a few months. One woman succumbed to the winter's chill and died. Copper Woman gathered wood for a pyre, and the two elders sang her on her journey. Then the second woman died a year later. As the third lay weakly on her mat, Copper Woman sobbed harder than ever, for she knew she would once again be alone.

"Lean close," the third woman said. "I have postponed my departure so I could teach you the greatest secret of all." She did, and as she said the words, her spirit flowed into Copper Woman's green eyes, and she was a part of Copper Woman forevermore.

Copper Woman now felt more isolated than ever. One day she cried so hard and long a ball of mucus piled on the beach. Embarrassed, she went to bury it, but she heard the elder whispering inside her: "There is no shame in feeling emotion. This too is sacred." So she stored it all in a mussel shell, and as it grew, she moved it into a clamshell, and then a crab's shell. From there a boy emerged, though badly fashioned, with mismatched bits that had formed inside the different shells.

She cared for him and lived with him, though, unformed as he was, he could not complete a task. He wove fish traps with gaping holes in the middle, he killed deer but could not dress them, he built fires that were either too hot or too cold. One night, he crawled under Copper Woman's blankets, and she, still lonely even with this companion, allowed him to love her. After that her body swelled like the moon, and she prayed that her child, whom she loved so much even before birth, would be born perfect, not jumbled like its father. At last, a girl was born, Mowita, and she was perfect.

Copper Woman had many more children, boys and girls, though the boys seemed like their father and easily distracted. Up above, Qolus, daughter of Thunderbird, smiled to see them at their daily tasks. She descended to earth, where she transformed herself into a man named Mah Teg Yelah and built a grand house on the beach. She sought and obtained the hand of Mowita in marriage, and they had children.

Mah Teg Yelah wished to return to the sky, but he stayed with his wife and children. Above, Thunderbird wept to see him looking so sad, and a great flood of those tears covered the earth. Mowita and all her children and sisters and animals piled into her great house, but her brothers remained outside, for they saw no harm in the rain. Copper Woman eyed the overcrowded house and shook her head. "I will be safe with my magic," she said. "It is time, anyway, for my skin to split, time you lived without being tied to your mother." So she left her bag of meat and bones on the beach and went off to visit her magical sisters.

The house floated through the flood, and at last the waters receded over a land of mountains, valleys, plains, and grasses. The sons of Mowita and Mah Teg Yelah went off with the daughters of Copper Woman, one couple in each of the four directions, and they became the parents of the black people and yellow people and white people and red people, and so we are all related, for we all come from the belly of Copper Woman.

Mowita looked at Mah Teg Yelah and knew he wanted to return to the sky. She told him his duties as a father were complete, and he turned back into Qolus and flew away.

Now Mowita was all alone. She cleaned and smoked the fish, she sewed and mended clothes, but the loneliness ached within her. One day as Mowita was sewing, she looked up and there was Copper Woman, back in new skin, back from visiting her sisters, back from the source of the sun, where it goes when it sinks beneath the horizon. Gladness swelled, and she ran to her mother and embraced her, and they laughed with joy.

Some months later, Mowita's gladness came forth as twin girls, one with the green eyes of her grandmother. The Children of Happiness grew strong and their laughter echoed, and Mowita in her gladness had many more children, and Copper Woman taught them all mystic secrets. The boys and girls were both more complete than Copper Women's first boy children, for Mah Teg Yelah had once been a woman, and so brought harmony to the household: A woman dwells within each man and a man dwells within each woman, so there is no need for conflict in marriage.

Copper Woman grew into Old Woman, and when she was so bent with age she could sweep the beach clean without even bending down, she knew it was again Time. Her skin split and she left her meat and bones on the beach, and she emerged from within, her Self freed. Mowita wept, wondering if she could be and do all Old Woman had done. Then she heard her green-eyed daughter chanting, asking Old Woman to enter her. And Old Woman did so.

And Mowita knew then that it was not necessary to be all her mother had been, since Old Woman was not Gone, only Changed, and would answer when needed. Someday she would travel on, and her daughter, but their wisdom would endure, if her daughter passed it on. When Time came for another Change, the women endured and told this story. And now it is almost Time again.[1]

This is the quintessential mystery of death, passed on by women in every culture: Death is not an ending. Copper Woman's wisdom passes to her daughter and granddaughter, her spirit watches over them in need, and her body regenerates, as she visits her daughter in her loneliness. Death is not a closed door, merely the next part of the cycle. Those who love us never truly leave us: the gifts they have passed are ours forever, until we offer them to others.

New Beginnings

Today, death and destruction fill the world. There is a fundamental distrust of the traitor or terrorist among us, the unseen enemy. Familial dysfunctions, chemical dependencies, short-lived relationships all are leading to disassociation from the earth and its protective healing. Gender tension grows as goddess worship reemerges and women take a greater role in the largely patriarchal culture. Contradictory feelings surround this chaotic phase of destruction. Some fear the devastation of the environment and the violence of the world. Others feel hope and optimism for the revival of the womanspirit.

But people don't realize chaos and conflict are as natural as the rest of the goddess cycle: Even the disappearance of the Dark Goddess was part of her ebb and flow, leading to regeneration and rebirth.

> During the closure phase of a 40,000-year cycle, the evolving feminine principle as the Goddess entered into a deep, incubatory sleep. Here she went into the darkness in order to distill the wisdom of the cycle into a new seed. The composting decay from her disintegrating culture provided the fertile soil to nourish the unlimited possibilities of the developing embryo.[2]

Darkness need not be evil: we begin in darkness, in the nurturance of our mothers' wombs. Seeds, too, generate in darkness, and only bloom when they have grown roots and stems. Only after nourishing ourselves in darkness, in obscurity, can we bloom in sunlight.

Corn Mother had many children, but they were crying, for they had nothing to eat. She told her husband to kill her, but in a very particular way: Her body must be dragged across barren ground until the bones were fleshless, and then must be buried for seven months. When her family returned after seven months they found the land blanketed in tasseled green plants: Corn that would nourish both body and spirit. Her children gathered the seeds each fall and buried them each spring, perpetuating the cycle of life.[3]

Many great goddesses reflected humanity's awe of winter and the closing of the season. Some were birds flying south with souls upon their wings, or wide-eyed owls watching through the night. Some were sleeping goddesses, stretched stiff or curled fetally, awaiting daylight. Some, like Baba Yaga, were bone goddesses surrounded by skulls, reminding visitors of their closeness to death. This goddess, dancing in the darkness, was the Basque Mari, Irish Morrigan, German Frau Holle, Australian Kalwadi.

The Greek Hera, too, periodically withdrew during the dark phase of the moon to the sacred spring of Kanathos. Wrapped in mourning clothes, she performed her most secret rituals of renewing her virginity. Far apart from men, the women who accompanied her would fast and tell stories of the ancient days. Cleansing themselves in the streams and encouraging the flow of sacred blood, they reveled in their new moon magic. As twilight descended, they would chant to Hera, summoning her in her manifestation as Anados, the Goddess Arising. All who beheld her received her blessing there in the circle of firelight, a pin-thin sliver of moon rising overhead. Thus Queen Hera was restored, and returned to Olympus as virgin and bride.[4]

The heroine's death elevates her to greater power as a guardian of the living, a source of magic and blessing for those who remain: "Dramatically, the maiden, like the sons of Inanna, Isis, Aphrodite, and Cybele, is the image of the new — the seed of corn, the seed of life — born from, lost, mourned, found, and reborn out of the old — the mother — in a cycle as continuous as the revolving of the moon."[5] This is the cycle of Persephone, surrender to the deepest unconscious of all and its mysteries, leading to undiscovered energy and triumph.

In China, Tiger Boy and Dragon Girl fell in love and decided to marry. As they approached the bridal chamber, however, black clouds enshrouded the moon. The Serpent King had long coveted Xiamen Island. He raided it, hissing and spitting, with many serpent demons. Tiger Boy picked up his bow, and Dragon Girl, her fish spear. For hours, they fought side by side, and finally Dragon Girl impaled the serpent in the chest. Dying, the Serpent King spat searing black water at her. But Tiger Boy leaped between them and shot the serpent in the eye. The Serpent King smashed to the ground so hard that he split the tip of Xiamen into another island, Gulangyu. And then Tiger Boy fell, dead from the Serpent's poison.

Dragon Girl sobbed over him, inconsolable. Then a beautiful girl appeared before her. "Dragon Girl, you mustn't cry," she said. "The Serpent King was only wounded, and he will return to kill all the villagers. Hurry to Putio Mountain and ask the Bodhisattva Kuan Yin to lend you a double-edged sword." Dragon Girl rowed for 49 days toward the Southern Ocean. There, she knelt before the Goddess of Mercy, who was moved, and offered Dragon Girl not a sword, but a beautiful lotus.

When Dragon Girl returned, she faced Serpent King's hissing army and held up the lotus. Shining waves of light burst from it, blinding the serpents, who fled to the bottom of the ocean. Serpent King fled with them, but the villagers knew he might return. "I will protect us all," said Dragon Girl. She knelt on a hill, lotus cupped in her hands, until she turned into a lotus herself, guarding the village forever.[6]

The Little Mermaid likewise dies in her story, but her journey is not complete. She becomes an air spirit, a creature far more powerful than ever, now closer to earning the soul she covets:

> She cast one more lingering, half-fainting glance at the prince, and then threw herself from the ship into the sea, and thought her body was dissolving into foam. The sun rose above the waves, and his warm rays fell on the cold foam of the little mermaid, who did not feel as if she were dying. She saw the bright sun, and all around her floated hundreds of transparent beautiful beings; she could see through them the white sails of the ship, and the red clouds in the sky; their speech was melodious, but too ethereal to be heard by mortal ears, as they were also unseen by mortal eyes. The little mermaid perceived that she had a body like theirs, and that she continued to rise higher and higher out of the foam. "Where am I?" asked she, and her voice sounded ethereal, as the voice of those who were with her; no earthly music could imitate it.[7]

Through dying, both mermaid and Dragon Girl become protective spirits, aiding mortals below. Though these heroines leave behind the world of life and love, they gain divinity.

After her assumption, the Virgin Mary was named Theotokos, literally the "God-bearer," or "Mother of God," a sacred interceder between humanity and the divine. Mary died surrounded by the apostles between three and 15 years after Christ's ascension. When the apostles later opened her tomb, it was found to be empty and they concluded that she had been assumed into Heaven. John of Damascus described her rising thus:

> The heavenly powers greet thee with sacred canticles and with joyous praise, saying: "Who is this most pure creature ascending, shining as the dawn, beautiful as the moon, conspicuous as the sun? How sweet and lovely thou art, the lily of the field, the rose among thorns; therefore the young maidens loved thee. We are drawn after the odor of thy ointments.... O gladness of angels and of all heavenly powers, sweetness of patriarchs and of the just, perpetual exultation of prophets, rejoicing the world and sanctifying all things.
>
> Watch over us, O Queen, the dwelling-place of our Lord. Lead and govern all our ways as thou wilt. Save us from our sins. Lead us into the calm harbor of the divine will. Make us worthy of future happiness through the sweet and face-to-face vision of the Word made flesh through thee.[8]

The new spirit-heroine has ultimate power: She can guide the mortals needing her counsel, especially children or the downtrodden. She can traverse the world in an eyeblink. She can intercede with God for the sake of mortals, like Mary, or bring Cinderella a glittering ballgown to make her dreams come true. She has reached an expanded consciousness, an understanding of how nature and the spirit, earth and air, are the same. The difference between death and life, fairy godmother and infant, is an imperceptible one, offering a barrier as tenuous as a breath. In her enlightened state, she understands how the cycle must continue and she can descend to earth to be reborn and claim her place in the unending ring of nature once again. With this, the heroine truly masters both worlds: mortal and goddess, corporeal and spiritual, enlightened one and guardian of others. This is the truest apotheosis.

Final Thoughts

The heroine's journey has always existed in epic myth and legend, though it was often understated: Antigone dies silently, walled up out of sight for her courage. Miao Shan generously sacrifices eye and arms to her father, and then ascends to heaven. Janet suffers all through the night, her beloved Tam Lin wrapped in her arms. Oonagh outwits a giant, and Macha seduces her would-be murderers. These are all tales of sacrifice, courage and brilliance, not to be discounted because so few mythic women are warriors.

Women have always had a power men lacked, leading to the early role as the Great Goddess who ruled supreme over all

> Women's power to create life, apparently out of their own substance, and to respond with fearful and mystical blood cycles to the phases of the moon, made them creatures of magic in the eyes of primitive men, who knew themselves unable to match such powers. Thus women took on the roles of intermediaries between humanity and spiritual powers. They became seers, priestesses, healers, oracles, lawmakers, judges, and agents of the Great Mother Goddess who gave birth to the universe.[1]

As women today read and write and create and craft and pray, they seek to tap this lost power, to become man's saviors and protectors, the rescuers of their children, the guardians of family, and thus, of the entire country and cosmos.

Many writers today are revising the old stories, arming girls with swords or inventing Cinder-lads and captive princes. But there is another way to balance the scales. The original pre–Victorian, pre–Disney heroines had plenty of courage and attitude, slaying giants with a needle and thread, or telling Scheherazade's tales, night after sleepless night. Heather Lyons in her article "Some Second Thoughts on Sexism in Fairy Tales," lists many assertive heroines including "the girl who rescues her sister; the girl as helper in the hero's flight; the clever peasant girl; the strong woman as bride; the change of sex; and the reinstatement of the standard banished woman."[2]

317

These are the heroines who must be celebrated, as they ascend into the sky to visit Mother Holle, or delve into death itself to face their shadow selves. As they evolve from seductresses to crones, they embody the magic of the spiritual, the natural forces, to accomplish their quests.

We no longer toil in fields and weave, wishing tiredly for a glimmer of enlightenment free of the body's aches and pains. Today we have time to think, to seek a path to higher thought, but we have completely divorced ourselves from the body and from the land, believing that food is sin, sex is sin, indulgence is sin, neglecting a career for children is a sacrifice, and "women's arts" are soft and weak. Life today involves dread of sex and its diseases, distance from nature and the growing cycle, isolation behind cubicles and cellphone speakers, competition between genders and races for at least ostensible equality.

But in this race to be as equal as possible, women must remember that their own path, celebrated in the great goddesses and their quieter fairytale sisters, is one of strength and dignity, once glorified beyond all others. We are still self-indulgent Inanna, kindly Kuan Yin, devastating Durga, heedless Hina, brave Brünnhild, sparkling Cinderella, and glorious Gaia, earth herself. We still whisper to our shadow-sister in the darkness, and ask her wishes in return for a fragment of her furious strength. For we are in ourselves the tri-part Goddess whom we must reintegrate. Only then can we grow into the whole person we are meant to be: the blossoming goddess on the heroine's path.

Appendix: Aarne-Thompson Folktale Types

The A–T Index covers only the Indo-European folktales. Yet, thanks to recurring motifs across cultures, most tales from other lands fit smoothly into the index. "The Maiden Without Hands" appears in Africa, Cinderella in China, and so forth. The list below is not complete but contains many popular tales, especially those relevant to this study.

SELECTED TYPES

Tales of Magic 300–745

SUPERNATURAL ADVERSARIES 300–399

AT 300	The Dragon Slayer
AT 301	The Three Stolen Princesses
AT 301A	Quest for a Vanished Princess
AT 302	The Ogre's (Devil's) Heart in the Egg
AT 303	The Twins or Blood-Brothers
AT 304	The Hunter
AT 305	The Dragon's Heart-Blood as Remedy for King
AT 306	The Danced-out Shoes (The Twelve Dancing Princesses)
AT 307	The Princess in the Shroud
AT 310	The Maiden in the Tower (Rapunzel)
AT 311	How the Devil Married Three Sisters (Fitcher's Bird)
AT 312	Bluebeard
AT 313	The Girl as Helper in the Hero's Flight (The Mastermaid)
AT 313H	Magic Flight from Witch (Baba Yaga)
AT 314	The Youth Transformed to a Horse
AT 315	The Faithless Sister
AT 316	The Nix of the Mill-pond
AT 317	The Stretching Tree

AT 317A	The Peasant Girl Rescues the Prince
AT 318	The Faithless Wife
AT 321	Eyes Recovered from a Witch
AT 325	The Magician and his Pupil
AT 326	The Youth Who Wanted to Learn What Fear Is
AT 327	The Children and the Ogre
AT 327A	Hansel and Gretel
AT 328	The Giant Killer (Jack and the Beanstalk or Molly Whuppie)
AT 330D	Bonhomme Misere
AT 332	Godfather Death
AT 332B	Death and Luck
AT 333	Red Riding Hood

SUPERNATURAL OR ENCHANTED RELATIVES 400–459

AT 400	The Swan Maiden
AT 402	The Animal Bride
AT 402A	The Marriage of Sir Gawain
AT 403	The Black and White Bride
AT 410	Sleeping Beauty
AT 425	The Search for the Lost Husband
AT 425A	Cupid and Psyche
AT 425C	Beauty and the Beast
AT 425J	The Heroine Serves in Hell for her Bridegroom
AT 425N	The Bird Husband
AT 432	The Prince as Bird
AT 440	The Frog Prince
AT 451	The Brothers Who Were Turned Into Birds (The Six Swans)

SUPERNATURAL HELPERS 500–559

AT 500	The Name of the Helper (Rumpelstiltskin)
AT 501	The Three Old Woman Helpers
AT 502	The Wild Man
AT 505	The Grateful Dead
AT 507A	The Monster's Bride
AT 510	The Persecuted Heroine (Love Like Salt)
AT 510A	Cinderella
AT 510B	The Dress of Gold, of Silver, and of Stars (Tattercoats)
AT 513	The Helpers
AT 514	The Shift of Sex
AT 519	Brunhilde, The Strong Bride
AT 530	The Princess on the Glass Mountain
AT 531	Ferdinand the True and Ferdinand the False
AT 533	The Goose Girl
AT 545B	Puss in Boots
AT 555	The Fisherman and His Wife

MAGIC OBJECTS 560–649

| AT 560 | The Magic Ring |
| AT 561 | Aladdin |

AT 612	The Three Snake-Leaves
AT 613	The Two Travelers
AT 621	The Louse Skin

SUPERNATURAL POWER OR KNOWLEDGE 650–699
AT 653A	The Rarest Thing in the World
AT 673	The White Snake
AT 676	Ali Baba

OTHER TALES OF THE SUPERNATURAL 700–749
AT 700	Tom Thumb
AT 703	The Artificial Child (The Snow Maiden)
AT 704	The Princess on the Pea
AT 706	The Maiden without Hands
AT 709	Snow White
AT 711	The Beautiful and the Ugly Twin
AT 720	The Juniper Tree

RELIGIOUS TALES 750–849
AT 756	The Three Green Twigs
AT 756B	The Devil's Contract
AT 759	God's Justice Vindicated
AT 766	Sleeping Hero Legends
AT 780	The Flower of Lily-Lo
AT 812	The Devil's Riddle

REALISTIC TALES 850–992A
AT 851	The Princess Who Cannot Solve the Riddle
AT 859	Poor Suitor Pretends to Wealth

THE HEROINE MARRIES THE PRINCE 870–879
AT 870	The Entombed Princess (Maid Maleen)
AT 873	The King Discovers his Unknown Son
AT 874	Ariadne
AT 875	The Clever Peasant Girl Who Solves the King's Riddles
AT 879	The Basil Maiden
AT 882	The Falsely Accused Wife
AT 883A	The Innocent Slandered Maiden
AT 888	The Faithful Wife
AT 891	The Man Who Deserts His Wife and Sets Her the Task of Bearing Him a Child
AT 900	King Thrushbeard
AT 901	Taming of the Shrew
AT 910B	The Servant's Good Counsels
AT 924	Sign Language Misunderstood
AT 926C	Wise Judges

TALES OF FATE 930–949
AT 931	Oedipus
AT 945	Luck and Intelligence

JOKES AND ANECDOTES 1200–1999

AT 1350	The Silence Wager
AT 1353	The Old Woman as Devil's Helper
AT 1354	Death for the Old Couple
AT 1360C	Old Hildebrand
AT 1364	The Blood-Brother's Wife
AT 1380	The Faithless Wife
AT 1408	Trading Places (family members exchange jobs with disastrous results)
AT 1418	The Equivocal Oath
AT 1539	Tricksters and their Victims
AT 1620	The Emperor's New Clothes
AT 1730	The Entrapped Suitors
AT 1741	A Woman Convinces a Guest that her Husband (or Employer) Wants to Cut Off his Ears

SELECTED MOTIFS

MYTHOLOGICAL MOTIFS

A0	Creator
A110	Origin of gods
A112	Birth of gods
A163	Contests among the gods
A188	Gods in love with humans
A220	Sun Deity
A220.1.1	Amaterasu
A240	Moon Deity
A301	Mother Earth conceived as mother of all things
A310	Deity of the world of the dead
A316	Persephone
A421.1.2	Sea Goddess
A483.1	Goddess of Mercy, Kuan Yin
A493.1	Pele
A510	Origin of the culture hero (demigod)
A526.7	Culture hero performs remarkable feats of strength and skill
A560	Culture hero's departure
A610	Creation of universe by creator
A673	Hound of hell
A736.1	Sun and moon as man and woman
A773	Origin of Pleiades
A800	Creation of earth
A822.2	Land created from dripping spear
A1010	Deluge
A1030	World-fire
A1150.2	Winter while Persephone is in underworld
A1231	First man descends from sky
A1241	Man made from clay

| A1270 | Primeval human pair |
| A1335 | Origin of death |

ANIMALS
B20	Beast-men
B50	Bird-men
B80.1	Seal-men
B81	Mermaid
B401	Helpful horse
B411	Helpful cow
B600.2	Animal husband provides characteristic animal food
B611.3	Horse paramour
B848.21	Lion's whisker

TABU
C12	Devil invoked appears unexpectedly
C30	Tabu: Offending supernatural relative
C31.1.2	Melusine
C32.1	Tabu: Looking at supernatural husband
C35.4	Tabu: Returning skin of animal wife
C321	Pandora
C400	Speaking taboo
C611	Forbidden chamber
C932	Loss of spouse for breaking taboo

MAGIC
D100	Transformation: Person to animal
D150	Transformation: Man to bird
D161.1	Transformation: Man to swan
D190	Transformation: Person to reptile
D300	Transformation: Animal to person
D361.1	Swan maiden
D361.1.1	Selkie bride
D454.3	Transformation: Cloth to other object
D672	Obstacle flight
D735	Disenchantment through kiss
D758.2	Disenchantment by maintaining silence for a year or more
D855.5	Magic object as reward for good deeds
D1611	Magic object answers for fugitive
D1652.8	Inexhaustible cloth
D1960.3	Sleeping Beauty

THE DEAD
E30	Resuscitation by arrangement of members
E234.3	Return from dead to avenge death
E235	Return from dead to punish indignities to corpse
E480	Abode of the dead
E632	The singing bone
E710	External soul

MARVELS

F17.1	Changing Woman
F81	Descent to lower world of the dead
F81.1	Orpheus
F81.1.0.1	Izanagi and Izanami
F92.2.1	Persephone
F251.4	Underworld people from children which Eve hid from God
F302.4	Animal brides
F321.3	Person enters fairyland to rescue a child
F324.3.1	Tam Lin
F329.1	Thomas the Rhymer
F848.1	Rapunzel
F1015.1.1	Twelve dancing princesses

OGRES

G10	Cannibalism
G200	Witch
G205	Witch stepmother
G211	Witch in animal form
G266	Witches steal
G271	Breaking spell
G284	Witch as helper
G412.1.	Hansel and Gretel
G530.2	The Mastermaid

TESTS

H36.1	Slipper Test
H41.1	Princess on the Pea
H56	Recognition by wound
H71.1	Star on forehead as a sign of royalty
H94	Recognition by ring
H121	Identification by cup
H310	Suitor tests
H465A	King Thrushbeard
H561.1	The clever peasant's daughter
H602.1.1	Symbolic meaning of numbers one to twelve (or other number)
H1091.1	Task: sorting grains: performed by helpful ants
H1091.2	Task: sorting grains: performed by helpful birds
H1199.12.4B	Maria Morevna
H1226.4	Pursuit of rolling ball of yarn leads to quest
H1242	Youngest child alone succeeds on quest
H1385.4	Wife seeks lost husband
H543	Riddle contest with the devil

THE WISE AND THE FOOLISH

J1185.1	Scheherazade
J1545.4	"Exiled wife's dearest possession"
J1675	Clever dealing with a king
J1795	Image in mirror mistaken

| J1804 | Conversation by sign language mutually misunderstood |
| J2461.1 | Literal following of instructions |

DECEPTIONS
K841	Substitute for execution obtained by trickery
K1310	Seduction by disguise or substitution
K1810	Deception by disguise
K1811	Gods in disguise visit mortals
K1814.5	Girl in disguise courted by husband
K1816.0.2.1	Maid Maleen
K1837.6.1	Mulan

REVERSAL OF FORTUNE
L13	Compassionate youngest son
L100	Unpromising hero or heroine
L310	Weak overcomes strong in conflict
L145.1B	Kate Crackernuts

ORDAINING THE FUTURE
M21	King Lear judgment
M300	Prophecies
M400	Curses

CHANCE AND FATE
N50	Wagers
N452	Secret remedy overheard in conversation of animals
N512	Treasure in underground chamber
N531	Treasure discovered through dream
N813	Helpful genie
N825.3	Old woman helper

SOCIETY
P17	Succession to the throne
P230	Parents and children
P250	Brothers and sisters
P253.2	Sister faithful to transformed brothers

REWARDS AND PUNISHMENTS
Q2	Kind and unkind
Q40	Kindness rewarded
Q65	Filial duty rewarded
Q86	Reward for industry
Q91	Cleverness rewarded
Q280	Unkindness punished

CAPTIVES AND FUGITIVES
R111.1.3C	The dragon slayer
R221	Heroine's threefold flight from ball (Cinderella)
R260	Pursuit

Unnatural Cruelty

S10	Cruel parents
S31	Cruel stepmother
S62.1	Bluebeard
S143	Abandoned in forest
S160	Mutilation
S241	Child unwittingly promised: "first thing you meet"

Sex

T54	Miraculous birth
T62	Princess to marry first man to ask her
T91	Unequals in love
T91.4.1.2	Lady Ragnell
T97	Father opposed to daughter's marriage
T111	Marriage of mortal and supernatural being
T121.3.1	Princess marries lowly man
T510	Miraculous conception

Traits of Character

W10	Kindness
W11	Generosity
W28	Self-sacrifice
W32	Bravery
W34	Loyalty
W121	Cowardice

Compiled from Margaret Read MacDonald, *The Storyteller's Sourcebook* (Detroit: Neal-Schuman Publishers, in association with Gale, 1982) and D.L. Ashliman, *A Guide to Folktales in the English Language* (New York: Greenwood Press, 1987).

Notes

Introduction

1. Joseph Campbell with Bill Moyers, *The Power of Myth* (New York: Doubleday, 1988), 123.

2. Joseph Campbell, *The Hero with a Thousand Faces* (Princeton: Princeton University Press, 1973), 120.

3. Simone de Beauvoir, *The Second Sex* (New York: Bantam Books, 1970), 171.

4. Joseph Campbell, *Pathways to Bliss: Mythology and Personal Transformation* (Novato, CA: New World Library, 2004), 145, 159.

5. Ibid., 159.

6. Ibid.

7. Madonna Kolbenschlag, *Kiss Sleeping Beauty Goodbye* (San Francisco: Harper & Row, 1979), 3.

8. Max Luthi, *Once Upon a Time: On the Nature of Fairy Tales*, translated by Lee Chadeayne and Paul Gottwald (New York: Fredrick Ungar, 1970), 135–136.

9. Sherna Gluck, "What's So Special About Women? Women's Oral His-tory," *Frontiers* 2/2:3–17. 1977:5

10. Clarissa Pinkola Estés, *Women Who Run with the Wolves* (New York: Ballantine, 1992), 264.

11. Jack Zipes, *The Brothers Grimm: From Enchanted Forests to the Modern World* (New York: Routledge, Chapman and Hall, 1988), 80–81.

12. Carol Schaefer, *Grandmothers Counsel the World* (Boston: Trumpeter Books, 2006), 138.

13. Ibid., 135.

Chapter 1

1. Hans Christian Andersen. "The Wild Swans," in *Hans Christian Andersen: The Complete Fairy Tales and Stories*, trans. Erik Christian Haugaard (New York: Anchor Books, 1983), 117–131.

2. A.B. Chinen, *Waking the World: Classic Tales of Women and the Heroic Feminine* (New York: Penguin Putnam, 1996), 166.

3. Jack Zipes, *The Brothers Grimm: From Enchanted Forests to the Modern World* (New York: Palgrave Macmillan, 1988), 40.

4. Sigmund Freud. "Family Romances," in *The Standard Edition of the Complete Psychological Works of Sigmund Freud*, ed. Anna Freud et al., trans. James Strachey (London: Hogarth, 1959), 237–41.

5. Maria M. Tatar, *The Hard Facts of the Grimms' Fairy Tales* (Princeton: Princeton University Press, 1987), 72.

6. Joseph Campbell with Bill Moyers, *The Power of Myth*, ed. Betty Sue Flowers (New York: Doubleday, 1988), 142.

7. "Inana's Descent to the Nether World," in The Electronic Text Corpus of Sumerian Literature, The ETCSL Project, edited by J.A. Black, G. Cunningham, E. Fluckiger-Hawker, E. Robson, and G. Zólyomi (Oxford: Oxford University Press, 2006), <http://www-etcsl.orient.ox.ac.uk>.

8. Campbell, *The Power of Myth*, 156.

9. Patrick Chamoiseau. "A Little Matter of Marriage," in *Creole Folktales*, trans. Linda Coverdale (New York: The New Press, 1994), 59.

10. Margaret Orbell. "Maori Mythology," in *The Feminist Companion to Mythology*, ed. Carolyne Larrington (London: Pandora, 1992), 299.

11. M. Esther Harding, *Women's Mysteries Ancient and Modern* (New York: Harper & Row, 1971), 16.

12. "Zi Ye," in *Women in Praise of the Sacred*, ed. Jane Hirschfield (New York: Harper Perennial, 1995), 21.

13. Starhawk and Hilary Valentine, *The Twelve Wild Swans* (San Francisco: HarperCollins, 2000), 194.

14. Ovid, *Metamorphoses*, trans. Brookes More (Boston: Cornhill, 1922), 6.5.571–73, The Theoi

Project, <http://www.theoi.com/Text/OvidMeta morphoses1.html>.

15. Karen E. Rowe. "To Spin a Yarn: The Female Voice in Folklore and Fairytale," in *Fairy Tales and Society*, ed. Ruth B. Bottigheimer (Philadelphia: University of Pennsylvania Press, 1986), 57.

16. Grimm Brothers. "Cinderella," in *Grimms Fairy Tales* (New York: Grosset & Dunlap, 1970), 160.

17. Ruth B. Bottigheimer. "Silenced Women in the Grimms' Tales," in *Fairy Tales and Society,* ed. Ruth B. Bottigheimer (Philadelphia: University of Pennsylvania Press, 1986), 119.

18. M.L. von Franz. "The Process of Individuation," in *Man and His Symbols*, ed. Carl G. Jung, (New York: Doubleday, 1964), 194.

Chapter 2

1. Richard Wagner, *The Ring of the Nibelung: Siegfried & The Twilight of the Gods*, trans. Margaret Armour (New York: Abaris Books, 1910), 77, The Internet Sacred Text Archive, <http://www.sacred-texts.com/neu/ron/index.htm>.

2. Ibid., 89.

3. Ibid., 110.

4. Ibid., 97.

5. Ibid., 110.

6. Ibid., 122.

7. Ibid., 132.

8. Ibid., 90.

9. *Kalevala*, trans. K. Bosley (Oxford: Oxford University Press, 1989), 22.

10. "*Sigrdrifumol*," *The Poetic Edda*, trans. Henry Adams Bellows (Princeton: Princeton University Press, 1936), 388, The Internet Sacred Text Archive, <http://www.sacred-texts.com/neu/poe/poe25.htm>.

11. Wagner, *The Ring of the Nibelung*, 83.

12. Joan Gould, *Spinning Straw into Gold* (New York: Random House, 2005), 98.

13. Ibid., 108.

14. Bruno Bettelheim, *The Uses of Enchantment* (New York: Alfred A. Knopf, 1977), 234.

15. Marion Woodman, *The Pregnant Virgin: A Process of Psychological Transformation* (Toronto: Inner City Books, 1985), 118–19.

16. Clarissa Pinkola Estés, *Women Who Run with the Wolves* (New York: Ballantine, 1992), 151.

17. N.J. Girardot, "Initiation and Meaning in the Tale of Snow White and the Seven Dwarfs," *Journal of American Folklore* (1977): 293.

18. Gould, *Spinning Straw into Gold*, 106.

19. Richard Wagner, *The Ring of the Nibelung: Siegfried & The Twilight of the Gods*, trans. by Margaret Armour (New York: Abaris Books, 1910), 8, The Internet Sacred Text Archive, <http://www.sacred-texts.com/neu/ron/index.htm>.

20. Ibid., 87.

21. Ibid., 89.

22. Ibid., 129.

Chapter 3

1. Maria M. Tatar, *The Annotated Classic Fairy Tales* (New York and London: W.W. Norton, 2002), 174.

2. Sydele E. Golston, *Changing Woman of the Apache: Women's Lives in Past and Present* (Danbury, CT: Grolier, 1996), 29–31.

3. Ibid., 46.

4. Brothers Grimm. "Cinderella," in *Grimms Fairy Tales* (New York: Grosset & Dunlap, 1970), 160.

5. Joan Gould, *Spinning Straw into Gold* (New York: Random House, 2005), 68.

6. Ibid., 193.

7. Ibid., 194.

8. Dorothy Dinnerstein, *The Mermaid and the Minotaur* (New York: Other Press, 1999), 17.

9. Gould, *Spinning Straw into Gold*, 41.

10. Hans Christian Andersen. "The Little Mermaid," in *Hans Christian Andersen: The Complete Fairy Tales and Stories*, trans. Erik Christian Haugaard (New York: Anchor Books, 1983), 58.

11. Ibid., 58.

12. Maureen Murdock, *The Heroine's Journey* (Boston: Shambhala, 1990), 19.

13. Marina Warner, *From the Beast to the Blonde* (New York: Farrar, Straus, and Giroux, 1994), 223.

14. Apuleius, *Cupid and Psyche*, trans. E.J. Kenney (Cambridge: Cambridge University Press, 1990), 97.

15. Patricia Reis, *Through the Goddess: A Woman's Way of Healing* (New York: Continuum, 1991), 137.

16. Silvia Brinton Perera, *Descent to the Goddess* (Toronto: Inner City Books, 1981), 42.

17. Gould, *Spinning Straw into Gold*, 65–66.

18. Jean Shinoda Bolen, *Goddesses in Everywoman* (New York: Quill, 2004), 259–261.

19. *Popol Vuh*, trans. Dennis Tedlock (New York: Simon and Schuster, 1996), 98–104.

Chapter 4

1. Merlin Stone. "Cerridwen," in *Ancient Mirrors of Womanhood* (Boston: Beacon Press, 1990), 58–60; "Taliesin," in *The Mabinogion*, ed. and trans. Lady Charlotte Guest (London: Bernard Quaritch, 1877), 471–494, The Internet Sacred Text Archive, February 2004, <http://www.sacred-texts.com/neu/celt/mab/index.htm>.

2. John Arnott MacCulloch, *The Religion of the Ancient Celts* (Edinburgh: T. & T. Clark, 1911), 118, The Internet Sacred Text Archive, February 2004, <http://www.sacred-texts.com/neu/celt/rac/index.htm>.

3. Ibid., 117.

4. Adrienne Rich, *Of Woman Born: Motherhood as Experience and Institution* (New York: Norton, 1976), 97.

5. Barbara G. Walker, *The Woman's Dictionary of Symbols and Sacred Objects* (San Francisco: Harper, 1988), 90.

6. Emma Jung and M-L. von Franz, *The Grail Legend*, trans. Andrea Dykes (New York: G.P. Putnam's Sons, 1970), 155.

7. Maria M. Tatar, *The Annotated Classic Fairy Tales* (New York and London: W.W. Norton, 2002), 193.

8. *The Mabinogion*, ed. and trans. Lady Charlotte Guest (London: Bernard Quaritch, 1877), 471–494, The Internet Sacred Text Archive, February 2004, <http://www.sacredtexts.com/neu/celt/mab/index.htm>.

9. William Thomas and Kate Pavitt, *The Book of Talismans, Amulets and Zodiacal Gems* (London: William Rider & Son, 1922), 89, The Internet Sacred Text Archive, <http://www.sacred-texts.com/sym/bot/index.htm>.

10. Ibid., 89.

11. Shahrukh Husain, *The Goddess* (Boston: Little, Brown, 1997), 144.

12. Merlin Stone, *Ancient Mirrors of Womanhood* (Boston: Beacon, 1990), 290.

13. Homer, *The Iliad, The Iliad of Homer & The Odyssey*, trans. Samuel Butler, ed. Robert Maynard Hutchins, XIV.214–218, in *Great Books of the Western World* 4 (Chicago: Encyclopædia Britannica, 1952, 1989).

14. Ibid., XIV.218–221.

15. *Nihongi: Chronicles of Japan from the Earliest Times to A.D. 697*, trans. W.G. Aston (Tokyo: Charles E. Tuttle, 1978), 83.

16. David Kinsley, *The Goddesses' Mirror: Visions of the Divine from East and West* (Albany: State University of New York Press, 1989), 71.

17. Barbara G. Walker, *The Woman's Dictionary of Symbols and Sacred Objects* (San Francisco: Harper, 1988), 82–83.

18. W.M. Hennessy, "The Ancient Irish Goddess of War," *Revue Celtique* 1 (1870): 32–37, The Internet Sacred Text Archive, <http://www.sacred-texts.com/neu/celt/aigw/aigw01.htm>.

19. Barbara G. Walker, *The Woman's Dictionary of Symbols and Sacred Objects* (San Francisco: Harper, 1988), 31.

20. Ibid., 31.

21. Jessie L. Weston, *From Ritual to Romance* (New York: Peter Smith, 1941), 71.

22. Jean Markale, *Women of the Celts* (Rochester, VT: Inner Traditions, 1986), 175.

23. Barbara G. Walker, *The Woman's Dictionary of Symbols and Sacred Objects* (San Francisco: Harper, 1988), 20.

24. Ibid., 2.

25. Mary Barnard, trans. *Sappho: A New Translation* (Berkeley: University of California Press, 1958), 37.

26. Joan Gould, *Spinning Straw into Gold* (New York: Random House, 2005), 74.

27. Sigmund Freud, *A General Introduction to Psychoanalysis* (New York: Routledge, Chapman and Hall, 1969), 156–177.

28. Carl Jung. "Psychological Aspects of the Mother Archetype," in *Collected Works*, trans. R.F.C. Hull, vol. 9, pt. 1, 2nd ed. (Princeton: Princeton University Press, 1968), 15.

29. Ibid., 15.

30. Ann G. Thomas, *The Women We Become: Myths, Folktales, and Stories about Growing Older* (Rocklin, CA: Prima, 1997), 131.

31. Annabel Williams-Ellis. "Clever Oonagh," in *British Fairy Tales* (Glasgow and London: Blackie and Son, 1976), 56–69.

32. Joseph Campbell with Bill Moyers, *The Power of Myth*, Betty Sue Flowers, ed. (New York: Doubleday, 1988), 125.

Chapter 5

1. The Rev. William Wyatt Gill, *Myths and Songs from the South Pacific* (London: Henry S. King, 1876), 91.

2. Ibid., 96.

3. Ibid., 88–98. Roslyn Poignant, "Two-Faced Tinarau," *Oceanic Mythology*, 50–53 (New York: Hamlyn, 1967), 50–53; A.W. Reed, "Hina-uri, Tinirau, and Kae," *Treasury of Maori Folklore* (New South Wales: Literary Productions, 1967), 145–147.

4. Patricia Reis, *Through the Goddess: A Woman's Way of Healing* (New York: Continuum, 1991), 195–196.

5. Gill, *Myths and Songs from the South Pacific*, 94.

6. Reis, *Through the Goddess*, 204.

7. Nor Hall, *The Moon and the Virgin: Reflections on the Archetypal Feminine* (New York: Harper & Row, 1980), 213–14.

8. Diane Purkiss, "Women's Rewriting of Myth" in *The Feminist Companion to Mythology*, ed. Carolyne Larrington, 441–458 (London: Pandora, 1992), 448.

9. Carl Jung, *Memories, Dreams, Reflections*, ed. Aniela Jaffé, trans. Clara Winston (USA: Vintage, 1989), 401.

10. Meri Lao, *Seduction and the Secret Power of Women: The Lure of Sirens and Mermaids*, trans. John Oliphant (Rochester, VT: Park Street, 1998), 37.

11. Barbara G. Walker, *The Woman's Dictionary of Symbols and Sacred Objects* (San Francisco: Harper, 1988), 350.

12. Andersen, Hans Christian, "The Little Mermaid" in *Hans Christian Andersen: The Complete Fairy Tales and Stories*, trans. Erik Christian Haugaard (New York: Anchor Books, 1983), 58.

Chapter 6

1. Merlin Stone. "Ix Chel," in *Ancient Mirrors of Womanhood* (Boston: Beacon, 1990), 92–96.

2. Jack Zipes, *The Brothers Grimm: From Enchanted Forests to the Modern World* (Routledge, Chapman and Hall: 1988), 115.

3. Betsy Cohen, *The Snow White Syndrome* (New York: Berkley, 1989), 9–10.

4. Bruno Bettelheim, *The Uses of Enchantment* (New York: Alfred A. Knopf, 1977), 76.

5. Dorothy Dinnerstein, *The Mermaid and the Minotaur* (New York: Other Press, 1999), 12.

6. Pierre Brunel, *Companion to Literary Myths, Heroes, and Archetypes*, trans. Wendy Allatson, Judith Hayward, and Trista Selous (New York: Routledge, 1992), 222.

7. Barbara G. Walker, *The Woman's Dictionary of Symbols and Sacred Objects* (San Francisco: Harper, 1988), 309.

8. Isabella Wylde, "Women Who Run with the Wolves: An Interview with Author and Analyst Clarissa Pinkola Estés," *Radiance* (Winter 1994), <http://radiancemagazine.com/issues/1994/wolves.html>.

9. Hilda Ellis Davidson, *Roles of the Northern Goddess* (London & New York: Routledge, 1998), 22.

10. Joseph Campbell, *The Masks of God: Creative Mythology* (New York: Viking Penguin, 1968), 118.

11. Shahrukh Husain, *The Goddess* (Boston: Little, Brown, 1997), 12–13.

12. W.M. Hennessy, "The Ancient Irish Goddess of War," *Revue Celtique* 1 (1870): 32–37, The Internet Sacred Text Archive, <http://www.sacredtexts.com/neu/celt/aigw/aigw01.htm>.

13. Robert Graves, *The Greek Myths*, Vol. 1 (New York: Penguin, 1955), 297.

14. Homer, *The Odyssey, The Iliad of Homer & The Odyssey*, trans. Samuel Butler, ed. Robert Maynard Hutchins, in *Great Books of the Western World* 4 (Chicago: Encyclopædia Britannica, 1952, 1989), XII.100.

15. Ibid., XII.100–101.

16. Ibid., XII.103–104.

17. Ibid., XII.103–104.

18. Susanna Rostas. "Mexican Mythology," in *The Feminist Companion to Mythology*, ed. Carolyne Larrington (London: Pandora, 1992), 383.

19. Ovid, *Metamorphoses*, ed. E.J. Kenney, trans. A.D. Melville (Oxford: Oxford University Press, 1987), 4.9.770.

20. Karen Randolph Joines, *Serpent Symbolism in the Old Testament* (Haddonfield, NJ: Haddonfield House, 1974), 111.

21. Krishanna Spencer, "Priestess Path: Under the Aegis of Athena," *The Beltane Papers* (Autumn 2002): 24.

22. Merlin Stone, *When God Was a Woman* (New York: Harcourt Brace, 1976), 199.

23. Mary Condren, *The Serpent and the Goddess* (San Francisco: Harper & Row, 1989), 8.

24. Joseph Campbell with Bill Moyers, *The Power of Myth*, ed. Betty Sue Flowers (New York: Doubleday, 1988), 45.

25. Roslyn Poignant, *Oceanic Mythology* (New York: Hamlyn, 1967), 93–94.

Chapter 7

1. "Tam Lin," collected by Francis James Child, in *The English and Scottish Popular Ballads*, Vol. 1 (New York: Dover, 1965), 336–7.

2. Marina Warner, *From the Beast to the Blonde* (New York: Farrar, Straus, and Giroux, 1994), 275.

3. M.L. von Franz. "The Process of Individuation," in *Man and His Symbols*, ed. Carl G. Jung (New York: Doubleday, 1964), 194.

4. Ella E. Clark, "The Maiden of Deception Pass," *Indian Legends of the Pacific Northwest* (Berkeley: University of California Press, 1953), 199–201.

5. Apuleius. "Cupid and Psyche," in *The Golden Ass*, trans. Robert Graves (New York: Farrar, Straus & Giroux, 1951), 111.

6. Apuleius, *Cupid and Psyche*, trans. E.J. Kenney (Cambridge: Cambridge University Press, 1990), 55.

7. Clarissa Pinkola Estés, *Women Who Run with the Wolves* (New York: Ballantine, 1992), 50.

8. Robert A. Johnson, *Owning Your Own Shadow* (San Francisco: HarperCollins, 1993), 62–63.

9. "The Farmer and the Barber," in *Folktales of India*, eds. Brenda Beck, Peter Claus, Goswami Praphulladatta, Jawaharlal Handoo (Chicago: University of Chicago Press, 1987), 42–45.

10. Apuleius, *Cupid and Psyche*, 75.

11. Erich Neumann, *Amor and Psyche: The Psychic Development of the Feminine*, trans. Ralph Manheim, Bollingen Series 54 (Princeton: Princeton University Press, 1956), 78–80.

12. Marina Warner, *From the Beast to the Blonde* (New York: Farrar, Straus, and Giroux, 1994), 274.

13. Terri Windling, "Beauty and the Beast," *The Journal of Mythic Arts*, The Endicott Studio (Summer 2007), <http://www.endicott-studio.com/rdrm/forbewty.html>.

14. Patrick Chamoiseau. "A Little Matter of Marriage," in *Creole Folktales*, trans. Linda Coverdale (New York: The New Press, 1994), 65.

15. Marion Woodman, *The Pregnant Virgin: A Process of Psychological Transformation* (Toronto: Inner City Books, 1985), 132.

16. Estés, *Women Who Run with the Wolves*, 64–65.

17. Bruno Bettelheim, *The Uses of Enchantment* (New York: Knopf, 1976), 307–308.

18. Angela Carter. "The Tiger's Bride," in *The Bloody Chamber* (New York: Penguin, 1990), 67.

19. Terri Windling, "Beauty and the Beast, " *The Journal of Mythic Arts*, The Endicott Studio (Summer 2007), <http://www.endicott-studio.com/rdrm/forbewty.html>.

Chapter 8

1. D. L. Ashliman, "Incest in Indo-European Folktales," (1997), Folklore and Mythology Electronic Texts, <http://www.pitt.edu/~dash/incest.html>.

2. Ibid.

3. Maria M. Tatar, *The Annotated Classic Fairy Tales* (New York and London: W.W. Norton, 2002), 215.

4. Helen Pilinovsky, "Donkeyskin, Deerskin, Allerleirauh: The Reality of the Fairy Tale," *The Journal of Mythic Arts*, The Endicott Studio (2001), <http://www.endicott-studio.com/fordnky.html>.

5. Jane Yolen. "Allerleirauh," in *The Armless Maiden, and Other Tales for Childhood's Survivors*, ed. Terri Windling, (New York: Tor Books, 1996), 37.

6. Pilinovsky, "Donkeyskin, Deerskin, Allerleirauh: The Reality of the Fairy Tale," 1.

7. Ibid., 1.

8. Tatar, *The Annotated Classic Fairy Tales*, 213.

9. Roslyn Poignant, *Oceanic Mythology* (New York: Hamlyn, 1967), 291.

10. Maria M. Tatar, *Off with their Heads! Fairy Tales and the Culture of Childhood* (Princeton: Princeton University Press, 1992), 133.

11. Marilyn Jurich, *Scheherazade's Sisters: Trickster Heroines and Their Stories in World Literature* (Westport, CT: Greenwood Press, 1998), 120.

12. Pilinovsky, "Donkeyskin, Deerskin, Allerleirauh," 4.

13. James Orchard Halliwell, *The Nursery Rhymes of England* (London, 1853), 22–31, Folklore and Mythology Electronic Texts, <http://www.pitt.edu/~dash/type0510b.html>.

14. Marion Woodman, *The Ravaged Bridegroom* (Toronto: Inner City Books, 1990), 126.

15. Ibid., 126.

16. Irina Zheleznova, ed. and trans. "The Frog Tsarevna," in *Folk Tales from Russian Lands* (New York: Dover, 1969), 1–9.

17. A.B. Chinen. "The Queen and the Murderer," in *Waking the World: Classic Tales of Women and the Heroic Feminine* (New York: Penguin Putnam, 1996), 3–7.

Chapter 9

1. Midori Snyder. "The Armless Maiden," in *The Armless Maiden, And Other Tales for Childhood's Survivors*, ed. Terri Windling (New York: Tor Books, 1996), 17–30.

2. Barbara Rush. "The Girl Swallowed Up by a Stone," in *The Book of Jewish Women's Tales* (Berkeley: University of California Press, 1994), 29–32.

3. Jack Zipes, *The Brothers Grimm: From Enchanted Forests to the Modern World* (New York: Routledge, Chapman and Hall, 1988), 120.

4. Valerie Paradiz, *Clever Maids: The Secret History of the Grimm Fairy Tales* (New York: Basic Books, 2005), 93.

5. Grimm Brothers. "The Girl without Hands," in *Grimms Fairy Tales* (New York: Grosset & Dunlap, 1970), 62–65.

6. D.L. Ashliman, "Incest in Indo-European Folktales," (1997), Folklore and Mythology Electronic Texts, <http://www.pitt.edu/~dash/incest.html>.

7. Gertrud Mueller Nelson, *Here All Dwell Free: Stories to Heal the Wounded Feminine* (New York: Doubleday, 1991), 43.

8. Zipes, *The Brothers Grimm*, 122–123.

9. Glen Dudbridge, *The Legend of Miao-shan* (London: Ithaca Press, 1978), 22–34.

10. Midori Synder. "The Hero's Journey," in *The Armless Maiden, and Other Tales for Childhood's Survivors*, ed. Terri Windling (New York: Tor Books, 1996), 32.

11. Maria M. Tatar, *Off with Their Heads! Fairy Tales and the Culture of Childhood* (Princeton: Princeton University Press, 1992), 123.

12. Ibid., 123.

13. "Psalm of Thirty-Four Verses, ascribed to Subhā," in *Psalms of the Sisters. Psalms of the Early Buddhists*, trans. Rhys Davids (London: Oxford University Press, 1909), XIV.381–383.

14. Ibid., XIV.366–399.

15. Nelson, *Here All Dwell Free*, 94.

16. Midori Synder, "The Hero's Journey," 32.

17. Hans Christian Andersen. "The Little Mermaid," in *Hans Christian Andersen: The Complete Fairy Tales and Stories*, trans. Erik Christian Haugaard (New York: Anchor Books, 1983), 57.

18. Maria M. Tatar, *The Annotated Classic Fairy Tales* (New York and London: W.W. Norton, 2002), 323.

19. Jack Zipes, *Fairy Tales and the Art of Subversion* (New York: Wildman, 1983), 84–85.

20. Andersen. "The Little Mermaid," 57.

21. Tatar, *Off with Their Heads!*, 125.

22. Nelson, *Here All Dwell Free*, 139.

23. Ibid., 150–51.

24. Katrin Hyman Tchana. "Sedna, Woman of the Sea," in *Changing Woman and Her Sisters* (New York: Holiday House, 2006), 22–29.

Chapter 10

1. "The Story of King Shahriyar, King Shah-Zeman, and Shahrazad the Wezeer's Daughter," in *The Arabian Nights' Entertainments or The Thousand and One Nights*, trans. Edward William Lane (New York: Tudor, 1944), 3–12.

2. Ibid., xvii.

3. Carl Jung. "Concerning the Archetypes, with

Special Reference to the Anima Concept," in *Collected Works*, trans. R.F.C. Hull, vol. 9, pt. 1, 2nd ed. (Princeton: Princeton University Press, 1968), 71.

4. Jerome W. Clinton. "Madness and Cure in the Thousand and One Nights," in *Fairy Tales and Society*, ed. Ruth B. Bottigheimer (Philadelphia: University of Pennsylvania Press, 1986), 41.

5. Karen E. Rowe. "To Spin a Yarn: The Female Voice in Folklore and Fairy Tale," in *Fairy Tales and Society*, ed. Ruth B. Bottigheimer.

6. Jack Zipes. "The Splendor of the Arabian Nights," in *When Dreams Came True: Classical Fairy Tales and Their Tradition* (New York: Routledge, 2007), 61.

7. Ibid., 59.

8. Ibid., 59–60.

9. "Pan Zhao," in *Women in Praise of the Sacred*, ed. Jane Hirschfield (New York: Harper Perennial, 1995), 28.

10. Autumn Stephens, *Wild Women: Crusaders, Curmudgeons and Completely Corsetless Ladies in the Otherwise Virtuous Victorian Era* (Berkeley, CA: Conari, 1992), 235.

11. Condren, *The Serpent and the Goddess*, 34–41.

12. Genesis 1:27.

13. "The Alphabet of Ben Sira," in *Rabbinic Fantasies: Imaginative Narratives from Classical Hebrew Literature* (Yale Judaica Series), ed. Professor David Stern and Mark Jay Mirsky (New Haven, CT: Yale University Press, 1998), 183.

14. Zora Neale Hurston. "Why Women Always Take Advantage of Men," *Mules and Men* (Bloomington: Indiana University Press, 1935), 33–39.

15. Robert A. Johnson, *Owning Your Own Shadow* (San Francisco: HarperCollins, 1993), 89.

16. Joseph L. Henderson. "Ancient Myths and Modern Man," in *Man and His Symbols,* ed. Carl G. Jung (New York: Doubleday, 1964), 134.

17. Vicki León, *Outrageous Women of Ancient Times* (New York: John Wiley & Sons, 1998), 89–91.

18. Barbara G. Walker, *The Woman's Dictionary of Symbols and Sacred Objects* (San Francisco: Harper, 1988), 182.

19. *The Epic of Gilgamesh*, trans. Maureen Gallery Kovacs (Wolf Carnahan, 1998), VI. i–ii.42–79.

20. Shahrukh Husain, *The Goddess* (Boston: Little, Brown, 1997), 156.

21. Andrew Harvey & Anne Baring, *The Divine Feminine* (Berkeley, CA: Conari, 1996), 150–151.

22. Saundaryalahari I II.7.24, in Miriam Robbins Dexter, *Whence the Goddess: A Source Book* (New York: Pergamon, 1990), 81.

23. "Devî Gita," in *Srimad Devî Bhagavatam*, trans. Swami Vijnanananda (India: Hari Prasanna Chatterji, 1921), 735, The Internet Sacred Text Archive, <http://www.sacred-texts.com/hin/dg>.

24. Haragovinda Sastri, ed., *Manusmrtih* (Varanasi: Chowkhamba Sanskrit Series, 1965), III.13.46.

25. Haunami-Kay Trask, *Eros and Power: The Promise of Feminist Theory* (Philidelphia: University of Pennsylvania Press, 1986), 161.

26. Merlin Stone, *When God Was a Woman* (New York: Harcourt Brace, 1976), 154–55.

27. Elizabeth Diab. "Hawaii," in *The Feminist Companion to Mythology,* ed. Carolyne Larrington (London: Pandora, 1992), 308.

28. Joseph Campbell, *The Masks of God: Oriental Mythology* (New York: Viking Penguin, 1962), 25.

Chapter 11

1. "Inana's Descent to the Nether World," J.A. Black, G. Cunningham, E. Fluckiger-Hawker, E. Robson, and G. Zólyomi, eds., t.1.4.1., The Electronic Text Corpus of Sumerian Literature, The ETCSL Project (Oxford: Oxford University, 2006), <http://www-etcsl.orient.ox.ac.uk>.

2. Elinor W. Gadon, *The Once and Future Goddess* (San Francisco: Harper & Row, 1989), 115.

3. Patricia Reis, "The Dark Goddess," *Woman of Power* 1, no. 8 (Winter 1988): 26.

4. Gadon, *The Once and Future Goddess*, 122.

5. Demetra George, *Mysteries of the Dark Moon: The Healing Power of the Dark Goddess* (New York: HarperCollins, 1992), 230.

6. Elizabeth Barrette, "Erishkegal: Goddess of Thankless Tasks," *SageWoman* 31 (Autumn 1995), <http://www.worthlink.net/~ysabet/spirit/erishkegal>.

7. Ibid.

8. Silvia Brinton Perera, *Descent to the Goddess* (Toronto: Inner City Books, 1981), 35.

9. George, *Mysteries of the Dark Moon*, 44.

10. "Descent of the Goddess Ishtar into the Lower World," in *The Civilization of Babylonia and Assyria*, ed. M. Jastrow (Philadelphia, London: J.B. Lippincott, 1915).

11. Reis, "The Dark Goddess," 26.

12. Silvia Brinton Perera, *Descent to the Goddess* (Toronto: Inner City Books, 1981), 70.

13. Patricia Reis, *Through the Goddess: A Woman's Way of Healing* (New York: Continuum, 1991), 64–65.

14. Miriam Robbins Dexter, *Whence the Goddess: A Source Book* (New York: Pergamon, 1990), 20.

15. Perera, *Descent to the Goddess*, 80.

16. Ibid., 91.

17. Elizabeth Prioleau, *Seductress: Women Who Ravished the World and Their Lost Art of Love* (New York: Penguin Group, 2004), 37.

18. Ibid., 412.

19. Neumann, *Amor and Psyche*, 112.

20. Karen Gernant, *Imagining Women: Fujian Folktales* (New York: Interlink, 1995), 254–262.

21. Apuleius, *Cupid and Psyche*, 105.
22. Ibid., 111.
23. Joan Gould, *Spinning Straw into Gold* (New York: Random House, 2005), 105–106.

Chapter 12

1. Pierre Brunel, *Companion to Literary Myths, Heroes, and Archetypes*, trans. Wendy Allatson, Judith Hayward, and Trista Selous (New York: Routledge, 1992), 241.
2. Susanna Rostas. "Mexican Mythology," in *The Feminist Companion to Mythology*, ed. Carolyne Larrington (London: Pandora, 1992), 371; Merlin Stone, "Coatlicue," in *Ancient Mirrors of Womanhood* (Boston: Beacon, 1990), 82–84.
3. Demetra George, "Mysteries of the Dark Moon," *Woman of Power* 1, no. 8 (Winter 1988): 33.
4. Susanna Rostas. "Mexican Mythology," in *The Feminist Companion to Mythology*, 371.
5. Ibid., 371.
6. Patricia Reis, *Through the Goddess: A Woman's Way of Healing* (New York: Continuum, 1991), 63.
7. Dorothy Dinnerstein, *The Mermaid and the Minotaur* (New York: Other Press, 1999), 161.
8. Ibid., 161.
9. Marie-Louise Von Franz, *Individuation in Fairy Tales* (Boston: Shambhala, 1990), 10.
10. Carl Jung. "Psychological Aspects of the Mother Archetype," in *Collected Works* Vol. 9, pt. 1, 2nd ed., trans. R.F.C. Hull (Princeton: Princeton University Press, 1968), 186.
11. Joseph L. Henderson. "Ancient Myths and Modern Man," in *Man and His Symbols*, ed. Carl G. Jung (New York: Doubleday, 1964), 118.
12. Aniela Jaffé. "Symbolism in the Visual Arts," in *Man and His Symbols*, ed. Carl G. Jung (New York: Doubleday, 1964), 267.
13. M.L. von Franz. "The Process of Individuation," in *Man and His Symbols*, ed. Carl G. Jung (New York: Doubleday, 1964), 170–71.
14. Wolfgang Lederer, *The Fear of Women* (New York: Grune & Stratton, 1968), 66.
15. Karen L. Rowe, "Feminism and Fairytales," *Women's Studies: An Interdisciplinary Journal* 6 (1979): 237–257, 5.
16. Maureen Murdock, *The Heroine's Journey* (Boston: Shambhala, 1990), 18.
17. Apuleius, *Cupid and Psyche*, trans. E.J. Kenney (Cambridge: Cambridge University Press, 1990), 97.
18. Ibid., 85.
19. Luis de Barandiaran Irizar, ed., *A View from the Witch's Cave: Folktales of the Pyrenees*, trans. Linda White (Reno: University of Nevada Press, 1991), 71–72.
20. Nancy Friday, *My Mother/My Self: The Daughter's Search for Identity* (New York: Delacorte, 1977), 38–39.

21. Ibid., 8.
22. Betsy Cohen, *The Snow White Syndrome* (New York: Berkley, 1989), 8.
23. Madonna Kolbenschlag, *Kiss Sleeping Beauty Good-Bye* (San Francisco: Harper & Row, 1979), 42.
24. Roger Sale, *Fairy Tales and After* (Cambridge, MA: Harvard University Press, 1978), 41–42.
25. Ibid., 41–42.
26. Kolbenschlag, *Kiss Sleeping Beauty Good-Bye*, 36.

Chapter 13

1. Louise Bogan. "Medusa," in *The Blue Estuaries: Poems 1923–1968* (New York: Farrar, Straus & Giroux, 1968), 4.
2. Deborah Pope, *A Separate Vision: Isolation in Contemporary Women's Poetry* (Baton Rouge: Louisiana State University Press, 1984), 34.
3. Hesiod, *Theogony*, trans. Hugh G. Evelyn-White, 270, Perseus Digital Library Project, ed. Gregory R. Crane, 2008, Tufts University, <http://www.perseus.tufts.edu>.
4. Ovid, *Metamorphoses*, ed. E.J. Kenney, trans. A.D. Melville (Oxford: Oxford University Press, 1987), 4.9.770.
5. Patricia Reis, *Through the Goddess: A Woman's Way of Healing* (New York: Continuum, 1991), 62.
6. Wolfgang Lederer, *The Fear of Women* (New York: Grune & Stratton, 1968), 3.
7. Ibid., 3.
8. Aeschylus, *Eumenides*, trans. Herbert Weir Smyth, Loeb Classical Library Volumes 145 & 146. (Cambridge, MA: Harvard University Press, 1926), 161, The Theoi Project, <http://www.theoi.com/Text/AeschylusEumenides.html>.
9. Thomas Taylor, *The Eleusinian and Bacchic Mysteries*, ed. Alexander Wilder (New York: J.W. Bouton, 1891), The Internet Sacred Text Archive, <http://www.sacred-texts.com/cla/ebm/ebm00.htm>.
10. Demetra George, *Mysteries of the Dark Moon: The Healing Power of the Dark Goddess* (New York: HarperCollins, 1992), 142.
11. Sigmund Freud. "Medusa's Head," in *Collected Papers*, vol. 5 (London: Hogarth, 1953), 105–6.
12. Jane Ellen Harrison, *Prolegomena to the Study of Greek Religion* (London: Merlin, 1962), 187.
13. Richard Geha, "For the Love of Medusa," *Psychoanalytic Review* 62, no.1 (1975): 3.
14. Barbara G. Walker, *The Woman's Dictionary of Symbols and Sacred Objects* (San Francisco: Harper, 1988), 81.
15. George, *Mysteries of the Dark Moon*, 160.
16. Herodotus, *The Histories*, trans. Henry Cary (New York: D. Appleton, 1899), 270.

17. Gaius Julius Hyginus, *Astronomica*, trans. Mary Grant, 2.13, The Theoi Classical E-Texts Library, <http://www.theoi.com/Text/HyginusFabulae1.html>.

18. Pausanias, *Description of Greece*, trans. W.H.S. Jones, Litt.D., and H.A. Ormerod (Cambridge, MA: Harvard University Press, 1918), XXIV.

19. Quintus Smyrnaeus, *The Fall of Troy*, trans. Arthur S. Way (Cambridge, MA: Harvard University Press, 1913), 14. 453 ff, Loeb Classical Library, <http://www.archive.org/stream/falloftroy00quin/falloftroy00quin_djvu.txt>.

20. H. Haarmann, "The Kinship of the Virgin Mary: Profile of a Cultural Archetype," *ReVision* 20, no. 3 (1998): 17–24.

21. Ovid, *Metamorphoses*, trans. Brookes More (Boston: Cornhill, 1922), 4.9.740, The Theoi Project, <http://www.theoi.com/Text/OvidMetamorphoses1.html>.

22. Pierre Brunel, *Companion to Literary Myths, Heroes, and Archetypes*, trans. Wendy Allatson, Judith Hayward, and Trista Selous (New York: Routledge, 1992), 36.

23. Aeschylus, *Prometheus Bound*, trans. Herbert Weir Smyth, Loeb Classical Library, <http://www.theoi.com/Text/AeschylusPrometheus.html>.

24. George, *Mysteries of the Dark Moon*, 160.

25. Dorothy Dinnerstein, *The Mermaid and the Minotaur* (New York: Other Press, 1999), 161.

26. George, *Mysteries of the Dark Moon*,166.

27. Emily Erwin Culpepper, "Gorgons: A Face for Contemporary Women's Rage," *Woman of Power* 3 (Winter/Spring 1986): 22–25.

28. Ibid.

29. Ibid.

30. Reis, *Through the Goddess*, 66.

31. Jane Caputi, *Gossips, Gorgons, and Crones* (Santa Fe: Bear, 1993), 197.

Chapter 14

1. Nancy Friday, *My Mother/My Self: The Daughter's Search for Identity* (New York: Delacorte, 1977), 379.

2. Joseph Campbell, *The Hero with a Thousand Faces* (Princeton: Princeton University Press, 1973), 190.

3. Ethel Johnston Phelps. "Fair Exchange," in *The Maid of the North: Feminist Folk Tales from Around the World* (New York: Holt, Rhinehart, and Winston, 1981), 25–34.

4. Campbell, *Hero with a Thousand Faces*, 193.

5. Merlin Stone, "Lia," in *Ancient Mirrors of Womanhood* (Boston: Beacon Press, 1990), 175–80.

Chapter 15

1. Suzanne I. Barchers. "The Witch," in *Wise Women: Folk and Fairy Tales from Around the World* (Englewood, CO: Libraries Unlimited, 1990), 91–93.

2. Joseph Campbell with Bill Moyers, *The Power of Myth*, ed. Betty Sue Flowers (New York: Doubleday, 1988), 129.

3. Marija Gimbutas, *The Language of the Goddess* (San Francisco: HarperCollins, 1989), 210.

4. Georgios A. Megas, ed., "Maroula," *Folktales of Greece*, trans. Helen Colaclides (Chicago: University of Chicago Press, 1970), 113–119.

5. Thomas Frederick Crane. "Snow-white-fire-red," in *Italian Popular Tales* (Boston: Houghton Mifflin, 1885), SurLaLune Fairytales, <http://www.surlalunefairytales.com/authors/crane/snowfirered.html>.

6. Marilyn Jurich, *Scheherazade's Sisters: Trickster Heroines and Their Stories in World Literature* (Westport, CT: Greenwood, 1998), 29.

7. Bapsy Pavry, *The Heroines of Ancient Persia* (Cambridge: Cambridge University Press, 1930), 75–79.

Chapter 16

1. Paul G. Zolbrod, *Diné bahané: The Navaho Creation Story* (Albuquerque: University of New Mexico Press, 1984), 175–275.

2. Sydele E. Golston, *Changing Woman of the Apache: Women's Lives in Past and Present* (Danbury, CT: Grolier, 1996), 23.

3. Ibid., 25–59.

4. Ibid., 48.

5. Mircea Eliade, *Myth and Reality*, trans. Willard R. Trask (New York: Harper & Row, 1963), 202.

6. Clarissa Pinkola Estés, *Women Who Run with the Wolves* (New York: Ballantine, 1992), 264.

7. Kathryn Theatana, "Priestess of Hecate," *Woman of Power* 1, no. 8 (Winter 1988): 36.

8. Joseph Campbell with Bill Moyers, *The Power of Myth*, ed. Betty Sue Flowers (New York: Doubleday, 1988), 146.

9. Ella E. Clark, "The Maiden Sacrificed to Winter," *Indian Legends of the Pacific Northwest* (Berkeley: University of California Press, 1953), 201–03.

10. J.F. Bierlein, "Marwe in the Underworld," *Parallel Myths* (New York: Ballantine, 1994), 203–204.

Chapter 17

1. Homer, *Hymn to Demeter*, trans. Hugh G. Evelyn-White, Perseus Digital Library Project, ed. Gregory R. Crane, 2008, Tufts University, <http://www.perseus.tufts.edu>.

2. Katherine G. Kanta, *Eleusis*, trans. W.W. Phelps (Athens: Traveler's, 1979), 15–16.

3. Karl Kerenyi, *Eleusis: An Archetypal Image of Mother and Daughter*, trans. Ralph Manheim (New York: Schocken, 1977), 93.

4. Demetra George, *Mysteries of the Dark Moon: The Healing Power of the Dark Goddess* (New York: HarperCollins, 1992), 255.

5. Ibid., 251.

6. Rosemary Radford Ruether, *Goddesses and the Divine Feminine* (Berkeley: University of California Press, 2005), 72.

7. Erich Neumann, *The Great Mother* (Whitefish, MT: Kessinger, 2004), 308–09.

8. Clarissa Pinkola Estés, *Women Who Run with the Wolves* (New York: Ballantine, 1992), 33.

9. Elinor W. Gadon, *The Once and Future Goddess* (San Francisco: Harper & Row, 1989), 158–59.

10. Estés, *Women Who Run with the Wolves*, 33.

11. Emily Kearns. "Indian Myth," in *The Feminist Companion to Mythology*, ed. Carolyne Larrington, 189–226 (London: Pandora, 1992), 214.

12. Ibid., 201.

13. M. Esther Harding, *Women's Mysteries Ancient and Modern* (New York: Harper and Row, 1977), 156–157.

14. *Devi-māhātmyam*, ed. Swami Jagadiswarananda (Madras: Sri Ramakrishna Math, 1969), II.7.31.

15. Patricia Monaghan, *The Book of Goddesses and Heroines* (New York: Dutton, 1981), 166.

16. Ibid., 65.

Section II: Archetypes

1. Riane Eisler, *The Chalice and the Blade* (New York: HarperOne, 1988), 25.

2. Jane Ellen Harrison, *Prolegomena to the Study of Greek Religion* (London: Merlin Press, 1962), 286.

3. Demetra George, "Mysteries of the Dark Moon," *Woman of Power* 1, no. 8 (Winter 1988): 33.

4. Miriam Robbins Dexter, *Whence the Goddesses: A Source Book* (New York: Pergamon, 1990), 177.

5. Toni Wolff, *Structural Forms of the Feminine Psyche*, trans. P. Watzlawik (Zurich: Students Association, C.G. Jung Institute, 1956), 4.

6. Ibid., 7.

7. Ibid., 14.

8. Ibid., 6.

9. Ibid., 4.

10. Ibid., 10.

11. Pamela S. Stevenson, "Wolff's Four Forms of the Feminine Psyche: Toward a Clinical Application" (Ph.D. dissertation, University of California-Berkeley, 1983), 44–90.

12. Simone de Beauvoir. "Introduction," in *The Second Sex* (New York: Bantam, 1970), xxviii.

Rising Moon: Maiden

1. Demetra George, "Mysteries of the Dark Moon," *Woman of Power* 1, no. 8 (Winter 1988): 33.

2. Jane Ellen Harrison, *Prolegomena to the Study of Greek Religion* (London: Merlin, 1962), 312.

3. Charlene Spretnak, *Lost Goddesses of Early Greece: A Collection of Pre-Hellenic Myths* (Boston: Beacon, 1992), 72.

4. Patricia Reis, *Through the Goddess: A Woman's Way of Healing* (New York: Continuum, 1991), 128.

5. René Malamud. "The Amazon Problem," trans. Murray Stein, in *Facing the Gods*, ed. James Hillman, 47–66 (Irving, TX: Spring Publications, 1980), 57.

Chapter 18

1. Merlin Stone. "Gum Lin," in *Ancient Mirrors of Womanhood* (Boston: Beacon, 1990), 36–42.

2. Robert D. San Souci. "Preface," in *Cut from the Same Cloth: American Women of Myth, Legend, and Tall Tale* (New York: Philomel, 1993), xii.

3. Robert D. San Souci. "Sal Fink," in *Cut from the Same Cloth: American Women of Myth, Legend, and Tall Tale*, 51–56.

4. Harold Courlander. "The Races between Payupki and Tikuvi," in *The Fourth World of the Hopis* (New York: Crown, 1971), 147–157.

5. Terri Windling, "Ashes, Blood, and the Slipper of Glass," *The Journal of Mythic Arts*, The Endicott Studio (Summer 2007), <http://www.endicott-studio.com/rdrm/forashs.html>.

6. Joseph Jacobs. "Molly Whuppie," in *English Fairy Tales* (London: David Nutt, 1890), the Internet Sacred Text Archive, <http://www.sacred-texts.com/neu/eng/eft/>.

7. Ibid.

8. John 20:1–3.

9. Mark 14:8.

10. John 20:14–16

11. Jean-Yves Leloup, *The Sacred Embrace of Jesus and Mary*, trans. Joseph Rowe (Rochester, VT: Inner Traditions, 2005), 4.

12. Ibid., 127.

13. Reidar Christiansen, ed. "The Finn King's Daughter," in *Folktales of Norway*, trans. Pat Shaw Iversen (Chicago: University of Chicago Press, 1968), 147–53.

14. Sophocles, *Antigone, The Oedipus Trilogy*, trans. F. Storr, 2006, EBook #31, <http//www.gutenberg.org/files/31/31-h/31-h.htm#antigone>.

15. Bapsy Pavry, *The Heroines of Ancient Persia* (Cambridge: Cambridge University Press, 1930), 35–41.

16. Joseph L. Henderson. "Ancient Myths and Modern Man," in *Man and His Symbols*, ed. Carl G. Jung (New York: Doubleday, 1964), 152.

Chapter 19

1. "Deirdre or, The Exile of the Sons of Usnech," in *The Book of Leinster*, ed. and trans. Douglas Hyde, 259b–261b, The CELT Project:

Corpus of Electronic Texts, <http:www.ucc.ie/celt>.

2. Barbara G. Walker, *The Woman's Dictionary of Symbols and Sacred Objects* (San Francisco: Harper, 1988), 89.

3. Grimm Brothers. "Little Snow White," in *Grimms Fairy Tales* (New York: Grosset & Dunlap, 1970), 4.

4. Starhawk and Hilary Valentine, *The Twelve Wild Swans* (San Francisco: HarperCollins, 2000), 5.

5. Moyra Caldecott, *Women in Celtic Myth* (Rochester, VT: Destiny, 1988), 150.

6. *The Nibelungenlied*, trans. A.T. Hatto (Baltimore: Penguin, 1965), 53.

7. Krishna-Dwaipayana Vyasa, *The Mahabharata*, trans. Kisari Mohan Ganguli (Columbia, MO: South Asia Books, 2004), 127.

8. Ibid., 127.

9. Ibid., 127.

10. Ibid., 128.

11. Patricia Monaghan, *The Book of Goddesses and Heroines* (New York: Dutton, 1981), 136; Vicki León, *Outrageous Women of Ancient Times* (New York: John Wiley & Sons, 1998), 39.

12. M. Esther Harding. "All Things to All Men," in *The Way of All Women* (New York: Putnam's, for the C.G. Jung Foundation for Analytic Psychology, 1970), 4.

13. Ibid., 4.

14. Susan Feldman, ed. "A Woman for a Hundred Cattle," in *The Story-Telling Stone* (New York: Dell, 1965), 304–311.

15. *Ramayana,* ed. and trans. William Buck (Berkeley: University of California Press, 1976), 415.

Chapter 20

1. Ruth M. Benedict. "The Rabbit Huntress," in *Zuni Mythology* (New York: AMS, 1960), 76–87.

2. Marilyn Jurich, *Scheherazade's Sisters: Trickster Heroines and Their Stories in World Literature* (Westport, CT: Greenwood, 1998), 223.

3. Bapsy Pavry, *The Heroines of Ancient Persia* (Cambridge: Cambridge University Press, 1930), 28–30.

4. David Kinsley, *The Goddesses' Mirror: Visions of the Divine from East and West* (Albany: State University of New York Press, 1989), 5.

5. Jean Shinoda Bolen, *Goddesses in Everywoman* (New York: Quill, 2004), 71.

6. Kinsley, *The Goddesses' Mirror*, 161.

7. Bolen, *Goddesses in Everywoman*, 163.

8. Homer, "Hymn to Aphrodite," ed. and trans. Hugh G. Evelyn-White, Perseus Digital Library Project, ed. Gregory R. Crane, 2008, Tufts University, <http://www.perseus.tufts.edu>, lines 8–33.

9. Lilas G. Edwards. "Joan of Arc: Gender and Authority in the Text of the Trial of Condemnation," in *Young Medieval Woman*, ed. Katherine J. Lewis, Noel James Menuge, & Kim M. Phillips (Stroud, UK: Sutton, 1999), 133–135.

10. W.S. Scott, trans. *Trial of Joan of Arc* (London: Associated Book Sellers, 1956), 104.

11. Lilas G. Edwards. "Joan of Arc: Gender and Authority in the Text of the Trial of Condemnation," in *Young Medieval Woman*, 145.

12. Ibid., 134.

13. Ibid., 67.

14. Hans H. Frankel, *The Flowering Plum and the Palace Lady: Interpretations of Chinese Poetry* (New Haven, CT: Yale University Press, 1976), 23.

15. Terry Woo. "Confucianism and Feminism," in *Feminism and World Religions*, ed. Arvind Sharma and Katherine K. Young (Albany: State University of New York Press, 1999), 135–136.

Chapter 21

1. Umberto Cassuto, *The Goddess Anath*, trans. Israel Abrahams (Jerusalem: The Magnes Press, 1971), 3.E.v.9–11.

2. Ibid., 3.E.v.30–33.

3. Ibid., 3.E.v.35–36.

4. *Canaanite Myths and Legends*, trans. G.R. Driver, ed. J.C.L. Gibson (Edinburgh: T. & T. Clark, 1977), 17.vi.16–19.

5. Ibid., 17.vi.39.

6. Ibid., 6.I.ii.31–38.

7. Rosemary Radford Ruether, *Goddesses and the Divine Feminine* (Berkeley: University of California Press, 2005), 57.

8. *Canaanite Myths and Legends*, 5.v.v.20–21.

9. Cassuto, *The Goddess Anath*, 87.

10. Ibid., 61.

11. Bapsy Pavry, *The Heroines of Ancient Persia* (Cambridge: Cambridge University Press, 1930), 84–88.

12. Jean Shinoda Bolen, *Goddesses in Everywoman* (New York: Quill, 2004), 62.

13. Marion Woodman, *The Pregnant Virgin: A Process of Psychological Transformation* (Toronto: Inner City Books, 1985), 85.

14. Judges 4:14.

15. Judges 5:24.

16. Emily Kearns. "Indian Myth," in *The Feminist Companion to Mythology*, ed. Carolyne Larrington (London: Pandora, 1992), 204.

17. Robert A. Johnson, *Owning Your Own Shadow* (San Francisco: HarperCollins, 1993), 73.

18. A.B. Chinen, *Waking the World: Classic Tales of Women and the Heroic Feminine* (New York: Penguin Putnam, 1996), 49.

Chapter 22

1. Jessica Amanda Salmonson. "Bearskin Woman and Grizzly Woman," in *The Giant Book of Myths and Legends*, ed. Mike Ashley (New York: Barnes and Noble, 1995), 17–18.

2. Judith C. Brown, *Immodest Acts* (New York: Oxford University Press, 1986), 6.

3. Beth Brant (Deganwadonti). "Coyote Learns a New Trick," in *Mohawk Trail* (Ithaca, NY: Firebrand, 1985), 31–35.

4. Robert M. Baum. "Homosexuality and the Traditional Religions of the Americas and Africa," in *Homosexuality and World Religions*, ed. Arlene Swidler (Valley Forge, PA: Trinity Press International, 1993), 22–24.

5. Haunani-Kay Trask, *Eros and Power: The Promise of Feminist Theory* (Philidelphia, University of Pennsylvania Press, 1986), 103.

6. Sandra A. Wawrytko. "Homosexuality and Chinese and Japanese Religions," in *Homosexuality and World Religions*, ed. Arlene Swidler (Valley Forge, PA: Trinity Press International, 1993), 202–203.

7. Ibid., 204.

8. Mantak Chia and Michael Winn, *Taoist Secrets of Love: Cultivating Male Sexual Energy* (Santa Fe, NM: Aurora, 1984), 206.

9. Paula Gunn Allen, *Grandmothers of the Light* (Boston: Beacon, 1991), 54–55.

10. Sandra A. Wawrytko. "Homosexuality and Chinese and Japanese Religions," in *Homosexuality and World Religions*, ed. Arlene Swidler (Valley Forge, PA: Trinity Press International, 1993), 213–214.

11. Michiko Y. Aoki. "Women in Ancient Japan," in *Women's Roles in Ancient Civilizations*, ed. Bella Vivante (Westport, CT: Greenwood, 1999), 70.

12. "Keiko," in *Nihongi: Chronicles of Japan from the Earliest Times to A.D. 697*, trans. W.G. Aston (Tokyo: Charles E. Tuttle, 1978), 190.

13. Walter L. Williams, *The Spirit and the Flesh: Sexual Diversity in American Indian Culture* (Boston: Beacon, 1986), 233.

14. S. Jacobs, W. Thomas, and S. Lang, eds., *Two-spirit People: Native American Gender Identity, Sexuality, and Spirituality* (Urbana: University of Illinois Press, 1997), 2–3.

15. Judy Grahn, "Strange Country This: Lesbianism and North American Indian Tribes," *Journal of Homosexuality* 12, no. 3 (1985): 53.

16. Nancy Oestreich Lurie, "Winnebago Berdache," *American Anthropologist* 55, no. 1 (1953): 708–712.

17. Robert M. Baum. "Homosexuality and Traditional Religions of the Americas and Africa," in *Homosexuality and World Religions*, ed. Arlene Swidler (Valley Forge, PA: Trinity Press International, 1993), 12.

18. Ibid., 8.

19. W.W. Hill cited in Walter L. Williams, *The Spirit and the Flesh: Sexual Diversity in American Indian Culture* (Boston: Beacon, 1992), 19.

20. Charles Downing. "The Girl Who Changed into a Boy," in *Armenian Folk-tales and Fables* (Oxford: Oxford University Press, 1993), 83–86.

21. *Sappho: A New Translation*, trans. Mary Barnard (Berkeley: University of California Press, 1958), 9.

22. Bella Vivante. "Women in Ancient Greece," in *Women's Roles in Ancient Civilization*, ed. Bella Vivante (Westport, CT: Greenwood, 1999), 246.

23. *Sappho*, 27.

24. Ibid., 64.

25. C.M. Bowra, *Greek Lyric Poetry* (Oxford: Clarendon, 1936), 187.

26. Vicki León. "Sappho," in *Uppity Women of Ancient Times* (Berkeley: Conari, 1995), 150–51.

27. *Sappho*, 93.

28. Ibid., 42.

29. Thomas Wentworth Higginson, "Sappho," *Atlantic Monthly*, July 1871, 1, Early Women Masters East and West, <http://www.earlywomenmasters.net/essays/authors/higginson/twh_sappho.html>.

30. *Sappho*, 23.

31. Ibid., 43

32. Bowra, *Greek Lyric Poetry*. 187.

33. Higginson. "Sappho," 6.

Chapter 23

1. Homer, "Hymn to Aphrodite," trans. Hugh G. Evelyn-White, ll.1–18, Perseus Digital Library Project, ed. Gregory R. Crane, 2008, Tufts University, <http://www.perseus.tufts.edu>.

2. Homer, *The Odyssey, The Iliad of Homer & The Odyssey*, trans. Samuel Butler, ed. Robert Maynard Hutchins, in *Great Books of the Western World* 4 (Chicago: Encyclopædia Britannica, 1952, 1989), VIII.306–320.

3. Elizabeth Prioleau, *Seductress: Women Who Ravished the World and Their Lost Art of Love* (New York: Penguin Group, 2004), 26.

4. David Kinsley, *The Goddesses' Mirror: Visions of the Divine from East and West* (Albany: State University of New York Press, 1989), 203.

5. Jules Cashford, Anne Baring, and Laurens Van Der Post, *The Myth of the Goddess: Evolution of an Image* (London and New York: Arkana, 1993), 363.

6. Ibid., 362.

7. Homer, *The Iliad, The Iliad of Homer & The Odyssey*, trans. Samuel Butler, ed. Robert Maynard Hutchins, in *Great Books of the Western World* 4 (Chicago: Encyclopædia Britannica, 1952, 1989), XIV.158–163.

8. Ibid., XIV.179–184.

9. Kinsley, *The Goddesses' Mirror*, 198–209.

10. Elinor W. Gadon, *The Once and Future Goddess* (San Francisco: Harper & Row, 1989), 288.

11. Riane Eisler, *The Chalice and the Blade* (New York: HarperOne, 1988), 115.

12. Susan A. Niles. "Women in the Ancient Andes," in *Women's Roles in Ancient Civilization*, ed. Bella Vivante (Westport, CT: Greenwood, 1999), 331.

13. Moyra Caldecott, *Women in Celtic Myth* (Rochester, VT: Destiny, 1988), 127–28.

14. Joris-Karl Huysmans, *À Rebours*, trans. Robert Bladick (New York: Penguin, 2003), 53.

15. Audre Lorde. "Uses of the Erotic: The Erotic as Power," in *Sister Outsider* (New York: The Crossing Press, 1984), 28.

16. Ibid., 55.

17. Marion Woodman, *The Pregnant Virgin: A Process of Psychological Transformation* (Toronto: Inner City Books, 1985), 85.

18. Dunn, Joseph, ed, *The Ancient Irish Epic Tale Táin Bó Cúalnge* (London: David Nutt, 1914), The Internet Sacred Text Archive, <http://www.sacred-texts.com/neu/cool/index.htm>.

19. Tristram Potter Coffin, *The Female Hero in Folklore and Legend* (New York: Seabury Press, 1975), 26.

20. Vicki León, *Outrageous Women of Ancient Times* (New York: John Wiley & Sons, 1998), 58–59.

21. William Shakespeare, *Antony and Cleopatra, The Riverside Shakespeare*, 2nd ed. (Boston: Houghton Mifflin, 1997), II.2.191–204.

22. Coffin, *The Female Hero in Folklore and Legend*, 30.

23. Prioleau, *Seductress: Women Who Ravished the World*, 201.

24. Haunani-Kay Trask, *Eros and Power: The Promise of Feminist Theory* (Philidelphia: University of Pennsylvania Press, 1986), 99.

25. A.B. Chinen, *Waking the World: Classic Tales of Women and the Heroic Feminine* (New York: Penguin Putnam, 1996), 175.

26. Elinor W. Gadon, *The Once and Future Goddess* (San Francisco: Harper & Row, 1989), 290.

27. Joseph Dunn, ed. *The Ancient Irish Epic Tale Táin Bó Cúalnge* (London: David Nutt, 1914), III.13.1.

28. Miriam Robbins Dexter, *Whence the Goddess: A Source Book* (New York: Pergamon, 1990), 161.

29. Vidagdhamadhava 7.44 in *Devi: Goddesses of India*, eds. John S. Hawley and Donna M. Wulff (Berkeley: University of California Press, 1996), 123.

30. Donna M. Wulff. "Radha: Consort and Conquerer of Krishna," in *Devi: Goddesses of India*, eds. John S. Hawley and Donna M. Wulff (Berkeley: University of California Press, 1996), 122.

31. Haunani-Kay Trask, *Eros and Power: The Promise of Feminist Theory* (Philidelphia, University of Pennsylvania Press, 1986), 98.

32. *The Epic of Gilgamesh*, trans. Maureen Gallery Kovacs (Stanford, CA: Stanford University Press, 1985), I.iv.8–15.

33. M. Esther Harding, *Women's Mysteries Ancient and Modern* (New York: Harper and Row, 1977), 144.

34. Merlin Stone, *When God Was a Woman* (New York: Harcourt Brace, 1976), 157.

Full Moon: Mother

1. Joseph Campbell with Bill Moyers, *The Power of Myth*, ed. Betty Sue Flowers (New York: Doubleday, 1988), 167.

2. Shahrukh Husain, *The Goddess* (Boston: Little, Brown, 1997), 18.

Chapter 24

1. John Bierhorst. "Crystal the Wise," in *Latin American Folktales: Stories from Hispanic and Indian Traditions* (New York: Pantheon, 2002), 137–141.

2. Marilyn Jurich, *Scheherazade's Sisters: Trickster Heroines and Their Stories in World Literature* (Westport, CT: Greenwood, 1998), 134.

3. Kalidasa. "Sakuntala and the Ring of Recollection," in *The Longman Anthology of World Literature*, Volume A: The Ancient World (New York: Pearson Education, 2004), 1027.

4. Ibid., 1027.

5. Barbara Rush. "He Who Has Found a Wife Has Found Good," in *The Book of Jewish Women's Tales* (Berkeley: University of California Press, 1994), 89–94.

6. Inea Bushnaq. "The Sultan's Camp-Follower," in *Arab Folktales* (New York: Pantheon, 1986), 339–343.

7. William Shakespeare, *All's Well That Ends Well, The Riverside Shakespeare*, 2nd ed. (Boston: Houghton Mifflin, 1997), 3.2.19–24.

8. Ibid., 3.2.28.

9. Ibid., 3.2.57–60.

10. Richard Erodoes and Alfonzo Ortiz, eds. "Iktome Sleeps with his Wife by Mistake," in *American Indian Myths and Legends* (New York: Pantheon, 1984), 372–374.

11. Rush. "The Garbage Girl Who Married the King," in *The Book of Jewish Women's Tales*, 48–51.

Chapter 25

1. E.A. Wallis Budge, ed. and trans. "The History of Isis and Osiris," in *Legends of the Gods: The Egyptian Texts* (London: Kegan Paul, Trench and Trübner, 1912), 198–229.

2. Neal Walls, ed. "The God and His Unknown Name," in *Desire, Discord and Death: Approaches to Near Eastern Myth* (Boston: American Schools of Oriental Research, 2001), 12.

3. William Thomas and Kate Pavitt, *The Book of Talismans, Amulets and Zodiacal Gems* (London: William Rider & Son, 1922), 56–57, The Internet Sacred Text Archive, <http://www.sacred-texts.com/sym/bot/index.htm>.

4. E.A. Wallis Budge, ed., *The Egyptian Book of the Dead* (New York: Dover, 1967), 54.

5. Marion Woodman, *The Ravaged Bridegroom* (Toronto: Inner City Books, 1990), 212.

6. David Kinsley, *The Goddesses' Mirror: Visions of the Divine from East and West* (Albany: State University of New York Press, 1989), 167.

7. Sharon Kelly Heyob, *The Cult of Isis among Women in the Graeco-Roman World* (Leiden: E.J. Brill, 1975), 48.

8. Kinsley, *The Goddesses' Mirror*, 175.

9. Jacob and Wilhelm Grimm. "Die Weiber zu Weinsperg," in *Deutsche Sagen*, Vol. 2 (Berlin: In der Nicolaischen Buchhandlung, 1818), no. 481, 180, trans. D.L. Ashliman, 2001, <http://www.pitt.edu/~dash/type0875ast.html>.

10. 1 Samuel 25: 1–44.

11. Irina Zheleznova, ed. and trans., *Folk Tales from Russian Lands* (New York: Dover, 1969), 134–147.

12. Tacitus, *Germania*, trans. A.J. Church and W.J. Brodribb (London: Macmillan, 1877), 7.4, 8.2–3, The Internet Medieval Sourcebook, <http://www.fordham.edu/halsall/source/tacitus1.html>.

13. Sean O'Sullivan, ed. and trans. "The Man Who Was Rescued from Hell," in *Folktales of Ireland* (Chicago: University of Chicago Press, 1966), 151–164.

Chapter 26

1. Kathleen Ragan. "Story of a Female Shaman," in *Fearless Girls, Wise Women, and Beloved Sisters* (New York: W.W. Norton, 1998), 147–48.

2. Ibid., 148.

3. Susanna Rostas. "Mexican Mythology," in *The Feminist Companion to Mythology*, ed. Carolyne Larrington (London: Pandora, 1992), 379.

4. Quoted in Nancy Huston. "The Matrix of War: Mothers and Heroes," in *The Female Body in Western Culture* (Cambridge, MA: Harvard University Press, 1986), 131.

5. Mary Condren, *The Serpent and the Goddess* (San Francisco: Harper & Row, 1989), 191.

6. Erich Neumann, *Amor and Psyche: The Psychic Development of the Feminine*, trans. Ralph Manheim, Bollingen Series 54 (Princeton: Princeton University Press, 1956), 140–141.

7. Dorothy Dinnerstein, *The Mermaid and the Minotaur* (New York: Other Press, 1999), 33.

8. Haunani-Kay Trask, *Eros and Power: The Promise of Feminist Theory* (Philidelphia: University of Pennsylvania Press, 1986), 149.

9. Merlin Stone, *When God Was a Woman* (New York: Harcourt Brace, 1976), 133.

10. Ibid., 142.

11. Samuel Noah Kramer, "The Weeping Goddess: Sumerian Prototypes of the Mater Dolorosa," *The Biblical Archeologist* 46, no. 2 (Spring 1983): 75, JSTOR, <http://www.Jstor.org/stable/3209643>.

12. Joseph Campbell and Bill Moyers, *The Power of Myth*, ed. Betty Sue Flowers (New York: Doubleday, 1988), 179.

13. Ibid., 179.

14. Merlin Stone, *When God Was a Woman* (New York: Harcourt Brace, 1976), 151.

15. Esther Harding, *Women's Mysteries Ancient and Modern* (New York: Harper & Row, 1971), 193.

16. Robert Briffault, *The Mothers* (New York and London: Macmillan, 1927), 48.

17. Euripides. "Bacchae," in *The Tragedies of Euripides*, trans. T.A. Buckley (London: Henry G. Bohn, 1850), The Perseus Digital Library Project, <http://www.perseus.tufts.edu/ lns 695–705>.

18. Patricia Reis, *Through the Goddess: A Woman's Way of Healing* (New York: Continuum, 1991), 196.

Chapter 27

1. Nathaniel B. Emerson, *Pele and Hi'iaka; a Myth from Hawaii* (Honolulu: Honolulu Star-Bulletin, 1915); Martha Beckwith, *Hawaiian Mythology* (New Haven, CT: Yale University Press, 1940), 160–02; King David Kalakaua. "Lohiau, the Lover of a Goddess," in *The Legends and Myths of Hawaii* (Rutland: Charles E. Tuttle, 1972), 483–497.

2. Elizabeth Diab. "Hawaii" in *The Feminist Companion to Mythology*, ed. Carolyne Larrington (London: Pandora, 1992), 323.

3. Homer, "To Earth the Mother of All," trans. Hugh G. Evelyn-White, lines 1–16, Perseus Digital Library Project, ed. Gregory R. Crane, 2008, Tufts University, <http://www.perseus.tufts.edu>.

4. *Devi-māhātmyam*, ed. Swami Jagadiswarananda (Madras: Sri Ramakrishna Math, 1969), 1.58.

5. Apuleius. "Cupid and Psyche," in *The Golden Ass*, trans. Robert Graves (New York: Farrar, Straus & Giroux, 1951), 208.

6. Jane Ellen Harrison, *Prolegomena to the Study of Greek Religion* (London: Merlin, 1962), 260–63.

7. Dorothy Dinnerstein, *The Mermaid and the Minotaur* (New York: Other Press, 1999), 161.

8. Joseph Campbell and Bill Moyers, *The Power of Myth*, ed. Betty Sue Flowers (New York: Doubleday, 1988), 167.

9. Shahrukh Husain, *The Goddess* (Boston: Little, Brown, 1997), 10–11.

10. J.M Adovasio, Olga Soffer & Jake Page, *The Invisible Sex* (New York: HarperCollins, 2007), 118–119.

11. LeRoy McDermott, "Self-Representation

in Upper Paleolithic Female Figures," *Current Anthropology* 37:2 (April 1996) 227.

12. M. Esther Harding, *Women's Mysteries Ancient and Modern* (New York: Harper and Row, 1977), 155.

13. Cynthia Ann Humes. "Vindhyavasini: Local Goddess Yet Great Goddess," in *Devi: Goddesses of India*, eds. John S. Hawley and Donna M. Wulff (Berkeley: University of California Press, 1996), 70.

14. Harrison, *Prolegomena to the Study of Greek Religion*, 274.

Chapter 28

1. *Kojiki: Record of Ancient Matters*, trans. Basil Hall Chamberlain (Rutland, VT: Charles E. Tuttle, 1981), 20.

2. Pierre Brunel, *Companion to Literary Myths, Heroes, and Archetypes,* trans. Wendy Allatson, Judith Hayward, and Trista Selous (New York: Routledge, 1992), 634.

3. Barbara Fass Leavy, *In Search of the Swan Maiden* (New York: New York University Press, 1994), 250.

4. Demetra George, *Mysteries of the Dark Moon: The Healing Power of the Dark Goddess* (New York: HarperCollins, 1992), 168.

5. The Koran, trans. N.J. Dawood, (New York: Penguin Books, 2000), 20:120–121.

6. Genesis 3:3, The Bible: Tikun Kor'im Hamefoar, eds. Nachum Y. Kornfeld and Abraham B Walzer, trans. Rabbi Aryeh Kaplan (Brooklyn: Simcha Graphic Associates, 2000).

7. Hesiod, *Works & Days*, trans. Hugh G. Evelyn-White, 54, The Theoi Project, ed. Aaron J. Atsma, 2008, <http://www.theoi.com/Heroine/Pandora.html>.

8. Ibid., 54.

9. Diodorus Siculus, *Library of History*, trans. C.H. Oldfather (Cambridge, MA: Harvard University Press, 1935), 3.56. 1–57.

10. Hesiod, *Theogony*, trans. Hugh G. Evelyn-White, Perseus Digital Library Project, ed. Gregory R. Crane, 2008, Tufts University, <http://www.perseus.tufts.edu>.

11. Merlin Stone, *When God was a Woman* (New York: Harcourt Brace, 1976), 220–21.

12. Ibid., 220.

13. Jules Cashford, Anne Baring, and Laurens Van Der Post, *The Myth of the Goddess: Evolution of an Image* (New York: Arkana, 1993), 335.

14. Carol Schaefer, *Grandmothers Counsel the World* (Boston: Trumpeter, 2006), 133.

15. Madonna Kolbenschlag, *Kiss Sleeping Beauty Goodbye* (San Francisco: Harper & Row, 1979), 200.

16. Simone de Beauvoir, *The Second Sex* (New York: Bantam, 1970), 171.

17. Rosemary Radford Ruether. "Sexism and God-talk," in *Women & Men: The Consequences of Power*, Selected Papers from the Bicentennial Conference "Pioneers for Century III," April 1976, Cincinnati, OH, 409–410.

18. Mary Condren, *The Serpent and the Goddess* (San Francisco: Harper & Row, 1989), 5.

19. Ibid., 5.

20. Kim M. Phillips. "Maidenhood as the Perfect Age of Woman's Life," in *Young Medieval Woman*, ed. Katherine J. Lewis, Noel James Menuge, & Kim M. Phillips (Stroud, UK: Sutton, 1999), 10.

21. de Beauvoir, *The Second Sex*, 170.

22. Patricia Reis, *Through the Goddess: A Woman's Way of Healing* (New York: Continuum, 1991), 63.

23. Adrienne Rich, *Of Woman Born: Motherhood as Experience and Institution* (New York: Norton, 1976), 285.

24. Geoffrey Ashe, *The Virgin Mary's Cult, and the Reemergence of the Sacred* (New York: Arkana, 1988), 80.

25. Augustine. "Literal Commentary on Genesis," IX:5–9, in Elizabeth A. Clark, *Women in the Early Church: Messages of the Fathers of the Church* (Collegeville, MN: The Liturgical Press, 1983), 28–29.

26. Genesis 3:16, The Holy Bible: 21st Century King James Version (Gary, IN: Deuel Enterprises, 1994).

Chapter 29

1. Angel Vigil, *The Corn Woman: Stories and Legends of the Hispanic Southwest* (Englewood, CO: Libraries Unlimited, 1994), 11–14.

2. Barbara Fass Leavy, *In Search of the Swan Maiden* (New York: New York University Press, 1994), 187.

3. Euripides. *Medea*, in *Euripides*, trans. David Kovacs (Cambridge: Harvard University Press), The Perseus Digital Library Project, <http://www.perseus.tufts.edu, lns 806–10>.

4. Ibid., lns 794–95.

5. Ibid., ln 817.

6. Ibid., ln 1391.

7. Ibid., lns 1345–46.

8. Ibid., ln 16.

9. Penelope Harvey. "South America: The Interpretation of Myth," in *The Feminist Companion to Mythology*, ed. Carolyne Larrington (London: Pandora, 1992), 399–400.

10. Nancy Friday, *My Mother/My Self: The Daughter's Search for Identity* (New York: Delacorte, 1977), 3.

11. Joan Gould, *Spinning Straw into Gold* (New York: Random House, 2005), 302.

12. Georg McCall Theal, *Kaffir Folk-Lore* (London: S. Sonnenschein, LeBas & Lawry, 1886) www.surlalunefairytales.com/books/africa/theal.

13. Maria M. Tatar, *Off with Their Heads! Fairy*

Tales and the Culture of Childhood (Princeton: Princeton University Press, 1992), 223.

14. Adrienne Rich, *Of Woman Born: Motherhood as Experience and Institution* (New York: Norton, 1976), 166.

15. Isobel White & Helen Payne. "Australian Aboriginal Myth," in *The Feminist Companion to Mythology*, ed. Carolyne Larrington (London: Pandora, 1992), 295–301.

16. "The Alphabet of Ben Sira," in *Rabbinic Fantasies: Imaginative Narratives from Classical Hebrew Literature* (Yale Judaica Series), eds. Professor David Stern and Mark Jay Mirsky (New Haven, CT: Yale University Press, 1998), 183–184.

17. Demetra George, *Mysteries of the Dark Moon: The Healing Power of the Dark Goddess* (New York: HarperCollins, 1992), 183.

18. Abolqasem Ferdowski. "The Legend of Seyavash," in *Shahnameh: The Persian Book of Kings*, trans. Dick Davis, 215–280 (New York: Penguin, 2007), 224.

19. Ibid., 217–224.

20. Ibid., 222.

Waning Moon: Crone

1. Demetra George, *Mysteries of the Dark Moon: The Healing Power of the Dark Goddess* (New York: HarperCollins, 1992), 227.

2. Ibid., 228.

Chapter 30

1. Sri Swami Sivananda, *Devi Māhātmya* (Shivanandanagar, India: The Divine Life Society, 1994), 5–7, <http://www.sivanandaonline.org/graphics/activities/navaratri_04/durga_saptasati.htm>.

2. David R. Kinsley. "Kali: Blood and Death Out of Place," in *Devi: Goddesses of India*, eds. John S. Hawley and Donna M. Wulff (Berkeley: University of California Press, 1996), 80.

3. Rita M. Gross. "Hindu Female Deities as a Resource for the Contemporary Rediscovery of the Goddess," in *The Book of the Goddess Past and Present*, ed. Carol Olson (Prospect Heights, IL: Waveland, 2002), 222–23.

4. Rachel Fell McDermott. "The Western Kali," in *Devi: Goddesses of India*, eds. John S. Hawley and Donna M. Wulff (Berkeley: University of California Press, 1996), 287–88.

5. Jane Caputi, *Gossips, Gorgons, and Crones* (Santa Fe: Bear, 1993), 281.

6. David Kinsley, *Hindu Goddesses: Visions of the Divine Feminine* (India: Motilal Banarsidass, 1987), 116.

7. Joseph Campbell, *The Masks of God: Oriental Mythology* (New York: Viking Penguin, 1962), 5.

8. Shahrukh Husain, *The Goddess* (Boston: Little, Brown, 1997), 156–157.

9. Linda E. Olds, "The Neglected Feminine: Promises and Perils," *Soundings: An Interdisciplinary Journal* 69, no. 3 (1986): 226–40, 234.

10. Campbell, *Oriental Mythology*, 165.

11. *The Gospel of Sri Ramakrishna*, trans. Swami Nikhilananda (New York: Rama-KrishnaVivekananda Center, 1942), 135–36.

12. Kinsley, *Hindu Goddesses*, 281.

13. Howard Norman. "The Woman Who Ate Men," in *Northern Tales: Traditional Stories of Eskimo and Indian Peoples* (New York: Pantheon, 1990), 226–28.

14. Barbara Smith. "Greece," in *The Feminist Companion to Mythology*, ed. Carolyne Larrington (London: Pandora, 1992), 81.

15. Patrick Chamoiseau. "The Person who Bled Hearts Dry," in *Creole Folktales*, trans. Linda Coverdale (New York: The New Press, 1994), 53.

16. Ibid., 51–53.

17. Ellen B. Basso, *In Favor of Deceit: A Study of Tricksters in an Amazonian Society* (Tucson: University of Arizona Press, 1987), 217.

18. M.L. von Franz. "The Process of Individuation," in *Man and His Symbols*, ed. Carl G. Jung (New York: Doubleday, 1964), 179.

19. Elinor W. Gadon, *The Once and Future Goddess* (San Francisco: Harper & Row, 1989), 83.

20. Rosemary Radford Ruether, *Goddesses and the Divine Feminine* (Berkeley: University of California Press, 2005), 195.

21. *Enuma Elish: The Epic of Creation*, in *The Seven Tablets of Creation*, trans. L.W. King, (London: Luzac, 1902), The Internet Sacred Text Archive, <http://www.sacred-texts.com/ane/stc>.

22. Ibid., 19.

23. Robert Bly and Marion Woodman, *The Maiden King* (New York: Henry Holt, 1998), 44.

24. Marija Gimbutas, *The Language of the Goddess* (San Francisco: HarperCollins, 1989), d 210.

25. Patricia Monaghan, *The Book of Goddesses and Heroines* (New York: Dutton, 1981), 40.

26. George, *Mysteries of the Dark Moon*, 146.

Chapter 31

1. "The Old Woman and the Devil," in *Arab Folktales*, ed. and trans., Inea Bushnaq (New York: Pantheon, 1986), 359–60.

2. Betty Friedan, *The Fountain of Age* (New York: Simon & Schuster, 1994), 139.

3. Barbara Meyerhof, "The Older Woman as Androgyne," *Parabola* 3, no. 4 (1978): 75–89, 75.

4. Demetra George, *Mysteries of the Dark Moon: The Healing Power of the Dark Goddess* (New York: HarperCollins, 1992), 222.

5. Friedan, *The Fountain of Age*, 86.

6. Simone de Beauvoir, *The Second Sex* (New York: Bantam, 1970), 589.

7. Ibid., 590.

8. George, *Mysteries of the Dark Moon*, 226.

9. Carl Jung. "Psychological Aspects of the Mother Archetype," in *Collected Works* Vol. 9, pt. 1, 2nd ed., trans. R.F.C. Hull (Princeton: Princeton University Press, 1968), 36.

10. Ibid., 36.

11. George, *Mysteries of the Dark Moon*, 222.

12. Jane Caputi, *Gossips, Gorgons, and Crones* (Santa Fe: Bear, 1993), 223.

13. "Voluspa," in *The Poetic Edda,* trans. Henry Adams Bellows (Princeton: Princeton University Press, 1936), II.9.6, The Internet Sacred Text Archive, <http://www.sacred-texts.com/neu/poe/poe00.htm>.

14. Patricia Reis, "The Dark Goddess," *Woman of Power* 8 (Winter 1988): 82.

15. Mary Condren, *The Serpent and the Goddess* (San Francisco: Harper & Row, 1989), 166.

16. W.M. Hennessy, "The Ancient Irish Goddess of War," *Revue Celtique* 1 (1870): 32–37, The Internet Sacred Text Archive, <http://www.sacred-texts.com/neu/celt/aigw/aigw01.htm>.

17. Ibid.

18. Jane Caputi, *Gossips, Gorgons, and Crones*, 226–27.

19. Hesiod, *Theogony*, trans. Hugh G. Evelyn-White (Cambridge, MA: Harvard University Press, 1914), lns 429–435, Perseus Digital Library Project, ed. Gregory R. Crane, 2008, Tufts University, <http://www.perseus.tufts.edu>.

20. Ibid., lns 440–449.

21. Nor Hall, *The Moon and the Virgin: Reflections on the Archetypal Feminine* (New York: Harper & Row, 1980), 65.

22. Ibid., 197.

23. Charles Downing. "The Mocker Mocked," in *Armenian Folk-tales and Fables* (Oxford: Oxford University Press, 1972), 6–9.

24. Paula Gunn Allen, *Grandmothers of the Light: A Medicine Woman's Sourcebook* (Boston: Beacon, 1991), 34.

25. Ibid., 34–36.

26. Barbara G. Walker, "Witches Past and Present," *Freethought Today* 25, no. 8 (Oct. 2008): 6–7.

27. Carol P. Christ. "Why Women Need the Goddess," in *Womanspirit Rising: A Feminist Reader in Religion,* eds. C. Christ and J. Plaskow (San Francisco: Harper & Row, 1979), 284.

28. Ursula K. Le Guin, "The Space Crone," *Co-Evolution Quarterly*, Summer 1976: 110.

29. Marion Woodman, *The Pregnant Virgin: A Process of Psychological Transformation* (Toronto: Inner City Books, 1985), 91.

30. Homer, "Hymn to Demeter," trans. Hugh G. Evelyn-White, Perseus Digital Library Project, ed. Gregory R. Crane, 2008, Tufts University, <http://www.perseus.tufts.edu>, II.101–102.

31. George, *Mysteries of the Dark Moon*, 221.

32. de Beauvoir, *The Second Sex*, 576.

Chapter 32

1. Barbara Rush. "A Woman of Valor — Crown of Her Husband," in *The Book of Jewish Women's Tales* (Berkeley: University of California Press, 1994), 229–231.

2. Lewis Hyde, *Trickster Makes This World* (New York: Farrar, Straus, and Giroux, 1998), 341.

3. Mahadeo L. Apte, *Humor and Laughter: An Anthropological Approach* (Ithaca: Cornell University Press, 1985), 74.

4. Ruth B. Bottigheimer, "Fertility Control and the Birth of the Modern European Fairy Tale Heroine," *Marvels and Tales: Journal of Fairy Tale Studies* 14, no. 1 (2000): 64–79, 71.

5. Hyde, *Trickster Makes This World*, 336.

6. Patricia Monaghan, *The Book of Goddesses and Heroines* (New York: Dutton, 1981), 42.

7. Homer, "Hymn to Demeter," trans. Hugh G. Evelyn-White, Perseus Digital Library Project, ed. Gregory R. Crane, 2008, Tufts University, <http://www.perseus.tufts.edu>.

8. Clement of Alexandria, *Athenians and the Rest of Greece*, trans. G.W. Butterworth, Loeb Classical Library (Cambridge, MA: Harvard University Press, 1919), 41.

9. A.B. Chinen, *Waking the World: Classic Tales of Women and the Heroic Feminine* (New York: Penguin Putnam, 1996), 176.

10. Luis de Barandiaran Irizar, ed., *A View from the Witch's Cave: Folktales of the Pyrenees*, trans. Linda White (Reno: University of Nevada Press, 1991), 107.

11. Kimberly A. Christen, *Clowns and Tricksters: An Encyclopedia of Tradition and Culture* (Denver, CO: ABC-CLIO, 1998), 58–59.

12. Marilyn Jurich, *Scheherazade's Sisters: Trickster Heroines and Their Stories in World Literature* (Westport, CT: Greenwood, 1998), 230.

13. Hyde, *Trickster Makes This World*, 342.

14. Ibid., 210.

15. Ellen B. Basso, *In Favor of Deceit: A Study of Tricksters in an Amazonian Society* (Tucson: University of Arizona Press, 1987).

16. Jurich, *Scheherazade's Sisters*, 33.

17. Ibid., 33–34.

18. Kimberly A. Christen, *Clowns and Tricksters: An Encyclopedia of Tradition and Culture* (Denver, CO: ABC-CLIO, 1998), 108–109.

19. Vicki Noble, "The Dark Goddess: Remembering the Sacred," *Woman of Power* 12 (Winter 1989): 57.

20. *Popol Vuh*, trans. Dennis Tedlock (New York: Simon and Schuster, 1996), 242.

21. Genesis 31:35.

22. Kathleen Ragan. "Molly Cotton-Tail Steals Mr. Fox's Butter," in *Fearless Girls, Wise Women, and Beloved Sisters* (New York: W.W. Norton, 1998), 160–164.

23. Jurich, *Scheherazade's Sisters*, 225.

New Moon: Spirit Guardian

1. Demetra George, "Mysteries of the Dark Moon," *Woman of Power* 1, no. 8 (Winter 1988): 33.

2. *Bhagavad Gita* 2.22 in *World Scripture: A Comparative Anthology of Sacred Texts*, ed. Andrew Wilson (New York: International Religious Foundation, 1991), 233.

Chapter 33

1. Andrew Lang. "The Witch in the Stone Boat," in *The Yellow Fairy Book*, ed. Brian Alderson (New York: Viking, 1980), 264–69.

2. Joan Gould, *Spinning Straw into Gold* (New York: Random House, 2005), 190.

3. Phyllis Chesler, *Women & Madness* (New York: Avon Books, 1972), 24.

4. Terri Windling, "Married to Magic: Animal Brides and Bridegrooms," *Journal of Mythic Arts*, The Endicott Studio (Summer 2004), <http://www.endicott-studio.com/rdrm/rr MarriedToMagic.html>.

5. Gould, *Spinning Straw into Gold*, 238.

6. George F. Schultz. "The Gambler's Wife," in *Vietnamese Legends* (Rutland, VT: Charles E. Tuttle, 1965), 36.

7. Ibid., 34–40.

8. Carl Jung. "The Phenomenology of the Spirit in Fairytales," in *Collected Works* Vol. 9, pt. 1, 2nd ed., trans. R.F.C. Hull (Princeton, Princeton University Press, 1968), 94.

9. Grimm Brothers. "The Juniper Tree," in *Grimms Fairy Tales* (New York: Grosset & Dunlap, 1970), 48.

10. Maria M. Tatar, *The Annotated Classic Fairy Tales* (New York and London: W.W. Norton, 2002), 159.

11. Carl Jung, "The Phenomenology of the Spirit in Fairytales," 86.

12. Biraago Diop, "Mali Poem," in *World Scrip-*

ture: A Comparative Anthology of Sacred Texts, ed. Andrew Wilson (New York: International Religious Foundation, 1991), 234.

13. George, *Mysteries of the Dark Moon*, 51–52.

Chapter 34

1. Anne Cameron, *Daughters of Copper Woman* (Vancouver, BC: Press Gang, 1981).

2. Demetra George, *Mysteries of the Dark Moon: The Healing Power of the Dark Goddess* (New York: HarperCollins, 1992), 98.

3. Tamara Agha-Jaffar. "Corn Mother," in *Women and Goddesses in Myth and Sacred Text* (New York: Pearson Education, 2005), 269.

4. Charlene Spretnack, *Lost Goddesses of Early Greece* (Boston: Beacon, 1992), 91–92.

5. Jules Cashford, Anne Baring, and Laurens Van Der Post, *The Myth of the Goddess: Evolution of an Image* (New York: Arkana, 1993), 368.

6. Karen Gernant, *Imagining Women: Fujian Folktales* (New York: Interlink, 1995), 180–187.

7. Hans Christian Andersen. "The Little Mermaid," in *Hans Christian Andersen: The Complete Fairy Tales and Stories*, trans. Erik Christian Haugaard (New York: Anchor, 1983), 58.

8. John of Damascus, "Sermon 1," *Three Sermons on the Dormition of the Virgin*, The Internet Medieval Sourcebook, ed. Paul Halsall, 2006, <http://www.fordham.edu/halsall/basis/john damascus-komesis.html>.

Final Thoughts

1. Barbara G Walker, "Witches Past and Present," *Freethought Today* 25, no. 8 (Oct. 2008): 6–7.

2. Heather Lyons. "Some Second Thoughts on Sexism in Fairy Tales," in *Literature and Learning* (London: Open University Press, 1978), 44.

Bibliography

Adovasio, J.M., Olga Soffer, and Jake Page. *The Invisible Sex*. New York: HarperCollins, 2007.

Aeschylus. *Eumenides*. Loeb Classical Library 145 & 146, translated by Herbert Weir Smyth. Cambridge, MA: Harvard University, 1926. The Theoi Project, <http://www.theoi.com/Text/AeschylusEumenides.html>.

_____. *Prometheus Bound*. Loeb Classical Library 145 & 146, translated by Herbert Weir Smyth. Cambridge, MA: Harvard University, 1926. The Theoi Project, <http://www.theoi.com/Text/AeschylusPrometheus.html>.

Agha-Jaffar, Tamara. *Women and Goddesses in Myth and Sacred Text*. New York: Pearson Education, 2005.

Allen, Paula Gunn. *Grandmothers of the Light: A Medicine Woman's Sourcebook*. Boston: Beacon, 1991.

"The Alphabet of Ben Sira," in *Rabbinic Fantasies: Imaginative Narratives from Classical Hebrew Literature Yale Judaica Series*, edited by Professor David Stern and Mark Jay Mirsky, 167–202. New Haven, CT: Yale University Press, 1998.

Andersen, Hans Christian. *Hans Christian Andersen: The Complete Fairy Tales and Stories*, translated by Erik Christian Haugaard. New York: Anchor, 1983.

Apte, Mahadeo L. *Humor and Laughter: An Anthropological Approach*. Ithaca, New York: Cornell University Press, 1985.

Apuleius. "Cupid and Psyche," in *The Golden Ass*, translated by Robert Graves. New York: Farrar, Straus & Giroux, 1951.

_____. *Cupid and Psyche*, translated by E.J. Kenney. Cambridge: Cambridge University Press, 1990.

Arabian Nights' Entertainments or The Thousand and One Nights, translated by Edward William Lane. New York: Tudor, 1944.

Ashe, Geoffrey. *The Virgin: Mary's Cult and the Re-Emergence of the Sacred*. New York: Arkana, 1988.

Ashley, Mike, ed. *The Giant Book of Myths and Legends*. New York: Barnes and Noble, 1995.

Ashliman, D.L. *A Guide to Folktales in the English Language*. New York: Greenwood, 1987.

_____. "Incest in Indo-European Folktales." Folklore and Mythology Electronic Texts, 1997, <http://www.pitt.edu/~dash/incest.html>.

Augustine. "Literal Commentary on Genesis," in *Women in the Early Church: Messages of the Fathers of the Church*, edited by Elizabeth A. Clark, 28–29. Collegeville, MN: The Liturgical Press, 1983.

Barchers, Suzanne I. *Wise Women: Folk and Fairy Tales from Around the World*. Colorado: Libraries Unlimited, 1990.

Barnard, Mary, trans. *Sappho: A New Translation*. Berkeley: University of California Press, 1958.

Barrette, Elizabeth. "Erishkegal: Goddess of Thankless Tasks." *SageWoman* 31 (Autumn 1995). <http://www.worthlink.net/~ysabet/spirit/erishkegal>.

Basso, Ellen B. *In Favor of Deceit: A Study of Tricksters in an Amazonian Society*. Tucson: University of Arizona Press, 1987.

Beck, Brenda, Peter Claus, Goswami Praphulladatta, and Jawaharlal Handoo, eds. *Folktales of India*. Chicago: University of Chicago Press, 1987.

Beckwith, Martha. *Hawaiian Mythology*. New Haven, CT: Yale University Press, 1940.

Benedict, Ruth M. *Zuni Mythology*. New York: AMS, 1960.

Bettelheim, Bruno. *The Uses of Enchantment*. New York: Alfred A. Knopf, 1977.

Bierhorst, John. *Latin American Folktales: Stories from Hispanic and Indian Traditions*. New York: Pantheon, 2002.

Bierlein, J.F. *Parallel Myths*. New York: Ballantine, 1994.

Bly, Robert, and Marion Woodman. *The Maiden King*. New York: Henry Holt, 1998.

Bogan, Louise. "Medusa," in *The Blue Estuaries: Poems 1923–1968*, 4. New York: Farrar, Straus & Giroux, 1968.

Bolen, Jean Shinoda. *Goddesses in Everywoman*. New York: Quill, 2004.

Book of Leinster, The, edited and translated by Douglas Hyde. The CELT Project: Corpus of Electronic Texts, <http:www.ucc.ie/celt>.

Botkin, B.A. *A Treasury of Mississippi River Folklore*. New York: Bonanza, 1978.

Bottigheimer, Ruth B., ed. *Fairy Tales and Society*. Philadelphia: University of Philadelphia Press, 1986.

_____. "Fertility Control and the Birth of the Modern European Fairy Tale Heroine." *Marvels and Tales: Journal of Fairy Tale Studies* 14, no. 1 (2000): 64–79.

Bowra, C.M. *Greek Lyric Poetry*. Oxford: Oxford University Press, 1936.

Brant, Beth Deganwadonti. *Mohawk Trail*. Ithaca, NY: Firebrand, 1985.

Briffault, Robert. *The Mothers*. New York and London: Macmillan, 1927.

Brown, Judith C. *Immodest Acts*. New York: Oxford University Press, 1986.

Brunel, Pierre. *Companion to Literary Myths, Heroes, and Archetypes*, translated by Wendy Allatson, Judith Hayward, and Trista Selous. New York: Routledge, 1992.

Budge, E.A. Wallis, ed. and trans. *Legends of the Gods: The Egyptian Texts*. London: Kegan Paul, Trench and Trübner, 1912.

Bulfinch, Thomas. *The Golden Age of Myth and Legend*. Hertfordshire, UK: Wordsworth Editions, 1993.

Bushnaq, Inea, ed. and trans. *Arab Folktales*. New York: Pantheon, 1986.

Caldecott, Moyra. *Women in Celtic Myth*. Rochester, VT: Destiny, 1988.

Cameron, Anne. *Daughters of Copper Woman*. Vancouver, BC: Press Gang, 1981.

Campbell, Joseph. *The Hero with a Thousand Faces*. Princeton: Princeton University Press, 1973.

_____. *The Masks of God: Creative Mythology*. New York: Viking Penguin, 1968.

_____. *The Masks of God: Oriental Mythology*. New York: Viking Penguin, 1962.

_____. *Pathways to Bliss: Mythology and Personal Transformation*, edited by David Kudler. Novato, CA: New World Library, 2004.

Campbell, Joseph, with Bill Moyers. *The Power of Myth*, edited by Betty Sue Flowers. New York: Doubleday, 1988.

Canaanite Myths and Legends, translated by G.R. Driver, edited by J.C.L. Gibson. Edinburgh: T. & T. Clark, 1977.

Caputi, Jane. *Gossips, Gorgons, and Crones*. Santa Fe: Bear, 1993.

Carter, Angela. *The Bloody Chamber*. New York: Penguin, 1990.

Cashford, Jules, Anne Baring, and Laurens Van Der Post. *The Myth of the Goddess: Evolution of an Image*. London and New York: Arkana, 1993.

Cassuto, Umberto. *The Goddess Anat*, translated by Israel Abrahams. Jerusalem: The Magnes Press, 1971.

Chamoiseau, Patrick. *Creole Folktales*, translated by Linda Coverdale. New York: The New Press, 1994.

Chesler, Phyllis. *Women & Madness*. New York: Avon, 1972.

Chia, Mantak, and Michael Winn. *Taoist Secrets of Love: Cultivating Male Sexual Energy*. Santa Fe: Aurora, 1984.

Chinen, Allan B. *Waking the World: Classic Tales of Women and the Heroic Feminine*. New York: Jeremy P. Tarcher, 1996.

Christ, Carol P. "Why Women Need the Goddess," in *Womanspirit Rising: A Feminist Reader in Religion*, edited by C. Christ and J. Plaskow, 273–87. San Francisco: Harper & Row, 1979.

Christen, Kimberly A. *Clowns and Tricksters: An Encyclopedia of Tradition and Culture*. Denver, CO: ABC-CLIO, 1998.

Christiansen, Reidar, ed. *Folktales of Norway*, translated by Pat Shaw Iversen. Chicago: University of Chicago Press, 1968.

Clark, Ella E. *Indian Legends of the Pacific Northwest*. Berkeley, CA: University of California Press, 1953.

Clement of Alexandria. *Athenians and the Rest of Greece*, translated by G.W. Butterworth. Cambridge, MA: Harvard University Press, 1919.

Coffin, Tristram Potter. *The Female Hero in Folklore and Legend*. New York: Seabury Press, 1975.

Cohen, Betsy. *The Snow White Syndrome*. New York: Berkley, 1989.

Condren, Mary. *The Serpent and the Goddess*. San Francisco: Harper & Row, 1989.

Courlander, Harold. *The Fourth World of the Hopis*. New York: Crown, 1971.

Crane, Thomas Frederick. *Italian Popular Tales.* Boston: Houghton Mifflin, 1885. SurLaLune Fairytales, <http://www.surlalunefairytales.com/authors/crane>.

Culpepper, Emily Erwin. "Gorgons: A Face for Contemporary Women's Rage," *Woman of Power* 3 Winter/Spring (1986): 22–25.

Curtin, Jeremiah. *Myth and Folk Tales of the Russians, Western Slavs, and Magyars.* New York: Benjamin Blom, 1971.

Davids, Rhys, trans. *Psalms of the Early Buddhists.* London: Oxford University Press, 1909.

Davidson, Hilda Ellis. *Roles of the Northern Goddess.* London & New York: Routledge, 1998.

de Beauvoir, Simone. *The Second Sex.* New York: Bantam Books, 1970.

"Descent of the Goddess Ishtar into the Lower World," in *The Civilization of Babylonia and Assyria*, edited by M. Jastrow. Philadelphia and London: J.B. Lippincott, 1915.

"Devî Gita." In *Srimad Devî Bhagavatam*, translated by Swami Vijnanananda. India: Hari Prasanna Chatterji, 1921. The Internet Sacred Text Archive, <http://www.sacred-texts.com/hin/dg>.

Devi-māhātmyam, edited by Swami Jagadiswaranand. Madras: Sri Ramakrishna Math, 1969.

Dexter, Miriam Robbins. *Whence the Goddesses: A Source Book.* New York: Pergamon, 1990.

Dinnerstein, Dorothy. *The Mermaid and the Minotaur.* New York: Other Press, 1999.

Douglas, Susan J. *Where the Girls Are: Growing Up Female with the Mass Media.* New York: Crown, 1994.

Downing, Charles. *Armenian Folk-tales and Fables.* Oxford: Oxford University Press, 1993.

Dudbridge, Glen. *The Legend of Miao-shan.* London: Ithaca, 1978.

Dundes, Alan, ed. *Cinderella, a Casebook.* New York: Wildman, 1983.

Dunn, Joseph, ed. *The Ancient Irish Epic Tale Táin Bó Cúalnge.* London: David Nutt, 1914. The Internet Sacred Text Archive, <http://www.sacred-texts.com/neu/cool/index.htm>.

Eisler, Riane. *The Chalice and the Blade.* New York: HarperOne, 1988.

Emerson, Nathaniel B. *Pele and Hi'iaka: A Myth from Hawaii.* Honolulu: Honolulu Star-Bulletin, 1915.

Enuma Elish: The Epic of Creation. In *The Seven Tablets of Creation*, translated by L.W. King. London: Luzac, 1902. The Internet Sacred Text Archive, <http://www.sacred-texts.com/ane/stc>.

The Epic of Gilgamesh, translated by Maureen Gallery Kovacs. Stanford: Stanford University Press, 1985.

Erodoes, Richard, and Alfonzo Ortiz, eds. *American Indian Myths and Legends.* New York: Pantheon, 1984.

Estés, Clarissa Pinkola. *Women Who Run with the Wolves.* New York: Ballantine, 1992.

Euripides. "Bacchae," in *The Tragedies of Euripides*, translated by T.A. Buckley. London: Henry G. Bohn, 1850. The Perseus Digital Library Project, <http://www.perseus.tufts.edu>.

_____. "Medea," in *Euripides*, translated by David Kovacs. Cambridge: Harvard University Press. The Perseus Digital Library Project, <http://www.perseus.tufts.edu>.

Evslin, Bernard. *Gods, Demigods & Demons: An Encyclopedia of Greek Mythology.* New York: Scholastic, 1975.

Farrer, Claire R. *Women and Folklore: Images and Genres.* Illinois: Waveland, 1975.

Feldman, Susan, ed. *The Story-Telling Stone: Traditional Native American Myths and Tales.* New York: Dell, 1965.

Fowke, Edith. *Tales Told in Canada.* Toronto: Doubleday Canada, 1986.

Frankel, Hans H. *The Flowering Plum and the Palace Lady: Interpretations of Chinese Poetry.* New Haven, CT: Yale University Press, 1976.

Freud, Sigmund. *A General Introduction to Psychoanalysis.* New York: Routledge, Chapman and Hall, 1969.

_____. "Medusa's Head," in *Collected Papers*, Vol. 5, 105–6. London: Hogarth, 1953.

_____. *Standard Edition of the Complete Psychological Works of Sigmund Freud*, Vol. 9, translated by James Strachey, edited by Anna Freud et al. London: Hogarth, 1959.

Friday, Nancy. *My Mother/My Self: The Daughter's Search for Identity.* New York: Delacorte, 1977.

Friedan, Betty. *The Fountain of Age.* New York: Simon & Schuster, 1993.

Gadon, Elinor W. *The Once and Future Goddess.* San Francisco: Harper & Row, 1989.

Geha, Richard. "For the Love of Medusa." *Psychoanalytic Review* 62, no. 1 (1975).

George, Demetra. *Mysteries of the Dark Moon: The Healing Power of the Dark Goddess.* New York: HarperCollins, 1992.

_____. "Mysteries of the Dark Moon." *Woman of Power* 1 no. 8 (Winter 1988): 30–34.

Gernant, Karen. *Imagining Women: Fujian Folktales.* New York: Interlink, 1995.

Gilgamesh, translated by R. Campbell Thompson. London: Luzac, 1928. The Internet Sacred Texts Archive, <http://www.sacred-texts.com/ane/eog/index.htm>.

Gill, the Rev. William Wyatt. *Myths and Songs from the South Pacific.* London: Henry S. King, 1876.

Gimbutas, Marija. *The Language of the Goddess.* San Francisco: HarperCollins, 1989.

Girardot, N.J. "Initiation and Meaning in the Tale of Snow White and the Seven Dwarfs." *Journal of American Folklore* (1977): 90.

Gluck, Sherna. "What's So Special about Women? Women's Oral His-tory." *Frontiers* 2, no. 2 1977: 3–17.

Golden Goddess, The: Ancient Egyptian Love Lyrics, translated by Raymond A. McCoy. Menomonie, WI: Enchiridion, 1972.

Golston, Sydele E. *Changing Woman of the Apache: Women's Lives in Past and Present.* Danbury, CT: Grolier, 1996.

Gould, Joan. *Spinning Straw into Gold.* New York: Random House, 2005.

Grahn, Judy. "Strange Country This: Lesbianism and North American Indian Tribes." *Journal of Homosexuality* 12, no. 3 (1985): 53.

Graves, Robert. *The Greek Myths,* Vol. 1. New York: Penguin, 1955.

Grimm, Jacob, and Wilhelm. "Die Weiber zu Weinsperg," in *Deutsche Sagen,* Vol. 2, no. 481, 180, translated by D.L. Ashliman. Berlin: In der Nicolaischen Buchhandlung, 1818. <http://www.pitt.edu/~dash/type0875ast.html>.

Grimm Brothers. *Grimms' Fairy Tales.* New York: Grosset & Dunlap, 1970.

Haarmann, H. "The Kinship of the Virgin Mary: Profile of a Cultural Archetype." *ReVision* 20, no. 3 (1998): 17–24.

Hall, Nor. *The Moon and the Virgin: Reflections on the Archetypal Feminine.* New York: Harper & Row, 1980.

Halliwell, James Orchard. *The Nursery Rhymes of England.* London, 1853. Folklore and Mythology Electronic Texts, <http://www.pitt.edu/~dash/type0510b.html>.

Hamilton, Edith. *Mythology: Timeless Tales of Gods and Heroes.* New York: New American Library, 1940.

Harding, M. Esther. *The Way of All Women.* New York: Putnam's, for the C.G. Jung Foundation for Analytic Psychology, 1970.

_____. *Women's Mysteries Ancient and Modern.* New York: Harper & Row, 1971.

Harrison, Jane Ellen. *Prolegomena to the Study of Greek Religion.* London: Merlin, 1962.

Harvey, Andrew, and Anne Baring. *The Divine Feminine.* Berkeley, CA: Conari, 1996.

Hawley, John S., and Donna M. Wulff, eds. *Devi: Goddesses of India.* Berkeley: University of California Press, 1996.

Hennessy, W.M. "The Ancient Irish Goddess of War." *Revue Celtique* 1 (1870): 32–37. The Internet Sacred Text Archive, <http://www.sacred-texts.com/neu/celt/aigw/aigw01.htm>.

Herodotus. *The Histories,* translated by Henry Cary. New York: D. Appleton, 1899.

Hesiod. *Theogony,* translated by Hugh G. Evelyn-White. Cambridge, MA: Harvard University Press, 1914. Perseus Digital Library Project, edited by Gregory R. Crane, 2008, Tufts University, <http://www.perseus.tufts.edu>.

_____. *Works & Days,* translated by Hugh G. Evelyn-White. The Theoi Project, edited by Aaron J. Atsma, 2008, <http://www.theoi.com/Heroine/Pandora>.

Heyob, Sharon Kelly. *The Cult of Isis Among Women in the Graeco-Roman World.* Leiden: E.J. Brill, 1975.

Higginson, Thomas Wentworth. "Sappho." *Atlantic Monthly* (July 1871). Early Women Masters East and West, <http://www.earlywomenmasters.net/essays/authors/higginson/twh_sappho.html>.

Hirschfield, Jane, ed. *Women in Praise of the Sacred.* New York: Harper Perennial, 1995.

Homer. "Hymn to Aphrodite," translated by Hugh G. Evelyn-White. Perseus Digital Library Project, edited by Gregory R. Crane, 2008, Tufts University, <http://www.perseus.tufts.edu>.

_____. "Hymn to Demeter," translated by Hugh G. Evelyn-White. Perseus Digital Library Project, edited by Gregory R. Crane, 2008, Tufts University, <http://www.perseus.tufts.edu>.

_____. *The Iliad of Homer & The Odyssey,* translated by Samuel Butler, edited by Robert Maynard Hutchins, in *Great Books of the Western World* 4. Chicago: Encyclopædia Britannica, 1952, 1989.

_____. "To Earth the Mother of All," translated by Hugh G. Evelyn-White. Perseus Digital Library Project, edited by Gregory R. Crane, 2008, Tufts University, <http://www.perseus.tufts.edu>.

Hurston, Zora Neale. *Mules and Men.* Bloomington: Indiana University Press, 1935.

Husain, Shahrukh. *The Goddess.* Boston: Little, Brown, 1997.

Huston, Nancy. "The Matrix of War: Mothers and Heroes," in *The Female Body in Western Culture,* edited by Susan Rubin Suleiman, 119–36. Cambridge, MA: Harvard University Press, 1986.

Huysmans, Joris-Karl. *À Rebours,* translated by Robert Bladick. New York: Penguin, 2003.

Hyde, Lewis. *Trickster Makes This World.* Farrar, Straus, and Giroux: New York, 1998.

Hyginus, Gaius Julius. *Astronomica,* translated by

Mary Grant. The Theoi Classical E-Texts Library, 2.13, <http://www.theoi.com/Text/HyginusFabulae1.html>.

"Inana's Descent to the Nether World," edited by J.A. Black, G. Cunningham, E. Fluckiger Hawker, et al. *The Electronic Text Corpus of Sumerian Literature*, The ETCSL Project. Oxford: University of Oxford, 2006, <http://www-etcsl.orient.ox.ac.uk>.

Irizar, Luis de Barandiaran, ed. *A View from the Witch's Cave: Folktales of the Pyrenees*, translated by Linda White. Reno, Nevada: University of Nevada Press, 1991.

Jacobs, Joseph. *English Fairy Tales*. London: David Nutt, 1890. The Internet Sacred Text Archive, <http://www.sacred-texts.com/neu/eng/eft/>.

Jacobs, S., W. Thomas, and S. Lang, eds. *Two-spirit People: Native American Gender Identity, Sexuality, and Spirituality*. Urbana: University of Illinois Press, 1997.

John of Damascus. "Sermon 1," *Three Sermons on the Dormition of the Virgin*. The Internet Medieval Sourcebook, edited by Paul Halsall, 2006, <http://www.fordham.edu/halsall/basis/johndamascus-komesis.html>.

Johnson, Robert A. *Owning Your Own Shadow*. San Francisco: HarperCollins, 1993.

Joines, Karen Randolph. *Serpent Symbolism in the Old Testament*. Haddonfield, NJ: Haddonfield House, 1974.

Jung, Carl. *Collected Works*, Vol. 9, pt. 1, 2nd ed., translated by R. F.C. Hull. Princeton, Princeton University Press, 1968.

_____, ed. *Man and His Symbols*. New York: Doubleday, 1964.

_____. *Memories, Dreams, Reflections*, edited by Aniela Jaffe, translated by Clara Winston. New York: Vintage, 1989.

Jung, Emma, and M-L. von Franz. *The Grail Legend*, translated by Andrea Dykes. New York: G.P. Putnam's Sons, 1970.

Jurich, Marilyn. *Scheherazade's Sisters: Trickster Heroines and Their Stories in World Literature*. Westport, CT: Greenwood, 1998.

Kabbala Denudata: The Kabbalah Unveiled, translated by S.L. MacGregor Mathers. New York: Theosophical Pub. Co., 1912. The Internet Sacred Text Archive, <http://www.sacred-texts.com/jud/tku>.

Kalakaua, King David. *The Legends and Myths of Hawaii*. Rutland: Charles E. Tuttle, 1972.

Kalevala, translated by K. Bosley. Oxford: Oxford University Press, 1989.

Kalidasa. "Sakuntala and the Ring of Recollection," in *The Longman Anthology of World Literature*, Vol. A, *The Ancient World*. New York: Pearson Education, 2004.

Kanta, Katherine G. *Eleusis*, translated by W.W. Phelps. Athens: Traveler's, 1979.

Kerenyi, Karl. *Eleusis: An Archetypal Image of Mother and Daughter*, translated by Ralph Manheim. New York: Schocken, 1977.

Kinsley, David. *The Goddesses' Mirror: Visions of the Divine from East and West*. New York: State University of New York Press, 1989.

_____. *Hindu Goddesses: Visions of the Divine Feminine*. India: Motilal Banarsidass, 1987.

Kluckhohn, Clyde, and Dorothea Leighton. *The Navaho*. New York: Doubleday, 1962.

Kojiki: Record of Ancient Matters, translated by Basil Hall Chamberlain. Rutland, VT: Charles E. Tuttle, 1981.

Kolbenschlag, Madonna. *Kiss Sleeping Beauty Goodbye*. San Francisco: Harper & Row, 1979.

Kramer, Samuel Noah. "The Weeping Goddess: Sumerian Prototypes of the Mater Dolorosa." *The Biblical Archeologist* 46, no. 2 (Spring 1983): 69–80. JSTOR, <http://www.Jstor.org/stable/3209643>.

Lang, Andrew. *The Yellow Fairy Book*, edited by Brian Alderson. New York: Viking, 1980.

Lao, Meri. *Seduction and the Secret Power of Women: The Lure of Sirens and Mermaids*, translated by John Oliphant. Rochester, VT: Park Street, 1998.

Larrington, Carolyne, ed. *The Feminist Companion to Mythology*. Great Britain: Pandora, 1992.

Leavy, Barbara Fass. *In Search of the Swan Maiden*. New York: New York University Press, 1994.

Lederer, Wolfgang. *The Fear of Women*. New York: Grune & Stratton, 1968.

Le Guin, Ursula K. "The Space Crone." *CoEvolution Quarterly* (Summer 1976): 108–110.

Leloup, Jean-Yves. *The Sacred Embrace of Jesus and Mary*, translated by Joseph Rowe. Rochester, VT: Inner Traditions, 2005.

León, Vicki. *Outrageous Women of Ancient Times*. New York: John Wiley, 1998.

_____. *Uppity Women of Ancient Times*. Berkeley: Conari, 1995.

Lewis, Katherine J., ed. *Young Medieval Woman*. Great Britain: Saint Martin's, 1999.

Lurie, Nancy Oestreich. "Winnebago Berdache." *American Anthropologist* 55, no. 1 (1953): 708–712.

Luthi, Max. *Once Upon a Time: On the Nature of Fairy Tales*, translated by Lee Chadeayne and Paul Gottwald. New York: Fredrick Ungar, 1970.

Lyons, Heather. "Some Second Thoughts on Sexism in Fairy Tales," in *Literature and Learn-*

ing, edited by Elizabeth Grugeon and Peter Waldon, 42–59. London: Open University Press, 1978.

The Mabinogion, edited and translated by Lady Charlotte Guest. London: Bernard Quaritch, 1877. The Internet Sacred Text Archive, <http://www.sacred-texts.com/neu/celt/mab/index.htm>.

MacCulloch, John Arnott. *The Religion of the Ancient Celts.* Edinburgh: T. & T. Clark, 1911. The Internet Sacred Text Archive, <http://www.sacred-texts.com/neu/celt/rac/index.htm>.

MacDonald, Margaret Read. *The Storyteller's Sourcebook.* Detroit, MI: Neal-Schuman, 1982.

Malamud, René. "The Amazon Problem," translated by Murray Stein, in *Facing the Gods,* edited by James Hillman, 47–66. Irving, Texas: Spring Publications, 1980.

Markale, Jean. *Women of the Celts.* Rochester, VT: Inner Traditions, 1986.

McDermott, LeRoy. "Self-Representation in Upper Paleolithic Female Figures." *Current Anthropology* 37 April (1996): 2.

Megas, Georgios A., ed. *Folktales of Greece,* translated by Helen Colaclides. Chicago: University of Chicago Press, 1970.

Meyerhof, Barbara. "The Older Woman as Androgyne." *Parabola* 3, no. 4 (1978): 75–89.

Minard, Rosemary. *Womenfolk and Fairy Tales.* New York: Houghton Mifflin, 1975.

Monaghan, Patricia. *The Book of Goddesses and Heroines.* New York: Dutton, 1981.

Murdock, Maureen. *The Heroine's Journey.* Boston: Shambhala, 1990.

Nelson, Gertrud Mueller. *Here All Dwell Free: Stories to Heal the Wounded Feminine.* New York: Doubleday, 1991.

Neumann, Erich. *Amor and Psyche: The Psychic Development of the Feminine.* Bollingen Series 54, translated by Ralph Manheim. Princeton: Princeton University Press, 1956.

_____. *The Great Mother,* translated by Ralph Manheim. Whitefish, MT: Kessinger, 2004.

Nibelungenlied, translated by A.T. Hatto. Baltimore: Penguin, 1965.

Nihongi: Chronicles of Japan from the Earliest Times to A.D. 697, translated by W.G. Aston. London: George Allen & Unwin, 1956.

Noble, Vicki. "The Dark Goddess: Remembering the Sacred." *Woman of Power* 1, no. 12 (Winter 1989).

_____. "Female Blood Roots of Shamanism." *Shaman's Drum* 1, no. 4 (Spring 1986): 15–20.

Norman, Howard. *Northern Tales: Traditional Stories of Eskimo and Indian People.* New York, Pantheon, 1990.

Olds, Linda E. "The Neglected Feminine: Promises and Perils." *Soundings: An Interdisciplinary Journal* 69, no. 3 (1986): 226–40.

Olson, Carol. *The Book of the Goddess Past and Present.* Prospect Heights, IL: Waveland, 2002.

O'Sullivan, Sean, ed. and trans. *Folktales of Ireland.* Chicago: University of Chicago Press, 1966.

Ovid. *Metamorphoses,* edited by E.J. Kenney, translated by A.D. Melville. Oxford, UK: Oxford University Press, 1987.

_____. *Metamorphoses.,* translated by Brookes More. Boston: Cornhill, 1922. The Theoi Project, <http://www.theoi.com/Text/OvidMetamorphoses1.html>.

Paradiz, Valerie. *Clever Maids: The Secret History of the Grimm Fairy Tales.* New York: Basic, 2005.

Pausanias. *Description of Greece,* translated by W.H.S. Jones, D. Litt, and H.A. Ormerod. Cambridge, MA: Harvard University Press, 1918.

Pavry, Bapsy. *The Heroines of Ancient Persia.* Cambridge: Cambridge University Press, 1930.

Perera, Silvia Brinton. *Descent to the Goddess.* Toronto: Inner City, 1981.

Phelps, Ethel Johnston. *The Maid of the North: Feminist Folk Tales from Around the World.* New York: Holt, Rhinehart, and Winston, 1981.

Pilinovsky, Helen. "Donkeyskin, Deerskin, Allerleirauh: The Reality of the Fairy Tale." *The Journal of Mythic Arts.* The Endicott Studio, 2001, <http://www.endicott-studio.com/fordnky.html>.

Pinsky, Mark I. *The Gospel According to Disney.* Louisville: Westminster, 2004.

The Poetic Edda, translated by Henry Adams Bellows. Princeton: Princeton University Press, 1936. The Internet Sacred Text Archive, <http://www.sacred-texts.com/neu/poe/poe00.htm>.

Pogany, Willy. *The Hungarian Fairy Book.* New York: Frederick A. Stokes, 1913.

Poignant, Roslyn. *Oceanic Mythology.* New York: Hamlyn, 1967.

Pope, Deborah. *A Separate Vision: Isolation in Contemporary Women's Poetry.* Baton Rouge: Louisiana State University Press, 1984.

Popol Vuh, trans. Dennis Tedlock. New York: Simon and Schuster, 1996.

Potter, Tristram. *The Female Hero in Folklore and Legend.* New York: Seabury Press, 1975.

Prioleau, Elizabeth. *Seductress: Women Who Ravished the World and Their Lost Art of Love.* New York: Penguin Group, 2004.

Ragan, Kathleen. *Fearless Girls, Wise Women, and Beloved Sisters.* New York: W.W. Norton, 1998.

Ramanujan, A.K., ed. *Folktales from India: A Selection of Oral Tales from Twenty-two Languages*. New York: Pantheon, 1991.

Ramayana, edited and translated by William Buck. Berkeley: University of California Press, 1976.

Reed, A.W. *Treasury of Maori Folklore*. New South Wales: Literary Productions, 1967.

Reis, Patricia. "The Dark Goddess." *Woman of Power* 1, no. 8, (Winter 1988): 24–27, 82.

_____. *Through the Goddess: A Woman's Way of Healing*. New York: Continuum, 1991.

Rich, Adrienne. *Of Woman Born: Motherhood as Experience and Institution*. New York: Norton, 1976.

Rowe, Karen E. "Feminism and Fairytales." *Women's Studies: An Interdisciplinary Journal* 6 (1979): 237–257.

Ruether, Rosemary Radford. *Goddesses and the Divine Feminine*. Berkeley: University of California Press, 2005.

_____. *Religion and Sexism*. New York: Simon & Schuster, 1974.

_____. "Sexism and God-talk," in *Women & Men: The Consequences of Power*. Selected Papers from the Bicentennial Conference "Pioneers for Century III," April 1976, Cincinnati, Ohio.

Rush, Barbara. *The Book of Jewish Women's Tales*. Berkeley: University of California Press, 1994.

Sale, Roger. *Fairy Tales and After*. Cambridge, MA: Harvard University Press, 1978.

San Souci, Robert D. *Cut from the Same Cloth: American Women of Myth, Legend, and Tall Tale*. New York: Philomel, 1993.

Sastri, Haragovinda, ed. *Manusmrtih*. Varanasi: Chowkhamba Sanskrit Series, 1965.

Schaefer, Carol. *Grandmothers Counsel the World*. Boston: Trumpeter, 2006.

Schultz, George F. *Vietnamese Legends*. Rutland, VT: Charles E. Tuttle, 1965.

Schwartz, Howard, ed. *Lilith's Cave: Jewish Tales of the Supernatural*. San Francisco: Harper & Row, 1988.

Shakespeare, William. *All's Well That Ends Well*, in *The Riverside Shakespeare*, 2nd ed. Boston: Houghton Mifflin, 1997.

_____. *Antony and Cleopatra*, in *The Riverside Shakespeare*, 2nd ed. Boston: Houghton Mifflin, 1997.

Sharma, Arvind, and Katherine K. Young, eds. *Feminism and World Religions*. Albany: State University of New York Press, 1999.

Smyrnaeus, Quintus. *The Fall of Troy*, translated by Arthur S. Way. Cambridge, MA: Harvard University Press, 1913. Loeb Classical Library, <http://www.archive.org/stream/falloftroy00quin/falloftroy00quin_djvu.txt>.

Sophocles. *Antigone. The Oedipus Trilogy*, translated by F. Storr. 2006. EBook #31. <http//www.gutenberg.org/files/31/31-h/31-h.htm#antigone>.

Spencer, Krishanna. "Priestess Path: Under the Aegis of Athena." *The Beltane Papers* 2 (Autumn 2002): 24.

Spencer, W.J., and F.J. Gillen. *The Northern Tribes of Central Australia*. London: Macmillan, 1904.

Spretnak, Charlene. *Lost Goddesses of Early Greece: A Collection of Pre-Hellenic Myths*. Boston: Beacon, 1992.

Starhawk, and Hilary Valentine. *The Twelve Wild Swans*. San Francisco: HarperCollins, 2000.

Stephens, Autumn. *Wild Women: Crusaders, Curmudgeons and Completely Corsetless Ladies in the Otherwise Virtuous Victorian Era*. Berkeley, CA: Conari, 1992.

Stevenson, Pamela S. "Wolff's Four Forms of the Feminine Psyche: Toward a Clinical Application." Ph.D. diss., University of California-Berkeley, 1983.

Stone, Kay F. "Things Walt Disney Never Told Us." *Journal of American Folklore* 88 (1975): 42–50.

Stone, Merlin. *Ancient Mirrors of Womanhood*. Boston: Beacon Press, 1990.

_____. *When God Was a Woman*. New York: Harcourt Brace, 1976.

Sturluson, Snorri. *The Prose Edda*, translated by Arthur Gilchrist Brodeur. New York: The American Scandinavian Foundation, 1916. The Internet Sacred Text Archive, <http://www.sacred-texts.com/ncu/pre>.

Swidler, Arlene, ed. *Homosexuality and World Religions*. Valley Forge, PA: Trinity Press International, 1993.

Tacitus. *Germania*, translated by A.J. Church and W.J. Brodribb. London: Macmillan, 1877. The Internet Medieval Sourcebook, <http://www.fordham.edu/halsall/source/tacitus1.html>.

Tatar, Maria M. *The Annotated Classic Fairy Tales*. New York and London: W.W. Norton, 2002.

_____. *The Hard Facts of the Grimms' Fairy Tales*. Princeton: Princeton University Press, 1987.

_____. *Off with Their Heads! Fairy Tales and the Culture of Childhood*. Princeton: Princeton University Press, 1992.

Taylor, Thomas. *The Eleusinian and Bacchic Mysteries*, edited by Alexander Wilder. New York: J.W. Bouton, 1891. The Internet Sacred Text Archive, <http://www.sacred-texts.com/cla/ebm/ebm00.htm>.

Tchana, Katrin Hyman. *Changing Woman and Her Sisters*. New York: Holiday House, 2006.

Theatana, Kathryn. "Priestess of Hecate." *Woman of Power* 1, no. 8 (Winter 1988): 35–37.

Thomas, Ann G. *The Women We Become: Myths, Folktales, and Stories about Growing Older*. Rocklin, CA: Prima, 1997.

Thomas, William, and Kate Pavitt. *The Book of Talismans, Amulets and Zodiacal Gems*. London: William Rider & Son, 1922. The Internet Sacred Text Archive, <http://www.sacred-texts.com/sym/bot/index.htm>.

"Thomas Rhymer: Child 39C," no. 3. *The Ancient and Modern Scots Songs*, 1769, 300. Tam Lin Balladry, <http://www.tam-lin.org/versions/39C.html>.

Trask, Haunami-Kay. *Eros and Power: The Promise of Feminist Theory*. Philidelphia: University of Pennsylvania Press, 1986.

Trial of Joan of Arc, translated by W.S. Scott. London: Associated Book Sellers, 1956.

Vigil, Angel. *The Corn Woman: Stories and Legends of the Hispanic Southwest*. Englewood, CO: Libraries Unlimited, 1994.

Vivante, Bella, ed. *Women's Roles in Ancient Civilizations*. Westport, CT: Greenwood, 1999.

Von Franz, Marie-Louise. *Fairy Tales and the Art of Subversion*. New York: Wildman, 1983.

_____. *The Feminine in Fairy Tales*. Boston: Shambhala, 2001.

_____. *The Grail Legend*, translated by Andrea Dykes. New York: G.P. Putnam's Sons, 1970.

_____. *Individuation in Fairy Tales*. Boston: Shambhala, 1990.

Vyasa, Krishna-Dwaipayana. *The Mahabharata*, translated by Kisari Mohan Ganguli. Columbia, MO: South Asia Books, 2004.

Waelti-Walters, Jennifer R. *Fairy Tales and the Female Imagination*. Montreal. Canada: Eden, 1982.

Wagner, Richard. *The Ring of the Nibelung: Siegfried & The Twilight of the Gods*, translated by Margaret Armour. New York: Abaris Books, 1910. The Internet Sacred Text Archive, <http://www.sacred-texts.com/neu/ron/index.htm>.

Walker, Barbara G. "Witches Past and Present." *Freethought Today* 25, no. 8 (Oct 2008): 6–7.

_____. *The Woman's Dictionary of Symbols and Sacred Objects*. San Francisco: HarperSanFrancisco, 1988.

Warner, Maria. *From the Beast to the Blonde*. New York: Farrar, Straus, and Giroux, 1994.

Weston, Jessie L. *From Ritual to Romance*. New York: Peter Smith, 1941.

Williams, Walter L. *The Spirit and the Flesh: Sexual Diversity in American Indian Culture*. Boston: Beacon, 1986.

Williams-Ellis, Annabel. *British Fairy Tales*. Glasgow and London: Blackie and Son, 1976.

Windling, Terri, ed. *The Armless Maiden and Other Tales for Childhood's Survivors*. New York: Tor Books, 1996.

_____. "Ashes, Blood, and the Slipper of Glass." *The Journal of Mythic Arts*, The Endicott Studio (Summer 2007), <http://www.endicott-studio.com/rdrm/forashs.html>.

_____. "Beauty and the Beast." *The Journal of Mythic Arts*, The Endicott Studio (Summer 2007), <http://www.endicott-studio.com/rdrm/forbewty.html>.

_____. "Married to Magic: Animal Brides and Bridegrooms." *The Journal of Mythic Arts*, The Endicott Studio (Summer 2004), <http://www.endicott-studio.com/rdrm/rrMarriedToMagic.html>.

Wolff, Toni. *Structural Forms of the Feminine Psyche*, translated by P. Watzlawik. Zurich: Students Association, C.G. Jung Institute, 1956.

Woodman, Marion. *The Pregnant Virgin: A Process of Psychological Transformation*. Toronto: Inner City Books, 1985.

_____. *The Ravaged Bridegroom: Masculinity in Women*. Toronto: Inner City Books, 1990.

Wylde, Isabella. "Women Who Run with the Wolves: An Interview with Author and Analyst Clarissa Pinkola Estés." *Radiance* (Winter 1994), <http://radiancemagazine.com/issues/1994/wolves.html>.

Zheleznova, Irina, ed. and trans. *Folk Tales from Russian Lands*. New York: Dover, 1969.

Zipes, Jack. *The Brothers Grimm: From Enchanted Forests to the Modern World*. New York: Routledge, Chapman and Hall, 1988.

_____. *When Dreams Came True: Classical Fairy Tales and Their Tradition*. New York: Routledge, 2007.

Zolbrod, Paul G. *Diné bahané: The Navaho Creation Story*. Albuquerque: University of New Mexico Press, 1984.

Websites

The CELT Project: Corpus of Electronic Texts <http://www.ucc.ie/celt>

Endicott Studio of Mythic Arts and Journal of Mythic Arts <http://www.endicott-studio.com/>

Folklore and Mythology Electronic Texts <http://www.pitt.edu/~dash/folktexts.html>

The Internet Classic Archive <http://classics.mit.edu/>

The Internet Medieval Sourcebook <http://www.fordham.edu/halsall/sbook.html>

The Internet Sacred Text Archive <http://www.sacred-texts.com/>

The Internet Women's History Sourcebook <http://www.fordham.edu/halsall/women/womensbook.html>

The Perseus Digital Library Project <http://www.perseus.tufts.edu/>

Project Gutenberg <http://www.gutenberg.org>

SurLaLune Fairytales <http://www.surlalunefairytales.com/>

The Theoi Project <http://www.theoi.com/>

For these and additional resources on myth and the heroine, please visit the author's website at www.vefrankel.com.

Index